The Making of an SS Killer

In this pioneering biography of a frontline Holocaust perpetrator, Alex Kay uncovers the life of SS Lieutenant Colonel Alfred Filbert, responsible as the first head of SS-Einsatzkommando 9, a mobile killing squad, for the murder of more than 18,000 Soviet Jews – men, women and children – on the Eastern Front. He reveals how Filbert, following the political imprisonment of his older brother, set out to prove his own ideological allegiance by displaying particular radicalism in implementing the orders issued by Hitler, Himmler and Heydrich. He also examines Filbert's post-war experiences, first in hiding and then being captured, tried and sentenced to life imprisonment. Released early, Filbert went on to feature in a controversial film in the lead role of an SS mass murderer. The book provides compelling new insights into the mindset and motivations of the men, like Filbert, who rose through the ranks of the Nazi regime.

ALEX J. KAY is Senior Academic Project Coordinator at the Institute of Contemporary History, Berlin. He is author of *Exploitation, Resettlement, Mass Murder: Political and Economic Planning for German Occupation Policy in the Soviet Union, 1940–1941* (2006) and co-editor of *Nazi Policy on the Eastern Front, 1941: Total War, Genocide, and Radicalization* (2012).

The Making of an SS Killer

The Life of Colonel Alfred Filbert, 1905–1990

Alex J. Kay

Institute of Contemporary History, Berlin

CAMBRIDGE
UNIVERSITY PRESS

CAMBRIDGE
UNIVERSITY PRESS

University Printing House, Cambridge CB2 8BS, United Kingdom

Cambridge University Press is part of the University of Cambridge.

It furthers the University's mission by disseminating knowledge in the pursuit of education, learning and research at the highest international levels of excellence.

www.cambridge.org
Information on this title: www.cambridge.org/9781107146341

First published 2016

Printed in the United Kingdom by Clays, St Ives plc

A catalogue record for this publication is available from the British Library

Library of Congress Cataloguing in Publication data
Kay, Alex J., author.
The making of an SS killer : the life of Colonel Alfred Filbert, 1905–1990 / Alex J. Kay.
New York : Cambridge University Press, [2016] | ©2016
LCCN 2015042443 | ISBN 9781107146341 (hardback)
LCSH: Filbert, Alfred, 1905–1990. | Nazis – Biography. | War criminals – Germany – Biography.
LCC DD247.H37 K39 2016 | DDC 940.53/18092–dc23
LC record available at http://lccn.loc.gov/2015042443

ISBN 9781107146341 Hardback

Contents

vi   Contents

Illustrations

Tables

x

Acknowledgements

The completion of a book brings with it the welcome opportunity to thank those who have assisted its author during the research, writing and publication process. Whilst I am unable to personally thank all those archival members of staff who lent me their expertise during the research phase, I would like to mention two in particular who were particularly accommodating: Eva-Marie Felschow of the Giessen University Archives and Margitta Nibbe of the BStU Central Archives in Berlin. Władysław Bułhak of the Institute of National Remembrance in Warsaw kindly provided copies of archival material, as did Felix Römer. Uwe Ruprecht and Alexandr Kruglov allowed me access to unpublished material. Manfred Kielhorn generously furnished me with copies of documents and other information during the research phase. Assistance was also provided by Rafał Wnuk, whilst Vadim Morochek aided me in deciphering handwritten Russian sources. Julia Schoen, Clemens Uhlig, Jochen Böhler, Katrin Paehler, Annette Weinke, Jean-Pierre Stephan and Ursula Langmann kindly read drafts of one or more individual chapters, whilst Wendy Lower, David Stahel and Pertti Ahonen were generous enough to read the entire draft manuscript. They all provided valuable feedback. My colleagues and friends Martin Holler (the first person with whom I discussed my proposed research project), Clemens Uhlig and David Stahel were the source of constant interest and encouragement throughout the research and writing phases, and the manuscript benefitted from numerous discussions with them. Martin and Clemens also kindly made available copies of archival material, whilst David put me in touch with the senior commissioning editor for history at Cambridge University Press, Michael Watson, whom I would also like to thank. I am obliged to the Maximilian Kolbe Foundation and zebis – Centre of Ethical Education in the Armed Forces for their invitation to present a paper on the subject of this book at one of their workshops in Oświęcim, Poland.

Several eyewitnesses to the life of Alfred Filbert agreed to answer my questions and recall their memories: his son, Dieter Filbert, answered some questions in writing; his nephew, Peter Filbert, invited me to his apartment in Weinheim and gave me copies of rare photographs of family members. Another nephew, Ralph Filbert, responded to my questions in writing via his wife, Erika, in spite of serious illness. Ralph sadly passed away shortly before the completion of the manuscript. Erika Filbert kindly also agreed to be interviewed on the telephone. Erika Kramer, widow of the director of *Notre Nazi*, Robert Kramer, gave of her time and answered my questions with great candour. In addition to reading a draft chapter of my manuscript, Ursula Langmann also generously gave of her time in recalling past events and answering numerous questions. I am extremely grateful to all of these people for their kindness and generosity. My warmest thanks are also due to my wife, Valentina, for her patience and support during the years of research and writing. This book is dedicated to my wonderful son, Cyrus, who provided the welcome and necessary contrast to the dark subject matter. He is my sunshine.

Abbreviations

BArch	Bundesarchiv ([German] Federal Archives)
BArch-MA	Bundesarchiv-Militärarchiv ([German] Federal Military Archives)
BND	Bundesnachrichtendienst ([German] Federal Intelligence Service)
BStU	Der Bundesbeauftragte für die Unterlagen des Staatssicherheitsdienstes der ehemaligen Deutschen Demokratischen Republik (The Federal Commissioner for the Records of the State Security Service of the former German Democratic Republic)
CIC	Counter Intelligence Corps
DHR	Deutscher Hochschulring (German University Circle)
dir.	directed by
DSt	Deutsche Studentenschaft (German Student Body)
ed.	editor / edited by / edition
eds.	editors
EG	Einsatzgruppe
EK	Einsatzkommando
EM	Ereignismeldung (Incident Report)
exp. ed.	expanded edition
fn.	footnote
FOIA	Freedom of Information Act
fol.	folio
fols.	folios
FRG	Federal Republic of Germany
Gestapa	Geheimes Staatspolizeiamt (Secret State Police Central Office)
Gestapo	Geheime Staatspolizei (Secret State Police)
GPU	Gosudarstvennoe Politicheskoe Upravlenie ([Soviet] State Political Administration)
HSSPF	Höhere(r) SS- und Polizeiführer (higher SS and police leader[s])

HStAD	Hessisches Staatsarchiv Darmstadt (Hessian State Archives, Darmstadt)
IfZ-Archiv	Archiv des Instituts für Zeitgeschichte (Archives of the Institute of Contemporary History), Munich
IMG	*Der Prozess gegen die Hauptkriegsverbrecher vor dem Internationalen Militärgerichtshof, Nürnberg, 14. November 1945 – 1. Oktober 1946*, 42 vols, Nuremberg, 1947–1949 (= IMT: The Trial of the Major War Criminals before the International Military Tribunal, Nuremberg)
IPN	Instytut Pamięci Narodowej (Institute of National Remembrance), Warsaw
IRR	Investigative Records Repository
ITS	International Tracing Service, Bad Arolsen
KGB	Komitet Gosudarstvennoi Bezopasnosti ([Soviet] Committee for State Security)
Komsomol	Vsesoyuzny Leninsky Kommunistichesky Soyuz Molodyozhi (All-Union Leninist Communist League of Youth); youth organisation of the Soviet Communist Party
Kripo	Kriminalpolizei ([German] Criminal Police)
LArch	Landesarchiv (Regional Archives)
NARA	National Archives and Records Administration, College Park, MA
Nbg. Doc.	Nuremberg Document
NCO	non-commissioned officer
n.d.	no date (of publication)
NKGB	Narodnyy Komissariat Gosudarstvennoi Bezopasnosti ([Soviet] Commissariat for State Security)
NKVD	Narodnyy Komissariat Vnutrennikh Del ([Soviet] People's Commissariat for Internal Affairs)
No.	number
n.pl.	no place (of publication)
NSDAP	Nationalsozialistische Deutsche Arbeiterpartei (National Socialist German Workers' Party / Nazi Party)
NSDStB	Nationalsozialistischer Deutscher Studentenbund (National Socialist German Student Union)
OKH	Oberkommando des Heeres (High Command of the [German] Army)
OKW	Oberkommando der Wehrmacht (High Command of the Wehrmacht)
p.	page
POW	prisoner of war

pp.	pages
R	reverse side
RAF	Rote Armee Fraktion (Red Army Faction)
rev. ed.	revised edition
RSHA	Reichssicherheitshauptamt (Reich Security Main Office)
SA	Sturmabteilung (Storm Detachment)
SD	Sicherheitsdienst (Security Service [of the SS])
SK	Sonderkommando
SS	Schutzstaffel
SSR	Soviet Socialist Republic
StArch	Staatsarchiv (State Archives)
TNA	The National Archives, Kew
TuLB	Tätigkeits- und Lagebericht(e) (Activity and Situation Report[s])
UAH	Universitätsarchiv Heidelberg (University Archives, Heidelberg)
UniA GI	Universitätsarchiv Gießen (University Archives, Giessen)
Vol.	volume
vols	volumes
VVN-BdA	Vereinigung der Verfolgten des Naziregimes – Bund der Antifaschistinnen und Antifaschisten (Association of Persecutees of the Nazi Regime – Federation of Antifascists)

Glossary

Einsatzgruppe	'operational group': unit of the Security Police and the SD deployed behind the Wehrmacht in the occupied territories
Einsatzkommando	'operational commando': subunit of an Einsatzgruppe deployed in the army group rear areas
General der Infanterie	'general of infantry': German regular army rank equivalent to a full general
Generalleutnant	German regular army rank equivalent to a major general
Hauptwachtmeister	German police rank equivalent to a non-commissioned officer in the military
Kriminalkommissar	German police rank equivalent to a detective inspector
Regierungsrat	'government councillor': German civil service grade
Reichsführer-SS	'Reich Leader SS': rank reserved for Heinrich Himmler as head of the SS
Reichstag	'imperial diet': lower chamber of the German parliament
Schutzstaffel	'protection echelon': elite paramilitary organisation of the Nazi Party
Sonderkommando	'special commando': subunit of an Einsatzgruppe deployed in the army rear areas
SS-Brigadeführer	SS officer rank equivalent to a brigadier
SS-Gruppenführer	SS officer rank equivalent to a major general
SS-Hauptsturmführer	SS officer rank equivalent to a captain
SS-Oberführer	SS officer rank between Standartenführer and Brigadeführer

SS-Obergruppenführer	SS officer rank equivalent to a lieutenant general
SS-Oberscharführer	SS rank equivalent to a warrant officer class I
SS-Obersturmbannführer	SS officer rank equivalent to a lieutenant colonel
SS-Obersturmführer	SS officer rank equivalent to a lieutenant
SS-Standartenführer	SS officer rank equivalent to a colonel
SS-Sturmbannführer	SS officer rank equivalent to a major
SS-Unterscharführer	SS rank equivalent to a sergeant
SS-Untersturmführer	SS officer rank equivalent to a second lieutenant
Waffen SS	armed branch of the Schutzstaffel
Wehrmacht	armed forces of Germany from 1935 to 1945

Introduction

Why write another biography of a Nazi perpetrator? Why not instead write a biography of a *victim* of Nazi mass murder? The victims were almost always innocent and helpless, they could alter little about their fate and they possessed no means of influencing decision-making processes.[1] The mindset and conduct of someone who kills requires considerably more explanation than the mindset and conduct of someone who *is killed*. As the historian Timothy Snyder has noted, 'It is less appealing, but morally more urgent, to understand the actions of the perpetrators. The moral danger, after all, is never that one might become a victim but that one might be a perpetrator or a bystander.'[2] In view of the estimated total of between 200,000 and 250,000 Germans and Austrians – predominantly, though not exclusively, men – directly involved in the mass murder of European Jewry,[3] the selection of a single subject is neither an easy nor an obvious choice. Over the last two decades, there has been a boom in biographies of leading Nazis.[4] Only to a limited extent, however, has this trend extended specifically to front-line Holocaust perpetrators. Direct killers have not been studied as individual subjects in similar depth to the major figures. Alongside the studies of the leading architects of the Holocaust, Himmler, Heydrich and 'Gestapo' Müller,[5] we have only a small handful of individual biographical accounts of mid-level SS (Schutzstaffel, i.e. Protection Echelon) and police functionaries heavily involved in the genocide of European Jewry, for example, on Odilo Globocnik, Walther Rauff or Theodor Dannecker.[6] It remains unclear, however, to what extent the findings made about a perpetrator like Werner Best can be applied to *front-line* executors of the Holocaust, a group to which Best did not belong.[7] In Ulrich Herbert's landmark biography of Best, furthermore, Werner Best the person runs the risk of disappearing behind his status as a member of a generational category.[8]

Alongside the boom in biographies of leading Nazis, research into Nazi crimes has increasingly focussed in recent years on the mid- and lower-level perpetrators.[9] Frequently, the results of this research have taken the form of collective biographical studies[10] or collections of short biographical sketches.[11] Despite their undeniable value, neither collective accounts nor collections of short sketches can replace in-depth individual biographies. As a result, we still lack biographies of many of the foremost protagonists within the SS, not least the Higher SS and Police Leaders, Heinrich Himmler's representatives in the German-occupied territories.[12] It can be observed furthermore that in scholarship on the Holocaust, there is a general dearth of biographies of SS officers who led commandos at the sites of mass murder.[13]

The lack of comprehensive individual biographies for direct perpetrators is particularly apparent when we look at the chiefs of the SS-Einsatzgruppen and their sub-units, the Einsatzkommandos and Sonderkommandos. In 2002, the historian Gerhard Paul noted that 'biographical portraits of individual commando chiefs are still rare'.[14] Well over a decade later, this remains true. Of the seventy-five men who commanded one of these groups or commandos in the German-occupied Soviet territories during the years 1941–1944,[15] biographies exist for merely three of them: head of Advance Commando Moscow (*Vorkommando Moskau*) within Einsatzgruppe B Professor Franz Alfred Six, commander of Einsatzgruppe B Arthur Nebe, and chief of Einsatzkommando 3 of Einsatzgruppe A Karl Jäger.[16] Ronald Rathert's treatment of Arthur Nebe's deployment in the East suffers considerably from the absence of any original documentation from the Einsatzgruppen or indeed from this five-month period *at all*, even though Rathert himself notes at one point that the almost daily incident reports compiled on the basis of reports sent back to Berlin by the Einsatzgruppen have been preserved intact.[17] Whilst Lutz Hachmeister's biography of Franz Six is altogether more comprehensive, Six's prominence was a result primarily of his position as Chief of Office II, later Office VII (Research on Enemies), in the Reich Security Main Office (*Reichssicherheitshauptamt*, or RSHA), just as Nebe is known first and foremost as the Director of the Reich Criminal Police (*Reichskriminalpolizei*).[18] Thus, whilst the third and most recently published of these three studies – Wolfram Wette's work on Karl Jäger – was marketed somewhat misleadingly as 'the first biography of a Nazi direct perpetrator in the field',[19] there is some truth in this claim, since Jäger (in contrast to Six and Nebe) was the subject of a biography primarily due to his activities in Lithuania as head of Einsatzkommando 3 between 1941 and 1943. Unfortunately, Wette's study suffers from a relative dearth of source material, which is limited to Jäger's SS personnel file, the notorious 'Jäger Report' and some survivor testimony, and which furthermore results in the exclusion of any coverage of Jäger's activity as an SS officer prior to his deployment in Lithuania or his role as a local police chief thereafter.[20]

In view of the aforementioned enormous number of direct perpetrators, why is this particular Nazi perpetrator – Alfred Filbert – the subject of this book? Although the historian Christian Gerlach counted him in 1999 among the 'most important leadership personnel' within the SS and police apparatus in German-occupied Belarus,[21] Alfred Filbert remains little known, even among subject specialists. Although he never joined the senior ranks of the SS, he nonetheless ended the war with the same SS rank as the far better known Adolf Eichmann.[22] As the subject of a biographical study, however, he is both interesting and important above all for two reasons. To begin with, as the first chief of Einsatzkommando 9 of Einsatzgruppe B, he was a particularly radical enforcer of the mass murder of Soviet Jewry and known within the Einsatzgruppe for being the first commander to also murder women and children. His conduct during the months June–October 1941 sheds light on the question – still contested by scholars – of orders for the murder of Soviet Jews and the expansion of these killings. The question of the timing of the issuing of orders to extend the murders to include *all* Soviet Jews and thus institute genocide can now in fact be answered for the first time, at least for Einsatzkommando 9.[23]

Second, Filbert's biography exhibits two unique features that are not in evidence for any other prominent SS officer. First of all, his own brother was imprisoned by the Nazi regime for expressing regret following the failure of the attempt on Hitler's life on 8 November 1939; he was subsequently incarcerated in a concentration camp and did not survive the war.[24] The fate of his brother became a constant and decisive factor in Filbert's post-war portrayal of himself as a victim. Moreover, I argue that his brother's arrest and imprisonment played a key role in motivating Filbert to actively participate in genocide. Second, Filbert portrayed an SS mass murderer, 'Dr S.' (i.e. himself – Filbert went into hiding after the war under the name 'Dr Selbert')[25] in the West German feature film *Wundkanal* (Gun Wound), which addressed the continuity of Nazi biographies in the Federal Republic of Germany. It was directed by Thomas Harlan, the son of Nazi director Veit Harlan, and premiered at the Venice International Film Festival in 1984. A documentary film *Notre Nazi* (Our Nazi) about the making of *Wundkanal* was shot simultaneously and is even more revealing than its inspiration.[26]

The life of Alfred Filbert spanned almost the entire twentieth century. His biography provides insights into the path to National Socialism taken by the so-called war youth generation (E. Günther Gründel) and the academic elite of the interwar years; the motivation of Nazi perpetrators for participating in mass murder and their involvement in the expansion of the same; the incorporation of Nazi criminals into post-war society in the Federal Republic of Germany and their prosecution (or, in many cases, their non-prosecution) by the West German judiciary; as well as the self-perception and self-portrayal of the perpetrators in the years and decades after the war.

Despite his unique life, not a single monograph, article or book chapter existed on Alfred Filbert when work was started on this biography. Since then only two scholarly articles specifically addressing Filbert have appeared, and both of these were penned by the current author.[27] Both a cause and a symptom of this anonymity is the unfortunate yet repeated misnaming of Filbert in the literature. This trend was started by the historian Michael Wildt in his well-received study on the leadership of the Reich Security Main Office, *Generation des Unbedingten*, in which Filbert is incorrectly referred to throughout as 'Albert'.[28] Regrettably, this error has been perpetuated by numerous historians since Wildt.[29] There is a contemporary precedent for the misnaming of Filbert as 'Albert', namely some of the official correspondence from 1974/75 concerning his early release from prison. This can be traced back to an error made by someone on the staff of the mayor of West Berlin at the time.[30] An earlier and more public precedent for misnaming him also exists: at the time of his arrest in 1959, he was sometimes referred to in the press as 'Georg Filbert'.[31]

***

One of the main questions I posed myself before embarking on the research for this book was the amount of original source material available on Filbert in light of his relative anonymity (though this should not be understood as a synonym for unimportance). In fact, for a mid-level Holocaust perpetrator and someone who remains, even for historians working in the field, relatively unknown, the source material is comparatively plentiful. One of the main sources used for this study are Filbert's trial records, comprising eighty-two files of defendant and witness testimony, prosecution and defence documents, and correspondence.[32] Naturally, testimony given in the framework of legal proceedings against Nazi perpetrators must be handled with great care – particularly that of defendants, from whom self-serving statements are to be expected.[33] With a total of six defendants and sixty-seven witnesses,[34] however, these documents contribute such a wealth of information that it would be foolish to overlook them as a historical source. If handled prudently and in conjunction with contemporary documentation, post-war testimony can provide important insights.[35]

Filbert's trial records were supplemented by documents from related legal proceedings,[36] but also by a substantial amount of contemporary documentation compiled by numerous German institutions and agencies – including the Reich Security Main Office and the 403rd Security Division (to which SS-Einsatzkommando 9 was assigned for logistical purposes) – addressing the period of Filbert's deployment with Einsatzkommando 9.[37] Original source material from the years of Filbert's employment in the SD and the Reich Security Main Office both prior and subsequent to his stint in the occupied Soviet territories was also utilised.[38] Party and state documents from the Nazi period were supplemented by a thick file from Filbert's days as a legal trainee in the People's State of Hesse, his doctoral file from his studies at the University of Giessen and his student file from the semester he spent at the University of Heidelberg.[39]

Three different archives provided documentation from the years of Otto Filbert's persecution, particularly in Buchenwald concentration camp, namely the International Tracing Service Archives in Bad Arolsen, the Archives of the Memorial Site Buchenwald in Weimar and the Institute of National Remembrance in Warsaw.[40] Important documents stored in the Residents' Registration Archives of Bad Gandersheim in the federal state of Lower Saxony were utilised for tracing Filbert's years in hiding under a false name after the war.[41] Berlin's Tegel Prison, where Filbert served his term of imprisonment, no longer possesses any records on its former inmate. What they did at one time possess was either destroyed or, in the case of files considered to be potentially of historical interest or significance, passed on to the Regional Archives in Berlin.[42] The surviving files were also used for this biography. The aforementioned and many other records from a total of thirty-three archives in seven different countries were accessed for this book.

In addition, the substantial number of so-called ego documents available in the source material cited above was rounded off by two interviews with Filbert, the first conducted by the British psychiatrist and psychoanalyst Dr Henry V. Dicks in July 1969 during Filbert's imprisonment,[43] and the second carried out during the filming of *Wundkanal* and included in the documentary *Notre Nazi*.[44] I was fortunate enough to be granted my own interviews with Filbert's nephew Peter; the interpreter on the set of *Wundkanal*, Ursula Langmann; the widow of the director of *Notre Nazi*, Erika Kramer; and a survivor of the Holocaust in Lithuania, Fania Brancovskaya.[45] These interviews were supplemented by correspondence with Filbert's eldest son, Dieter, and Filbert's nephew Ralph (with the assistance of his wife, Erika).[46] Unfortunately (though understandably), Dieter Filbert did not feel comfortable being interviewed on the subject of his late father, and declined my request to this effect. The information provided by these eyewitnesses to the life of Alfred Filbert nonetheless added much to the story told in these pages. When Filbert's widow died in 2003, the children cleared out their parents' apartment. No personal documents belonging to Filbert, such as letters or notebooks, were found. Thus, a self-contained collection of private papers belonging to Filbert evidently does not exist.[47] However, letters from Filbert himself and also from his father contained in other, aforementioned, archival collections were utilised for this book.

The main bulk of the archival material in German was supplemented by sources in Russian[48] and English. Published source material was consulted in German, Russian, English and French. Alongside the wealth of German-language literature, works in English, Russian, French and, to a considerably lesser extent, Italian were also drawn on. Survivor testimony was provided in Yiddish.

Once the research has been carried out, how should the historian approach the structuring of a biographical study? For assistance in answering this question, we can draw on the thoughts of the nineteenth-century Danish philosopher, Søren Kierkegaard, who wrote,

> It is quite true what philosophy says: that life must be understood backwards. But then one forgets the other principle: that it must be lived forwards. Which principle, the more one thinks it through, ends exactly with the thought that temporal life can never properly be understood precisely because I can at no instant find complete rest in which to adopt the position: backwards.[49]

Perhaps we, in hindsight, can succeed in understanding a person's life backwards by retelling it in the same way it was lived: forwards. As the French sociologist Pierre Bourdieu has noted, a human life constitutes a whole, a coherent and orientated ensemble. Like a story, a human life has a beginning and an end, and a chronological ordering of this life (in the form of a biography) is thus also a logical ordering.[50] This biography is therefore structured chronologically and expands on events, which combine to form sequences that allow for an intelligible analysis of relations and thus of the life as a whole. Of course, the chronological ordering is not in all cases strictly adhered to, as this – to borrow once again from Bourdieu – runs the risk of the narrative thread being lost.[51] Ultimately, however, we can, like Bourdieu, regard the pursuit of a chronological portrayal as inherent in the representation of life as history.[52] This realisation is also implicit in Kierkegaard's reflections on temporal life.

Although this biography covers the whole 85-year span of Filbert's life (1905–1990), the two longest chapters are those addressing his four-month stint as chief of a mobile killing squad in the German-occupied Soviet territories from June to October 1941. There are two reasons for this principle focus: first, the atrocities committed by Filbert during this period were the reason for his arrest in 1959, for him spending a total of sixteen years in prison and for him being cast in the role of an SS murderer in the film *Wundkanal* in the 1980s. Thus, his function as commando chief at the age of 35/36 decisively shaped the remaining forty-nine years of his life. Second, major historiographical debates continue to surround aspects of the National Socialist mass murder of Soviet Jewry, not least the escalation of the killing to include women and children, in effect marking the transition to genocide. For these reasons, the months of June–October 1941 require even more in-depth treatment than the other periods of Filbert's life. As such, the chapters in question furthermore constitute a systematic and thorough portrayal of the activities of one of the sub-commandos of SS-Einsatzgruppe B during the first four months of the German-Soviet war.[53]

1 'I went to school with quite a number of Jewish co-religionists and never knew hatred for Jews'

Childhood, youth and early adulthood, 1905–1932

On 14 November 1903, the 24-year-old professional soldier Corporal (*Unteroffizier*) Peter Filbert of the First Grand Ducal Hessian Lifeguards Infantry Regiment No. 115 (*Leibgarde-Infanterie-Regiment (1. Großherzoglich Hessisches) Nr. 115*) married the 22-year-old Christiane Kühner, an ironing woman, in Darmstadt.[1] Both were Protestant, as were their respective parents, with the exception of Kühner's mother, Franziska Kühner, née Weiß, who was Catholic.[2] The Lifeguards Infantry Regiment No. 115, garrisoned in Darmstadt, had been founded on 11 March 1621 and was as such the oldest of all German infantry regiments (see Figure 1).[3]

At ten o'clock on the morning of 8 September 1905, Karl Wilhelm Alfred was born in Darmstadt as the youngest of the three children of Peter and Christiane Filbert.[4] Their first child, Lina (see Figure 2), had been born on 26 July 1902 – almost sixteen months before her parents married – in Heidelberg,[5] the birthplace of her mother.[6] Their second child, Alfred's older brother Otto (see Figure 3), had been born on 10 May 1904 in Darmstadt.[7] Alfred would spend the first six years of his life in the Darmstadt garrison of the Lifeguards, at which his father was stationed.[8] During this time his father was promoted to company sergeant major (*Kompaniefeldwebel*, also known by the slang term *Spieß*).[9] Filbert would later state, 'We had a good life then. Of course I wanted to become a soldier. [...] After all – the Guards! I was enthusiastic [...] as a child.'[10] In 1911, when Alfred was six, Peter Filbert was taken on by the postal administration as a telegraph inspector. This meant that the family had to leave Darmstadt and move to nearby Worms.[11] It was here that Karl Wilhelm Alfred, known simply as Alfred, went to school. After attending the junior school (*Mittelschule*) and the upper secondary school (*Oberrealschule*) in Worms, he left the latter with his secondary school certificate (*mittlere Reife*) in March 1922 and began an apprenticeship at the *Commerz– und Privatbank* in Mannheim on 1 April of the same year. During this time he lived with his parents in Worms.[12]

Figure 1 Members of the Lifeguards Infantry Regiment No. 115 posing in front of their Darmstadt barracks, around 1910. (Source: Hessisches Staatsarchiv Darmstadt, R 4, Nr. 31736 UF, 'Soldaten, gruppiert vor Fassade der Infanterie-Kaserne, Darmstadt, um 1910'. Photographer: Geschwister Strauss, Darmstadt. Reproduced with permission of the Hessisches Staatsarchiv Darmstadt.)

Filbert would later describe his upbringing as 'proper' (*korrekt*).[13] In his home and family life, he knew only 'command and order' (*Befehl und Ordnung*). Nevertheless, he regarded his father as kind and warm-hearted, looked up to him and missed him terribly as a child during his absence on active service, including during the First World War,[14] during which he served as a captain (*Hauptmann*) and company commander.[15] It was in fact left to his mother to be the disciplinarian; she, however, was 'too strict'. To prove his point, Filbert recalled that during one of his father's absences he had suffered a bad fall and lay on the ground yelling in considerable pain. His mother came out and beat him with a stick for weeping. Only then did she look at his leg and discover that it was broken. She then took him into the house. Filbert put his mother's strictness down in part to her being so busy looking after three children. It was his soldier father with whom Filbert identified and whom he would later attempt to make proud.[16] The historian Wendy Lower notes that whilst historians

Figure 2 Lina Filbert, elder sister of Alfred, about 1930. (Reproduced with permission of Peter Filbert, Weinheim.)

cannot put their subjects on the couch or into a laboratory, 'it is worth pointing out that most Germans of the Nazi era were raised in authoritarian households where regular beatings – certainly not inductive reasoning – were employed to discipline and motivate children'.[17]

Filbert would recall many years later that he and his older brother, Otto, had loved each other 'very much' as children.[18] Allowing for potential nostalgia, Otto was and would remain a key figure for his younger brother throughout the latter's life. In 1926, Otto Filbert left Germany for the United States, where he would remain for twelve years.[19] He departed

Figure 3 Otto Filbert, elder brother of Alfred, about 1930.
(Reproduced with permission of Peter Filbert, Weinheim.)

on 8 April 1926 as a third-class passenger on the steamship *Columbus* from Bremen to New York via Southampton and Cherbourg.[20] Otto's future wife, Wilhelmina Koskamp, born in Bottrop, departed on 13 June 1926 – two months after her future husband – as a third-class passenger on the steamship *Bremen* from Bremen to New York, where she arrived on 24 June. Her uncle, Henry Bente, lived in New Haven, Connecticut.[21]

Asked in 1960, during the preliminary investigations for his subsequent trial, what his attitude towards Jews and Judaism had been during his youth, Filbert replied,

I spent my youth in Worms [on the] Rhine, a city with a large Jewish community, with families who had lived there for centuries. Many were known to me. I went to school with quite a number of Jewish co-religionists and never knew hatred for Jews. During the time I spent taking dance lessons I was often invited to visit Jewish families and my brother, who was a year older than me, used to socialise with Jewish families.[22]

By claiming he had been friendly with Jews, Filbert was no doubt attempting to appeal to the prosecutor and the judge at his trial. Nonetheless, Filbert's contact with Jews during his youth is itself interesting not least because many later Holocaust perpetrators had in fact never encountered Jews before they started killing them under the Nazi regime.[23]

Worms was located on the left bank of the Rhine River. In order to reach Mannheim, where he was engaged in his bank apprenticeship, Filbert had to cross over to the right bank. Those parts of the People's State of Hesse (the successor state to the Grand Duchy of Hesse-Darmstadt following the revolution of 1918) on the left bank of the Rhine, that is, the province of Rhenish Hesse (*Rheinhessen*), were occupied by French troops until 1930 in accordance with the terms of the Versailles peace treaty of 1919. The blockade of the bridges across the river in the French-occupied Rhineland in 1923 caused Filbert 'considerable difficulties' that led him to abandon his apprenticeship in Mannheim after a year and a half and instead complete it at the *Rheinische Kreditbank* in Worms.[24] It is not known what, if any, kind of *political* response these 'considerable difficulties' aroused in the 18-year-old Filbert, though it is certainly conceivable that the French occupation of the Rhineland and everything this entailed may have led to the development of revisionist nationalism within him. Of those German territories termed by the sociologist Michael Mann as 'regions adjacent to "threatened borders"', it was in fact the western territories, the Rhineland among them, that were most over-represented in Mann's analysis of over 1,500 biographies of perpetrators of Nazi genocide,[25] which is the largest and most representative sample of Nazi mass murderers yet studied. The upheaval of the French occupation of the Rhineland during the 1920s potentially offered Filbert decisive political experiences that may have shaped his ideological outlook.

Having completed his bank apprenticeship and unable to find employment in a bank due to the prevailing economic crisis, Filbert managed to obtain temporary work at the tax office in Worms. The then director of the tax office suggested to Filbert that he return to school in order to sit his school-leaving examinations so as to be hired afterwards by the tax office as a salaried employee.[26] Filbert followed this advice and, in autumn 1925, began attending a private school in Mainz, which also belonged to the province of Rhenish Hesse within the People's State of Hesse, governed from Darmstadt. During the months of October, November and December 1925, Filbert also attended the *Handelsinstitut Lust-Dickescheid* in Worms in order to learn shorthand.[27] After one and a half years at the private school in Mainz, Filbert sat his school-leaving examinations (*Abitur*) at the upper secondary school in Mainz as an external candidate.[28] Filbert's school-leaving certificate from March 1927 demonstrated that his best subjects were German and – perhaps ironically in view of later events – civic studies (*Staatsbürgerkunde*), in both of which he obtained the grade 'good' (*gut*). In the subjects French, mathematics, geography, natural history (*Naturkunde*) and physics he received the somewhat lower grade of 'on the whole good' (*im ganzen gut*). In English, history and chemistry he managed to obtain the grade 'sufficient' (*genügend*).[29] Despite his status as an external candidate, Filbert was apparently the best in his examination group. On the basis of his good examination results, Filbert's father 'allowed' him to commence university studies in law and economics rather than seek employment, as planned, at the tax office in Worms.[30] Thus, the career disruption that had threatened Filbert a couple of years earlier due to his inability to find work in a bank as a result of the prevailing economic crisis had led him to return to education and commence a university degree. He now had the prospect of a career in law. In Filbert's case, therefore, 'career disruption' does not appear to have been the cause of him joining the Nazi Movement.[31]

Filbert began his law studies in the summer semester of 1927 at the University of Giessen (*Hessische Landesuniversität zu Gießen*), where he enrolled on 30 April 1927.[32] He interrupted his nine semesters there to spend one semester, the summer semester of 1929, at the University of Heidelberg (*Ruprecht-Karls-Universität Heidelberg*),[33] the birthplace of his mother.[34] Filbert later claimed to have also studied at the University of Marburg.[35] The university archives in Marburg, however, do not contain any indication of an enrolment on the part of Filbert. Given the relative proximity of Giessen and Marburg, it is possible that he attended lectures in Marburg during his time at the University of Giessen, though without ever enrolling there.[36] Filbert spent less than three months in Heidelberg, enrolling on 2 May and leaving on 25 July 1929, during which time he lived at 15 Zwingerstraße.[37]

By the beginning of the 1930s, National Socialist students at German universities were already a force to be reckoned with, not least in Heidelberg. As early as the summer semester of 1930, a year after Filbert had been there, the National Socialist German Student Union (*Nationalsozialistischer Deutscher Studentenbund*, or NSDStB) obtained seventeen of forty-six seats in the elections to the General Student Committee (*Allgemeiner Studentenausschuss*, or AStA) at the University of Heidelberg. In the elections for the winter semester 1932/33, which were held on 19 and 20 January 1933, the NSDStB received eighteen of thirty-nine seats. This constituted a percentage of 46.7 per cent, as compared with the national average of 41.3 per cent.[38] These elections took place less than a fortnight before the Nazi assumption of power in Germany. Later that year, on 30 October 1933, another prominent future SS officer enrolled at the University of Heidelberg to study law, namely, Hanns Martin Schleyer.[39] Schleyer would go on to become an occupation official under Reinhard Heydrich in the Protectorate of Bohemia and Moravia during the war. He served in the 1970s as president of both the Confederation of German Employers' Associations and the Federation of German Industries until his murder by the Red Army Faction (*Rote Armee Fraktion*, or RAF) in October 1977.[40]

When Filbert began studying at the University of Giessen in summer 1927, a certain Heinz Jost was in his final semester there and in the process of completing his law studies.[41] Like Filbert, Jost had been born in the province of Hesse, in the small town of Holzhausen.[42] He would later be Filbert's immediate superior for a total of five years as Chief of Office III (Counterintelligence) in the Main Office of the SS Security Service (*Sicherheitsdienst*, or SD) and, later, as Chief of Office VI (Foreign Intelligence) in the Reich Security Main Office (*Reichssicherheitshauptamt*, or RSHA). During that one semester in Giessen, the two of them lived a stone's throw away from each other, Filbert at 67 Goethestraße and Jost at 30 Ludwigstraße.[43] It is unclear, however, whether the two of them already knew each other at this stage. They probably met for the first time several years later via the SS in Worms.[44] Between summer 1927 and winter 1929, Filbert resided at no fewer than three other locations in Giessen (20 Landmannstraße, 29 Asterweg and 36 Gnauthstraße).[45]

In the final examination in autumn 1933, known as the First Legal Exam (*Erste Juristische Prüfung*), Filbert received the overall grade 'sufficient' and the same grade in both the written and oral exams,[46] just as Jost had done six years previously.[47] It ranks among the traditional characteristics of the training for German lawyers that the grading is extremely stingy. Most successful examinations are evaluated only with 'sufficient'. Unlike Jost, however, it was Filbert's fourth attempt at passing the exam for legal trainees, although only *three* attempts were officially permitted. Filbert at the time put his failure to pass at the third attempt in summer 1932 down to his preparation being hampered by his 'political activities for the National Socialist Movement'.[48] If this was true, it would mean that Filbert was already active in the Nazi Movement prior to joining the

Nazi Party itself in August 1932. Indeed, in his curriculum vitae from January 1937 he confirmed, 'even before joining the Party I supported the Movement'.[49] The fact that the responsible ministry in Hesse even allowed Filbert to sit the exam a fourth time indicates that he received preferential treatment,[50] in all likelihood due to his dedication to the National Socialist Movement, which by that time was in power in Germany.

Many years later, Filbert would describe his childhood and his student years as 'my loveliest' (*meine schönste*) time.[51] His identity card from the University of Heidelberg shows a handsome man of almost twenty-four with short cropped hair and prominent ears (see Figure 4).[52] In his very first semester at the University of Giessen, he joined the student fraternity (*Burschenschaft*) Alemannia, which obliged each and every member to engage in at least six fencing matches.[53] As a member of the Alemannia, Filbert obtained the facial scars that he would carry for the rest of his life (see Figures 5 and 6). The Alemannia had been founded as a student union (*Studentenverein*) in December 1861, obtained in January 1862 the status of an association (*Verbindung*) and from November 1864 that of a fraternity. Its colours were blue, red and gold and its motto 'Unity creates power' (*Einheit schafft Macht*).[54] Heinz Jost was also a member of a student association, namely, the Corps Hassia-Gießen in nearby Mainz, where Filbert had attended upper secondary school.[55]

By the winter semester 1920/21, there existed at all universities in Germany so-called university circles (*Hochschulringe*), which sought to unite all nationalistic corporation and non-corporation students in a single organisation. These were in turn united in a German University Circle (*Deutscher Hochschulring*, or DHR), which had been founded in July 1920. At the centre of the ideology of the DHR students was an invocation of the *Volk*, which they understood to refer to all those with a 'shared ancestry, history and culture'. The main practical characteristics of this way of thinking can be summed up as pan-Germanic and anti-Semitic. Radical anti-Semitism thus functioned within the student fraternities of the DHR as an offensive expression of a radical nationalistic disposition and as a symbol of membership in the ethnic-nationalistic (*völkisch*) camp. This led already at the beginning of the 1920s to demands for the exclusion of Jews from any bodies representing German students. At the fourth congress of the German Student Body (*Deutsche Studentenschaft*, or DSt), the DHR, which had a two-thirds majority, forced through a statute accepting the racial–biological principle of membership already prevalent in Austria and the Sudetenland, and according to which Jews were barred from membership. The statute was incorporated into the charter of the DSt. Even when, at the end of 1926,

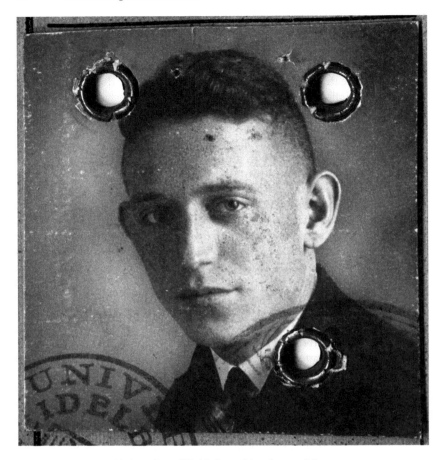

Figure 4 University of Heidelberg identity card for summer semester
1929. (Source: Universitätsarchiv Heidelberg, StudA, Filbert, Alfred
(1929), 'Erkennungskarte'. Reproduced with permission of the
Universitätsarchiv Heidelberg.)

the Prussian Minister for Education threatened to cancel the state's
recognition and funding of the DSt if the executive board did not revoke
the racist membership statute, 77 per cent of the students at Prussian
universities voted to retain the clause.[56] The outcome of the voting is
significant because it indicates how deeply many students, even in the
calm phase of the Weimar Republic, cherished ethnic-nationalist ideas.
As the historian Ulrich Herbert has correctly noted, a large number of the

Figure 5 Alfred Filbert (second row from the bottom, furthest left) with other members of the Giessen student fraternity Alemannia, 1927. (Reproduced with permission of Peter Filbert, Weinheim.)

academically educated leadership under the National Socialists were recruited from precisely these age groups.[57]

***

In 1932, E. Günther Gründel published an influential book, *Die Sendung der jungen Generation* ('The Calling of the Young Generation'), identifying three generational groups with reference to the First World War: the young front generation (*junge Frontgeneration*), born between 1890 and 1900; the war youth generation (*Kriegsjugendgeneration*), born between 1900 and 1910; and the postwar generation (*Nachkriegsgeneration*), born after 1910. Gründel regarded the war youth generation as the most important of these three groups. Although they had not personally experienced the Great War at the front, the childhood of the males belonging to this generation – of which Gründel himself, born 1903, was one – had been shaped by the hopes, despair and fallout of the war. Their fathers' world had collapsed and with it everything they had known. Revolution and the so-called revaluation of all values (a term borrowed

Figure 6 Alfred Filbert, 1927. (Reproduced with permission of Peter Filbert, Weinheim.)

from Friedrich Nietzsche) were followed straight after leaving school by the struggle for a job and in life in general.[58] Gründel correctly recognised the importance of childhood and youth experiences in shaping the character of the protagonists,[59] and he identified the most prominent characteristic of the war youth generation as 'dispassion' (*Sachlichkeit*). By this he meant that they did not wear their hearts on their sleeves, instead hated any form of verbal altruism, verbal moralisation or verbal patriotism, and ranked the objective above the personal. 'We [the war youth generation] seek not so much the best viewpoints as the best methods.'[60]

The publicist Sebastian Haffner (born 1907), another contemporary, also stressed in the memoirs of his youth, composed in 1939, the formative nature of the German schoolboys' experiences of the First World War, in which he saw the roots of National Socialism: 'The actual generation of Nazism, though, are those born in the decade 1900–1910, who, entirely untroubled by its actuality, experienced the war as one big game.'[61] Echoing Gründel, the historian Ulrich Herbert terms this group of young men the 'dispassionate generation' (*Generation der Sachlichkeit*).[62] In the same year as Gründel's work appeared, the publisher Peter Suhrkamp wrote an essay titled 'Sons without Fathers and Teachers', in which he characterised the same generation as 'the most unsettled, the most unclear and the most adventurous' in bourgeois society, as well as 'the fiercest opponents of liberalism'. He added, 'The most remarkable thing about them is their lack of humanity, their carelessness towards that which is human.'[63] These words would prove to be prophetic. Without exception, all twenty-four defendants at the Nuremberg SS-Einsatzgruppen trial of 1947/48 emphasised during proceedings how big the impact of the First World War, the German defeat and the immediate aftermath had been on their lives, although the vast majority were in fact far too young to have actually participated in the war.[64]

Having been born in 1905, Filbert was likewise too young to fight in the First World War or with the post-war *Freikorps* paramilitary militias, yet he was old enough to join the Nazi Movement before it came to power, and this he did. Following a lengthy interview with Filbert in July 1969, the British psychiatrist and psychoanalyst Dr Henry V. Dicks concluded,

His was a 'we' response [...] to the social pressures of that time on a young man typically pre-disposed to identify himself with the Nazi Movement which promised to heal Germany's divisions, hunger and humiliated soldierly pride and to realize such mens' [*sic*] hate-laden aims to exterminate its real and imaginary opponents and enemies.[65]

It was to the war youth generation and to the dispassionate generation that Filbert belonged. He also belonged to the young leadership of the National Socialist state who had been educated at academic institutions in the 1920s. Although he did not complete his university studies until late 1933, it was only as a result of a three-and-a-half-year interlude between him obtaining his secondary school certificate and embarking on his school-leaving examinations that his university studies were considerably delayed till 1927. Whilst still studying, he became active in the

Nazi Movement and joined both the Party and the SS.[66] Filbert was very much a part of the dispassionate generation and would remain so. As we will see, however, his generation was not the only or even the most decisive factor in explaining why he became an enthusiastic advocate of National Socialism and a radical enforcer of Nazi policies.

2 'In terms of his character he is irreproachable in every respect'

Nazi Party membership and career in the SS Security Service, 1932–1939

On 23 August 1932, more than a year before the end of his university studies in Giessen and five months prior to the Nazi takeover of power in Germany, Alfred Filbert joined the SS, which was still officially a sub-organisation of the SA (*Sturmabteilung*, i.e. Storm Detachment), in Worms.[1] His SS identity card carried the number 44,552.[2] Only days after joining the SS, Filbert also joined the National Socialist German Workers' Party (*Nationalsozialistische Deutsche Arbeiterpartei*, or NSDAP) in Worms.[3] His NSDAP membership number was 1,321,414.[4] It is tempting to surmise that Filbert may have been one of the 30,000 people who attended Adolf Hitler's speech of 12 June in the Wormatia Stadium on Alzeyer Straße.[5]

According to Filbert's SS certificate of service (*Dienstleisstungszeugnis*) from 15 December 1934:

During this period he performed his duties at all times gladly and to the satisfaction of all his superiors. It is in particular to be cited with praise that he thoroughly proved himself as a member of the SS during the main years of struggle in formerly red Worms in the year 1932 until the takeover of power. He was always a good comrade.[6]

During the period in question, from August 1932 to December 1934, Filbert belonged to the SS-Sturm 4/II/33, later renamed the SS-Sturm 8/33.[7] A *Sturm*, literally meaning 'storm' was a sub-unit of the SS corresponding to a company in the regular army and contained between 70 and 120 members. On Shrove Tuesday (28 February) 1933, Filbert was 'in the front line' during the 'heavy fighting' in Worms, though he was incapacitated from 23 March to mid-May of the same year by a serious case of liver poisoning.[8] In view of the date on which Filbert's incapacitation began, it is tempting to speculate that this may have been caused by excessive alcohol consumption in celebrating the passing of the Enabling Act (*Ermächtigungsgesetz*) on 23 March. The Enabling Act allowed the German government under Hitler to enact legislation without the participation of the German parliament, the Reichstag.[9] Filbert's involvement in the 'heavy fighting' in Worms on Shrove Tuesday 1933 provided him with an opportunity to 'distinguish' himself within the Nazi Movement by engaging in (pre-war) physical violence.

During his membership of the SS-Sturm 4/II/33, Filbert also completed six weeks of training at the SS sports school in the Bavarian town of Fürth (27 May–11 July 1934), for which his actual employer, the Hessian Ministry of State, granted him holidays.[10] The course participants were assessed on their personality and on their performance in the categories of office work, classroom tuition, drill, outdoor sports and shooting.[11] The same year, in addition to his training at the SS sports school, Filbert spent a further four weeks with the auxiliary police.[12] Another leave of absence from 30 August till 9 September was necessitated by Filbert's attendance of the annual Nazi Party rally in Nuremberg.[13] By February 1934 at the latest, Filbert had shown an interest in joining the political police and submitted an application to this end.[14] In response to the enquiries of the police,[15] the NSDAP in Hesse-Nassau confirmed, 'There are no concerns about the national dependability of the aforementioned.'[16]

It was in Worms via the SS that Filbert first met the man who would later become his direct superior, Heinz Jost.[17] Jost was acting police chief there between March and September 1933.[18] Following a subsequent spell as police chief in Giessen, where Filbert, as we know, was in the process of completing his university studies, Jost began his full-time career with the SS Security Service (*Sicherheitsdienst*, or SD) in Berlin in July 1934.[19] It is perhaps no coincidence that Filbert also began work as a full-time employee of the SD Main Office in Berlin not long thereafter, on 1 March 1935.[20] Before that, however, he continued his education to become a qualified lawyer. After passing the First Legal Exam on 20 December 1933, he began his legal traineeship (*Vorbereitungsdienst*) for junior lawyers in Hesse on 27 January 1934.[21] His first posting was at the local court in Worms,[22] where he commenced his duties on 29 January 1934.[23] Here he spent the next eight months,[24] and received the overall grade of 'satisfactory' (*befriedigend*),[25] before being sent to the small local court in Alzey in the province of Rhenish Hesse (*Rheinhessen*). He never reported for work there, however, because by that time he had already been granted an extended period of leave in order to work on his doctoral thesis at the University of Giessen.[26] On 30 October 1934, at Filbert's request, the president of the higher regional court in Hesse took the unusual step of granting Filbert leave from his legal traineeship, initially until the end of October 1935. The president explained his decision by pointing to 'the current circumstances' (*den vorliegenden Verhältnissen*).[27]

To which 'current circumstances' he was referring can be established from Filbert's written request of 27 October 1934:

As I have received the assurance of the Minister of State that I will be assigned in the near future to the police service and my summoning could take place any day, I request a leave of absence from the legal traineeship in order that I can sit the doctoral examination at the University of Giessen in the time remaining until my summoning. I request, in due consideration of my particular situation, that my request be granted.[28]

The Minister of State in Hesse was Dr Philipp Wilhelm Jung, formerly NSDAP circuit leader in Worms.

In fact, it was not just the 'police service' to which Filbert was assigned but in fact the SD – the Security Service of the SS. He began working for the SD Main Office in the Prinz-Albrecht-Palais at 102 Wilhelmstraße in Berlin on 1 March 1935 (see Figure 7).[29] Two days before starting work for the SD, the qualification of a Doctor of Laws was officially conferred on Filbert.[30] The doctoral thesis had been accepted in December 1934 and published early the following year. It was a mere twenty printed pages in length and entitled 'Can the Right of Refusal of the Trustee of the Conditional Seller be eliminated by means of the Prospective Entitlement of the Buyer to the Purchase of a Property?' (*Kann das Ablehnungsrecht des Konkursverwalters des Vorbehaltsverkäufers mit der Anwartschaft des Käufers auf den Eigentumserwerb ausgeräumt werden?*).[31] Filbert's doctoral supervisor was Erich Bley, professor of civil law and the philosophy of law in Giessen from 1932 to 1940, when he was appointed to a professorship in Graz. Bley had joined the NSDAP in May 1933 and would go on to write reports for the SD during the war years.[32] The subject matter of Filbert's thesis is nonetheless almost entirely apolitical and the historian Christian Ingrao has noted that Filbert's thesis – like that of other Nazis with a legal background, such as Hans Nockemann[33] – 'did not highlight its author's ethnic-nationalist commitment'.[34] This is for the most part true, though Filbert does refer in a prominent place in his thesis (page one) to the period 'before the national uprising' (*vor der nationalen Erhebung*), by which he meant the National Socialist takeover of power. This phrase doubtlessly exhibits undertones of right-wing ideology, as it was by no means a term used across the political spectrum to describe the event in question.

In the SD Main Office, Filbert was earmarked for SD domestic intelligence, specifically for a job that entailed keeping student corporations under surveillance. As a corporation student himself, however, Filbert had misgivings. He requested time to consider and sought advice from Dr Werner Best, head of Office I in the State Police Office

Figure 7 The Prinz-Albrecht-Palais, headquarters of the SD Main
Office, at 102 Wilhelmstraße, Berlin, in spring 1941. (Source:
Brandenburgisches Landesamt für Denkmalpflege und Archäologisches
Landesmuseum, Zossen, Messbildarchiv, 44 L 37 / 7204.26, 'Fassade
des Prinz-Albrecht-Palais in der Wilhelmstraße 102, 1941'.
Reproduced with permission of the Brandenburgisches Landesamt für
Denkmalpflege und Archäologisches Landesmuseum.)

(*Staatspolizeiamt*). Best, like Filbert, came from the province of Hesse and
the two of them knew each other from there.[35] Best took Filbert to SD
chief Reinhard Heydrich, to whom Filbert repeated his concerns.
Heydrich decided to assign Filbert instead to SD foreign intelligence
under Heinz Jost.[36]

On 2 January 1936, Filbert wrote to the president of the higher
regional court in Hesse to inform him that it would be impossible for
him to recommence his legal traineeship in Hesse but that he intended
to complete his training instead in Prussia. To this end, he announced
that he had arranged for the next phase of his training to be with the

Secret State Police Central Office (*Geheimes Staatspolizeiamt*, or Gestapa) in Berlin.[37] A week later, the higher regional court also approved this course of action.[38] Thus, on 20 February 1936 Filbert commenced the next phase of his training as a junior lawyer in the Gestapo Central Office in Berlin.[39] There he remained for six months.[40] At the end of this time, the personnel officer in the Gestapo Central Office, Hans Tesmer, conferred on Filbert the overall grade of 'good'. According to Tesmer, Filbert possessed good legal skills; had augmented this with considerable knowledge of adminis-tration; and was perceptive, industrious, conscientious and depend-able. Filbert furthermore showed great interest in the work of the political police.[41] Tesmer concluded,

Dr Filbert was thoroughly instructed in all important fields of activity of the Secret State Police. He handled the tasks assigned to him carefully and skilfully. In his judgement of political correlations he demonstrated a clear focus and a good understanding. His aptitude and suitability for the remit of the political police emerged in his case in a welcome way. Dr Filbert possesses an assured and able manner, which particularly came across in his oral presentation. His conduct towards colleagues testified to his sense of camaraderie. His draft reports were fluid and well thought through. In terms of his character [he is] irreproachable in every respect; he promises to become a capable senior administrative officer. His conduct on and off duty was impeccable.[42]

Filbert's performance in his legal studies had been agreeable and rounded off with the doctor title. Now, his training in the judiciary was comple-mented by an assignment to the executive, and here he appeared to have found in the political police a niche in which he could distinguish himself.

Following completion of his training with the Gestapo Central Office, the next step for Filbert would have been an eight-week period of training in a camp for legal trainees in Jüterbog in the Prussian province of Brandenburg.[43] All freshly qualified lawyers were required to undergo this National Socialist indoctrination in the Hanns Kerrl Communal Camp (*Gemeinschaftslager Hanns Kerrl*).[44] Upon his return from a four-week holiday in September 1936, however, Filbert informed the president of the higher regional court in Darmstadt that he was meanwhile employed full-time in the SD and requested that he therefore be granted another leave of absence from his legal traineeship until further notice.[45] In fact, Filbert was no longer merely a full-time SD employee: on 1 July 1936, he had been promoted to SS officer rank, and exactly a month later appointed head of Main Department 22 (Enemy Intelligence Services) within Office III (Counterintelligence) of the SD Main Office.[46] The requested leave of absence was granted, initially for half a year until April 1937.[47] At Filbert's request, however, it was extended to the end of August 1937[48] and then a third time until 31 August 1938.[49] On 14 November 1938, Filbert then requested that he be discharged entirely from the legal traineeship, as he was now to be 'accepted for good into the Secret State Police Central Office' (endgültig in das Geheime Staatspolizeiamt übernommen).[50] His request was granted four days later.[51] As a full-time employee of the SD since 1 March 1935, Filbert was embedded in an institutional sub-culture 'already favourable to tough physical, legal, and biological remedies for social ills years before genocide was initiated'. As the sociologist Michael Mann has pointed out, the Nazi regime 'could more easily accomplish genocide wielding such a willing core' of perpetrators.[52] Filbert's training in law had furthermore already provided him with experience of 'a conducive sub-culture in which Nazi ideology could resonate', as the Nazis were heavily over-represented in the legal profession.[53]

In his analysis of over 1,500 biographies of perpetrators of Nazi genocide, Mann identifies 'disrupted employment' as a characteristic that affected 24 per cent of his sample, though he adds that 'at most 16% of the sample might have suffered career disruptions that conceivably could lead through "the psychology of hard times" to extremist reactions'.[54] As noted in the previous chapter, the upheaval of the French occupation of the Rhineland during the 1920s certainly led Filbert to abandon his bank apprenticeship in Mannheim and instead to complete it in Worms; it furthermore potentially offered him decisive political experiences that may have shaped his ideological outlook. It is doubtful, though, that Filbert's joining of the Nazi Movement was a consequence of career disruption. Whilst indisputable in itself, Filbert's career disruption was nonetheless not particularly grave when compared with the German population of the time as a whole. Moreover, although never a brilliant law student, he could feasibly have had a career in law, had he not followed his ambition and ideology in opting for the SD.

***

In 1937, the SD Main Office commenced with the establishment of an information network in south-eastern Europe, Czechoslovakia and Austria.[55] Prior to this, intelligence work on Czechoslovakia, for example, had been sketchy and heavily reliant on press service digests.[56] By making use of the facilities provided by the SD district offices close to the German frontiers, Office III (Counterintelligence) in the SD Main Office – to which Filbert had been assigned two years earlier – established contact with pro-Nazi circles among Sudeten Germans and Austrians in order to gather intelligence on developments in these places. Office III played a substantial role in the preparation and execution of the Anschluss, the annexation of Austria by the Reich in March 1938.[57] As an officer in the foreign intelligence service, Filbert was required to make trips abroad. During the early autumn of 1938, he spent several weeks in the Sudetenland on official business.[58] At the beginning of October the Sudetenland was occupied by German troops.[59] Filbert's presence in the Sudetenland was understandable, as it was Office III that at the end of June had drafted plans for the deployment of SD members in the wake of German troops in the event of an advance into Czechoslovakia.[60] Department III 225, specially created for the task, led the SD operation.[61] Analogous to its duties in the Reich, the SD was to follow directly behind the advancing troops and provide for the consolidation of political life in the newly occupied territories as well as all industries required for the war economy.[62] Office III thus fixed the routes to be taken by the Einsatzgruppen in their advance across the border. The Sudetenland Medal (*Sudetenland-Medaille*), commemorating the union of this territory with Germany, was conferred on Filbert in recognition of his deployment there.[63]

Filbert was away on official business a lot during this period, for example in September 1939, when he spent – he later alleged – fourteen days in Budapest. Filbert claimed, after the war, to have been in Berlin on 1 September, when the Wehrmacht invaded and overran Poland, unleashing the Second World War,[64] but away on his birthday, 8 September. According to his testimony, he found upon his return a telegram from Heydrich congratulating him on his 34th birthday, which he had supposedly spent in the Hungarian capital.[65] During the time of Filbert's alleged two-week absence in Budapest, however, he was actually in Berlin attending meetings of the office heads of the future Reich Security Main Office (*Reichssicherheitshauptamt*, or RSHA) on 7, 12 and 19 September.[66] At the third of these meetings, on 19 September, and indeed as the first item on the agenda, Filbert was taken to task by Heydrich:

C [= Chief, i.e. Heydrich] told SS-Obersturmbannführer Dr Filbert in a clear way that the foreign reports are poor and must be considerably altered. In their current form they are a poor collage of newspaper and radio reports from foreign stations. He demands an invigoration of the work and desires only reports that have resulted from direct intelligence work.[67]

In front of his peers, Filbert – and by extension Jost – had been unequivocally warned.

On 21 September, Heydrich hosted a further meeting in Berlin of the office heads of the future Reich Security Main Office, who were joined this time by the chiefs of the Einsatzgruppen operating at the time in

Poland. Adolf Eichmann, then head of the Central Office for Jewish Emigration (*Zentralstelle für jüdische Auswanderung*) in Vienna, was also present. Again, Filbert also attended the meeting, representing Office VI (SD Overseas) of the emergent RSHA, which would replace Office III of the SD Main Office.[68] Heydrich summarised his instructions in four points:

1. Jews into the cities as quickly as possible,
2. Jews from the Reich to Poland,
3. the remaining 30,000 Gypsies to Poland as well,
4. systematic sending forth of the Jews from the German territories with freight trains.[69]

Filbert would later dispute having ever been present at this important meeting,[70] but the meeting's minutes tell a different story.[71] This meeting served as an introduction for Filbert to the planning for the deportation and ghettoisation of Eastern European Jews. Within two years he would be directly responsible for the shooting of Jews in their thousands.

Filbert was not present at all such meetings between 7 and 27 September. Of the seven meetings of future RSHA office heads that took place during this three-week period, Filbert attended five. Interestingly, those meetings he did not attend – on 8 and 14 September – were not attended by his boss Heinz Jost either, at least not according to the respective minutes.[72] Thus, Filbert was not so much representing Jost during the meetings he did attend, but was rather the only representative of Office III/VI to attend *any* of these meetings during the period in question. This suggests that Filbert was less a mere deputy for Jost in the latter's absence and more *the* key figure in SD foreign intelligence. Accordingly, in Filbert's absence through illness – as on 29 September – it was not Jost or Jost's representative who attended such meetings, but in fact Filbert's own deputy, SS-Sturmbannführer August Finke.[73]

At the meeting on 27 September, which Filbert also attended,[74] Heydrich announced that the decree for the reorganisation of the security apparatus had been signed by Himmler.[75] With effect from 1 October 1939, the Main Office of the Security Police, the Security Service of the Reichsführer-SS, the Secret State Police Central Office and the Reich Criminal Police Office were combined to form the Reich Security Main Office.[76] This decree thus officially fused the SD – a Party organisation – with the Security Police (i.e. Secret State Police and Criminal Police) – a state organisation. In this way, the SD was accounted for by the budget of the Reich Finance Minister, whilst still retaining its independence.[77] More than any other institution in Nazi Germany, the RSHA would become synonymous over the next six years with repression, terror and annihilation. As mentioned earlier, Office III of the SD Main Office now became Office VI (SD Overseas) of the RSHA.[78] Filbert was appointed both deputy head of Office VI under Heinz Jost,[79] his former superior in Office III, and head of the subordinated Group A, General Tasks (*Allgemeine Aufgaben*).[80] In this capacity he was responsible for personnel, administration, workshops and general intelligence tasks.[81] As such, Filbert was also the plenipotentiary of Office VI for reviewing all intelligence liaisons, including securing communications and courier lines and deploying intelligence resources at home and abroad.[82] Office VI was the largest of all seven RSHA offices,[83] and between September 1939 and June 1941, when he assumed command of Einsatzkommando 9, Filbert was the key figure in foreign intelligence. Jost did not possess experience in foreign intelligence and was dependent in this respect on his deputy.[84] In an interview after the war, their former colleague Dr Wilhelm Höttl said, 'He [Jost] relied on his very capable chief of staff, Dr Filbert; he had the then Office III [of the SD Main Office] by and large in his grip.'[85] The Interrogation Section of the Third US Army concluded in July 1945 that Filbert had not only been 'Jost's closest collaborator' but also 'the most able man in the section'.[86] His name was 'intimately connected with almost all phases of German intelligence operations during the first period', that is, until Jost's removal in September 1941.[87]

3 'Pity that the scoundrel didn't perish'
Brother's imprisonment and career stagnation, 1939–1941

In spite of Heydrich's aforementioned clear rebuke of September 1939 to the effect that the SD's foreign intelligence reports required improvement, Filbert had enjoyed a rapid rise through the SD and the ranks of the SS during the period 1935–1939. After becoming a full-time employee of Jost's Office III (Counterintelligence) in the SD Main Office on 1 March 1935, he had been promoted to the first SS officer rank, namely Untersturmführer (equivalent to second lieutenant), on 1 July 1936 (see Figures 8, 9 and 10).[1] Exactly one month later, he had been appointed head of Main Department 22 (Enemy Intelligence Services) within the SD Main Office. Further promotions followed on 30 January 1937 to Obersturmführer (lieutenant) and on 12 September 1937 to Hauptsturmführer (captain).[2] On 1 March 1938, his superior in Office III, SS-Oberführer Rudolf Fumy, had given Filbert the following appraisal:

SS-Hauptsturmführer Dr Filbert heads Main Department III 22 with considerable prudence and vigour. Under his leadership, Main Department III 22 has been expanded in an exemplary fashion. His knowledge and achievements are far above the average.
In view of the position as Main Department head and the exemplary achievements, it is proposed that he be promoted to SS-Sturmbannführer.[3]

Filbert's promotion to Sturmbannführer (major) followed eleven days later. On 30 January 1939 he was promoted again to Obersturmbannführer (lieutenant colonel).[4] With the creation of the RSHA in October 1939, Filbert had been appointed both deputy head of Office VI (SD Overseas), and head of the subordinated Group A, General Tasks. It was at this point, in autumn 1939, that his SS career stagnated. Although it would be more than six years before the Nazi regime collapsed, Filbert would remain at the rank of Obersturmbannführer (see Table 1). The reasons for this sudden halt to his rapid ascent are to be sought less in his professional performance and more in his family circumstances, as we will see.

Figure 8 Alfred Filbert in SS uniform wearing the insignia of an SS-Untersturmführer, 1937. (Source: Bundesarchiv Berlin-Lichterfelde, VBS 283/6010010064, RuSHA-Akte Dr. Alfred Filbert. Reproduced with permission of the Bundesarchiv Berlin-Lichterfelde.)

The years 1937–1939 in particular also saw notable developments in Filbert's personal life. On 15 May 1937 he married Käthe Ilse Frieda Bernicke,[5] born on 4 April 1910 in Groß Rhüden in Lower Saxony (see Figures 11 and 12).[6] The couple's first son, Dieter, was born a year later in Berlin on 21 May 1938.[7] On 27 February 1940, Käthe Filbert would give birth to their second son, Günter.[8] According to Filbert's SS officer file, Bernicke was not herself a member of the Nazi Party,[9] and neither were her parents.[10] Käthe Bernicke had been a supervisor in the German Red Cross and was still an active member as of early 1937.[11] In view of her new husband's status within the Nazi Movement, however, it is

Figure 9 Alfred Filbert in SS uniform wearing the insignia of an SS-Untersturmführer and the cuff title of the SD Main Office, 1937. (Source: Bundesarchiv Berlin-Lichterfelde, VBS 283/6010010064, RuSHA-Akte Dr. Alfred Filbert. Reproduced with permission of the Bundesarchiv Berlin-Lichterfelde.)

Figure 10 Alfred Filbert in SS uniform wearing the insignia of an SS-
Untersturmführer and a peaked cap with the SS death's head badge,
1937. (Source: Bundesarchiv Berlin-Lichterfelde, VBS 286/
6400010138, SSO-Akte Dr. Alfred Filbert. Reproduced with
permission of the Bundesarchiv Berlin-Lichterfelde.)

reasonable to assume that her own political loyalties may have been
similar. By 1937, the German Red Cross had long ceased to be an
independent organisation. The executive president was SS-Oberführer
Dr Ernst-Robert Grawitz, the Reich's most senior SS physician
(*Reichsarzt-SS*) and responsible for numerous atrocities in the years that

Table 1 *Comparative table of ranks (1941)*

German ministerial bureaucracy	SS	German army	British army
Reichsminister	Reichsführer-SS	Generalfeldmarschall	Field Marshal
Staatssekretär	[no equivalent]	Generaloberst	General
Unterstaatssekretär	SS-Obergruppenführer	General	Lieutenant General
Ministerialdirektor	SS-Gruppenführer	Generalleutnant	Major General
[no equivalent]	SS-Brigadeführer	Generalmajor	Brigadier
Ministerialdirigent	SS-Oberführer	[no equivalent]	[no equivalent]
Ministerialrat	SS-Standartenführer	Oberst	Colonel
Regierungsdirektor	SS-Obersturmbannführer	Oberstleutnant	Lieutenant Colonel
Oberregierungsrat	SS-Sturmbannführer	Major	Major
Landrat	[no equivalent]	[no equivalent]	[no equivalent]
Regierungsrat	[no equivalent]	[no equivalent]	[no equivalent]
Amtsrat	SS-Hauptsturmführer	Hauptmann	Captain
Oberinspektor	SS-Obersturmführer	Oberleutnant	Lieutenant
Inspektor	SS-Untersturmführer	Leutnant	Second Lieutenant
Obersekretär	SS-Hauptscharführer	Oberfeldwebel	Warrant Officer Class I
Sekretär	SS-Oberscharführer	Feldwebel	Warrant Officer (Class II)
Verwaltungsassistent	SS-Scharführer	Unterfeldwebel	Staff Sergeant
Assistent	SS-Unterscharführer	Unteroffizier	Sergeant
Ministerialamtsgehilfe	SS-Rottenführer	Obergefreiter	Corporal
Amtsgehilfe	SS-Sturmmann	Gefreiter	Lance Corporal
[no equivalent]	SS-Mann	Soldat	Private

Source: Alex J. Kay, Jeff Rutherford and David Stahel, eds., *Nazi Policy on the Eastern Front, 1941: Total War, Genocide, and Radicalization* (Rochester, NY: University of Rochester Press, 2012), p. 321.

Figure 11 Käthe Bernicke, future wife of Alfred Filbert, in her SS
marriage application, 1937. (Source: Bundesarchiv Berlin-Lichterfelde,
VBS 283/6010010064, RuSHA-Akte Dr. Alfred Filbert. Reproduced
with permission of the Bundesarchiv Berlin-Lichterfelde.)

followed, including medical experiments on concentration camp
inmates.[12]

Filbert's own father had joined the NSDAP in Worms on 1 May 1933[13]
and in fact rose to become a circuit training officer (*Kreisausbildungsleiter*)
in the Party, whilst Filbert's mother – like his mother-in-law[14] – was in the
National Socialist Women's League (*NS-Frauenschaft*).[15] Not everyone

Figure 12 Käthe Bernicke, future wife of Alfred Filbert, in her SS
marriage application, 1937. (Source: Bundesarchiv Berlin-Lichterfelde,
VBS 283/6010010064, RuSHA-Akte Dr. Alfred Filbert. Reproduced
with permission of the Bundesarchiv Berlin-Lichterfelde.)

in the Filbert family was a committed National Socialist, however.
According to testimony Filbert gave in 1960, his parents had persuaded
his older brother Otto to return to Germany from the United States,
where he had been living for the previous twelve years and had worked

as an engineer for the Pullman Works in Philadelphia. He returned to Germany, together with his wife of five years[16] and two sons (Ralph, born 1934, and Peter, born 1936),[17] in 1938 for one year on a trial basis.[18] According to Filbert, his brother Otto was unable to adapt to the new way of life in Nazi Germany and resolved to return to the United States. Otto had already obtained from the US consulate in Hamburg the relevant papers for his departure, when he learnt of an order from Hitler that prevented German citizens wherever possible from emigrating. Despite the twelve years he had spent in the United States, Otto Filbert had remained a German citizen.[19] He could not leave Germany. This left him in a state of considerable embitterment. In response to the failure of the assassination attempt on Hitler's life made by the carpenter Georg Elser on 8 November 1939, Otto commented to a colleague at the Junkers Aircraft Factory in Dessau, where he worked, 'Pity that the scoundrel didn't perish.'[20] This comment was promptly reported by Otto's colleague and Otto was arrested by the Magdeburg Gestapo on 13 November.[21] A regular court of law in Dessau then sentenced him to four years' imprisonment for 'treachery' (*Heimtücke*), although he did not have any previous convictions.[22] He was thus convicted on the basis of the Law against Treacherous Attacks on State and Party and for the Protection of Party Uniforms (*Gesetz gegen heimtückische Angriffe auf Staat und Partei und zum Schutz der Parteiuniformen*) of 20 December 1934.[23] Otto's father, Peter Filbert, chose not to pay for the costs of his son's defence counsel.[24]

Filbert later claimed to have done everything he could to help his brother, including visiting him several times in prison and speaking with the prison warden. No one, however, was able to help Otto, apparently, since Himmler had personally decreed that after serving his sentence Otto should be sent to a concentration camp. In view of Himmler's leadership style and frequent personal intervention in the private and professional affairs of his officers,[25] it is entirely plausible that he issued such a directive. According to Filbert, it was this affair with his brother that put a stop to any further promotion for him within the SS.[26] Heinz Jost's former adjutant, SS-Hauptsturmführer Paul Lehn, likewise later testified to this effect.[27] The historian Michael Wildt casts doubt on this assertion in light of the rank Filbert had already reached.[28] Yet it is precisely for this reason that Filbert's claim seems plausible: in the space of two-and-a-half years he had been promoted five times; yet over the next six-and-a-half years he would not be promoted again. Filbert would remain at the rank of SS-Obersturmbannführer, to which he had been promoted in January 1939. He was not promoted even after his four-month spell commanding an SS task force in the East, although it was not uncommon for replaced commando or group chiefs to be promoted upon their return to Germany in recognition of their completion of a stint in the field.[29]

***

For the time being, Filbert remained with Office VI of the RSHA. At the end of March 1940, he received the Memel Medal (*Memel-Medaille*)[30] in commemoration of the bloodless annexation to Germany of Memel Territory (now the Klaipėda Region) from Lithuania on 22 March 1939.[31] On 5 June of the same year, head of Office I (Administration and Law) of the RSHA Dr Werner Best, his old acquaintance from Hesse, drew up a proposal for Filbert's appointment as government councillor (*Regierungsrat*) in the German ministerial bureaucracy and thus his admission into the senior civil service.[32] The advantages of such an admission for the RSHA were manifold: intake and training of candidates for the civil service; the creation and administration of permanent posts; promotions, secondments or transfers; fixed incomes and secure pensions.[33] Best justified his proposal to promote Filbert as follows: 'By virtue of his rich experience in the foreign intelligence service and his countless personal contacts abroad, the contribution of Dr Filbert is of inestimable value from the perspective of the State Police. There is therefore an urgent professional interest in his admission to the civil service.'[34] The proposal was to be submitted to Hitler.[35] Whether it got that far, however, is unclear. Best appears not to have been able to provide the Reich Ministry of Finance with a satisfactory description of Filbert's proposed position.[36] There is in any case nothing in Filbert's SS personnel file to suggest that the appointment was made.[37] The constellation of Best and Filbert was an unfortunate one; both of them were having trouble with Heydrich and Himmler. Following a disagreement with Heydrich over future recruitment practice in the RSHA, Best departed a month after submitting the proposal for Filbert's appointment and reported for duty in the Wehrmacht.[38] Best was not alone among prominent members of the RSHA in seeking deployment at the front. The head of Office II[39] (Ideological Research on Opposition), SS-Standartenführer Professor Franz Alfred Six, had voluntarily joined the Waffen SS in May 1940.[40] Filbert used a vacation in July 1940 to also join a Waffen SS regiment, though he did not see combat due to the swift German victory in the French campaign in June and returned instead to the RSHA in Berlin. Filbert later explained that he had joined the Waffen SS regiment because of the difficulties he was experiencing within the RSHA as a result of his brother, and that he had hoped to serve at the front.[41] The regiment in question was the SS-Death's Head Infantry Regiment 14

(*SS-Totenkopf-Infanterie-Regiment 14*), which Filbert joined with the rank of SS-Unterscharführer (equivalent to sergeant).[42]

Filbert would eventually get to see combat, though perhaps not under quite the circumstances he had in mind in July 1940. That very same month, Germany's political and military leaderships began to discuss the possibility of invading the Soviet Union the following spring.[43] Filbert himself was not involved in preparations until March 1941. On 26 March, Reinhard Heydrich met with Reichsmarschall Hermann Göring. Following the meeting, Heydrich noted down in a series of points what had been discussed. Points 10 and 11 read:

10. Regarding the solution to the 'Jewish Question' I briefly reported to the Reichsmarschall and presented him with my draft, of which, with an alteration regarding the jurisdiction of [Alfred] Rosenberg, he approved and ordered resubmission.

11. The Reichsmarschall said to me, among other things, that in the event of an operation in Russia we should prepare a very short, 3–4-page briefing that the troops could get, about the dangerousness of the GPU organisation, the political commissars, Jews etc., so they more or less know whom they have to put up against the wall.[44]

Heydrich sent the original version of these notes to Himmler and copies to Chief of Office IV (Gestapo) of the RSHA SS-Brigadeführer Heinrich 'Müller (also for Eichmann's information)'; to head of Group E (Counter-Espionage) in Office IV SS-Sturmbannführer Walter Schellenberg; to Chief of Office I (Personnel) of the RSHA SS-Brigadeführer Bruno Streckenbach; to Chief of Office III (SD Domestic) of the RSHA SS-Standartenführer Otto Ohlendorf, later head of Einsatzgruppe D in the southern Ukraine; and to 'Filbert (for SS-Brif. [= Brigadeführer] Jost)'. The information contained therein was 'strictly confidential' (*streng vertraulich*).[45] The most likely explanation for Filbert being directly sent a copy of these important notes is that he had long since to all intents and purposes replaced his nominal superior, Heinz Jost, as the leading figure in Office VI of the RSHA. Perhaps he had also already been earmarked by Heydrich for deployment with the Einsatzgruppen in the campaign against the Soviet Union.

The fact that SS-Obersturmbannführer Adolf Eichmann, the head of IV B 4, the RSHA's section on Jewish affairs, and principal organiser of transports, was to be informed of the contents of Heydrich's notes indicates that Heydrich and Göring discussed deportations. When this is combined with the knowledge that the two men also discussed 'the solution of the "Jewish Question"' in conjunction with the jurisdiction of Alfred Rosenberg, who was at this point in time slated to head the civil administration in the territories later to be conquered from the Soviet

Union,[46] it becomes clear that Heydrich's reflections on a solution to the 'Jewish Question' were in terms of a territorial solution in the occupied Soviet territories after the war. Thus, by the end of March 1941 at the latest, this course of action – the draft for which had been 'approved' by Göring – was the intended policy towards Europe's Jewish population.[47] Point 11 in Heydrich's notes makes it clear, however, that certain groups had been earmarked for execution during the – already resolved upon – invasion of the Soviet Union, Jews among them. Filbert was thus among a small group of perhaps around ten men who were privy to German plans for the fate of both Soviet Jewry and European Jewry as a whole. His hands-on involvement was about to increase.

After the war, Filbert claimed that he first learnt of plans to invade the Soviet Union during a discussion with Heydrich in March or April 1941. Aside from himself and Heydrich, the aforementioned Müller and Streckenbach, as well as Chief of Office V (Criminal Police) of the RSHA SS-Brigadeführer Arthur Nebe, later head of Einsatzgruppe B in Belarus, were allegedly present.[48] Filbert was the only participant below the rank of SS-Brigadeführer (equivalent to brigadier). This could be understood as a testament to his importance. Filbert himself later claimed that he was merely representing the absent Jost,[49] but it is striking how often Filbert deputised for Jost between 1939 and 1941.

Similarly to the preparations for the deployment of the Einsatzgruppen in the Polish campaign two years earlier,[50] at the meeting in spring 1941 Filbert learnt that commandos of the Security Police and the SD would be deployed alongside security divisions of the Wehrmacht in order to 'cleanse' (*säubern*) the regions between the three advancing army groups of scattered enemy soldiers and partisans.[51] Nebe, Müller, Streckenbach and Filbert all volunteered for service in the impending operation, though apparently unaware, according to Filbert, that their activity would include carrying out executions of, among others, Jews.[52] When he first made this claim to ignorance, Filbert was under arrest for the mass murder of Soviet Jews. His assertion should be viewed in this context. Heydrich's memorandum of 26 March – a copy of which was sent to Filbert – furthermore made it clear that the German leadership expected Jews to be among those who would be 'put up against the wall'. Filbert knew precisely what a commission in the East would entail and he volunteered for it. On 20 April, quite possibly in recognition of him volunteering to serve with the SS forces in the Soviet campaign, the War Merit Cross 2nd Class with Swords (*Kriegsverdienstkreuz II. Klasse mit Schwertern*) was conferred on Filbert.[53]

Heydrich's adjutant subsequently instructed Filbert to repair to the town of Pretzsch in the Prussian province of Saxony, where he would assume command of the unit Einsatzkommando (EK) 9.[54] The first head of Sonderkommando 7a, SS-Obersturmbannführer Dr Walter Blume, claimed after the war that he had initially been chosen to command EK 9 but that he requested Streckenbach to instead give him 'a small commando at the front', a wish that was then granted.[55] The case of SS-Sturmbannführer Ernst Ehlers demonstrates that it was possible to reject an appointment to lead such a commando and not suffer any negative consequences. Ehlers was originally appointed head of Einsatzkommando 8, like EK 9 a sub-commando within Einsatzgruppe (EG) B, but he requested redeployment before the invasion began.[56] This was granted: Ehlers was instead appointed to head departments IV and V in the staff of EG B, a post he held from June until his departure from Russia on 14 October 1941.[57] He was replaced as head of EK 8 by SS-Sturmbannführer Dr Otto Bradfisch. From May 1941 onwards, the personnel of the Einsatzgruppen gathered in the town of Pretzsch, where the Border Police Academy (*Grenzpolizeischule*) was located, and in the neighbouring towns of Düben and Bad Schmiedeberg.[58] As head of personnel within the RSHA, it was Streckenbach – incidentally chief of Einsatzgruppe I during the Polish campaign[59] – who was responsible for assembling the Einsatzgruppen. He often visited and inspected those gathered in Pretzsch.[60] According to Streckenbach, it was Heydrich who made suggestions for the senior positions, that is, those of EG and EK chiefs, and Himmler who personally made the final decision.[61] On 16 June 1941, six days before the invasion of the Soviet Union and evidently after the decision had been made to appoint Filbert to command EK 9, Streckenbach returned Filbert's personnel and examination files from his time as a legal trainee to the president of the higher regional court in Darmstadt.[62]

Following his appointment as head of EK 9, Filbert returned to Berlin to settle his official affairs in the RSHA[63] and then attend a meeting of the commando and group chiefs – analogous to the approach taken for the Polish campaign[64] – hosted by Heydrich on 17 June at his headquarters in the Prinz-Albrecht-Palais.[65] It was most likely here, on this day, that the EG and EK chiefs were expressly informed that their commission in the area of operations would involve the decimation of Soviet Jewry.[66] Based on the evidence for the approach of the Einsatzgruppen during the first five weeks of the military campaign, Heydrich had probably specified that the Jewish intelligentsia and as many male Jews of military service age as possible be killed, since these target groups were regarded by the German leadership as likely Communist activists and potential partisans.[67] As the historian Klaus-Michael Mallmann has convincingly argued, if there had been a pre-invasion order to kill *all* Soviet Jews,[68] the course of action taken by all the commandos during the first five weeks of the campaign would have amounted to insubordination.[69]

During the planning phase for the German invasion of the Soviet Union – codenamed 'Operation Barbarossa' – Hitler, Himmler and Heydrich could not have been certain how the Wehrmacht would react to large-scale massacres of Soviet Jews – that is, non-combatants – within its own area of operations. It seems reasonable to assume, therefore, that the pre-invasion orders issued *in writing* to the Einsatzgruppen were roughly compatible with the instructions issued by the High Command of the Wehrmacht (*Oberkommando der Wehrmacht*, or OKW) to the regular troops.[70] These instructions, later referred to as 'the criminal orders', called for the execution of political functionaries (Red Army commissars) and those offering any kind of resistance.[71] Indeed, the instructions contained in Heydrich's oft-cited 2 July written communication to Himmler's most senior representatives in the occupied Soviet territories, the Higher SS and Police Leaders (*Höhere SS– und Polizeiführer*, or HSSPF) – which claimed to summarise the instructions Heydrich had already issued verbally to the Einsatzgruppen at the afore-mentioned meeting of 17 June – called for the execution specifically of 'Jews in Party and state positions' (*Juden in Partei– und Staatsstellungen*).[72]

At the same time, the wording of Heydrich's written instructions from 2 July left the group and commando chiefs considerable discretion of inter-pretation. Since Communist Party functionaries had already been mentioned at the top of Heydrich's list of those to be executed, the additional reference to 'Jews in Party and state positions' placed particular emphasis on Jews. Furthermore, the instructions included, in the list of those to be executed, 'all [. . .] other radical elements (saboteurs, propagandists, snipers, assassins, agitators, etc.)'.[73] Thus, it appears that Heydrich expected, and indeed intended, that his instructions be interpreted broadly; how, for example, were the terms 'propagandists' and 'agitators' to be defined? Even the last word on the list, 'etc.', demonstrates that those who came under the heading 'other radical elements' were by no means clearly specified. The key point here is that, although Heydrich stipulated *in writing* only that Jews in Party and state positions were to be killed, by emphasising Jews *at all* here (when such Jews were already subsumed under Communist Party functionaries), and by making other entries in the list very vague, he was – between the lines – leaving sig-nificant leeway for his subordinates, including Filbert, to go beyond his written instructions.

4 'So, we've finished off the first Jews'
SS-Einsatzkommando 9 and deployment in the East,
June–July 1941

Although the SS-Einsatzgruppen had been deployed in previous military campaigns, they operated during the invasion of the Soviet Union in June 1941 for the first time officially under the title 'Einsatzgruppen of the Security Police and the SD'.[1] Three of the Einsatzgruppen, A to C, were assigned to each of the three Army Groups, North (for the Baltic), Centre (for Belarus) and South (for northern and central Ukraine), whilst the fourth – Einsatzgruppe D – was assigned to the German 11th Army, which was set to advance together with the two Romanian armies through southern Ukraine, the Crimea and the Caucasus. Einsatzgruppe (EG) B, with an initial strength of 655 men,[2] was assigned to Army Group Centre (see Figure 13).[3] In accordance with the agreement reached between the High Command of the Army (*Oberkommando des Heeres*, or OKH) and the RSHA in the spring, its two Sonderkommandos (SK), 7a and 7b, would operate in the army rear areas (*rückwärtige Armeegebiete*), where they would be responsible for securing specific materials and card indexes as well as important individuals ('leading emigrants, saboteurs, terrorists etc.'), whilst its two larger Einsatzkommandos (EK), 8 and 9, would be deployed further back in the army group rear areas (*rückwärtige Heeresgebiete*), where they would investigate and tackle movements hostile to Germany – to the extent that these movements did not constitute part of the enemy's armed forces – and provide information to the Wehrmacht on political developments.[4] An Advance Commando Moscow (*Vorkommando Moskau*), which was to fulfil special tasks in the Soviet capital, was also part of EG B.

At the time of its departure from Pretzsch,[5] Einsatzkommando 9 contained a total of 144 people. Of these, fifteen were SS officers. A further eighty-three were officials of non-officer rank in the Gestapo, the Criminal Police, the SD or the Waffen SS, of which fifty-one were non-commissioned officers (NCOs). As many as forty-six drivers and baggage personnel also belonged to the commando. This contingent included a platoon of Waffen SS reservists. A platoon of the Order Police (*Ordnungspolizei*) – the 3rd platoon of the 2nd company of Reserve Police Battalion 9 – also joined the commando in Warsaw. This platoon

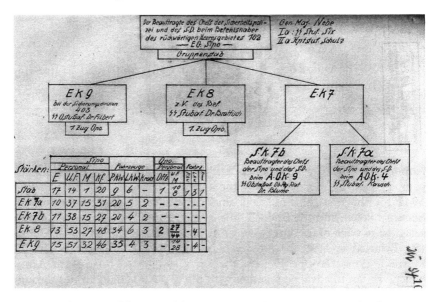

Figure 13 Diagram of the structure and personnel strength of
Einsatzgruppe B at the outset of Operation Barbarossa, June 1941.
(Source: Bundesarchiv-Militärarchiv, Freiburg im Breisgau, RH 22/
224, fols. 107–108, 'Anlage zum Korpsbefehl Nr. 18 vom 24.6.41', here
fol. 108. Reproduced with permission of the Bundesarchiv-
Militärarchiv.)

totalled forty-two men, of which fourteen were NCOs and twenty-eight
from the rank and file.[6] The addition of the police platoon took the
strength of EK 9 to a combined total of 186 men. Both the Waffen SS
reservists and the Order Police platoon functioned as 'guard forces'
(*Sicherungskräfte*). In actuality, this meant that they were to be predominantly used for carrying out arrests and for shooting operations.[7] Like the
other groups and commandos, EK 9 was fully motorised and had thirty-
five cars, four trucks and three motorcycles at its disposal as of 24 June.[8]
The Order Police platoon had an additional four trucks.[9]

   The allocation of duties within the commando was based on that of the
Reich Security Main Office: it contained a personnel specialist (Section
I), a specialist for household and financial affairs (Section II), an SD
specialist (Section III), a Gestapo specialist (Section IV) and a Criminal
Police specialist (Section V).[10] It was not unusual within the different
formations of the Einsatzgruppen for the same person to head both
Sections IV and V and, thus, to function in effect as an overarching 'police

specialist', as for instance in EK 9, the staff of EG B or the staff of EG A.[11] It was the responsibility of the police specialist to keep a record of the killings and at regular intervals of perhaps a week to submit figures for those killed to the commander, who – in the case of EK 9 – was Filbert. It was then the responsibility of the latter to pass these figures on to the staff of Einsatzgruppe B. From there, the reports of all the commandos subordinated to Einsatzgruppe B were sent on to the RSHA in Berlin, where they formed the basis of the almost daily 'Incident Reports USSR' (*Ereignismeldungen UdSSR*, or EM).[12] Reports from sub-commandos (*Teilkommandos*) reached the commando staff by courier or by radio, whilst teletype was additionally employed to send the more comprehensive reports of the commando staff itself on to Berlin.[13]

Filbert's deputy in EK 9 was the 41-year-old Wilhelm Greiffenberger, who headed a sub-department (*Unterreferat*) in Office I (Personnel) of the Reich Security Main Office.[14] Filbert had initially intended to utilise Greiffenberger as an interpreter, as the latter had been born in St Petersburg, Russia, into a family with German roots. However, in view of his rank of Sturmbannführer in the SS, which meant he was the highest-ranking officer in the commando after Filbert, Greiffenberger was appointed at his own request as deputy to Filbert, as well as head of Section I (Personnel) and Section II (Financial Affairs).[15] Head of Sections IV and V in the commando and thus responsible for the tasks of the Gestapo and the Criminal Police was the 27-year-old Gerhard Schneider, who was a detective inspector (*Kriminalkommissar*) in the Gestapo. Although Schneider was one of the youngest officers in the commando, Filbert appointed him to this position on account of his brisk military bearing and his zeal. Like Filbert, Schneider was the son of a professional soldier.[16] Instead of using the formal and more customary *Sie*, the two of them communicated per *Du*.[17] It was perhaps no coincidence that it was the most radical of his officers with whom Filbert was on this familiar footing.

As head of Section IV, it was Schneider who was in charge of anti-Jewish measures.[18] During his deployment with EK 9, Schneider wore the uniform of an SS-Obersturmführer, which corresponded to his rank in the Gestapo.[19] A dozen members of the Security Police – that is, Gestapo and Criminal Police – belonged to the police section.[20] Among those subordinated to Schneider within the police section was Heinrich Tunnat, a 28-year-old probationary detective inspector in the Berlin Criminal Police and SS-Untersturmführer. After the commando departed from Pretzsch, Tunnat was entrusted with the leadership of the aforementioned Waffen SS platoon, which did not have an officer of its own.[21] Head of the SD section in EK 9 was SS-Obersturmführer

Friedrich 'Fritz' Klein of the SD.[22] Among other things, the SD section
was required to deal with political matters in the area of operations.[23]
According to Greiffenberger, Klein had 'a distinctly hard time of it with
Filbert'.[24] All of the aforementioned – Filbert, Greiffenberger, Schneider,
Tunnat and Klein – were assigned to Einsatzkommando 9 already in
Pretzsch.[25]

***

On the morning of 23 June, the day after the launch of the German
invasion of the Soviet Union, Einsatzkommando 9 left Pretzsch together
with the rest of Einsatzgruppe B. After a stopover in Poznań, which was
reached the same day, it arrived on 28 June in Warsaw, where the aforementioned Order Police platoon (the 3rd platoon of the 2nd company of
Reserve Police Battalion 9), led by the 33-year-old non-commissioned
officer Hauptwachtmeister Richard Neubert, was attached to it (see
Figure 14). It departed again a day later, however, for the operations
area of the 403rd Security Division, to which it was assigned (see
Figure 15).[26] The commando overnighted along the way in the small
East Prussian border town of Treuburg (now Olecko, Poland).[27] Here
Filbert assembled the entire commando and informed them of the so-
called Führer order (*Führerbefehl*), according to which the
Einsatzkommandos in the rear areas also had the task of shooting Soviet
Jews.[28] Both Greiffenberger and Tunnat later testified – independently
of one another – that they interpreted the order at the time as being
limited to Jewish men.[29] The order provoked neither objections nor
discussions.[30] At least two members of EK 9 later testified that the
order also extended to 'Gypsies', whilst one of these furthermore recalled
the inclusion of 'other subversive elements' and the other remembered
specifically 'commissars and functionaries'.[31]

After overnighting in Treuburg, the commando crossed the German-
Soviet border and reached – on 30 June – the town of Varina, 70 km
south-east of Vilnius, capital city of the Lithuanian Soviet Socialist
Republic (Lithuanian SSR). There the unit spent the night in a camp in
the forest.[32] From here, Filbert – acting on the orders of Einsatzgruppe B –
instructed a fifteen- to twenty-man-strong advance party under the 32-
year-old SS-Obersturmführer Richard Haupt, who belonged to the commando's police section, to march to Vilnius via the Belarusian cities of
Grodno and then Lida and for these two localities to be 'swept by the
Security Police' (*sicherheitspolizeilich zu überholen*).[33] In Lida, the
Wehrmacht had already gathered together all Jews between 15 and 60
years of age, before then releasing them.[34] On 5 July, in accordance with
Filbert's instructions, Haupt and another SS officer, SS-Obersturmführer

Figure 14 Members of the 2nd company of Reserve Police Battalion 9, assigned to Einsatzgruppe B in Warsaw. (Source: Staatsarchiv Ludwigsburg, EL 48/2 I Bü 678. Reproduced with permission of the Staatsarchiv Ludwigsburg.)

Kurt Schulz-Isenbeck, arrested almost 300 men in Lida, whom locals had denounced as Jews. Of these men, ninety – those who had attended a university or technical college – were then taken to a location around two kilometres outside the town, where they were shot from behind, five at a time, into bomb craters.[35] According to one of the drivers of the sub-

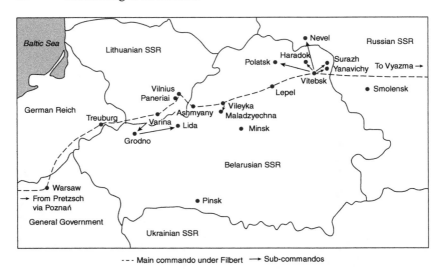

--- Main commando under Filbert ⟶ Sub-commandos

Figure 15 Route taken by EK 9 and its sub-commandos between June and October 1941. (Drawn by the author.)

commando, the wives and children of the murdered men witnessed the shooting of their husbands and fathers, as they had followed the prisoners at a distance of 50–100 m.[36] This operation appears to have been the first mass shooting of Jews carried out by members of Einsatzkommando 9. Six political commissars of the Red Army had already been shot by the commando in Grodno.[37]

Whilst the EG and EK heads had a great deal of latitude, their actions were also monitored by their superiors. In a written order from Heydrich dated 1 July and issued to all four Einsatzgruppen chiefs, EG B commander SS-Brigadeführer Arthur Nebe was rebuked because during a visit to Grodno that same day Himmler and Heydrich had found 'no member of the SP [= Security Police] and the SD in this locality'.[38] As Nebe himself put it in a subsequent report to Berlin, 'only 96 Jews' (*nur 96 Juden*) had been executed in Grodno and nearby Lida during the first days of the presence of Haupt's sub-commando there. Nebe announced that he had accordingly issued the order 'to considerably intensify' (*erheblich zu intensivieren*) shootings in the area.[39] As the responsible commando chief, it can be assumed that Nebe in turn rebuked Filbert for his initial oversight in Grodno.

***

BИ.ІЬІІА — WILNO. Георгіевскій просиектъ — Prospekt Śto. Jerski

Figure 16 40 Gedimino Prospektas (right) in Vilnius, 1905/1906. The building subsequently became the NKVD headquarters. From July 1941, it housed the majority of EK 9, as well as the Gestapo prison. (Source: Lietuvos Centrinis Valstybės Archyvas, Vilnius, 12843. Reproduced with permission of the Lietuvos Centrinis Valstybės Archyvas.)

On 1 July, the main commando reached Vilnius.[40] The 'Jerusalem of Lithuania' was one of the most important centres of Jewish life in Eastern Europe[41] and around 80,000 Jews (60,000 Vilnius Jews and about 20,000 Jewish refugees from Poland) inhabited the city on the eve of the German occupation.[42] Whilst the majority of EK 9 was quartered in what had been the local Soviet political police (NKVD) building[43] at 40 Gedimino Prospektas, which also housed the Gestapo prison (see Figure 16), Filbert and most of those members of the commando holding the rank of officer in the SS were accommodated in a nearby hotel.[44] According to a post-war statement by his orderly at the time, Filbert arranged for two Jewish women to clean his hotel room, though he forbade members of his Einsatzkommando from conversing with these workers.[45] In Vilnius, the Lithuanian police force was disbanded and those members of it deemed suitable were subordinated to EK 9.[46] Prior to the arrival of EK 9, another unit of Einsatzgruppe B, Sonderkommando 7a, had already passed through Vilnius[47] and encouraged the locals to engage in anti-Jewish excesses. Upon arriving in Vilnius, Filbert learnt that Lithuanian locals had done just that by shooting a large number of Jews in a mixed forest outside the city. Filbert then arranged for a member of the police section of his commando, the Austrian SS-Obersturmführer Franz Schauschütz, to assume control of the shooting operations against Vilnius Jews outside the city.[48] According to EM 21:

> The Lithuanian security force, which was subordinated to the Einsatzkommando following the dissolution of the Lithuanian political police, was instructed to participate in the liquidation of the Jews. For this purpose, 150 Lithuanian officials were assigned, who arrest the Jews and bring them to concentration camps, where they are subjected to special treatment (*Sonderbehandlung*) on the same day. This work has now begun and in this way continuously around 500 Jews, incl. saboteurs, are liquidated every day.[49]

Although the Lithuanians – about 150 volunteers, most of them soldiers, known as the 'Ypatingas Būrys' (special squad)[50] – continued to do the actual shooting, Schauschütz, in agreement with Filbert, directed operations and used members of Einsatzkommando 9 to cordon off the area and, in some cases, to guard the victims.[51] Mass shootings were being carried out there under the direction of EK 9 no later than 4 July, a mere two days after the unit had reached Vilnius. On 4 July fifty-four Jews were 'liquidated' and on 5 July ninety-three Jews.[52] Returning to headquarters after attending the first shooting, Filbert said to some Wehrmacht officers waiting for him in the antechamber to his office: 'So, we've finished off the first Jews.'[53] Filbert's orderly, who overheard this remark, concluded that Filbert was a 'sadist'.[54] No later than 7 July, SS-Obersturmführer Haupt's sub-commando, which had carried out the earlier mass shooting in Lida, re-joined the rest of EK 9 in Vilnius.[55] By 8 July, no fewer than 321 Vilnius Jews had been killed by EK 9 in the mixed forest.[56]

Whilst the murder of hundreds of Jews continued on an almost daily basis in the forests outside the city, 300 further Jewish men were shot at another location. The ostensible cause for this operation was five or six shots that had been fired at the accommodation of Einsatzkommando 9 in Vilnius during the night of 12–13 July. No one had been killed or even injured in the incident and the shooter could not be found.[57] In the morning, however, Filbert ordered that the neighbourhood inhabited predominantly by Jews be combed and that some Jewish men be arrested and valuables confiscated. Filbert then ordered that some of those arrested be shot by officers of the Einsatzkommando – who were meant to lead by example – and members of the Order Police platoon. It was Filbert himself who selected a shooting site on the outskirts of the city and instructed SS-Untersturmführer Tunnat to take a work detachment consisting of Jews to the site and to dig a pit that was suitable to be used as a mass grave.[58]

On Sunday, 13 July,[59] the Einsatzkommando's leadership and members of the police platoon drove in trucks to the shooting site with the Jews who were to be killed. The victims were led to the pit in groups of five, where they were shot by a ten-man firing squad. Following consultation with Filbert, it was Tunnat who gave the command for the first salvo. The next two salvos were commanded by Filbert himself and a fourth by SS-Obersturmführer Schneider.[60] One of those required to shoot, a member of the 3rd platoon of the 2nd company of Reserve Police Battalion 9, was so nervous that Filbert spotted this, suddenly came over to him and said, 'What's going on with the target dolls. You don't need to tremble like that!'[61] Filbert himself and Schneider both actively participated in the shooting as part of the firing squad on at least one occasion. Whether either of them actually killed one (or more) of the victims by their own hand cannot be verified, as there were always two shooters for each victim.[62] At his trial in 1962 and during the proceedings leading up to it, Filbert claimed to have intentionally missed his target.[63] Given that the purpose of the officers' active participation was to lead by example, however, the court came to the reasonable conclusion that Filbert would not have risked missing his target in case the other shooter had also missed.[64]

Thus, the assumption that the Einsatzgruppen and Einsatzkommando chiefs themselves did not fire a weapon during the mass shootings in the occupied Soviet territories[65] is unfounded. Prior to, during and subsequent to his trial, Filbert testified that the Einsatzgruppen had received a pre-invasion order to the effect that each and every member of the units was obliged 'to actively participate' in at least one shooting.[66] Furthermore, Filbert actually admitted to having personally taken part in the shooting operation described earlier in fulfilment of this order.[67] Not only Filbert but also the other Einsatzkommando chief in Einsatzgruppe B, SS-Sturmbannführer Dr. Otto Bradfisch, took active part in several shooting operations,[68] as did other commando chiefs.[69] In the opinion of Yitzhak Arad, 'in all likelihood' Filbert himself 'staged' the incident on the night of 12–13 July in order to ensure the implementation of the order that each member of the unit personally take part in at least one execution.[70] Whilst there is no evidence to support this theory, Filbert certainly exploited the situation to its fullest extent.

In a report from mid-July, the staff of the 403rd Security Division noted,

Secret Field Police and Security Service (SD) are collaborating in combatting Jewish attacks. All Jews are now distinguished by badges. A large number of shootings has already taken place. I have agreed with the very loyal head of the

SD, Obersturmbannführer Dr Filbert, that these shootings will take place as unobtrusively as possible and remain hidden from the troops.[71]

This did not prevent, however, a short notification about the shooting from appearing in the soldiers' newspaper issued by the Wehrmacht propaganda company stationed in Vilnius, *Der Durchbruch* (The Breakthrough).[72]

Following the so-called hostage shooting of mid-July,[73] further shootings were carried out at the same location by members of the police platoon and the Waffen SS platoon of EK 9.[74] One of these shootings took place on 15 July, on which day 219 Jews were shot in a joint operation between EK 9 and the Lithuanian security force set up earlier in the month.[75] Each and every deployment of members of his commando was ordered personally by Filbert himself. He specified who would lead the individual operation, described that person's task to him and instructed him on how many men he was permitted to use. Whilst these shootings were being carried out, the aforementioned massacres led by SS-Obersturmführer Schauschütz continued, though now in a pine forest near the locality of Paneriai (Ponary), situated around 8 km southwest of Vilnius.[76] Filbert ordered members of his commando to remove Jews from their dwellings in Vilnius and force them to the pits in Paneriai Forest. Schauschütz streamlined the killing operations here in such a way that it was possible to shoot several hundred people within a single hour.[77] According to the diary of Kazimierz Sakowicz, a Polish journalist living in Paneriai (see Figure 17), executions by shooting took place for nine consecutive days from 11 till 19 July. After three days of quiet, executions continued on 23 July and occurred every day until the end of the month, with the exception of Sunday, 27 July. Sakowicz put the number of people shot during July at 'around 5,000'.[78] Although the shooting site in Paneriai Forest was cordoned off, members of the 96th Infantry Division, a regular German Army unit, were able to observe on three consecutive days not only the arrival in columns of at least 400 victims each but also the shootings themselves.[79] One of them was even able to take photographs of the proceedings (see Figures 18 and 19).[80] Those Jews still in Vilnius were not aware at the time that their fathers, brothers, husbands and sons were being shot in the Paneriai Forest.[81] The Polish–Jewish librarian Herman Kruk noted in his diary entry for 20 July, however, that rumours had reached the Jewish Council (*Judenrat*) as early as 10 July and then again five days later to the effect that people were being shot in Paneriai, but that the Jewish Council dismissed the rumours on both occasions as unfounded.[82] Around the same time as the so-called hostage shooting and the subsequent shootings at the same location, six

Figure 17 The house of Kazimierz Sakowicz on the edge of the Paneriai Forest, from which he witnessed the executions carried out nearby from July 1941 onwards. (Photograph taken on 30 May 2012 by the author.)

Russian prisoners were shot who had been handed over to EK 9 by the Wehrmacht's Secret Field Police (*Geheime Feldpolizei*, or GFP) after allegedly having been caught directing Bolshevik propaganda and training.[83]

On 13 July, Nebe issued an order for Einsatzkommando 9 to send an advance party to the Belarusian town of Vileyka,[84] which was then implemented three days later.[85] According to Nebe, it had become increasingly apparent that the main workload in terms of locating resistance movements, partisans, Communist functionaries and Jews was to be dealt with by the Einsatzkommandos in the army rear areas.[86] In Nebe's estimation, cooperation in the rear areas – where, for Nebe, 'the most important executive Security Police task' resided – between the Einsatzkommandos and the security divisions, field headquarters and local headquarters of the regular German Army in the first three weeks of the campaign had been 'excellent' (*ausgezeichnet*). During the same period, cooperation with the Wehrmacht's Secret Field Police and

Figure 18 Lithuanian militiamen under the command of EK 9 marching Jews, with their heads covered, to their death in Paneriai, July 1941. (Source: Yad Vashem Archives, Jerusalem, Photo number 4613/916. Photographer: Otto Schroff. Reproduced with permission of the Yad Vashem Archives.)

Figure 19 One of the pits in Paneriai Forest, now part of the memorial site there. (Photograph taken on 30 May 2012 by the author.)

counterintelligence troops (*Abwehr III*) in the operations area of Army Group Centre had been 'the best imaginable' (*die denkbar beste*). Moreover, 'the activity of my Einsatzgruppe is acknowledged and promoted by all Wehrmacht departments in every way'. Nebe's 'measures' had been met with 'the most complete understanding' (*das vollste Verständnis*) by the leadership of Army Group Centre. The Secret Field Police had even provided troops to support the 'liquidations', that is, mass shootings.[87]

Between 4 July and 23 July, when EK 9 departed from Vilnius,[88] Filbert had arranged for the murder of at least 5,000 Jewish inhabitants of the city either by members of his own commando or Lithuanian nationalists.[89] Both Greiffenberger and Schneider later testified that Schauschütz was left in Vilnius with a small sub-commando, whilst the main commando of EK 9 departed collectively from Vilnius.[90] Following its departure from Vilnius, EK 9 then killed no fewer than 527 Jewish men in the Belarusian town of Ashmyany, situated 25 km south-east of Vilnius on the road to Vileyka.[91] This may have been the first time that EK 9 killed the entire male Jewish population in a given locality.[92] According to

EM 34 from 26 July, the Wehrmacht's security divisions had made 'urgent requests' for the systematic capture by the EKs of partisans, saboteurs and Communist functionaries in the army rear areas and 'exceptionally appreciate[d]' (*außerordentlich begrüßen*) the presence of the Security Police there.[93]

5 'In Vileyka, the Jews had to be liquidated in their entirety'
Genocide of Belarusian Jewry, July–October 1941

Einsatzkommando 9 arrived no later than 25 July in the town of Vileyka,[1] where it remained for several days. Up to this point, during the first five weeks of Germany's military campaign against the Soviet Union, EK 9 – like the other commandos of the four Einsatzgruppen – had targeted primarily Jewish men of military service age.[2] This would change dramatically from Vileyka onwards. According to post-war testimony by Gerhard Schneider and Wilhelm Greiffenberger, it was here, on 29 July,[3] that Filbert gave a talk to the officers of his commando, during which he explained that – on the orders of higher authorities – Jewish women and children were to be included in future shooting operations.[4] The reason Filbert cited was that the unit's execution figures had been criticised as too low.[5] Schneider testified after the war:

Coming from Vilnius, we had just arrived in Vileyka when Dr Filbert, returning from a meeting of commando heads at another location, called a meeting of the officers. One could sense that he was himself agitated, bitter and very serious. He informed us that he was returning from a meeting of commando heads, at which either Heydrich himself must have been present or new orders of Heydrich's were announced. In any case, he was given a dressing down. EK 9 had attracted the negative attention of Heydrich in particular because its activity in fulfilling the shooting order had been far too limited. Furthermore, as the inclusion of women and children in the shooting operations had been ordered, he could now simply no longer avoid mandating the intensified deployment of his commando. Pointing at me, he then ruled: 'You assume command tomorrow.' He likewise ordered one or two other officers to participate.[6]

Greiffenberger's post-war testimony corroborated Schneider's statement regarding timing, context and nature of the new orders and the location of their communication to the commando:

We had been in Vileyka only a few days when Filbert held a staff meeting with a small group of officers. I believe that, aside from Filbert and me, Schneider and Klein were present at this meeting. During the course of this staff meeting, Filbert disclosed to us that he had received the order from a higher authority to shoot Jewish women and children as well in the future. Furthermore, Filbert took this opportunity to point out that the reported shooting figures had been criticised in high places as too low.[7]

It is very doubtful that the sluggish fulfilillment of execution quotas was the real reason for the issuing of orders to include women and children in the shooting operations. After all, at this point in time, EK 9 had shot and killed more people than any of the other commandos belonging to Einsatzgruppe B.[8] One member of the staff of EG B, SS-Untersturmführer Andreas von Amburger, testified after the war that 'in Einsatzgruppe B it was common knowledge that EK 9 was particularly rigorous in its approach to the liquidation of the Jewish population'.[9] We must also keep in mind that neither Schneider nor Greiffenberger had been present when the new orders were issued to Filbert. In their post-war testimony, they were simply relaying what Filbert had told them in Vileyka. Perhaps anticipating misgivings on the part of some of his officers regarding the murder of women and children – misgivings that were indeed voiced[10] – Filbert may have presented the new orders less as a conscious expansion of an ideological or racial programme of mass murder and more as an inescapable chastisement for EK 9's (supposed) tardiness hitherto.

Concerning Filbert's own receipt of the new commission, Schneider spoke after the war of an 'issuing of orders' (*Befehlsausgabe*), 'at which either Heydrich himself was present or at which a direct order of Heydrich's was conveyed'.[11] According to Greiffenberger's post-war testimony:

We had radio contact with Einsatzgruppe B. On several occasions Filbert was ordered to attend meetings with the group staff. [...] To my knowledge, the RSHA [in] Berlin intervened in the matter of the shootings of Jews at a later date, when we were situated in Vileyka, on one single occasion, regarding the matter of also shooting women and children in the future.[12]

As Heydrich was the head of the Reich Security Main Office (*Reichssicherheitshauptamt*, or RSHA) and, in this capacity, in charge of the Einsatzgruppen, there is a high probability that the new orders had indeed come from him. If Heydrich had issued the order directly, as Schneider indicated, then Filbert must have travelled to Berlin to receive it. On 20 July, the same day as EK 9's departure from Vilnius, Heydrich had begun a three-day trip to the southern part of the Soviet front near Yampil in Ukraine. There he re-joined Fighter Squadron 77, with which he had already flown in air raids over Norway the previous year. He then returned to Berlin.[13] His next trip to the occupied Soviet territories does not appear to have taken place until the beginning of September, when he visited Himmler's eastern headquarters at Hegewald near Zhytomyr.[14] It was not unusual for members of a commando to travel back to the Reich during the course of their deployment in the occupied Soviet territories. Greiffenberger, for example, had travelled back to Germany in mid-July in order to send parcels with furs to the families of commando personnel.[15] It thus appears that Heydrich issued the new orders to Filbert in person in Berlin during the week between 23 July, when Heydrich returned to the German capital, and 29 July, when Filbert communicated these orders to his officers.[16]

In order to combat the misgivings voiced in the wake of the meeting on 29 July by some of the officers, including Schneider and Tunnat, to the effect that those members of the commando who were fathers or were particularly young could not be expected to kill women and children, Filbert announced he himself would lead the first shooting operations in Vileyka. He accordingly selected from the police battalion those men who appeared most suitable.[17] The following day, 30 July, at least 350 Jewish victims who had been arrested two days earlier during a combing of the town, including – for the first time – women, were driven out of the city and shot under Filbert's command.[18] Filbert also made the preparations for the next shooting operation, but transferred the command to Greiffenberger, as the next highest-ranking officer. During the course of this operation, which lasted approximately three hours, at least 100 Jewish men, women and – again for the first time – children aged 15 were killed.[19] A member of the 3rd platoon of the 2nd company of Reserve Police Battalion 9 later estimated the total number of victims of the two shooting operations in Vileyka at between 300 and 500.[20] Greiffenberger also subsequently put the number of Jews murdered in Vileyka at 500 and believed that 'all Jews who had resided in Vileyka' had thus been shot by EK 9.[21] EG B felt sufficiently certain of this at the time to report back to Berlin: 'In Vileyka, the Jews had to be liquidated in their entirety.'[22] The report did not elaborate on why this 'had to be' done. If all remaining Vileyka Jews *were* indeed killed by EK 9, it stands to reason – particularly as Sonderkommando 7a of EG B had already 'combed' the town prior to EK 9's arrival and shot between 130 and 150 Jewish men aged 15–60 years there on 12 July[23] – that a substantial proportion of EK 9's victims in Vileyka – larger in fact than the available sources and testimony indicate – were women and children.

According to testimony given by one member of the police platoon of EK 9:

I can only say that the situation in Commando 9 was a different one as of Vileyka than previously. From our stay in Vileyka onwards, small sub-commandos under the command of different SS and SD officers were pulled off Filbert's main commando with increasing frequency for special tasks unknown to me, so that [the size of] the regular commando diminished ever further.[24]

In EM 43, dated 5 August, Nebe made reference to the Jewish population and also noted 'the Security Police sweeps, which have become more comprehensive of late' (*die umfassender gewordenen sicherheitspolizeilichen Überholungen in letzter Zeit*).[25] This was an understatement – the Vileyka massacres at the end of July in fact marked the transition to genocide against Soviet Jewry.[26] As such, EK 9 was not only the first commando within EG B to begin systematically killing Jewish women and children, but in fact the first commando of *any* of the Einsatzgruppen to do so.[27]

Filbert commissioned Schneider to lead the next shooting operation, which took place in the nearby town of Maladzyechna, located approximately 70 km north-west of the capital of the Belarusian Soviet Socialist Republic (Belarusian SSR), Minsk. Early on the morning of the shooting, Schneider ordered the members of his commando – approximately half of the entire strength of EK 9[28] – to haul at least 100 Jews, around 70 men and 30 women, from their dwellings, where most of them were still sleeping, and to bring them to the execution site, an open field near the town. The shooters were supplied by the police platoon, led by Hauptwachtmeister Neubert, though it was Schneider – evidently having overcome his misgivings from the end of July regarding the murder of Jewish women – who each time gave the command to shoot. The operation lasted two to three hours.[29] Filbert commanded Tunnat to lead a further shooting operation in the vicinity of Vileyka. Around seventy Jewish men were taken from a nearby village and brought to the execution site along with ten or twelve female Jewish teachers, who had already been arrested. After being stripped either completely naked or down to their underpants, the women were shot first using tracer ammunition. The men were then shot into a second pit, which had been dug on Tunnat's orders.[30]

***

Einsatzkommando 9 departed Vileyka and arrived no later than 2 August in the badly damaged city of Vitebsk, not far from the border with the Russian Soviet Federative Socialist Republic (RSFSR). There its members found a Jewish ghetto, which had been erected by the field headquarters of the German Army as early as July[31] and was already overcrowded. Nevertheless, the commando promptly rounded up further Jews from the vicinity of Vitebsk and brought them to the ghetto.[32] Shortly after arriving in Vitebsk, Filbert expressly ordered the resumption of the mass shooting of Jews there. During the first ten days of the commando's stay in the city, at least two shooting operations took place against Jews, women among them. The first operation claimed the lives of 332 Jews, including five Bolshevik functionaries. In the second operation, twenty-seven Jews were publicly shot, allegedly 'because they refused to go to work'.[33] Members of the police platoon cordoned off the execution site during these two operations, whilst Gestapo officials from the police section of EK 9 were called upon as shooters.[34] According to one of the policemen who cordoned off the execution site during the second shooting operation, all the male and female victims were forced to remove their clothing in its entirety before being shot. The clothing was then burned where it had been left.[35] One Jewish woman was publicly hanged in Vitebsk for allegedly requesting a German soldier to open a door, causing the soldier's lower arm to then be blown off by a concealed explosive charge.[36]

The historian Helmut Krausnick has noted that EK 9's activities in September consisted more than before in combatting partisans,[37] yet the source material suggests that this transition may have already begun earlier, in August. Nebe had already noted at the beginning of the month that partisans were disrupting supplies, attempting to sabotage the economy in the rear areas and disseminating 'subversive Bolshevist propaganda' (*bolschewistische Zersetzungspropaganda*), and thus constituted 'a serious threat' (*eine ernste Gefahr*) for the continuation of the war. He added that the EKs would, therefore, be required to participate actively in combatting the partisans as soon as the required forces were available.[38] Between 9 and 16 August, EK 9 carried out four large operations against partisans in the forested areas around Vitebsk. A 'substantial number of partisans' (*größere Anzahl Partisanen*) were taken by surprise and killed.[39] A further, strong commando sent the following week into the woods near Moskalevo, twenty kilometres north of the town of Haradok, failed to seize partisans due to the sheer size of the forested area.[40] Another anti-partisan search operation carried out the same week by a sub-commando of EK 9 in the vicinity of Gramki, around ninety kilometres from Vitebsk, resulted in the capture and slaying of an alleged Communist informant.[41]

Around 12 August, Filbert sent Schneider with a sub-commando to the area around Surazh, located north-east of Vitebsk close to the Belarusian–Russian border. The sub-commando had the task of finding and destroying a partisan camp in the forest. After searching for several hours, however, Schneider abandoned the search without having found the camp and instead carried out a mass shooting of Jews in Surazh itself. According to one of the policemen in the sub-commando, the order had been issued to arrest all Jews in the town, men, women and children. A unit of German sappers stationed in Surazh provided volunteers to help search the locality and round up the victims. The pit prepared by

Schneider and likewise a natural hollow nearby proved to be too small for
the victims, who numbered at least 200 but probably as many as 500–600.
After completing the shooting, Schneider's commando departed the
crime scene without covering the corpses and returned to Vitebsk that
same night. The aforementioned sappers assured Schneider, however,
that they would detonate the pits the following day.[42] According to one of
the policemen in the sub-commando, a third of those shot in Surazh were
men and two-thirds women and 'children of all ages'. All 'delinquents' (as
the ex-policeman described them), men, women and children, had to
strip naked at the collection point.[43] Depending on whether EK 9 had
succeeded in killing all Jews in Vileyka, as Greiffenberger believed, the
operation in Surazh may have been the first time that EK 9 killed the
entire Jewish population in a given locality. Evidently, Filbert and EK 9
had now commenced with the indiscriminate killing of Jews, irrespective
of age or gender.[44] A few days after leading this operation, as a result of
requests he had submitted to Nebe's adjutant, Schneider was transferred
to the staff of Einsatzgruppe B in Smolensk. He thereafter had nothing
more to do with the mass shooting of Jews until his recall to Berlin at the
end of September.[45]

Filbert himself led a sub-commando during a further mass shooting of
Jews in August in a small town, possibly Lepel,[46] on the road between
Vileyka and Vitebsk. Around 100 Jewish men were seized and taken to the
edge of a nearby forest, where Tunnat supervised the cordoning off of the
execution site and Filbert himself commanded the shooters. Two men
managed to flee; though one of them was shot and killed whilst running
across an open field, the other was able to escape.[47] The same month, a
political commissar of the Red Army who had escaped from the prison
camp in Lepel and procured civilian clothing was found wandering about
in the villages and the woods. 'In view of his political dangerousness
he was subjected to special treatment', that is, killed.[48] Also in August,
397 male Jews from the civilian internment camp (*Zivilgefangenenlager*) in
Vitebsk were delivered by the Wehrmacht to EK 9, who then shot them. A
Major Brotbrück, the adjutant of the commander of the 9th Army
Generaloberst Adolf Strauß, who attended the shooting at his own
request, commended the 'soldierly bearing' (*soldatische Haltung*) of the
commando and concluded that this practice of annihilation was without
doubt a 'humane form of implementation' (*humane Durchführungsart*).[49]
In the second half of August, nineteen male and female Jews were shot in
Vitebsk on account of arson. As Nebe stated in a report dated 25 August
and intended for presentation to Army Group Centre, three German
soldiers had been shot on 12 August in the vicinity of Vitebsk. During a
'pacification operation' by the Wehrmacht, these nineteen Jews were then

found 'wandering about' in the forest where the soldiers had been killed. Suspected of carrying out the attack and furthermore 'exposed' as arsonists in Vitebsk, the nineteen were executed by EK 9.[50] Nebe then added the 'gratifying fact' (*erfreuliche Tatsache*) that the local population was becoming ever more receptive as a result of the way in which the Security Police 'keenly and justly' (*scharf und gerecht*) took care of things and that the local population supported the work of the Security Police by reporting Communists.[51] During the same period, EK 9 announced that criminality in Vitebsk had returned to a normal level and that Vitebsk could now be regarded as a pacified city. In a population of around 50,000 inhabitants, there were as a rule 25 criminal cases a day, most of which were minor instances of theft.[52]

By late August, a sub-commando of EK 9 was stationed in the northern Belarusian city of Polatsk.[53] The eight-man commando was made up of Waffen SS men and led by SS-Untersturmführer Tunnat.[54] The vast majority of the inhabitants, including the Jewish population, had still been in the badly damaged city at the time of its occupation by German forces.[55] The Jews were concentrated in a ghetto consisting of an outdoor enclosure fenced in by barbed wire.[56] Women and children were among the victims of a massacre there in August.[57] A member of the sub-commando later testified that Tunnat's commando shot ten or twelve male and female Jews, who were members of Komsomol, the Soviet Communist Party's youth organisation.[58] At the end of August, shortly after arriving in Polatsk, EK 9 killed a Russian woman who had been found on railway property in the vicinity of a large fuel depot 'in suspicious circumstances' (*unter verdächtigen Umständen*). She had been carrying a small sack containing powdered leaf and a box of matches. EK 9 came to the conclusion that she intended to set fire to the fuel depot.[59]

At the end of August, EK 9 reported to EG B that in all localities occupied by the Security Police the Jews were housed in ghettos, marked with an identifying symbol and forced to carry out communal work.[60] In fact, this applied across EG B's area of operations, and indeed to a far greater extent than in the territory in which the neighbouring Einsatzgruppe A was deployed.[61] As in Polatsk, the Jewish inhabitants of the town of Haradok, located 30 km north of Vitebsk, were concentrated in a ghetto consisting of an outdoor enclosure fenced in by barbed wire.[62] In the month of August, Wehrmacht anti-aircraft gunners voluntarily assisted the SS in massacring as many as 2,000 Jews here.[63] The following month, four Soviet soldiers and two Jews were arrested during a sweep of two villages east of Haradok. The Jews were accused by witnesses of spying for the partisans and then 'liquidated' by EK 9, whilst the four Soviet soldiers – in the absence of any evidence suggesting a link to the partisans – were sent to a prison camp.[64] Reported sightings of the Soviet Marshal Grigory Kulik in the forests of the Haradok District (*raion*) led a small sub-commando from EK 9 to venture through the marshes and woods on twelve one-horse carriages. Ten men without identity papers were apprehended near the village of Pribilnye. They were 'specially treated' (*sonderbehandelt*) as partisans.[65]

The 403rd Security Division noted an increase in the activity of 'partisan gangs' (*Partisanen-Banden*) during September, and the SD collaborated closely with the regular troops in rapidly implementing defensive measures.[66] At the beginning of the month, the division encountered 'a disguised partisan gang' (*eine getarnte Partisanenbande*) in Polatsk. It succeeded in capturing the leader of the partisans and securing an ammunition and explosives dump belonging to them.[67] At the end of the month, the division felt able to report that the pacification of its then area of operations could be regarded in the main as completed.[68] Whilst EK 9 was stationed in Vitebsk, its platoon of Order Police was detached from the commando and replaced by a second platoon of Waffen SS made up of very young men.[69] In September, Filbert placed Tunnat in charge of a twenty-man-strong sub-commando that included the young Waffen SS members and was then stationed in the Russian town of Nevel because of the presence of partisans in the vicinity.[70] There, as in the other occupied cities, a Jewish Council had been set up in August and tasked with registering all Jews, male and female. The Jews had then been assigned to work commandos and made to clean the town.[71] During the first half of September, seventy-four Jews were shot in Nevel.[72] Around the same time, the local headquarters of the German Army brought Tunnat's attention to a Jewish ghetto located outside the town. Tunnat passed this information on to Filbert, who promptly commissioned him to 'dissolve' the ghetto, that is, to shoot its inhabitants. Tunnat nevertheless delayed carrying out this order for two weeks, in spite of repeated exhortations from Filbert, and then claimed not to have sufficient manpower. Filbert instructed him to obtain assistance from the local army headquarters and exhorted him to implement the order forthwith. At the end of September, Tunnat began preparations to dissolve the ghetto. The 640 victims of the shooting operation were men, women and children as young as five years. The firing squad was made up of five to eight men equipped with sub-machine guns. Tunnat led the operation in the suburban park Golubaya Dacha and gave the command to fire. He apparently fulfilled the wishes of the local German Army commander by including in the massacre two men from a nearby prisoner of war camp, who were executed for sabotage. Once the shooting operation was over, the ghetto itself was razed to the ground.[73] A few days after the dissolution of the ghetto and the murder of its inhabitants, Tunnat was called back to Berlin. He embarked on the return journey together with three other EK 9 officers: Schneider, Fritz Klein and Kurt Schulz-Isenbeck. Greiffenberger did not return to Berlin until December, thus making him the longest serving of the officers assigned to EK 9 in Pretzsch.[74]

In a similar operation to that in Nevel, 1,025 people were killed during the second half of September during the dissolution of the ghetto in the Belarusian village of Yanavichy, situated about 15 km south of Surazh.[75] EM 92 appeared to boast about the slaughter of 1,025 people by a commando of only twelve men led by SS-Obersturmführer Karl Rath: 'The operation was carried out merely by one officer and 12 men.'[76] According to eyewitnesses – peasants in the nearby village of Zaitsevo, where the massacre apparently took place – the first batch of victims brought to the execution site from the ghetto consisted of young girls, whom the members of the commando raped before shooting.[77] In the case of both the Nevel and Yanavichy ghetto dissolutions, the killers cited contagious diseases as the reason for annihilating the ghettos' inhabitants.[78] In the second half of August, prior to the dissolution of the ghetto, EK 9 had already killed 149 Jews in Yanavichy as 'NKGB informants and political functionaries' (*NKGB-Spitzel und politische Funktionäre*).[79] In this instance, the commando was responding to a tip from the commandant of Army Group Rear Area (Korück) 582.[80] Another innovation occurred in September 1941: the first proven murder operation against Soviet Roma by EG B (and only the second by any of the Einsatzgruppen).[81] In this case, the Field Headquarters (*Feldkommandantur*) 181 of the Wehrmacht handed over 23 Roma (13 males and ten females) near Lepel to EK 9 'because they had terrorised the rural populace and committed numerous acts of theft'.[82] These twenty-three 'Gypsies' (*Zigeuner*) were then shot by EK 9.[83] The murder of these Roma does not, however, appear – at least at this stage – to have been part of a systematic programme to annihilate all Soviet Roma. In his post-war testimony, Filbert stated that he had not been issued with such an order parallel to the order to kill Soviet Jews.[84] This seems likely, as Roma were neither among those earmarked for execution according to Heydrich's written instructions of 2 July to the Higher SS and Police Leaders[85] nor were they mentioned in Heydrich's guidelines of 17 July for sifting Soviet prisoner of war camps.[86]

The former head of an issuing authority for passports in a neighbourhood of Vitebsk was arrested in September by EK 9 and 'liquidated' as a close associate of the NKVD. Three Jews were shot for not entering the ghetto and for concealing their 'Jewish ethnic origin' (*jüdische Rassenzugehörigkeit*). A Russian man who had stolen and slaughtered a cow from a collective farm was 'liquidated'.[87] Before the end of the month, three partisans were shot and killed in the area of Ivniki. Eight youths from Vultshina and Bikovtshina aged between 16 and 22 were arrested on the suspicion of being partisans. Some of them were members of Komsomol. Suspected of collecting weapons for the partisans, they were all 'specially treated' when three sub-machine guns, fifteen rifles, several thousand rounds of ammunition, a number of hand grenades and several parcels of poison gas were discovered. Two partisans were arrested during a sweep of the area around Yeseritshe. One of them was armed with a double-action revolver and a hand grenade, and was shot on the spot. During a sweep of the woods around Pletni, one Red Army soldier was shot and killed.[88]

Also in September, a delegate of the Supreme Soviet of the Belarusian Soviet Republic 'convicted' (*überführt*) of arson in Vitebsk was shot by EK 9 'after a thorough interrogation' (*nach eingehender Vernehmung*). A member of the Communist Party was arrested and 'liquidated' in Tikhanovo in the Surazh District. He was accused of calling on the agricultural workers to stop working for the Germans because the Soviets would soon return. An NKVD official and Komsomol leader from Dvoritsha was 'specially treated' (*sonderbehandelt*) for his inhumane conduct during interrogations. EK 9 arrested a Russian man accused of stabbing and killing a German soldier who was arbitrating in a dispute between two Russians. The man was handed over to the Wehrmacht's Secret Field Police, who publicly hanged him. Two members of the Vitebsk security services were 'liquidated' for abusing their positions to engage in looting. In Haradok, three Russians, who had allegedly plundered large quantities of flour and grain, were shot and killed.[89]

At the end of September, in the area of Ostrova, a sub-commando of EK 9 seized and 'liquidated' three Jews accused of providing partisans with 'shuttle services' (*Zubringerdienste*). The same sub-commando discovered a partisan hidden in a wooded area near Budianka. As he was suspected of participating in a partisan attack on the EK 9 sub-commando stationed in Surazh and furthermore admitted to actively working for the Communist Party, he was 'subjected to special treatment' (*der Sonderbehandlung unterzogen*). During an operation against partisans on 25 September in Truhovagara and Osyatno, 20 km north-east of Polatsk, a Russian woman was 'liquidated' for repeatedly harbouring partisans. Another operation against partisans near Vyeryetshe led to the capture of five people who were in contact with partisans and had supplied them with food. The five were shot, as was a partisan discovered during a sweep of Sastarinya. A further partisan, who pretended to have been imprisoned by the Soviets for political reasons, was 'liquidated'. A third partisan was executed after attempting to escape into the woods.[90]

On 1 October, fifty-two Jews, who had fled from Haradok south-east to Vitebsk and supposedly 'produced unrest among the populace by spreading rumours', were killed by EK 9.[91] By early October, the infamous SS Cavalry Regiment 2 was also deployed in and around Haradok and Vitebsk.[92] EK 9 shot four Jews in Vitebsk the same month for roving about outside the ghetto, removing the yellow star and supporting themselves by begging. In the village of Borovlyany, EK 9 executed a five-person Jewish family for allegedly spreading anti-German rumours. In Ostrovno, 30 km west of Vitebsk, EK 9 shot 169 Jews for supposedly not following German orders. In the village of Tronkavichi, EK 9 arrested a village elder for assisting the NKGB in Lepel. After being interrogated, he was shot.[93] EK 9's September operations in Nevel and Yanavichy were the first ghetto dissolutions cited for any unit of Einsatzgruppe B in either the daily Incident Reports or the fortnightly (later monthly) Activity and Situation Reports (*Tätigkeits–und Lageberichte*, or TuLB),[94] and were the precursor for a similar but much larger operation by EK 9 in Vitebsk the following month. As noted earlier, the ghetto had been erected in July by the German Army, and by the beginning of October between 5,000 and 10,000 inhabitants of the ghetto had already died from starvation and disease, especially typhus.[95] This was a consequence of the complete failure to supply the ghetto population, for which the 403rd Security Division and its subordinated Field Headquarters were responsible.[96] Sofiya Isidorovna Ratner, a Jewish teacher, wrote to her four children – who had presumably succeeded in leaving Vitebsk before the arrival of the Germans – from within the ghetto:

Dear children! Marusen'ka, Atochka, Viten'ka, Ninochka, adieu! I am dying. What we are going through in the ghetto cannot be described. It is better to die. [...]
My dears, my beloved, my infinitely beloved children: adieu.
I do not even know if you are all still alive. We have no idea what is happening around us; we are completely cut off from the world. I am here with Aunt Fanya and of course with all the remaining Jews of Vitebsk. And once more, adieu, my dears! How difficult it is for me to say goodbye to you forever.
Your mother, who loves you infinitely!
6 / IX '41
We are still alive. The ghetto is being enclosed with barbed wire. We are condemned to death by starvation.
8 / IX '41[97]

Thus, in September and October 1941, the ghettoised Jews of Vitebsk were suffering a similar fate to millions of non-Jews in the German-occupied Soviet territories, who were the victims of a systematic, state-sponsored policy of death by starvation.[98] Whilst the killings of some Soviet Jews may have been linked to this planned reduction and redistribution of food supplies, this was not a decisive factor in the mass murder of Jews.[99] The principal victims of the starvation strategy were ultimately captive Red Army soldiers and the inhabitants of major urban centres such as Leningrad and Kharkiv.[100]

On one occasion, Greiffenberger and two young Waffen SS officers entered the Vitebsk ghetto and inspected the cellar of one of the buildings in its northern part: 'The sight we were presented with in this cellar was terrible. In this room lay about ten Jews, reduced to skeletons, some of whom had in the meantime died from hunger, and others with thick bellies and ulcers.'[101] At this point, Filbert ordered the dissolution of the ghetto, that is, the killing of the remaining Jews,[102] with the justification that there was a 'danger of epidemics' (*Seuchengefahr*)[103] – a situation that the actions of EK 9 itself, in sending ever more Jews into the already overcrowded ghetto, had helped to bring about in the first place. Filbert's order was promptly implemented: the first shooting, with at least 250 victims – men, women and 40 children aged between 2 and 8 years – was carried out by Waffen SS men under the command of Greiffenberger and lasted from nine in the morning till four in the afternoon. The children were led by the hand to the pit and then shot in the back of the neck. After the completion of the operation, Greiffenberg drove back to base in Vitebsk and reported to Filbert the shooting of 250 Jews from the ghetto.[104] That same evening, one of the young Waffen SS officers who had taken part in a shooting operation for the first time and had killed children, had a screaming fit. Whilst Greiffenberger attempted to compose him, Filbert merely remarked, 'And something like that wants to be an SS officer. He should be sent straight back home with a corresponding appraisal.'[105]

Filbert was present at the next operation, which cost the lives of at least 750 people, women among them. During the operation led by Greiffenberger and the subsequent operation attended by Filbert, the shooters were permitted – evidently for the first time – to drink schnapps.[106] This adaptation to the requirements of the task at hand occurred in spite of instructions issued to the group and commando chiefs prior to the invasion, according to which excessive alcohol consumption was 'strictly prohibited' (*strengstens untersagt*) for all members of the Einsatzgruppen.[107] One week later, at least 800 people – including mothers carrying infants and a group of 'crying and screaming 10- to 12-year-old children' – were shot, on Filbert's orders, by a commando led by the 33-year-old Kriminalkommissar Bodo Struck,[108] an instructor in criminalistics at the Border Police Academy in Pretzsch and Schneider's replacement as head of EK 9's police section.[109] Filbert observed proceedings with other officers.[110] On 5 October, the Commander of the Rear Area of Army Group Centre, General der Infanterie Max von Schenckendorff, was in Vitebsk to inspect the 403rd Security Division, whose commanding officer Generalleutnant Wolfgang von Ditfurth particularly stood out as a result of his open anti-Semitism. On this occasion, von Schenckendorff partook of a social evening with the Higher SS and Police Leader for Russia Centre, SS-Obergruppenführer Erich von dem Bach-Zelewski.[111] It was von Schenckendorff who had shortly before initiated the infamous anti-partisan warfare seminar in Mogilev on 24–26 September, the result of which was the slogan: 'Where there is a partisan, there is a Jew, and where there is a Jew, there is a partisan.' (*Wo der Partisan ist, ist der Jude und wo der Jude ist, ist der Partisan*). In the words of historian Jörn Hasenclever, he was a 'willing ally of the SS'.[112] Bach-Zelewski, for his part, was a man who according to Hitler could 'wade through a sea of blood' and was 'even more severe and brutal' than Heydrich.[113] It is reasonable to assume that the presence of these two men in Vitebsk encouraged a radical approach on the part of EK 9.

Beginning on 8 October and finishing on 10 October, EK 9 completed the annihilation of the inhabitants of the Vitebsk ghetto by shooting between 4,000 and 8,000 Jews.[114] They were brought to the Ilovskii ravine and shot there.[115] The teacher Sofiya I. Ratner was among those who perished.[116] As far as is known, not a single Jewish person survived the mass slaughter in the ghetto, which impedes the ascertainment of an exact death toll.[117] Greiffenberger later testified that in Vitebsk men, women and children had been shot 'without distinction'.[118] Members of the regular German Army were at least witnesses to this massacre, as demonstrated by a later conversation between two NCOs in British captivity:

[Bernd] Faller: In Russia I've seen many times how they knock off Jews there. That was really horrible. First of all, before they were ready to be shot, they had to undress themselves etc., and one then saw when they exposed their torso that they'd been beaten beforehand. They had broad streaks as wide as this, swollen as wide as this, swollen to a centimetre, badly bruised streaks, crisscrossed all over, it was awful. They let themselves be led away, they went everywhere they had to, everywhere they were sent. But they were beaten like anything on the way there. I've seen how the SS ... sleeves rolled up, cudgel in hand, it was really quite something, and always 'give him here', constantly beating all the men. One of them was over eighty, well over eighty, almost ninety, he could barely walk, they chased him, he fell on his face and remained lying there, and they beat him as he lay. Two other men, old geezers as well, picked him up and carried him away; he

had a beard this long, a terribly old man, they almost beat him to death. The youngest who was shot was thirteen and the oldest was over ninety.

21 Y: And women and girls too?

Faller. Everyone. [In] one camp, an epidemic broke out in it because the people couldn't look after themselves, or anything. They got nothing to eat, nothing at all. Naturally disease broke out, and so on, so they gunned down the whole camp with machine guns, they were simply blown away, in Vitebsk. About 5,000 people. Men, women, children, the whole kit and caboodle, everyone.

21 Y: When was that?

Faller. That was in '41. After that we got out of there.[119]

The events of October 1941 in Vitebsk were evidently very memorable for this particular NCO, who recalled them in detail to his comrade three years later, in November 1944.

On 20 October, shortly after the dissolution of the Vitebsk ghetto, Filbert was relieved as commander of Einsatzkommando 9.[120] Before returning to Berlin, Filbert personally handed over command of the unit to his successor SS-Sturmbannführer Oswald Schäfer.[121] Around the same time, EK 9 received the order to advance to the Russian city of Vyazma, which it then did on 25 October.[122] It is possible that, upon his return to Berlin, Filbert personally presented Heydrich with an album containing photographs of the members of EK 9 but also of mass shootings of Jews. Greiffenberger later testified to this effect:

In Vilnius, Filbert had a photo album put together on the advance and the deployment of EK 9 with the photographs of all officers and the entire commando and labelled in white writing. I can no longer say today whether Filbert had pictures of Jew shootings (*Judenerschießungen*) pasted into this album. I know that Filbert had pictures taken of such scenes of Jew shootings. To my knowledge, this album had not yet been completed in Vilnius; it was rather the case that Filbert wanted after its completion to hand over the album from Vitebsk to Obergruppenführer Heydrich on a festive occasion, probably a birthday. I assume that Filbert took this book with him when he was ordered back from Vitebsk and personally presented it to Heydrich.[123]

This album does not appear to have survived, but Filbert's compilation of it indicates a considerable pride in his work and that of his subordinates.

According to the figures submitted by EK 9 itself to Einsatzgruppe B and then forwarded on to Berlin, the commando shot a total of 11,449 Soviet Jews during Filbert's four-month stint as commander.[124] This averaged out at more than ninety-four people each and every day. Filbert asserted at his trial that EK 9 had killed 'only' around 1,000 Jews during this period. After the war, defendants testified that it had been commonplace to round up the figures for those killed before passing them on to Einsatzgruppe B, in order to create an impression of particular efficiency. Nebe, in turn, supposedly exaggerated the figures he then passed on to the RSHA in Berlin.[125] There is good reason to believe, however, that such claims were merely part of some defendants' defence strategy. As head of departments IV and V in the staff of EG B, it was the task of SS-Sturmbannführer Eduard Holste to gather the reports of the individual commandos and compile them in a single report for the RSHA. He testified after the war:

I never doubted the accuracy of the figures reported to us. I also never heard that the numbers of those shot were randomly increased by commando chiefs. I personally never ventured an increase in the figures for the shootings and was also never instructed by Nebe or Neumann[126] or anyone else to 'touch up' the figures reported by the commandos.[127]

Greiffenberger's testimony corroborated Holste's statements: 'If Filbert had reported higher figures than [the number of] Jews actually shot, I would basically have learned of this. I never heard that Filbert prompted Schneider or any other official from Section IV to report incorrect shooting figures.'[128] Both Holste and Greiffenberger incriminated themselves with their testimony.[129] The same applies to the head of EK 8, Otto Bradfisch, who testified: 'The reports of figures submitted by my commando ought to be correct'.[130] The historians Gert Robel and Christian Gerlach in fact conclude that the execution figures submitted by the commandos tended to be too *low* rather than too high.[131] They are not alone: in his concluding statement, the presiding judge at Filbert's trial, Karlheinz Meyer, estimated the number of victims of EK 9 under Filbert to be as high as 15,000.[132] Let us take the following example: the reported figure of 11,449 killed up to Filbert's replacement is unrealistic not least because EK 9 – according to its own figures – had already killed 10,269 people as of 28 September,[133] and an increase of 1,180 over the course of the next three weeks evidently does not take into account the many thousands annihilated in the Vitebsk ghetto, or at least not in their entirety.[134] Based on the research carried out for this and the preceding chapter, EK 9 killed *at a conservative estimate* just over 18,000 people during the four months it was under Filbert's command, though it might easily have been several thousands more. Of these 18,000 people, the vast majority – over 99 per cent – were Jewish men, women and children. The remainder were Roma, Red Army commissars, other Soviet POWs, former Soviet officials, alleged Communist informants and alleged partisan accomplices (see Table 2). An unidentified number of genuine partisans can be added to the death toll. This figure of around 18,000 dead confirms that – at least in the case of EK 9 under Filbert – the figures reported back to Berlin, as suspected by Judge Meyer, were in fact too low. It was as

Table 2 *Table of victims killed by EK 9 under the command of Alfred Filbert between 22 June and 20 October 1941*

Date	Location (in Belarus unless other- wise stated)	Figure	Identity	Remarks
Early July	Grodno	6	Red Army commissars	
5 July	Lida	90	Jewish men	Intelligentsia
4–8 July	Vilnius, Lithuania	321	Jewish men	In a mixed forest outside the city
13 July	Vilnius, Lithuania	300	Jewish men	The so-called hostage shooting
15 July	Vilnius, Lithuania	219	Jewish men	
Mid-July	Vilnius, Lithuania	6	Russian prisoners (of war?)	
11–19 July	Vilnius, Lithuania	4,500	Jewish men	In Paneriai Forest
Late July	Ashmyany	527	Jewish men	Entire male Jewish population of town
30 July	Vileyka	350	Jewish men and women	Women included for the first time
End of July	Vileyka	100 (at least)	Jewish men, women and children aged 15	Entire Jewish population of town?
Early August	Maladzyechna	100 (at least)	Jewish men and women (70:30)	
Early August	Near Vileyka	80 or 82	Jewish men and ten or twelve female Jewish teachers	Tracer ammunition used
2–12 August	Vitebsk	332	Jewish men and women, incl. five Bolshevik functionaries	
2–12 August	Vitebsk	27	Jews	Shot in public
August	Vitebsk	1	Jewish woman	Hanged in public
12 August	Surazh	500–600	One-third Jewish men, two-thirds Jewish women and children of all ages	Entire Jewish population of town; voluntary assistance from Wehrmacht
First half of August	Haradok	2,000	Jews	Voluntary assistance from Wehrmacht
9–16 August	Forests around Vitebsk	?	Substantial number of partisans	
17–23 August	Near Gramki	1	Alleged Communist informant	

Table 2 (*cont.*)

Date	Location (in Belarus unless otherwise stated)	Figure	Identity	Remarks
August	Small town between Vileyka and Vitebsk	100	Jewish men	
Late August		1	Red Army commissar	Escapee from prison camp in Lepel
August	Vitebsk	397	Jewish men	Delivered by Wehrmacht from civilian internment camp
Second half of August	Vitebsk	19	Jewish men and women	
Second half of August	Yanavichy	149	Jews	
August	Polatsk	?	Jewish men, women and children	
Late August	Polatsk	10 or 12	Jewish male and female youths	Komsomol members
Late August	Polatsk	1	Russian woman	
First half of September	Nevel, Russia	74	Jews	
End of September	Nevel, Russia	640 (at least)	Jewish men, women and children, and two men from a POW camp	Ghetto dissolved
Second half of September	Yanavichy	1,025	Jewish men, women and children	Ghetto dissolved
September	Near Lepel	23	13 male and 10 female Roma	Handed over by Wehrmacht
September	East of Haradok	2	Jews	
September	Near Pribilnye, Haradok District	10	10 men (alleged partisans)	
September	Vitebsk	1	Man (alleged NKVD associate)	
September	Vitebsk	3	Jews	
September	Vitebsk	1	Man	For stealing and slaughtering a cow
September	Near Ivniki	3	Partisans	
September	Vultshina and Bikovtshina	8	Youths	Komsomol members among them

Table 2 (*cont.*)

Date	Location (in Belarus unless otherwise stated)	Figure	Identity	Remarks
September	Near Yeseritshe	1	Partisan	
September	Near Pletni	1	Red Army soldier	
September	Vitebsk	1	Supreme Soviet delegate	
September	Tikhanovo	1	Communist Party member	
September	Dvoritsha	1	NKVD official	
September	Vitebsk	2	Security personnel	For looting
September	Haradok	3	Russians	For looting
Late September	Near Ostrova	3	Jews	
Late September	Near Budianka	1	Partisan	
25 September	North-east of Polatsk	1	Russian woman	For harbouring partisans
Late September	Near Vyeryetshe	5	'People'	For supplying partisans with food
Late September	Sastarinya	3	Partisans	
1 October	Vitebsk	52	Jews	Fled from Haradok
Early October	Vitebsk	4	Jews	
Early October	Tronkavichi	1	Village elder (alleged NKGB informant)	
Early October	Borovlyany	5	Jewish family	
Early October	Ostrovno	169	Jews	
Early October	Vitebsk	250 (at least)	Jewish men, women and children	From the ghetto
Early October	Vitebsk	750 (at least)	Jewish men and women	
Early October	Vitebsk	800 (at least)	Jews, incl. women and children	
8–10 October	Vitebsk	4,090–8,000	Jewish men, women and children	Ghetto dissolution completed
	Total number	**18,071 – 22.085** (at least)		

if, in response to the imprisonment of his brother and the stagnation of his own career thereafter, Filbert wanted with his zeal in the campaign against the Soviet Jews, the alleged pillars of the Jewish–Bolshevik system, to prove to the RSHA and SS leaderships his commitment to the National Socialist cause and his ideological reliability.

The relatively low number of Soviet commissars killed by EK 9 may have been in large part due to the particularly zealous implementation of the Commissar Order on the part of the 403rd Security Division. It reported for the month of July 1941 a total of 62 'dispatched' (erledigt) political commissars, divided into those who were disposed of by the troops themselves, civilian commissars 'liquidated' by the subordinated Secret Field Police for 'guerilla activity' and civilian commissars who were handed over to the SD.[135] In the month of August, nine military commissars were killed by the troops and twenty-seven were disposed of in the subordinated transit camps for POWs (Durchgangslager, or Dulags), whilst eighty-nine civilian commissars were killed by the troops and a further two handed over to the SD.[136] In September, one military commissar was killed by the troops and six were disposed of in the transit camps, whereas 108 civilian commissars were killed by the troops and a further three handed over to the SD.[137] In October, fifty-one military commissars were disposed of in the transit camps, twelve civilian commissars were killed by the troops and another two handed over to the SD.[138] In fact, of all the verifiable shootings of Soviet commissars by regular German troops in the rear areas (as opposed to the front) between June 1941 and May 1942, more than half were killed by a single security division, namely the 403rd.[139] This was in spite of the procedure prescribed by the Commissar Order, which required the Wehrmacht to kill Red Army commissars found in the operations area, whereas commissars 'seized in the army group rear areas due to dubious conduct' were instead to be handed over 'to the Einsatzgruppe or Einsatzkommandos of the Security Police (SD)'.[140] As the statistics cited here demonstrate, the 403rd Security Division handed over only a handful of commissars to EK 9 during the four-month period in question; it preferred to take care of them itself. The radical approach of the unit in this matter was evidently a result of additional orders issued by its commanding officer, the aforementioned Generalleutnant Wolfgang von Ditfurth.[141]

***

Alfred Filbert was recalled to Berlin on or around 20 October 1941.[142] There is some reason to believe that Filbert requested his recall to Berlin, as was the case with his superior SS-Brigadeführer Arthur Nebe less than a fortnight later.[143] For example, he subsequently claimed to have written a letter to Heinz Jost's former adjutant, SS-Hauptsturmführer Paul Lehn, requesting him to intervene with Jost in order to bring about his recall to Berlin. Lehn confirmed that he had received such a letter from Filbert.[144] Given his zealous conduct as commando chief, however, it seems probable that Filbert's desire to return was not because he fundamentally disapproved of his commission to kill the Soviet Jews but rather because of the emotional strain of leading a mobile killing unit over a prolonged period of time.[145] During his imprisonment in the 1960s, Filbert in fact confessed to having suffered a 'nervous collapse' whilst with EK 9, the symptoms of which he cited as trembling and weeping fits.[146] Beyond Filbert's own post-war claims, there is no evidence to suggest that he really did suffer a breakdown whilst commanding EK 9. Even if he did, however, the historian Richard Rhodes is correct in pointing out that psychological trauma on the part of the perpetrators 'in no way mitigates the crime. Indeed, such mental conflict is indirect evidence that the men of the Einsatzgruppen were well aware that what they were doing was criminal and evil even if the highest authority of the German state had ordered it.'[147] Filbert was by no means the first of the commando chiefs within EG B to return to Berlin. SS-Oberführer Professor Franz Alfred Six, chief of the Advance Commando Moscow, had returned to the capital as early as the second half of August, whilst SS-Obersturmbannführer Dr Walter Blume, head of Sonderkommando 7a, had followed in September.[148]

According to the 1962 judgement at Filbert's trial in Berlin, his conduct during his deployment in the east had been 'that of a committed National Socialist' (*das eines überzeugten Nationalsozialisten*). This description had been used by Bodo Struck, who also added that Filbert 'advocated one hundred per cent the aims of the regime of the time' (*sich hundertprozentig für die Ziele des damaligen Regimes einsetzte*).[149] The court concluded furthermore that Filbert had been 'an energetic, even very strict commander' (*ein energischer, sogar sehr strenger Kommandoführer*) who insisted on the exact implementation of his orders. One trial witness described him as 'the engine of the Einsatzkommando' (*der Motor des Einsatzkommandos*). Co-defendants Schneider and Greiffenberger satisfied the court that shooting operations had only taken place on Filbert's express orders and that he had taken care of everything in the unit, even down to the last detail. Each and every mass killing operation had been preceded by a talk with the officers of the Einsatzkommando, during which Filbert had stipulated who would lead the operation.[150] Filbert himself had personally led no fewer than three separate shooting operations: the first operation in Vilnius itself in mid-July; the first massacre in

Vileyka, during which women were shot for the first time; and the shooting in August in a small town on the road between Vileyka and Vitebsk.[151] Greiffenberger described Filbert as a 'brutal and ruthless commando chief, who only had his own advancement in mind and thus rigorously advocated the shootings of Jews'.[152] The court concluded that the hearing of evidence had clearly revealed 'that Dr Filbert strove to have shot all Jews he could get hold of and that he acted inhumanely towards the Jews'.[153]

6 'Was it thinkable that I, a jurist and a soldier, would do such a thing?'
Suspension from the Reich Security Main Office and reinstatement until the war's end, 1941–1945

On 2 July 1941, shortly after departing for the Soviet Union at the head of Einsatzkommando 9, Filbert had been replaced by Walter Schellenberg as group leader and deputy head of Office VI of the RSHA under Heinz Jost.[1] In the second half of October, upon his return to Berlin from his stint in the east, Filbert was accused of having misappropriated RSHA funds. The affair impacted not only on Filbert but also on other senior members of Office VI, namely Jost – who had been fired by Heydrich as early as the beginning of September[2] – and SS-Obersturmbannführer Friedrich Vollheim, head of Group VI C. The charges were used to remove the three of them from office.[3] The specific charges against Filbert were twofold: first, it was claimed that Filbert had illegally retained 60,000 Reich marks in foreign currency in his office safe for his own personal use; second, he was accused of taking out 'a dubious loan' (einen zweifelhaften Kredit) for the purchase of a house.[4] The interest rate agreed on for the mortgage was supposedly half a per cent lower than the rate generally applied.[5] The house in question was a villa at 34 Waltharistraße in the Berlin suburb of Wannsee, which Filbert had moved into in 1941 (and would then ultimately purchase in 1943).[6] Proceedings were initiated against him and he was questioned by an SS court in Berlin.[7] He later disputed his guilt with the words: 'Was it thinkable that I, a jurist and a soldier, would do such a thing?'[8]

Filbert was only one of many Nazi criminals who admitted in their post-war testimony to having committed murder (albeit often on a scale much smaller than had actually been the case) but disputed having ever enriched themselves materially or financially. Franz Stangl, the former commandant of Treblinka extermination camp, endeavoured after the war to make it clear that no theft had taken place under his command.[9] During the post-war investigation of crimes committed at the Meseritz-Obrawalde psychiatric clinic in occupied Poland, one nurse charged with poisoning patients explained:

[...] I would never have committed theft. I know that one is not supposed to do something like that. During the bad times [pre-war depression years] I was a saleswoman and I would have had easy opportunities back then to do that. But I never did such a thing because I simply knew that one is not allowed to do that. Even as a child I had learned: you are not allowed to steal.[10]

Another nurse testified, 'If I am asked whether I would have carried out theft in response to a corresponding order, I must say that I would not have done so. The administration of medication, even for the purpose of killing the mentally ill, however, I regarded as my official duty, which I was not allowed to refuse.'[11]

Contrary to popular belief, however, corruption was in fact a wide-spread phenomenon among state and Party agencies during the Nazi era.[12] Nowhere was this more visible than in the context of the persecution of the Jews. The historian Frank Bajohr has termed the Aryanisation (*Arisierung*), namely the theft of Jewish assets and their transfer to so-called Aryans, the 'focal point of the corruption'.[13] According to the perverse SS moral codex, 'decency' could be reconciled with mass murder if a murderer carried out his tasks without pursuing his own personal interests.[14] In his notorious speech to a gathering of SS generals in Poznań on 4 October 1943, Heinrich Himmler claimed, 'We had the moral right, we had the duty to our people, to kill these people who wanted to kill us. We do not have the right, however, to enrich ourselves with even one pelt, with one watch, with one Mark, with one cigarette or with anything else.'[15] To name just one example, the commandant of Buchenwald concentration camp, SS-Standartenführer Karl Otto Koch, was arrested in August 1943 'for embezzlement, falsification and destruction of documents, coercion of officials, intimidation, and other serious offences' committed during his time in Buchenwald, and sentenced to death by an SS court in December 1944. Koch was accused not only of personal enrichment but also of committing several murders in an attempt to cover up his other criminal activities. On Himmler's orders he was executed in Buchenwald at the beginning of April 1945.[16] The punishment of personal enrichment did not preclude mass corruption, however, provided this served the collective aims of the regime. Furthermore, in practice the aforementioned SS code of conduct was widely and frequently ignored on an individual level. As the historian Klaus-Michael Mallmann has demonstrated, the process of annihilating the Jews always possessed 'a highly materialistic dimension'.[17]

Concerns about individual cases of corruption were raised within the Reich Security Main Office on more than one occasion. On 22 December 1940, Heydrich wrote to all RSHA office and department heads, all Gestapo and Criminal Police headquarters, all SD sections, the Officer

School of the Security Police (*Führerschule der Sicherheitspolizei*) and the Higher SS and Police Leaders, among others, on the subject of the 'Prevention of corruption within the Security Police and the SD'. He noted that of late various public authorities had been guilty of a large number of cases of malfeasance in the assignment of public commissions. Various private industry firms had succeeded in obtaining delivery orders by donating cash and other gifts. Heydrich hoped that such abuses were not in evidence within departments of the Security Police and the SD: 'Should I learn that members of the Security Police and the SD have requested or received benefits of any kind, I will proceed most ruthlessly against the persons concerned.'[18] On 12 August 1941, Heydrich sent an express letter to a similar group of recipients on the 'Handling of cases of corruption in the Wehrmacht, in public authorities and public bodies, in the NSDAP, its organisations and associated formations'. He informed his readers that since the beginning of the war a considerable increase had been recorded in the number of cases of corruption. For an effective combatting of corruption, he continued, a ruthless clampdown was necessary, 'irrespective of the person' (*ohne Ansehen der Person*) concerned.[19] At the time the letter was sent, Filbert was in Vitebsk. We can assume it still reached him though, as the 'Einsatzkommandos of the Security Police and the SD' were among the addressees.

Filbert himself had first-hand experience of Aryanisation. In June 1941, the new issue of the Berlin telephone book was delivered. It would be the last complete Berlin telephone book to appear until after the war. The entries reflect information valid as of February 1941. The 1,574 pages contained entries for around 315,000 telephone connections, meaning that almost every third household in Berlin – with a total population of 4,242,501 (as of June 1933) – already owned a telephone.[20] Alfred Filbert was listed under 'Filbert, Dr', without a first name. His private address was also listed: the aforementioned 34 Waltharistraße in the Berlin suburb of Wannsee.[21] 34 Waltharistraße was a villa built in 1905 and called *Villa Olga*.[22] Between 1925 and 1941, the house had belonged to and been inhabited by Paul Cahn, a Jewish manufacturer.[23] Cahn would later be deported with his wife Eva to Theresienstadt concentration camp in June 1942, where he would die the following year. Eva Cahn would die in Auschwitz.[24] Filbert was able to purchase the villa in 1943.[25] The suburb of Wannsee, more specifically another villa at 56/58 Am Großen Wannsee, would be the location for the infamous Wannsee Conference of 20 January 1942.

In the specific case of Filbert's suspension, however, it seems probable that the charges were largely fabricated. Dr Henry V. Dicks, the British psychiatrist and psychoanalyst who interviewed Filbert in prison in July

1969, doubted the substance of the charges. He was convinced that Filbert's 'type of character would not have contained the capacity for such a common crime'. He believed instead that the SS had responded to the 'nervous collapse' Filbert had allegedly suffered whilst on the eastern front 'by framing him as a thief'.[26] A more likely explanation, however, is that Heydrich had been waiting for an opportunity to get rid of Heinz Jost. Not only had Filbert been the driving force in Office VI under Jost, but he – like Jost – was tarnished by his association with Werner Best, who had been forced out of the RSHA by Heydrich as early as June 1940. Filbert, Jost and Best all originated from Hesse and had known each other for years. Once Schellenberg had replaced Filbert as Jost's deputy in July 1941, Jost's days as chief of Office VI were also numbered.[27] Jost later testified, 'The money was in fact all there, right down to the last penny, which was known to Heydrich as well, without him taking the opportunity to clear up the matter in favour of Filbert or myself.'[28] In Filbert's case, it was not only his association with Best and Jost that cost him his post in Office VI but also the arrest of his brother in November 1939 and Otto's subsequent imprisonment. Both these factors contributed to tarnishing Filbert to the extent that his position was no longer tenable.

***

For two years after his suspension from the SD, Filbert was on unemployed leave at home.[29] Filbert described it himself as 'house arrest' (*Hausarrest*).[30] His suspension evidently constituted a major loss of pride for Filbert: 'Can you imagine how I felt as a soldier – the whole neighbourhood knew – night after night, seeing me sitting with my wife in the air raid shelter – what would all those women say: "Why isn't he at the front – that's where he should be"?'[31] In his SS officer file the box for 'SS penalties' (*SS-Strafen*) is blank and the file makes no mention of his suspension.[32] Filbert's post-war assertions to the effect that he was suspended from duty in the RSHA for two years are almost certainly authentic, however, since they were confirmed independently after the war by more than one of Filbert's former colleagues. An alternative explanation, then, for his file not containing any mention of the suspension is that the charges were never proven and Filbert did not receive any punishment beyond being suspended whilst the charges were investigated.

In the autumn of 1943, Filbert was completely rehabilitated and reinstated in the RSHA, though not in SD-Overseas. Instead, he was appointed to the Criminal Police (*Kriminalpolizei*, or *Kripo*), Office V.[33] Here he served once again under Arthur Nebe, the former head of Einsatzgruppe B. Nebe assigned him to Department V B 2 under Karl Schulz, which dealt with Fraud (*Betrug*).[34] Filbert's reinstatement was no doubt helped by the death in the meantime of the man who, it seems, had been behind his suspension from the RSHA in the first place: Reinhard Heydrich.[35] Less than a year later, on 4 July 1944, Filbert was then promoted to head the newly created Group Economic Crime (*Wirtschaftskriminalität*, V Wi), containing six departments and set up in order to provide for 'a unified centralisation of all departments for combating economic criminality'.[36] Even Filbert himself could later see the irony of this appointment to the head of a section dealing with corruption, given the reasons for his suspension almost three years earlier: 'The 60,000 Reichsmark was a good recommendation for a start', as he jestingly told the aforementioned Dicks in 1969.[37] Following the arrest of SS-Obersturmbannführer Hans Lobbes in the wake of the 20 July 1944 plot to kill Hitler, Filbert assumed control of Group V B, which dealt with Operations (*Einsatz*).[38] The hitherto head of Department V B 2, Karl Schulz, replaced Filbert as head of Group V Wi.[39] Lobbes was evidently the only member of the Criminal Police whom Nebe had confided in regarding the plans to assassinate Hitler.[40] His failure to approach Filbert, although the latter had been suspended from the RSHA for two years, tends to once more negate Filbert's post-war claims that he distanced himself from the regime following the arrest of his brother, Otto. Although Otto had been arrested in 1939, Filbert demonstrated complete commitment to the ideological objectives of the regime during his deployment as chief of EK 9 two years later. Though suspended in autumn 1941, Filbert was assigned to the Kripo in 1943, promoted to group leader in 1944 and then given fresh responsibility following the reshuffle in the wake of the 20 July bomb plot, that is, at a time when the regime had to know exactly whom it could and could not count on. There was no question, however, where Filbert's loyalties lay. On 12 September 1944 Heinrich Himmler conferred on him the War Merit Cross 1st Class with Swords (*Kriegsverdienstkreuz I. Klasse mit Schwertern*).[41] Filbert remained as head of Group V B until the German capitulation in May 1945.[42]

In summer 1944, Filbert visited Sachsenhausen concentration camp north of Berlin together with Nebe's successor as chief of the Criminal Police, SS-Oberführer Friedrich Panziger, in order to lend support to the members of a special commission that had been set up by the Criminal Police in order to investigate cases of corruption involving concentration camp personnel.[43] More specifically, the task of the special commission was to expose profiteering with Wehrmacht commodities, including motor vehicle parts and radios. Filbert was called in to support the special commission after it had come under fire from the Gestapo, which had its own commission operating on unrelated business in Sachsenhausen. The Criminal Police's special commission continued its work in Sachsenhausen until the autumn.[44]

***

Having served a four-year prison sentence in Dessau,[45] Otto Filbert was transferred by the Magdeburg Gestapo on 6 December 1943 to Buchenwald concentration camp, situated near the city of Weimar, the focal point of the German Enlightenment. Weimar's concrete history from 1890 at the latest developed in such a way that the subsequent good neighbourly relations between city and concentration camp are not an inexplicable, bewildering phenomenon: cultural arrogance, ethnic nationalism and anti-Semitism found fertile soil here.[46] Otto Filbert's status in Buchenwald was that of a 'political prisoner'. He was given prisoner number 29092 (see Figure 20).[47] A week after arriving in Buchenwald, Otto was transferred from block 17 to block 63 along with fifty-nine other prisoners, overwhelmingly Eastern Europeans.[48] As of 1 January 1944, the camp counted 37,000 inmates. Six months later, on 1 July, this number had risen to 61,000.[49] By October 1944, there were 85,000 prisoners in Buchenwald.[50]

Filbert later testified that Otto had sent his last message to the family from Buchenwald concentration camp in winter 1944 or spring 1945. Otto was thereafter missing without trace.[51] In fact, Otto Filbert left Buchenwald before winter 1944. He was released from the main concentration camp on 20 October 1944, only to be transferred to an external camp detachment in Weimar.[52] For the next five-and-a-half weeks he performed forced labour for the Fritz Sauckel Works.[53] On 28 November, Otto was then released from Buchenwald entirely. This by no means meant that he was free, however. On the contrary, he was assigned to serve in the Waffen SS Dirlewanger formation, a penal battalion.[54] All his effects were sent to his father Peter Filbert in Worms.[55]

The Dirlewanger Brigade was one of the most notorious of all SS formations. The core of the unit, which had been set up in 1940 under the command of SS-Obersturmführer Dr Oskar Dirlewanger, consisted of convicted poachers. Dirlewanger was himself a habitual criminal.[56] The historian Knut Stang characterises him furthermore as 'a sadistic, amoral alcoholic'.[57] As early as July 1942, and increasingly from 1943, concentration camp inmates were assigned to the unit.[58] The administration of the concentration camps even proposed that political prisoners be recruited.[59] It was Dirlewanger himself who submitted this idea to Himmler, and political prisoners were then indeed recruited from autumn 1944 onwards.[60] In his letter from 7 October 1944, Dirlewanger told Himmler that the concentration camps contained men

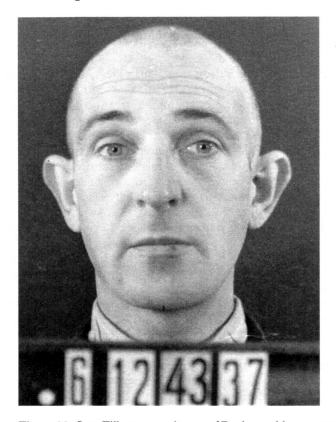

Figure 20 Otto Filbert as a prisoner of Buchenwald concentration camp. (Source: International Tracing Service Archives, Bad Arolsen, 1.1.5.3 KZ Buchenwald, 'Häftlings-Personal-Karte' [Doc. ID # 5856617]. Reproduced with permission of the International Tracing Service Archives.)

who had remained true to their political convictions at the time of the Nazi takeover of power in 1933 and in this way 'showed character, in contrast to the many hundreds of thousands' (*Charakter zeigten, im Gegensatz zu den vielen Hunderttausenden*) who had sided with the stronger forces, that is, the Nazis, 'despite inner opposition' (*trotz innerlicher Gegnerschaft*). In order to be recruited, however, it was necessary for these political prisoners to have 'altered themselves inwardly' (*sich innerlich gewandelt*) and to possess the desire to demonstrate this alteration 'through participation in the struggle of the Greater German Reich' (*durch Teilnahme am Kampf des Großdeutschen Reiches*).[61]

A total of almost 2,000 political prisoners from various camps were assigned to the Dirlewanger Brigade in November 1944 and early 1945.[62] All German and Austrian political prisoners in Buchenwald, including members of the illegal German Communist Party (*Kommunistische Partei Deutschlands*, or KPD), but also Wehrmacht soldiers, were ordered to attend a muster, at which the camp commandant, SS-Oberführer Hermann Pister, addressed the assembled prisoners. Aside from threats, it seems that no force was applied in Buchenwald in the attempted recruitment of political prisoners. Those who did join the Dirlewanger Brigade appear to have volunteered.[63] Otto Filbert was among the approximately 100 Buchenwald prisoners who joined the unit, 'almost all unwitting newcomers' (*fast alles ahnungslose Neuzugänge*), in the words of Buchenwald inmate Eugen Kogon.[64] It should by no means be assumed, however, that the prisoners volunteered out of enthusiasm for the war or the regime. They most likely saw it as providing a potential opportunity to escape the horrors of Buchenwald, or at least as an alternative to these horrors.

The new recruits were transported via Kraków to Slovakia, where they received brief military training.[65] In the view of historian Hellmuth Auerbach, the imprisonment of opponents of a political regime by this regime and then their compulsion to defend the regime with arms is a singular phenomenon in modern European history.[66] Former concentration camp inmates in the Dirlewanger Brigade were treated with particular rigour. They were not given ammunition until directly before their deployment at the front and any attempt to absent oneself from the brigade was punished by shooting. By order of Himmler, Dirlewanger was permitted to exert power over the life and death of the men under his command during hostilities. For the former concentration camp inmates, however, this power applied at all times, even in non-combat situations.[67]

Following deployment for anti-partisan warfare in Belarus from February 1942 to summer 1944, where it had been one of the most murderous of all formations and killed at a conservative estimate 30,000 civilians,[68] the Dirlewanger Brigade was transferred to Warsaw at the beginning of August 1944 to assist in suppressing the Warsaw Uprising. At the same time, overall command of the operation was placed in the hands of the aforementioned Erich von dem Bach-Zelewski, Himmler's Chief of Anti-Partisan Formations (*Chef der Bandenkampfverbände*) and another veteran of the fighting in Belarus.[69] The Dirlewanger Brigade continued in Warsaw where it had left off in Belarus. As early as 5 August, it commenced with the mass slaughter of both combatants and non-combatants, children included, in the Warsaw neighbourhood of Wola. In the course of two days alone, the unit killed between 30,000 and 40,000 people, overwhelmingly civilians. During their advance west through the city, they used women and children as human shields and destroyed each and every building they passed, using gasoline and hand grenades.[70] The capitulation of the surviving Polish forces was signed on 2 October 1944. A total of perhaps 150,000 Polish non-combatants had been killed by the Germans in August and September alone. The remainder of the civilian population was expelled from Warsaw along with the Polish POWs. The empty city was then systematically destroyed by German forces.[71]

In October 1944, the 6,500-man-strong brigade, now known as the SS Storm Brigade Dirlewanger (*SS-Sturmbrigade Dirlewanger*),[72] was relocated to Slovakia to put down the national insurgency there.[73] In December, the unit – now including the political prisoners from the concentration camps – was deployed on the Hungarian front against the advancing Red Army. It is probable that the political prisoners from Buchenwald (as well as those from Auschwitz, Ravensbrück, Groß-Rosen, Neuengamme and Flossenbürg concentration camps) were assigned to the four companies of the 2nd Battalion of SS Regiment 2. The political prisoners comprised around a third of each of the approximately 180-man-strong companies of the 2nd Battalion.[74] Of the almost 770 former political prisoners deployed in the 2nd and 3rd Battalions of SS Regiment 2, roughly 480 – for the most part former members of the Communist Party – deserted to the Soviets by 18 December.[75] Of the remainder, around 200 men were either wounded, had been taken ill or had fallen victim to the executions within the unit.[76] Whether Otto Filbert was among those who escaped across the front lines is impossible to say. It is just as likely that he had already died as a result of either the brutal treatment within the brigade itself or the hostilities in Hungary. As of January 1945, the unit was back in Slovakia, though it was transferred back to Germany the same month.[77] One month later, Hitler personally ordered that the Dirlewanger Brigade be expanded to a division.[78]

It has often been assumed that Otto Filbert died in Buchenwald concentration camp.[79] This supposition is based on an acceptance of Alfred Filbert's own assumption, voiced after the war, about the fate of his brother and on a failure to examine the original documentation from Buchenwald. This documentation makes it quite clear that Otto Filbert was released from Buchenwald, as discussed earlier. His wife, Wilhelmina, heard from her husband for the last time on 28 November 1944, the day he was released from Buchenwald and transferred to the Dirlewanger formation. On 16 May 1951 she applied for him to be declared dead as of 28 November 1944. Five months later, on 15 October 1951, the local court in Bottrop, where Otto's family lived, pronounced Otto Filbert dead and – lacking more exact data – gave the obviously fictitious date and time of death as midnight on 31 December 1945.[80] In addition to his wife, Otto Filbert left behind three sons (Kurt had been born in 1938 in Germany),[81] one of whom, Peter, was then raised by Otto's sister Lina in Mannheim.[82]

Although Filbert was aware of Otto's almost twelve-month incarceration in Buchenwald concentration camp, there is no indication that he learnt either at the time or at a later date of his brother's brief deployment with the Dirlewanger Brigade. In the testimony he provided at various times after the war, his allusions to the fate of his brother were generally made in a sober and matter-of-fact way. Frequently, this was coupled with the utilisation of Otto's suffering first and foremost as evidence of Filbert's own suffering. This victim mentality was evident throughout Filbert's trial, during his imprisonment and indeed subsequent to his release.[83] Beyond responding to Otto's arrest and imprisonment in 1939 by demonstrating a renewed, complete commitment to the ideological objectives of the Nazi regime, as argued earlier, it remains unclear what the extended torment of his only brother actually meant to Filbert at the time on a personal level.

***

The Reich Security Main Office was officially dissolved on 22 April 1945 and Office V along with it.[84] At this point, the institutions of the SS and police divided themselves into two groups, one of which went south to the so-called Alpine Fortress around Hitler's former mountain retreat of Berchtesgaden, whilst the other – comprising Himmler, the Main Office Order Police, Offices III, V and VI of the RSHA, as well as several former Higher SS and Police Leaders – made its way to the so-called Fortress North in the state of Schleswig-Holstein.[85] Thus, among those institutions that went north to the vicinity of Flensburg in Schleswig-Holstein were parts of Office V of the RSHA, including the head of Group V B, Alfred Filbert.[86] According to a British report dated 2 July 1945, 'FILBERT is suspected to have gone underground in [the] FLENSBURG area.'[87]

7 'My son, who has not yet returned home from the war'
Post-war submergence and reintegration into West German society, 1945–1959

On the day of the capitulation of the German armed forces, 8 May 1945, Filbert took leave of his colleagues from the Criminal Police in Flensburg and 'hiked', as he put it, to the state of Thuringia in central Germany. His aim was to learn how his family was, for they had been staying with Filbert's parents-in-law at the potash works in Volkenroda.[1] Filbert thus remained loyal to Hitler's regime until well after the latter's suicide on 30 April and, in so doing, avoided the fate of many Germans who were in favour of surrendering without a struggle in order to prevent unnecessary destruction or loss of life, or simply so as to make a good impression on the new power holders, and were therefore murdered in the final weeks of the war by those still loyal to the regime.[2] After he had verified that his wife and sons were still alive, Filbert went to the town of Bad Gandersheim in what is now the neighbouring federal state of Lower Saxony.[3] There, under the assumed name of 'Alfred Selbert', he registered with the local authorities in the neighbourhood of Heckenbeck on 2 June 1945. His place of abode was listed as the Hilprechtshausen manor (*Gut Hilprechtshausen*), his profession as 'agricultural worker' and his marital status as 'single'.[4] Filbert selected the name 'Selbert' because he had operated under this name during his time with the SD and still retained the corresponding identity papers.[5] Apparently, Filbert always possessed several ID cards.[6] Filbert would remain in Bad Gandersheim for the next six years. During the immediate post-war months, both the US Army and the British Military Mission in Denmark, successor to the Supreme Headquarters, Allied Expeditionary Force (SHAEF) Mission (Denmark), were evidently interested in locating Filbert. The description of Filbert in the relevant US Army file ran as follows: 'Born 8 Sep 1905 in GIESSEN [*sic*]; height 5'11" (1.80 m); thin build; small chest; dark brown hair; grey-blue eyes; long thin face, pale complexion, large pointed nose, very visible duel scars on chin; wears SS uniform and badly fitting civilian clothes.'[7]

As of 25 June 1945, Filbert's wife, Käthe, registered with the local authorities in Bad Gandersheim along with her two sons at 8 Burgstraße ('c/o Timmermann'). According to her local registration card, Käthe Filbert was 'married'.[8] From 1946, Käthe's parents were also registered at this address.[9] In Bad Gandersheim, Filbert was 'immediately' taken on as a lawyer by the well-known industrialist Heinrich Pferdmenges.[10] In Filbert's own words:

[A]s his activities were rather paralysed as a result of conditions at that time though, I initially kept myself busy at his then residence, the Hilprechtshausen manor close to Bad Gandersheim. We intended [...] to set up a settlement and carpentry workshops where refugees would be settled. In order to prepare myself for this, I worked in the relatively small workshop, which was located at the manor, as a bench and machine carpenter. We then established the Leinetal firm, a furniture factory, with a corresponding settlement. I assumed commercial, in particular financial, control under a managing director.[11]

From 1946, the furniture and textile business Leinetal was set up in the so-called sheepfold at the Hilprechtshausen manor, where it specialised in the production of domestic radios and gramophones. A year or two later, the furniture factory and the houses of the settlement were completed in a cleared, former forested area belonging to the manor located 2 km away on the banks of the Leine River. The factory Leinetal (literally *Leine valley*) was then relocated to this area. The firm existed until 1979. Today, the premises belong to the firm Treppenmeister Leinetal, which is likewise a woodworking enterprise.[12]

There is no evidence for a prior relationship between Filbert and Pferdmenges for the period before June 1945.[13] Instead, Filbert – as Selbert – was registered along with many others that year on a list of 'Evacuees and Refugees' who had settled in Heckenbeck and at the Hilprechtshausen manor.[14] Filbert remained at the Hilprechtshausen manor beyond the death of Heinrich Pferdmenges in 1947.[15] During his time in Hilprechtshausen, Filbert/Selbert appears to have lived very reclusively. He was never a member in any of the societies or clubs that were revived in nearby Heckenbeck in 1947 and 1948, for example, the choral society, the fire brigade, the football club or the table tennis club.[16] Between April and November 1946, another prominent Nazi lived in the manor house at Hilprechtshausen with his wife and two children: Professor Gerhard von Mende.[17] During the Nazi period, von Mende had been employed in the NSDAP's Foreign Policy Office (*Außenpolitisches Amt*, or APA) under Alfred Rosenberg and was subsequently appointed by the latter to head Department I 5 overseeing the Caucasus in the Reich Ministry for the Occupied Eastern Territories.[18]

The move to Heckenbeck was facilitated by the Georgian Misha Alshibaya, whose sister lived in Munich and was friends with Heinrich Pferdmenges's own daughter.[19] It is unclear whether Filbert and von Mende knew each other from the war or what kind of relationship the two had at the Hilprechtshausen manor. Von Mende's two children were later unable to recall Filbert (or, for that matter, 'Selbert').[20]

After almost four years in Heckenbeck, Filbert departed on 23 February 1949 and moved to 2 Rathenowstraße in the nearby borough of Kreiensen, where he registered with the local authorities on 28 February 1949 as a 'commercial employee' (kaufmännischer Angestellter), again under the name 'Alfred Selbert' (though now using his doctor title) and still 'single'.[21] On 22 July 1949, Filbert's mother died in Worms, aged 68.[22] As Filbert had been living away from his family under an assumed name, it is conceivable that he had not seen his mother over the course of the preceding four years, since the war had ended, and perhaps longer.

On 25 April 1951, Filbert – still registered as 'Selbert', though now listed under the profession 'self-employed business consultant' (selbständiger Wirtschaftsberater) – departed from Kreiensen for Mannheim in the federal state of Baden-Württemberg.[23] During the almost six years that Filbert and his family had lived in Bad Gandersheim, though admittedly at separate addresses, his sons had seen him on only a few occasions.[24] This limited contact with his family must have served to prevent Filbert from being discovered; his wife Käthe was, after all, registered in Bad Gandersheim under her real name. Filbert registered in Mannheim on 27 April as a business consultant and, for the first time in almost six years, under his real name and as a married man. The address he provided was 2a Parkring, where he lived with his sister, Lina, and her husband Adolf Hille, a former bank manager eighteen years her senior whom Lina had married on 16 September 1930 in Worms.[25] Otto Filbert's son, Peter, born 1936, was living at the time with his aunt Lina in Mannheim. Upon the arrival of his uncle Alfred, due to the limited space in his aunt's apartment it appears that Peter was sent to stay with his grandfather, Peter Filbert, in Worms.[26]

Filbert may have felt the time was right to reassume his real name because of the amnesty resulting from the Law on the Granting of Impunity from Prosecution (Gesetz über die Gewährung von Straffreiheit),[27] passed by the West German government – despite considerable misgivings on the part of the Allied High Commission – on the last day of 1949. At first glance, the law applied only to minor offences for which a prison sentence of up to one year had been passed.[28] At the same time, however, it also explicitly benefitted those who had eluded internment and denazification at the end of the war by assuming a false identity.[29] Filbert, of course, was one of these so-called illegals. Filbert's decision to reassume his real name – sixteen months after the Law on the Granting of Impunity from Prosecution had been passed – may also have been connected to the announcement of sentence modifications for those convicted by a US military court in the Nuremberg Einsatzgruppen trial of 1947/48. On 31 January 1951, US High Commissioner for Germany John J. McCloy reduced sixteen of twenty convictions, including commuting nine death sentences to prison terms of varying lengths, ranging from ten years to life.[30] McCloy furthermore amnestied all those who had been sentenced at the various Nuremberg trials to jail terms of less than fifteen years for crimes committed under the Nazis.[31]

After less than seven months in Mannheim, Filbert left the city on 9 November 1951[32] and returned to the state of Lower Saxony, where he registered five days later in Hanover at the address 8 Landschaftstraße.[33] On 15 October, whilst Filbert was living with his sister Lina, their brother Otto was pronounced dead by the local court in Bottrop.[34] The court in Bottrop was responsible because this was where Otto's wife and children had been living at the time of both his incarceration in Buchenwald and his transfer to the Dirlewanger Brigade.[35] The German agency responsible for maintaining records on the fate of former German members of the Wehrmacht and the Waffen SS has neither a missing person report nor a death note for Otto Filbert in its files. According to a search request submitted by his wife in 1953, two years after Otto had been pronounced dead, he had sent his last message from Buchenwald in November 1944 at precisely the time when he was released from the concentration camp and assigned to the Dirlewanger Brigade.[36]

Alfred Filbert, having discarded his false identity and resumed using his real name, began working in 1951 as a casual employee (*Aushilfskraft*) for the *Braunschweig-Hannoversche Hypothekenbank* in Hanover. Filbert's new employer was apparently unaware of his activities during the war or of his membership in the SS,[37] which the International Military Tribunal had classified as a 'criminal organisation' at the post-war Trial of the Major War Criminals in Nuremberg. In 1953, Filbert moved from 8 Landschaftsstraße to 1 Borkumer Straße, where he registered on 21 November.[38] This was the only time he moved apartment during the more than six years he spent in Hanover.[39] For a period of two years, from November 1951 to November 1953, Filbert lived alone in Hanover before his family joined him. As of 14 November 1953, Käthe Filbert and her two sons – having left Bad Gandersheim after over eight years there – were also registered in Hanover, though at a different address, namely 42a Ferdinand-Wallbrechtstraße.[40] Nevertheless, this address was only a couple of streets away from Filbert's abode at 1 Borkumer Straße and, moreover, a branch office of the *Sparkasse Hannover* bank is located to this day at 42a Ferdinand-Wallbrechtstraße, suggesting that the family may have been registered in company housing.[41] It seems likely, however, that 42a Ferdinand-Wallbrechtstraße was merely the address given by Käthe Filbert at the time of her move from Bad Gandersheim:[42] according to an annotation from 25 November 1953 recorded on her Bad Gandersheim registration card, her new address in Hanover was in fact 1 Borkumer Straße, that is, the very address at which her husband had registered four days earlier.[43] Their eldest son, Dieter, confirmed that the family indeed lived together in Hanover.[44]

In spring 1956, Filbert – apparently by chance – encountered his former subordinate in EK 9, Gerhard Schneider, in Hanover. Schneider had been appointed to a post in the Ministry of Economics and Transport in the federal state of Lower Saxony, and was in the process of searching for an apartment in Hanover. He asked Filbert for assistance in finding one.[45] Schneider was one of two former EK 9 members whom Filbert met 'by chance' (*zufällig*) in the years after 1945.[46] It is hardly surprising that Filbert and Schneider were at large in Hanover (and even able to meet) given the identity of the head of the criminal police there at the time: Dr Walter Zirpins, formerly SS-Sturmbannführer and chief of the criminal police in the Łódź Ghetto in occupied Poland.[47] In an article from 1941, Zirpins had described the German crackdown on illegal attempts to survive on the part of the Jews of Łódź as 'above all' a 'professionally rewarding, that is, satisfying', task.[48]

Over the course of a few years following his move to Hanover in November 1951, Filbert managed to work his way up the career ladder to the point that he was named manager of the West Berlin branch of the *Braunschweig-Hannoversche Hypothekenbank* in 1958. He began working in his new position in Berlin on 1 January 1958. His family then joined him in Berlin three months later, on 1 April of the same year.[49] Filbert's place of work was located at 13a Tauentzienstraße.[50] His monthly gross income as a West Berlin bank manager was 1,250 German marks including housing allowance.[51] Filbert initially lived in Berlin-Wilmersdorf,[52] but later moved to a three-room apartment at 49 Bamberger Straße in Berlin-Schöneberg (see Figure 21).[53]

If it is assumed that Filbert did not have any contact with his parents whilst he was in hiding, it remains unclear at which point – if at all – he re-established contact with his father, whom he had so idolised as a child. A letter written by Peter Filbert to the University of Giessen dated 30 March 1951 suggests that even then, almost six years after Filbert had gone underground and a month before he recommenced using his real name,

Figure 21 49 Bamberger Straße in the West Berlin district of
Schöneberg, where Alfred Filbert lived in a three-room apartment from
1958 until his arrest in 1959 and again from 1975 until his death in
1990. (Photograph taken on 15 January 2012 by the author.)

father and son were still not in touch. In the letter, Filbert senior, who still resided in Worms, requested that he be sent the 'authenticated certificates' attesting to his son's successful completion of his legal traineeship and attainment of the qualification of a doctor of laws 'for the purpose of completing the paperwork lost as a result of the war'. Most interesting in his letter is the way Filbert senior refers to his son: 'my son, who has not yet returned home from the war' (*meinen aus dem Kriege noch nicht zurückgekehrten Sohn*).[54] True enough, Peter Filbert *was* the father of a son who had not returned home from the war, but his name was Otto, not Alfred. Did Peter Filbert, six years after the end of the war, really not know anything about the whereabouts of his only remaining son? On the other hand, this could conceivably have been a ruse in order to mislead the authorities as to whether Filbert junior was still alive or not. It is not unlikely that Filbert himself requested his father to obtain these certificates in order that he could pass them on to his new employer. On the last day of 1956, Filbert's father died in Worms, aged 77.[55]

***

According to Thomas Harlan, who devoted much of his life to tracking down and uncovering mid-level Nazi perpetrators and their post-war careers and would later direct Filbert in the feature film *Wundkanal*, Filbert, after he went to ground when the war ended – under the name 'Selbert' – worked for the Central Intelligence Agency (CIA) in Bolivia in the struggle against communism.[56] The United States did indeed initiate a campaign to prevent the spread of communism in the wake of the Bolivian National Revolution of 1952.[57] By the time of the National Revolution, some form of US-Nazi cooperation vis-à-vis Bolivia was already in place: with the help of the Counter Intelligence Corps (CIC), in whose pay he had been since 1947, the notorious 'Butcher of Lyon' and former SS-Hauptsturmführer Klaus Barbie had succeeded in fleeing to Bolivia in 1951.[58] Under the Nazi War Crimes Disclosure Act of 1998, the CIA declassified and released a total of 1,309,200 pages of documents, of which 109,200 pages were from the post-1947 CIA era.[59] The approximately 50,000 pages released prior to January 2005 alone (775 name files and 36 subject files) revealed that five associates of Adolf Eichmann had worked for the CIA and that at least a further twenty-three Nazis and/or war criminals had been approached by the CIA for recruitment.[60] Among those whose files were released were Heinz Tunnat, Wilhelm Greiffenberger and Konrad Fiebig, all three of whom served as officers in EK 9 under Filbert. Fiebig has been described as '[t]he man with the most blood on his hands in the Gehlen Organization', that is, the forerunner of the *Bundesnachrichtendienst* (BND), Germany's foreign intelligence agency. He was retired by the BND in 1962 for falsifying the autobiography he had submitted at the time of being hired.[61] Files on Filbert were not among those released by the CIA.

A request by the author to be granted access to records held in the archives of the CIA pertaining to Alfred Filbert and the CIA under the Freedom of Information Act (FOIA) was denied by the agency's Information and Privacy Coordinator, who determined that the CIA could 'neither confirm nor deny the existence or nonexistence of records' pertaining to Filbert and the CIA.[62] An appeal to the Agency Release Panel (ARP) was also denied.[63] A subsequent request by the author for a Mandatory Declassification Review (MDR) under the terms of Executive Order (EO) 13526 of all records relating to Alfred Filbert held in the CIA archives was cancelled with reference to the denial of the earlier FOIA request and the author's 'right to seek judicial review of this determination in a United States district court'.[64] Based on these rejections, it is impossible to determine whether the CIA is or is not in possession of records pertaining to a relationship between that agency and Filbert during the early post-war period. If so, however, then it would appear that those records are sufficiently sensitive to warrant a refusal to grant access to them more than half a century after the events in question. An FOIA request submitted by the author to the National Archives and Records Administration, on the other hand, *was* granted and two personal files on Filbert located among the records of the US Army Staff were declassified, one of the files originating from the CIC and one from US Army, Europe (USAREUR).[65] Unfortunately, these two files do not provide an answer to the question as to whether Filbert was recruited or even approached by either the CIA or the CIC.

8 'A trial of this magnitude has never previously taken place before a German court'
Arrest and trial, February 1959–June 1962

The year 1958 witnessed a turning point in the prosecution in West Germany of violent crimes committed by the Nazi regime and its representatives, above all in Eastern Europe. The so-called Ulm Einsatzgruppen trial (*Ulmer Einsatzgruppenprozess*) against ten members of the Einsatzkommando Tilsit, which had murdered more than 5,000 Jews in the German-Lithuanian borderlands in the summer of 1941,[1] provoked a startled and appalled response across sections of the West German public and media regarding the magnitude and savagery of the crimes committed. Among the West German authorities, it also led to the realisation of the necessity of a systematic and coordinated nationwide investigation and prosecution of National Socialist crimes. A direct consequence of the Ulm trial was the establishment of the Central Office of the Judicial Authorities of the Federal States for the Investigation of National Socialist Crimes (*Zentrale Stelle der Landesjustizverwaltungen zur Aufklärung nationalsozialistischer Verbrechen*) in the city of Ludwigsburg later the same year. Like Ulm, Ludwigsburg was located in the federal state of Baden-Württemberg. The main focus of the investigations carried out by the *Zentrale Stelle* were the crimes committed by the Einsatzgruppen and its subordinated commandos in the occupied Soviet Union and by units of the Security Police and the Order Police and by ethnic German battalions in Poland.[2]

The year of the Ulm Einsatzgruppen trial and the founding of the *Zentrale Stelle* also ushered in a turning of the tide for Filbert. According to Thomas Harlan, someone had blown the whistle on Filbert; another participant of the regular meetings of former SS men in Berlin.[3] In the autumn of 1958, the West Berlin Public Prosecutor's Office initiated an investigation into former members of Reserve Police Battalion 9, some of whom had been assigned to Einsatzkommando 9 in the summer of 1941. During the questioning of a police official, Filbert's name was mentioned.[4] Preliminary proceedings against almost 250 members of Reserve Police Battalion 9 were ultimately discontinued in early 1960

Figure 22 Alfred Filbert following his arrest by the West Berlin police, 1959. (Source: Landesarchiv Berlin, B Rep. 058, Nr. 3016. Reproduced with permission of the Landesarchiv Berlin.)

because their plea of having acted under superior orders (*Befehlsnotstand*) could not be disproven. The investigation against Filbert and other members of Einsatzkommando 9, on the other hand, continued.[5]

In the second half of February 1959, a few days before Filbert's arrest in Berlin, police officers were in Bad Gandersheim enquiring after his whereabouts.[6] At 7 o'clock on the morning of 25 February 1959, Filbert was arrested by two members of the Criminal Police in his West Berlin apartment at 49 Bamberger Straße.[7] A search of the apartment was carried out, but nothing was found. Filbert was then taken to the police station,[8] where he was questioned (see Figures 22 and 23).[9] The following day, the charge of murder of an 'unknown number of persons of Soviet nationality' was brought against Filbert by the chief of police in Berlin.[10] At 3 o'clock on the afternoon of the same day, Filbert was transferred to the remand centre at 12a Alt Moabit, where he was given the prisoner number 782/59. The remand centre noted in Filbert's prisoner book that he had 'suicidal tendencies'.[11]

On 4 March, Filbert was transferred to the tuberculosis infirmary of the Plötzensee detention centre at 7 Heckerdamm in Berlin-Charlottenburg.[12] During May and June, the questioning of Filbert nevertheless continued with a series of hearings.[13] On 1 June, Filbert appointed Dr Paul Ronge as his defence counsel.[14] In mid-June, Dr Ronge expressed 'serious concerns due to the state of health of my client, who is known to suffer from pulmonary tuberculosis'.[15] The head doctor at the tuberculosis infirmary, who was also treating Filbert, submitted a report later the same month in which he concluded that, despite

Figure 23 Alfred Filbert following his arrest by the West Berlin police, 1959. (Source: Landesarchiv Berlin, B Rep. 058, Nr. 3016. Reproduced with permission of the Landesarchiv Berlin.)

the tuberculosis in both lungs, Filbert – who weighed only 65.2 kg at a height of 182 cm (5 feet 11 1/2 inches) – was fit enough to remain detained because he was receiving the required medical and medicinal treatment in the infirmary.[16] On 20 July 1960, Filbert was transferred from the Plötzensee detention centre, where he had been since March 1959, to the Moabit remand centre, where he was booked in as prisoner number 2970/60.[17]

On 21 May 1959, a second former member of Filbert's Einsatzkommando 9, head of sections IV and V Gerhard Schneider, was also arrested.[18] On 10 July, the Institute of Contemporary History (*Institut für Zeitgeschichte*) in Munich sent the Berlin police the incident reports of the Einsatzgruppen on four microfilms, and the police set about working its way through the 3,000 pages.[19] On 19 December, the Chief Public Prosecutor of the Regional Court in Berlin applied for preliminary investigations to be opened against Filbert.[20] This was granted and preliminary investigations were opened nine days later. Filbert was accused

[...] during the period from July 1941 to April 1942 in Russia, Lithuania and Poland, in the central section of the army group rear area [...] of having jointly with others [...] by means of several independent actions with base motives, maliciously and cruelly killed or of having had killed by persons subordinated to him a not yet established number of people, mostly of Jewish faith [...].[21]

Over the course of the next two years, the Public Prosecutor's Office was able to ascertain exactly when Filbert had commanded EK 9, where it had been deployed and, at least approximately, how many people it had murdered.

Further charges were brought against Filbert on 18 August 1959 for the murder of twenty-seven prisoners of Sachsenhausen concentration camp on 11 October 1944.[22] Three-and-a-half weeks earlier, the East German newspaper *BZ am Abend* (now the *Berliner Kurier*) had already reported that Filbert had been among the murderers in Sachsenhausen of the former Reichstag delegates for the Communist Party Ernst Schneller and Mathias Thesen, as well as 25 other anti-Nazis, including Siegmund Sredzki and Heinz Bartsch, and jointly responsible for the deportation of a further 103 prisoners to Mauthausen concentration camp in Austria.[23] During a hearing on 3 March 1960, Filbert disputed not only any involvement in the murder of the twenty-seven prisoners but indeed any knowledge at all of their shooting.[24] It was concluded at the beginning of 1961 that Filbert had neither perpetrated nor arranged for the murders in October 1944 and proceedings against him were ended.[25]

The indictment for Filbert's role in the killings of EK 9, however, was not long in coming. On 21 November 1961, Filbert was indicted, along with the other former members of EK 9 Gerhard Schneider, Bodo Struck, Wilhelm Greiffenberger, Heinrich Tunnat and Konrad Fiebig. Filbert was accused

[...] during the period from the beginning of July to 20 October 1941 in the area of Vilnius, Grodno, Lida, Vileyka, Maladzyechna, Nevel and Vitebsk acting jointly with Hitler, Himmler, Heydrich and others in at least 11,000 cases of having with premeditation from base motives, maliciously and cruelly killed people or of having arranged their killing by subordinates.[26]

The main trial took place over the course of eighteen days: 14, 16–18, 21, 23–24, 28, 30 May, 1, 4, 7, 12–14, 18, 20 and 22 June 1962.[27] One German newspaper wrote, 'A trial of this magnitude has never previously taken place before a German court.'[28] Indeed, a German court had never before sat in judgement on a more than 10,000-fold murderer.[29] During these eighteen days, a total of sixty-seven witnesses testified.[30] Many of these witnesses had themselves taken active part in the mass shootings of the Einsatzgruppen, either as members of EK 9 or one of the other commandos, including Erwin Schulz (first chief of EK 5 of EG C), Dr Walter Blume (first chief of SK 7a), Dr Otto Bradfisch (first chief of EK 8) and Karl Rath (head of the sub-commando that dissolved the Yanavichy ghetto and murdered its 1,025 inhabitants).[31] The findings of the court have already flowed into Chapters 4 and 5 and will not be discussed again here. Merely a few of the most notable incidents from the eighteen-day trial will be recapped here.

Filbert began his statement on the first day of the trial, Monday 14 May, with a grievance to the effect that he was subject to strict night-time observation at the Moabit remand centre and then proceeded to complain that he had lived a 'very, very difficult life' (*sehr, sehr schweres Leben*). This expression of self-pity prompted considerable murmuring amongst the spectators in the courtroom, which was filled to capacity.[32] Throughout the proceedings, Filbert constantly pleaded superior orders, insisted he had made every effort to moderate these orders and claimed to have reported inflated kill counts to Berlin.[33] Filbert's defence strategy was thus based on the assertion that he had been bound by the general order 'to kill all Jews' (*alle Juden zu töten*),[34] and that he had received this comprehensive killing order prior to the invasion.[35] Filbert's legal argumentation was thus in line with most of the officers and men in the dock at the Nuremberg SS-Einsatzgruppen trial of 1947/48 and the subsequent West German trials and proceedings against commando and group chiefs.[36] It is now generally accepted by historians that this testimony was false and part of a legal defence strategy of binding orders.[37] As the historian Klaus-Michael Mallmann has convincingly argued, if there had been a pre-invasion order to kill *all* Soviet Jews, the course of action taken by all the commandos during the first five weeks of the campaign would have amounted to insubordination. Second, the failure to follow such an order strictly, and the limiting of the shooting operations to Jewish men of military service age, would have presented an ideal defence strategy during the post-war trials of commando and group chiefs. Not one of the defendants, however, many of whom were furthermore doctors of law, made use of this defence in court.[38] As discussed in Chapters 3, 4 and 5, the evidence clearly shows that the order to kill *all* Soviet Jews, regardless of age or gender, was not issued until the campaign was well under way.

Of the other defendants at the trial of Filbert and other former members of EK 9, Schneider likewise insisted that he had reported inflated kill counts and furthermore claimed to have only participated in the mass killings 'because he would have had to fear injury or death in the event of a refusal to obey orders'.[39] To this day, however, after decades of legal proceedings, not a single case has been documented for the National Socialist period in which a person who refused to partake in a killing or an execution was actually punished by death or even, for example, transferred to a penal battalion.[40] On the third day of proceedings, the accused Wilhelm Greiffenberger testified. He had already been captured by the Soviets in May 1945 and sentenced by a Soviet military tribunal in December 1949 to death, though not for his involvement in the killings of EK 9 – which he had concealed – but rather for his membership in the SS, which the International Military Tribunal had classified as a 'criminal organisation' at the Trial of the Major War Criminals in Nuremberg. This sentence had subsequently been commuted to twenty-five years of hard labour. He was then released in September 1953 and returned to Germany.[41] In considering the evidence, the Berlin court later concluded, 'The accused Greiffenberger has confessed. The Assize Court is convinced that from his first hearing on he has honestly endeavoured to openly convey what he still recalled from past events and to correct lapses of memory.'[42] Indeed, Greiffenberger was the only defendant who had 'from the outset unreservedly admitted what he did' (*von Anfang an rückhaltslos eingestanden, was er getan hat*).[43] During his testimony to the court on 17 May 1962, Greiffenberger stated, 'We are talking here as though dealing with the sale of meat. Everything sounds so clinical. But no-one can relieve us of the burden and responsibility that we bear.' According to one correspondent, he was then so moved that he was unable to talk for a minute and had to fight back tears before he was able to continue.[44] During Greiffenberger's testimony, one reporter of Jewish descent, whose relatives had been murdered by the Nazis, struck his head against the bench and sobbed.[45]

It was the events of this, the third day of proceedings from a total of eighteen, which were addressed in the single article published on the trial by the *Darmstädter Echo*, a regional newspaper based in Filbert's city of birth. The newspaper did not even publish an article announcing the verdict or the sentences. In the one article from 18 May, no mention was made of Filbert having been born in Darmstadt. Four of the accused are mentioned by name in the article, including Filbert, though he is the only one of the four whose first name is not mentioned.[46] What was the reason for this? Was it because he was the principal defendant? Or, more likely, in spite of him being the principal defendant? The daily newspaper *Darmstädter Tagblatt*, which has since been discontinued, went even further than its competitor and failed to print a single article on the Filbert trial.[47] Outside of Darmstadt, however, there was extensive coverage of Filbert's trial in nationwide and regional newspapers. These included the national daily *Frankfurter Rundschau*, the national weeklies *Die Zeit* and the *Allgemeine Wochenzeitung der Juden in Deutschland* (now the *Jüdische Allgemeine*), the West Berlin daily *Der Tagesspiegel,* the East Berlin daily *Berliner Zeitung*, the Hamburg weekly *Die Andere Zeitung*, and the dailies *Stuttgarter Nachrichten* and *Stuttgarter Zeitung*. No fewer than seven articles appeared in the daily *Augsburger Allgemeine* alone. Clearly, Filbert's trial was not entirely overshadowed by the upholding of the judgement in the Jerusalem trial of Adolf Eichmann on 29 May and his execution two days later. The Eichmann trial had been followed by the media worldwide with great interest.[48] Around 800 articles appeared on the Eichmann trial in the German national daily newspapers the *Frankfurter Allgemeine Zeitung*, the *Süddeutsche Zeitung, Die Welt* and the *Frankfurter Rundschau* alone.[49]

On the eighth day of proceedings against Filbert and his co-defendants, the witness Dr Georg Fleischmann, formerly deputy head of the Gestapo in the staff of EG B and at the time of the trial head of the Criminal Police in Ludwigshafen,[50] raised his hand to be sworn in. Instead of raising his hand to take an oath, however, he raised his outstretched arm and gave the so-called Hitler salute. There was murmuring among the spectators in the courtroom. Only then, after a second or two, did Fleischmann realise his error and correct himself.[51] Another of the witnesses was Richard Neubert, who had led the Order Police platoon attached to EK 9 and thus taken active part in several shooting operations. Karlheinz Meyer, the presiding judge at Filbert's trial, described Neubert's conduct before the court as 'shameless and impudent' (*frech und dreist*) although he was just as guilty as the accused:[52] 'He works in this building but he actually belongs in the dock as well.'[53] Neubert was not sitting with the other defendants in the dock, however, for the simple reason that in 1941 he had only been a *Hauptwachtmeister*, that is, a non-commissioned officer and not a full officer like Filbert and his co-defendants. Instead of being on trial, Neubert was now an official of the judiciary in the same West Berlin criminal court in which Filbert and the others were being tried.

Regarding the cost in human lives of the actions of those on trial, Judge Meyer stated that the court did not see its task as engaging in a 'macabre calculation'. However, as discussed in Chapter 4, Meyer did estimate the number of those killed by EK 9 under Filbert at 'around 15,000' and not, as contained in the RSHA's incident reports, 11,000 people.[54] The court concluded that Filbert had acted 'from base motives and with fore-thought' (*aus niedrigen Beweggründen und mit Überlegung*):

Dr Filbert has demonstrated in a series of individual cases that his actions and his decisions were determined by hatred of Jews. Thus, he forbade members of his Einsatzkommando to converse with Jewish workers who cleaned the accommo-dation of the commando in Vilnius and Vitebsk. He objected to such Jewish workers being served coffee or tea from the stocks of the commando, and expressed himself indignantly about the Jews having also been provided with drinking vessels that had been used by members of the commando.[55]

On 22 June 1962, twenty-one years to the day since the German invasion of the Soviet Union had been launched and with it the massacres of the Einsatzgruppen, Filbert was sentenced to life imprisonment for participa-tion in murder; Schneider to ten years in prison as an accessory to murder; Greiffenberger to three years for the same offence; and Struck and Tunnat to four years apiece, also as accessories to murder. Fiebig was acquitted due to lack of evidence. Filbert's civil rights were furthermore revoked for life; those of Schneider for a period of five years; and those of Struck, Tunnat and Greiffenberger for three years each. Those defen-dants who were convicted were obliged to pay for the costs arising from the trial.[56] Judge Meyer stated in his judgement that the 'inner conviction' of the defendants at the time of their crimes should be decisive in deter-mining the sentences meted out to them.[57] Filbert is reported to have wept during sentencing.[58]

The day after sentencing, Filbert's attorney, Dr Ronge, appealed against the verdict.[59] On 9 April 1963, the West German Federal Supreme Court rejected Filbert's appeal and thus confirmed the verdict against him as legally binding.[60]

'A limited, lower middle class, status-
and-promotion seeking philistine'
Imprisonment and early release, 1962–1975

When the verdict against Filbert was confirmed as legally binding, the former head of EK 9 had already spent just over four years in prison. He was now facing a life sentence in West Berlin's Tegel Prison (*Strafanstalt Tegel*, today *Justizvollzugsanstalt Tegel*) at 39 Seidelstraße, where he was given the prisoner number 1251/63.[1] At this time in the Federal Republic of Germany, a distinction was made between different types of imprisonment: penal servitude (*Zuchthaus*); prison (*Gefängnis*); confinement (*Einschließung*); and detention (*Haft*). Filbert had received a sentence of life in *Zuchthaus*. The *Zuchthaus* had emerged as a form of incarceration in the Netherlands and northern Germany in the late sixteenth and early seventeenth centuries. It combined the twin purposes of chastisement through labour and the opportunity for re-socialisation.[2] In June 1969, the distinction between different types of imprisonment was abolished in the Federal Republic of Germany, and the *Zuchthaus* along with it. Thus, life sentences in *Zuchthaus* and in *Gefängnis* were now both altered to the more generic sentence of 'life imprisonment' (*lebenslange Freiheitsstrafe*).[3] This alteration to the Criminal Code also applied to sentences already imposed but not yet, or not yet fully, served.[4] Thus, Filbert's own sentence of life in *Zuchthaus* was affected by these changes. The provisions came into effect on 1 April 1970.[5]

On 15 January 1964, the Justus Liebig University in Giessen resolved to strip Filbert of the Doctor of Laws title he had obtained on 27 February 1935, as it considered Filbert unworthy of using the doctor title in light of the judgement passed against him by the Regional Court in Berlin.[6] On 12 February 1964, the university wrote to Filbert to inform him of its decision.[7] On 2 March, in a four-and-a-half-page handwritten letter to the university, Filbert filed an objection. In his letter he claimed that he had been appointed head of EK 9 as retribution for the conduct of his brother Otto, who had been imprisoned by the regime for political reasons. He furthermore claimed that refusal to carry out the mass shootings against Jews and other Soviet citizens had been punishable by death. He claimed thus to have had no choice but to commit the crimes of which the Regional Court in Berlin had found him guilty. As he had throughout the legal proceedings against him, he again pleaded superior orders.[8] Filbert then added,

Unfortunately I must point out that High Court Justice Meyer, presiding judge of the Assize Court, is a Jew and his family suffered considerably during the Hitler period. I leave it to the university to decide whether a judge in such a case can make an objective decision or whether he is prejudiced.[9]

Karlheinz Meyer had been born in Berlin in 1922 as the son of a banker and his Jewish wife. Due to the National Socialist racial laws, he was prevented from studying until after the end of the Second World War.[10] On 14 July 1964, the Justus Liebig University rejected Filbert's objection as unsubstantiated. Filbert was obliged to bear the costs of the proceedings.[11]

In March 1966, Filbert was back in court, this time as a witness in the trial for murder of four other members of Einsatzkommando 9, two of whom were his successors as commander, Oswald Schäfer and Wilhelm Wiebens.[12] Wiebens had replaced Schäfer in February 1942.[13] Also in the dock was Karl Rath, who – as a subordinate of Filbert's – had led the twelve-man-commando that had dissolved the Yanavichy ghetto in September 1941 and murdered its 1,025 inhabitants. Wiebens was sentenced to life imprisonment for two cases of murder, whilst Rath received a five-year sentence as an accessory to murder in two cases; Schäfer, on the other hand, was acquitted.[14] Rath was not convicted for carrying out the dissolution of the Yanavichy ghetto – a fact that was presumably unknown to the court – but rather for leading two shooting operations in January 1942, in which a total of at least fifty-eight Jews were killed. The court stated that the fact that the number of victims of these two operations was 'rather considerable' (*recht erheblich*) had the effect of 'stiffening the sentence' (*strafschärfend*).[15]

On 25 April 1966, one month since Filbert had given testimony in the trial of Schäfer and Wiebens, preliminary investigations against him in the context of a proposed – but ultimately abandoned – complex of trials of several hundred former members of the RSHA were temporarily discontinued, and in January 1968 they were permanently ended. In the context of investigations into the involvement of Heydrich's former deputy Werner Best in the organisation of the Einsatzgruppen for Poland and the issuing of orders to them for the extermination of the Polish intelligentsia, evidence could not be found to the effect that Filbert had contributed in a concrete way to the drawing up and issuing of orders for the execution of Polish citizens, beyond his attendance of the meetings of future RSHA office heads on 7, 12, 19, 21 and 27 September 1939.[16] By the end of 1969, the year after the abandonment of proceedings against Filbert, the entire complex of proposed RSHA trials had also been derailed once and for all.[17]

In April 1969, the Main Department IX/11 within the Ministry of State Security in East Berlin, which was responsible for the 'Solving and Prosecution of Nazi and War Crimes' (*Aufklärung und Verfolgung von Nazi–und Kriegsverbrechen*),[18] provided information to the Soviet KGB (Committee for State Security) in response to a request submitted by the latter regarding an investigation into the death of the head of the Vitebsk anti-fascist resistance movement. It was suspected that Filbert had been involved in her death.[19] It is not clear from the available documentation what came of this investigation. In any case, the Ministry of State Security did not have any documents at its disposal on the Vitebsk anti-fascist resistance movement or its members, and was thus unable to pass any such information on to the KGB.[20]

Three months later, in July 1969, a British psychiatrist and psycho-analyst, Dr Henry V. Dicks, interviewed Filbert at length in his prison cell.[21] Dicks, who did not smoke, was unable to offer Filbert a cigarette. Filbert responded unhappily to the effect that he could no longer afford cigarettes, that his wife was poor and also ill with diabetes.[22] His sister Lina sent him paints and canvasses in order to allow him to pursue his hobby of painting.[23] According to Dicks, 'a not very good copy' by Filbert of *The Man with the Golden Helmet* (formerly attributed to Rembrandt)[24] hung on the wall of the prison governor's office.[25] Much of what Filbert then went on to say during the course of the interview consisted of griping aimed at various people whom he felt were to blame for his predicament. He once again used the fate of his brother to present himself to Dicks as a victim, before referring again to Judge Meyer as being Jewish by marriage. The arrest of his brother, he continued, had led to intrigues against him within the RSHA, ultimately resulting in his two-year suspension. Greiffenberger, he complained, had insisted on being his deputy in EK 9 and then betrayed him as a crown witness.[26] Filbert's anti-Semitism was in evidence on several occasions during the interview, for example when referring to those Jews from Eastern Europe who had settled in Germany after the First World War as an 'alien element'.[27]

Dicks summarised his findings as part of *A Socio-Psychological Study of Some S.S. Killers*. He wrote,

At no time did I feel that I was conversing with an educated or cultivated person. [...] PF[28] had never been other than a limited, lower middle class, status-and-promotion seeking philistine with a good-boy 'underling' mentality. His cold, inhuman eyes that wept only for himself were an accurate pointer to his psycho-logical make-up.[29]

Dicks classified Filbert as 'a real fanatic'. Significantly, Dicks recognised that Filbert 'felt uniquely singled out'.[30] This victim mentality was evident throughout Filbert's trial, during his imprisonment (as Dicks's conclusions illustrate) and indeed subsequent to his release. To what extent, if at all, was Filbert justified in feeling 'uniquely singled out'? During his interview with Dicks, Filbert contrasted his own fate with that of his opposite number in EK 8, Dr Otto Bradfisch: he 'only got a ten years' sentence' at Munich. 'He denied nothing, but stood up in court simply affirming "Those were my orders".'[31] Bradfisch, from June 1941 to April 1942 the first chief of EK 8,[32] another sub-commando within EG B, and witness at Filbert's trial, was indeed sentenced to ten years in prison by the Regional Court in Munich in July 1961.[33] Particularly interesting – and, at first glance, baffling – in the case of Bradfisch is that he was convicted of being an *accessory to* murder and not, like Filbert, of murder. He was also convicted in 15,000 cases, more than twice as many as Filbert.[34] The respective judgements make it clear, however, that the disparity in the two sentences resulted from the subjective interpretation of the respective courts regarding the extent to which the defendant had received a concrete order and to what extent the order allowed for the taking of initiative on the part of the recipient.[35] In November 1963, the Regional Court in Hanover convicted Bradfisch furthermore as an accessory to the murder of at least 22,000 people as Gestapo chief in the Polish city of Łódź from 1942 to 1944 and added a further three years on to his earlier conviction.[36] Thus, compared with Bradfisch, Filbert was justified in claiming to have been more severely treated by the German legal system. Filbert was furthermore one of only four former senior members of the Reich Security Main Office whom German courts convicted in the twenty years following the war for committing Nazi crimes.[37] These facts tell us less about the justness of Filbert's treatment, however, than about the failures of the Federal German legal system in prosecuting Nazi crimes of violence. In view of the magnitude of his own crimes, Filbert had little reason to complain.

During his aforementioned interview with Dr Dicks, Filbert had told the British psychiatrist that he was in the process of preparing an appeal.[38] The federal state government in Berlin rejected a request for a pardon for Filbert on 17 February 1970.[39] On 31 May 1972, Filbert applied for proceedings to be reopened at his own expense. His request was rejected as inadmissible by the Regional Court in Berlin on 1 November 1973.[40] An appeal for clemency submitted by Filbert on 25 February 1974 was likewise rejected by Berlin's federal state government.[41] Although Filbert's requests for a pardon, a retrial and clemency were not granted, it would in fact be little more than fifteen months before he was released. On 5 June 1975, after serving more than sixteen years in prison, he was released from Tegel Prison. An examination by a medical specialist had confirmed that the 69-year-old was not fit enough to remain locked up.[42] It was Filbert's deteriorating eyesight that spared him having to serve his full life sentence.[43] An eye examination had established on 10 October 1974 that the vision in his right eye had already been reduced by more than 50 per cent and a progressive deterioration was expected.[44] At a further eye examination on 16 January 1975 it had then been established that the remaining vision was drastically endangered by prison conditions and Filbert's release was recommended.[45] A week later, the director of the prison had followed this recommendation in a letter sent to the Public Prosecutor's Office in Berlin:

The conduct of the prisoner during his imprisonment so far has never given cause for complaint; his behaviour towards members of staff was always faultless. [...] I therefore apply for the enforcement of the custodial sentence against the prisoner Filbert to be suspended due to him being unfit to serve his prison sentence in accordance with §§ 45 and 46 of the Criminal Enforcement Regulations.[46]

Following another eye examination on 15 May, the eye specialist concluded, 'It must, therefore, be noted emphatically that under the current circumstances the patient is threatened with blindness in the near future.'[47] At 3 o'clock on the afternoon of 5 June, Filbert was released from Tegel Prison and allowed to return home to 49 Bamberger Straße.[48]

According to Thomas Harlan, Filbert had spent some time in the secure wing of Stuttgart's Stammheim Prison (*Haftanstalt Stuttgart-Stammheim*, today *Justizvollzugsanstalt Stuttgart*) towards the end of his imprisonment in Tegel Prison.[49] In 1975, the year of Filbert's release, a multi-purpose building containing the secure wing was built especially for the imprisonment of leading members of the radical left-wing Red Army Faction (*Rote Armee Fraktion*, or RAF). As of 2012, however, Filbert was unknown to the director of the JVA Stuttgart, who also confirmed that the prison did not possess any records on Filbert. If any records from 1975 had existed, they would have been either destroyed or passed on to the State Archives in Ludwigsburg.[50] As of September 2012, however, the State Archives in Ludwigsburg did not possess any such records relating to Filbert, either.[51] One potential explanation for this was offered by Harlan: Filbert was not in Stammheim as a prisoner but rather in an advisory capacity:

And we asked him about the death of Ulrike Meinhof [on 9 May 1976] and requested him to tell us and to show us what he knew about her death and how Ulrike Meinhof had taken her own life. Strangely enough, he knew everything that one must know and he even spoke like an insider, because at a specific moment he pulled back and said: 'I don't want to comment on that', as though he were keeping a secret, although, as far as we knew, he had nothing to do with the death of Ulrike Meinhof and thus nothing to hide, and in this way, with his help, we could link him to the death of Ulrike Meinhof.[52]

In an interview given after the release of *Wundkanal*, Harlan stated, 'Filbert [. . .] was not really a murderer in Stammheim; he merely possessed a type of guru function among his old comrades.'[53] How plausible is some kind of involvement on Filbert's part in the death of Ulrike Meinhof, even if 'only' in an advisory capacity? He had after all been convicted of thousand-fold murder by a *German* court – would the Federal German judicial authorities of 1975 really have associated themselves with him? Yet he was also the former deputy head of German intelligence, and thus in certain respects a well-informed man with certain 'talents'. All we have to go on, however, is what Harlan claimed Filbert had told him and, importantly, *upon enquiry*; Filbert had not volunteered the information himself (though why should he?). It was Harlan who had raised the subject of Ulrike Meinhof and asked Filbert what he knew about her death. Given what we have learnt about Filbert's need for admiration and recognition, it is feasible that Filbert puffed himself up and told Harlan what he wanted to hear.

Interestingly enough, Filbert *had* briefly spent time in Stammheim as a prisoner. Following three days of treatment in the Hohenasperg Prison Hospital (*Vollzugskrankenhaus Hohenasperg*) in the federal state of Baden-Württemberg, Filbert had been transferred on 18 July 1969 to Stammheim Prison, likewise in Baden-Württemberg, to be then returned to Berlin.[54] Yet this was long before the arrest of the RAF leadership or the construction of the secure wing at Stammheim.

10 'A chess game of egos'
Wundkanal and aftermath, 1975–1990

Following his release from prison for health reasons in June 1975, Filbert lived for another fifteen years. He returned to 49 Bamberger Straße in West Berlin, where he would remain until his death in 1990.[1] In 1983, Filbert's pre-1945 biography was the subject of a request for information submitted by the District Administration for State Security in Rostock in East Germany to the Main Department IX/11 within the Ministry of State Security, commonly known as the Stasi, in East Berlin.[2] The request was made in the context of the 'processing of operative material' (*Bearbeitung eines operativen Materials*).[3] The backdrop to the request appears to have been the fact that the District Administration for State Security in Rostock had become aware 'that in the FRG a film is being made with the professional advice of Fillbert [*sic*]' (*daß in der BRD ein Film unter Fachberatung des Fillbert gefertigt wird*).[4] In fact, Filbert was providing much more than specialist advice: he was acting in the lead role.

The former SD officer, RSHA member and Italy specialist Karl Haß – whose wife had officially declared him dead in 1953 – had played small supporting roles in various feature films during the 1960s, including a bit part in Luchino Visconti's *La caduta degli dei* ('The Damned', 1969), generally as a member of the SA or the SS.[5] The only time a convicted Nazi mass murderer has played a mass murderer in a feature film, however, was in 1984 in the film *Wundkanal – Hinrichtung für vier Stimmen* ('Gun Wound – Execution for Four Voices'). According to the film's closing credits, it stars 'Alfred F.' in the lead role of 'Dr S.'.[6] This was Alfred Filbert, wearing a toupee and, intermittently, a false moustache. The character's name was no coincidence. Filbert had once before been known under the name 'Dr S.': Dr Selbert, the name he had used for the first six years after the war. In *Wundkanal*, Filbert was in many ways playing himself. The director and producer was Thomas Harlan, son of Veit Harlan, director of the notorious Nazi anti-Semitic propaganda film *Jud Süß* ('The Jew Süss'). Harlan junior devoted his life, initially in the Polish archives, later in films and novels, to tracking down and uncovering mid-level Nazi perpetrators and their post-war careers; men like his father, men like Filbert. He ultimately brought criminal charges against more than 2,000 Nazi perpetrators who were still alive.[7] As Harlan stated in an interview after the release of *Wundkanal*: 'The film is a work about the plural; I merely start with my [own] father'.[8]

The shooting of the film *Wundkanal* began in 1981, initially in Hungary with the actor Erwin Geschonneck, a former concentration camp prisoner and one of East Germany's most celebrated actors. According to Harlan, the West German embassy managed to have the film shoot stopped, however, on the grounds that Harlan and his crew were allegedly engaging in propaganda for terrorism.[9] The abrupt termination of the shoot led to a legal dispute between the production firm Quasar Film and Hungarofilm.[10] After returning to East Berlin, Harlan decided to shoot *Wundkanal* with a real perpetrator in the lead role: Alfred Filbert.[11] Harlan and Heike Geschonneck, the fourth wife of the aforementioned Erwin Geschonneck and executive producer[12] of *Wundkanal*, came across Filbert's name whilst at the Central Office of the Judicial Authorities of the Federal States for the Investigation of National Socialist Crimes (*Zentrale Stelle der Landesjustizverwaltungen zur Aufklärung nationalsozialistischer Verbrechen*) in the German city of Ludwigsburg.[13] This, however, was not the first time that Harlan had been acquainted with the name Alfred Filbert: two decades earlier, Harlan had corresponded with the Chief Public Prosecutor attached to the Regional Court in Berlin, regarding the trial against Filbert. The Public Prosecutor's Office had been at the time in the process of preparing the indictment against Filbert and his co-defendants.[14]

Harlan met with Filbert over coffee and cake in the latter's West Berlin apartment at 49 Bamberger Straße. According to Harlan, Filbert

[...] was touched by a visit from the son of Harlan, the son of the great consoler, and it was already clear on this first day of our acquaintance that he was prepared to speak; whether [he was also prepared] to act, this no-one could know. And later it lasted two weeks before we noticed that he had no taken the bait and wanted to become an actor; it was on the day when we are standing in the desert with him and he is prepared to hold the pistol how Andreas Baader is supposed to have held it to his neck, but could not have held it.[15]

This comment (see Figure 24) was a reference to Harlan's theory that the leadership of the radical left-wing RAF had not in fact committed suicide in Stuttgart's Stammheim Prison on the night of 18 October 1977 but instead had been murdered. Baader, for example, was supposed to have shot himself in cell 719 in the base of the neck so that the bullet exited through his forehead. Tests indicated, however, that it was virtually

Figure 24 Alfred Filbert (wearing a toupee) and Thomas Harlan on the
set of *Wundkanal*, 1983. (Still image from *Notre Nazi*, directed by
Robert Kramer [France/Germany: Reass Films/Quasar Film, 1984],
00:54:35.)

impossible for a person to hold and fire a pistol in such a way at the
distance necessary to cause the powder burns found on the skin of
Baader's neck. Harlan concluded that one's own arm is too short.[16] His
conclusions are reflected in the opening credits of *Wundkanal*: 'IN THE
NECK AT A DISTANCE LONGER THAN A MAN'S ARM / AT A
DISTANCE OF 30.5 CENTIMETERS FROM THE WOUND / THE
BULLET BEING FIRED INTO THE NECK BY STRANGERS'.[17] In
Wundkanal, Dr S. compels another man, whom he has just finished
interrogating, to shoot himself in precisely the same way in which
Baader was supposed to have killed himself. The title of the film,
Wundkanal, is based on this idea: the 'Wundkanal', or wound channel,
is the trajectory taken by a bullet in a body (in this case, a skull) between
the point of entry and the point of exit.[18] On other occasions, Harlan
argued that the RAF leadership had indeed killed themselves, though only
'in order to prove that they were to be murdered'.[19] One of the principal
concerns of the RAF was also Harlan's principal concern and the real
subject of the film: the continuity of Nazi biographies in the Federal

Republic of Germany and of murder in the name of the state. Harlan was, by his own admission, less concerned with the murder of Jews than with the *murderers* of Jews.[20]

Following his return from Hungary, Harlan wanted to resume shooting in the Peruvian jungle, though the state of Filbert's health did not permit this.[21] Instead, shooting took place at Exposure Studios in Charenton outside Paris.[22] The shoot began on 22 August 1983[23] and lasted for eight weeks.[24] According to the French journalist Pierre Joffroy, during his Parisian outings, Filbert carefully avoided certain quarters, where there were surviving witnesses to the Holocaust, and he insisted that the production car that took him from his hotel to the studio and back stick to the same route every day; otherwise, he panicked and was afraid the driver might be attempting to abduct him.[25] The interpreter on set, Ursula Langmann, relates a very different and telling story. She was responsible not only for translating between Filbert and the largely French crew (only Thomas Harlan and Heike Geschonneck spoke German) but also for taking care of Filbert on and off the set, including picking him up from his hotel on the Rue Kepler in the morning, driving him back to the hotel in the evening, eating with him, attending costume fittings, etc.[26] One Saturday, Langmann had to accompany Filbert to a costume fitting at a tailors in the 9th arrondissement in Paris, where the costume designer had ordered a couple of suits for the film shoot. Afterwards, around lunchtime, Filbert was hungry and wanted to eat something. Langmann suggested various restaurants at more conventional tourist locations in Paris in order that they could leave that particular quarter of the city as soon as possible. The reason for her desire to go elsewhere was that at the time around the cabaret music hall *Folies Bergère* there were predominantly restaurants belonging to Tunisian or Moroccan Jews and Langmann wanted to reach what she termed 'neutral ground' with Filbert. As Filbert was a little hard of hearing and therefore spoke very loudly, the thought was anathema to Langmann that Filbert might trumpet something about his past in one of the restaurants. Yet Filbert, 'stubborn' as he was, could not be persuaded to eat elsewhere. The two of them ended up in a Jewish couscous restaurant, where the food was admittedly very tasty but where Langmann soon lost her appetite at the site of the large families gathered there on the Sabbath, unaware of who was sitting at the neighbouring table. Eventually, Langmann asked Filbert if he knew where they had ended up: he, of course, knew that the restaurant was run by North African Jews and that he was surrounded first and foremost by Jewish families, eating their lunch. Yet this did not bother Filbert in the slightest: 'No qualms, not the least sense of guilt ... In his eyes, it had nothing whatsoever to do with him or his past.'[27]

In the film *Wundkanal* itself, 'Dr S.', a war criminal, is kidnapped by a group of four young people, heirs to Andreas Baader and Ulrike Meinhof, and imprisoned in a room filled with mirrors and monitors, where he is constantly confronted with his own image. The four voices, belonging to the unseen kidnappers, one of whom speaks English (the American filmmaker Robert Kramer) and one of whom is a woman (Heike Geschonneck), interrogate him in a mock trial scenario, force him to pass judgement on himself and attempt to elicit a confession of guilt. Ultimately, whereas the prisoner is released, the film ends with the four kidnappers lying dead on the floor, evidently in reference to the fate of the four RAF members in Stammheim: Baader, Meinhof (or, alternatively, Irmgard Möller, who survived the night of 18 October 1977), Gudrun Ensslin and Jan-Carl Rasspe. Harlan dedicated the film to the memory of Giangiacomo Feltrinelli,[28] the Italian publisher and left-wing revolutionary who had financed his research on Nazi perpetrators and their post-war careers. The release of Dr S. also prefigures Harlan's advocacy of and admiration for the Truth and Reconciliation Commission created by Nelson Mandela and established in South Africa after the abolition of apartheid. Harlan later noted, 'The truth that must no longer be concealed has the greatest power.' He contemplated what might have happened, had the National Socialists testified before a truth commission: it would have created in German society an awareness of the crimes committed. A truth commission would have contrasted significantly with the criminal courts, before which the perpetrators felt compelled to deny their complicity.[29] Historical scholarship on National Socialist crimes would surely have benefitted immeasurably from a conception of justice that prioritised truth over guilt.

The film *Wundkanal* mixes fact and fiction to such an extent that it is unclear to the viewer which is which. Filbert is mentioned for the first time during the opening credits, which include the following text (in English):

> DR ALFRED SELBERT ALIAS PAULSSEN ALIAS GRODNOW
> BORN SEPT. 8, 1906 AT HEIDELBERG (W. GERMANY)
> FORMER CHIEF SS INTELLIGENCE DEPT. 6.
> NOW IN LA PAZ, BOLIVIA, DIRECTOR SINCE 1971
> FEDERAL INTELLIGENCE AGENCY B.N.D. (W. GERMANY)
> LOCAL REPRESENTATIVE.[30]

Filbert had, of course, lived for the first six years after the war under the name 'Dr Alfred Selbert' and this was the man – thus, in effect, himself – whom he was now playing in *Wundkanal*. He was indeed born on 8 September, though in the year 1905, not 1906. Later in the film, however, Filbert – as Selbert – correctly states that he was born on 8

September 1905. Though his mother had been born in Heidelberg, Filbert himself was born in Darmstadt. Filbert was not the former chief of SS intelligence, department 6, but rather the former *deputy* chief of Office VI of the RSHA. The Bolivian connection was potentially also not far from the truth, depending on whether one believes Harlan's afore-mentioned claim that Filbert had worked for the CIA in Bolivia after the war. Without any hard evidence to this effect, however, his assertion must be regarded as tenuous. Although Filbert was still in Berlin's Tegel Prison in 1971, the holding of a function in the BND either prior to or subse-quent to his imprisonment is not in itself entirely unlikely in light of the high number of former Nazis in the BND[31] and also the close working relationship between the CIA and the BND (including its forerunner, the Gehlen Organisation).[32]

The slight inconsistencies contained in the information given are not accidental, they are not errors. They are, on the contrary, intentional and have the purpose of disorientating the viewer, of persuading the viewer to accept the possibility that everything he/she sees is factual or, conversely, that nothing is factual at all. The very real continuity of Nazi biographies in the Federal Republic of Germany is merged with the possibility of foul play in the Stammheim deaths but also with clearly fictitious elements such as the figure of Colonel Humphrey Ian Donald Calleigh, director of the 'Office of Peace Planning & Security' of British Military Intelligence in Hertfordshire, England.[33] This approach allows Harlan to play with the accepted conventions of documentary filmmaking and to straddle the boundary between fact and fiction.

When Filbert is mentioned for a second time during the opening credits, it is his real name that is used:

> PAUL WERNER[34] ALFRED FILBERT PAUL WERNER
> THE AUTHORS OF THE 1939–1945 GENOCIDE
> NOW STILL ACTIVE & INVOLVED IN
> THE GERMAN PRISON KILLINGS (1977 . . .)[35]

The 1977 'German prison killings' were, of course, the aforementioned deaths of the RAF leadership in Stuttgart's Stammheim Prison. Just over halfway through the film, Dr S. is instructed to read an abridged but verbatim passage on the liquidation of the Vitebsk ghetto from the actual judgement against Filbert from 1962.[36] The only alteration made to the passage is that the words 'Dr Filbert' are replaced with 'Dr S.', though Filbert is on the verge of saying 'Dr Selbert' (!) and only at the last moment corrects himself. Even Greiffenberger is mentioned by name during the reading of the passage. Confronted with his own image on another monitor, Dr S. concludes the passage by removing his spectacles and saying: 'Yes, what can I say to that? All sorts of things could be said to that.'[37]

Wundkanal thus offers the viewer a total of six different identities for Filbert: 1. The name 'Dr Alfred Selbert', as used in the opening credits; 2. 'Paulssen', a pseudonym for 'Dr Alfred Selbert'; 3. 'Grodnow', likewise a pseudonym for 'Dr Alfred Selbert'; 4. The name 'Alfred Filbert', also used in the opening credits; 5. 'Dr S.', who – as the closing credits make clear – is the name of the character we see on the screen, and who is also referred to during the reading of the (real) judgement against Filbert and seen written on various sketches laid out on the floor; and 6. 'Alfred F.', the name of the actor playing 'Dr S.', according to the closing credits.[38] So many identities evidently confused the organisers of the Berlin International Film Festival, at which the film was shown in February 1985, as in a data sheet containing crew, cast and plot they listed the actor playing the part of 'Dr S.' as 'Alfred Selbert' and even added that the role of 'Dr S. II' was played by 'Aldred [sic] Selbert'.[39] Or was this merely a ploy on the part of Thomas Harlan to further confuse his audience? It was he, after all, who was cited as the editor of the data sheet.[40]

As soon as Harlan decided to replace Erwin Geschonneck with Filbert, that is, an actor with a real perpetrator, *Wundkanal* ceased to be a fictional film. Instead, it became an experiment. From this point on, the entire crew was only concerned with Filbert the person, with his crimes and with the question of his guilt. The making of the film became the actual event, rather than the film itself. For this reason, the documentary *Notre Nazi* ('Our Nazi'), which was shot at Harlan's request by the American filmmaker Robert Kramer parallel to the shooting of *Wundkanal* and designed to document the whole process, became just as important as *Wundkanal* and considerably more interesting. Harlan and Kramer had met each other during the mid-1970s in Portugal, where both men were making films about the Carnation Revolution of 1974, *Torre Bela* (1975) and *Scenes from the Class Struggle in Portugal* (1977), respectively. Harlan subsequently visited Kramer at his home in San Francisco in the late 1970s, but it was only later, after Kramer and his family had moved to France, that Harlan invited him to document the filming of *Wundkanal*. Kramer accepted the offer, though he remained very independent from Harlan and shot less a companion piece to *Wundkanal* than a film of his own, which can be watched in its own right.[41]

Why did Filbert agree to star in a film in which he not only played himself as a recognised mass murderer but in which he was also subjected to an intensive interrogation over twenty years after his trial in Berlin? First of all, Filbert was paid a fee of 150,000 French francs (or 50,000

Figure 25 Alfred Filbert on the set of *Wundkanal*, 1983. (Still image from *Notre Nazi*, directed by Robert Kramer [France/Germany: Reass Films/Quasar Film, 1984], 00:04:32.)

German marks) for his involvement in the film.[42] Above and beyond that, however, there are several indications to the effect that Filbert did not realise what he was getting himself into. Towards the end of *Wundkanal*, when asked to make a confession, Dr S. refuses, adding 'I've had enough' (*Mir hat's genügt*). The viewer has the feeling that it is not (just) Dr S. who has had enough but in fact the actor Filbert himself. Before shooting began, Harlan – by his own admission – had deceived Filbert into believing that he wanted to make a film *about* him. By means of this tactic, Harlan succeeded in persuading Filbert to take part in the film Harlan actually wanted to make, which was not in fact about Filbert as such.[43] Harlan and his crew treated Filbert so well, paid him so much attention and gave him a feeling of importance that he had not enjoyed for decades, that Filbert was soon prepared to become an actor (see Figure 25). Harlan later said that 'little pressure and a whole lot of seduction' had brought this about.[44] 'He feverishly waited to be made up again the next day.'[45]

Ursula Langmann was effectively Filbert's 'chauffeur', among other things, and she drove him around every day in a mid-range rental car.[46] On Filbert's birthday, which fell during the shoot, Harlan arranged flowers and a cake for him.[47] Erika Kramer, Robert Kramer's widow, spent a great deal of time on set and later described the interaction between Harlan and Filbert as 'a chess game of egos'. She cites three things as the principal motivations for Filbert agreeing to take part in the film: money, his identification with whom Harlan was (i.e. the son of Veit Harlan) and a belief on Filbert's part that any guilt had been expiated because he had served his time in prison.[48] In an interview that he gave Pierre Joffroy from the French daily newspaper *Libération* at the time, Filbert stated that he had obeyed Harlan like he had once obeyed Heydrich.[49] This, in the words of the film critic Ekkehard Knörer, demonstrated the willingness of an authoritarian character to do as he is told.[50]

Although Dr S. is released at the end of *Wundkanal* without any physical harm being done to him, the film shoot did not conclude quite so peacefully. On the final day of shooting, Harlan's Algerian assistant director, Aziz Bel Milloud, allegedly broke five of Filbert's ribs. This incident cost Harlan and his crew 5,000 German marks, 1,000 for each rib.[51] Filbert did not require inpatient treatment,[52] however, and Ursula Langmann suspected that Filbert obtained a falsified medical certificate attesting to the five broken ribs in order to be freed from his contract.[53] How the injury came about can be seen in *Notre Nazi*. The backdrop to the injury was a discussion initiated by Harlan about a massacre of 100 Jewish men in Belarus in August 1941. Filbert had personally commanded the shooters.[54] Harlan also notes that two prisoners had managed to flee the execution and escape. The viewer sees Harlan briefing a group of six Jewish men, telling them about Filbert: '[T]his barbarian, who has remained a barbarian. You are not facing a man here. It is the remnant, the mortal remains of somebody who does not exist anymore, and who existed forever as a child. It is one of the worst individuals that the earth has seen, which has the misfortune not to know it.'[55] Filbert does not want to talk about the massacre in question, which he in any case denies being involved in, instead making Tunnat responsible. He stands up and attempts to leave the set; a physical confrontation ensues. Filbert is confronted by the men briefed by Harlan, Holocaust survivors, one of whom may or may not be one of those who fled the massacre. One of the men then rolls up his sleeve and shows Filbert a tattoo on his arm, which he says came from Auschwitz, where his entire family was murdered. Filbert responds by saying, 'My brother was in Buchenwald and he is dead.'[56]

It was not the first time during the shooting of *Wundkanal* that Filbert had presented himself as a victim on account of the fate of his brother. On another occasion he explains his imprisonment not as a result of the atrocities he had committed in Lithuania and Belarus but instead as a result of his brother expressing regret at the failure of the attempt on Hitler's life in November 1939: 'I had to as a result of my brother, as a result of this statement [following the attempt on Hitler's life], I had to sit in prison for 18 [*sic*] years. I lost my eyesight in the process, I lost my honour, the nervous strain. Yes, thanks a lot!'[57] In Filbert's eyes, it was 'a crime under constraint' (*ein erzwungenes Verbrechen*).[58] This response was aimed at Robert Kramer, who described Filbert as 'guilty of one of the greatest crimes against humanity possible'.[59] On another occasion, Filbert weeps whilst talking about the fate of his brother. It initially appears to the viewer that Filbert's show of emotion is on account of the suffering and death of his brother, before it becomes clear that he is in fact weeping – at least in part – for himself and his damaged career in the SS: 'I naturally suffered a lot from this.'[60] In his bestselling book *The Road Less Travelled*, psychiatrist M. Scott Peck describes a not dissimilar situation he encountered during an interview with the parents of a schizophrenic patient, Susan. Describing to them Susan's great progress in therapy, Peck was surprised to find Susan's mother crying. It soon became clear that these were not tears of joy but tears of sadness. He eventually realised that Susan's mother 'was not crying for Susan but for herself'. Peck defined this failure to perceive the separateness of another person on an emotional level and the use of the other as a vehicle to express one's own needs as narcissism.[61] Henry V. Dicks also characterised Filbert as a 'narcissistic prig'.[62] In Filbert's case, it was his brother Otto whom he was using as a vehicle to express his own needs.

The two films, *Wundkanal* and *Notre Nazi*, should be watched consecutively,[63] and Harlan indeed drew up a legal contract to prevent *Notre Nazi* from being shown without *Wundkanal*.[64] Harlan, who also produced *Notre Nazi*,[65] later explained the film's purpose:

A film that unmasks *Wundkanal*. *Wundkanal* is a film about guilt, and *Nôtre Nazi* is a second film about guilt. The film about guilt merges into the film about the origins of guilt. This newly formed guilt, which *Nôtre Nazi* deals with, was our guilt. It was no wonder that this self-exposure had to be punished by the audience sooner or later.[66]

Harlan was referring here to the public reaction when the two films were premiered at the Venice International Film Festival (*Mostra Internazionale d'Arte Cinematografica di Venezia*) at the end of August 1984. The film provoked anger, uproar, fits of dizziness and shattered glass doors.[67] Harlan was beaten at the exit to the cinema.[68] As Harlan himself well knew, the shock provoked by the film was because of the perceived hounding of an old man:

> Here, a grandfather is kidnapped, not a father, and interrogated and tormented. And the grandfather is likeable; the grandchildren cannot stand to see how a seasoned forebear – even if he has much to answer for – is persecuted for a second time at his age; they shudder to see the patriarch encircled and questioned about 40-year-old murders and suicides, especially when they then watch Robert Kramer's *Our Nazi*, the mirror image of WUNDKANAL: here, we expose ourselves and show how the persecutors quickly assume the attributes of the persecuted; we become revolting, above all myself. [...] *Our Nazi*, that is then myself.[69]

It was a similar story at the Berlin International Film Festival (*Internationale Filmfestspiele Berlin*) in February 1985, though the two films did share the Prize of the Readers' Jury of the alternative Berlin magazine *Zitty*.[70] The films were also shown at the Strasbourg International Film Festival on Human Rights (*Festival International du Film des Droits de l'Homme de Strasbourg*) in 1984.[71] Lengthy articles appeared in the national weekly newspaper *Die Zeit* and the weekly news magazine *Der Spiegel* following the premiere in Venice.[72] Hans-Dieter Seidel from the conservative *Frankfurter Allgemeine Zeitung* found the juxtaposition of Auschwitz and Stammheim to be scandalous and 'completely obscene' (*vollends widerwärtig*). This in turn provoked a response by the Hamburg-based, left-wing monthly magazine *konkret* in its October 1984 issue.[73]

***

In spite of the commotion that took place on the final day of the shoot and the resulting alleged injury to his ribs, Filbert stated his willingness to return and continue shooting. Some months later, a member of the crew happened to see Filbert in Berlin. Filbert confided in him that his experience of the movies had been the single greatest moment of his life.[74] Karl Wilhelm Alfred Filbert died in Berlin's Saint Gertrude Hospital at 11:30 on the morning of Wednesday, 1 August 1990, five-and-a-half weeks short of his 85th birthday.[75] Although Filbert had been stripped of his doctor of laws title more than twenty-six years previously, he was still adorned with the qualification on his death certificate. He outlived his brother's widow, Wilhelmina, by almost six years. She had passed away on 10 September 1984 in Bottrop.[76] Filbert's own wife, Käthe, survived her husband by thirteen years and died in 2003.[77]

At the time of writing, Filbert's two sons, Dieter and Günter, were living in Berlin and Stuttgart, respectively. They both have children of their own.[78] Dieter enjoyed a very close relationship with his cousins, the sons of Otto Filbert.[79] Otto's eldest son, Ralph, returned to the United States after the war and resided for many years near Philadelphia, where the family had lived in the 1920s and 1930s.[80] He passed away at his home on 24 February 2014.[81] Otto's only surviving son, Peter, remained in Germany and lives today in Weinheim, in the federal state of Baden-Württemberg.[82]

Concluding thoughts

'But the active ones, they were all National Socialists.'[1] This is how Filbert assessed the nature of participation in the Nazi Movement almost forty years after the end of the war. Filbert actively pursued a career in the Nazi security apparatus. He volunteered for service in the SS-Einsatzgruppen in the war of annihilation against the Soviet Union, and he displayed particular radicalism in implementing his commission to murder Soviet Jewry. Filbert can be regarded as falling into at least one (and quite possibly four) of the five categories of 'ordinary people' identified by the sociologist Michael Mann in his analysis of over 1,500 biographies of perpetrators of Nazi genocide: he was a 'materialist killer' (or careerist).[2] In the words of Dr Henry V. Dicks, the British psychiatrist and psychoanalyst who interviewed Filbert at length in his prison cell in July 1969, Filbert was a 'status-and-promotion seeking philistine'.[3] His deputy in Einsatzkommando 9, Wilhelm Greiffenberger, concluded that Filbert 'only had his own advancement in mind'.[4] Simultaneously, however, Filbert also belonged to what Mann terms the 'real Nazis', that is, those who were 'committed to extreme nation-statism radicalized into murderous ethnic/political cleansing. They were *ideological* killers'.[5] Dicks classed Filbert 'as a real fanatic. To persevere in accepting zealously and unquestioningly any assignment the Party offered him [...] seems to me the hallmark of SS dedication.'[6] Indeed, the social psychologist Stanley Milgram has noted that '[i]deological justification is vital in obtaining *willing* obedience, for it permits the person to see his behavior as serving a desirable end'.[7] Filbert's motivations for pursuing a career in National Socialism, culminating in active participation in crimes on a mass scale, were both careerist *and* ideological. In fact, Filbert's ambition and craving for recognition were strengthened and, significantly, *justified* by his ideology and his belief that he belonged to the 'master race'. His ideology persuaded him that the career advancement, status and recognition he sought were no more than his due; he felt he had a right to success. Ideology and egotism were mutually reinforcing.

The prosecutor in the trial of Adolf Eichmann in Jerusalem in 1961, Gideon Hausner, was keen for the transcripts of the interviews Eichmann had given the Dutch journalist and former SS officer Willem Sassen from 1956 to 1960 to be admitted to evidence, 'since they included remarks revealing of Eichmann's own sense of self-importance and his anti-Semitism in contrast to his carefully crafted statements to the contrary in court'.[8] This combination of a sense of self-importance and anti-Semitism, egotism and ideology, appears decisive for explaining the mindset of many Holocaust perpetrators. It thus becomes clear that, whilst helpful, the explanatory approach of the 'war youth generation', the 'dispassionate generation' (Herbert) or the 'unconditional genera-tion' (Wildt) has limitations and is in itself insufficient to take into account either the various motivations of a man such as Filbert or the diversity of the perpetrators in general, and thus falls short as an expla-natory model.[9] After all, the embrace of radical alternatives was not restricted to the young, as the examples of Karl Jäger (born 1888) and Paul Blobel (born 1894) – two of the most fanatical commando chiefs in the East – demonstrate. What we can say about the males of the war youth generation, as young men in the early stages of their careers in 1933, is that 'if they were ambitious and wanted to make an impact thereafter, they were well advised to hitch their wagon to the Nazi star'.[10]

The conduct of the Holocaust perpetrators cannot be explained in terms of their ideology alone, and yet cannot be understood without it, for anti-Semitism provided at all times a general absolution for the actions of the perpetrators. The unity of ideological convictions and sanctioning from above, on the one hand, and the material and career interests and opportunities, on the other, can feasibly explain the conduct not only of Filbert but of a great many direct perpetrators of the Holocaust.[11] There is no empirical basis for dismissing or downplaying the role of ideology as a motivational factor for direct perpetrators of the Holocaust or for making the 'breezy assertion' (Mallmann) that anti-Semitism was more the exception than the rule.[12] On the contrary, the explicit and visceral hatred of Jews exhibited in private letters sent home by *regular* Wehrmacht soldiers involved either directly or indirectly in the mass murder in the East speak a clear language.[13] There can be little doubt, in the words of historian Thomas Kühne, of 'the crucial role of popular anti-Semitism in the Holocaust'.[14] The case of Alfred Filbert – who displayed particular radicalism in pursuing the annihilation of Soviet Jews – furthermore demonstrates the importance of supplementing the question as to why people participate in mass murder with the enquiry as to how extensive and enthusiastic this participation is.[15]

A further factor in explaining Filbert's participation in Nazi mass crimes was the – real or perceived – threat to his brother, which made him a 'fearful killer'.[16] He was less fearful for the welfare of his brother, however, and more fearful for his own jeopardised career chances. In fact, it was the feeling that his own commitment to the regime might be called into question that spurred Filbert not only to volunteer to lead a commando in the East but also to implement his tasks with particular zeal. As the social psychologists Roy F. Baumeister and W. Keith Campbell have concluded, people with favourable views of themselves who feel these views are being questioned, undermined or attacked are the most likely to behave aggressively in response.[17] The results of studies carried out by Baumeister and Brad J. Bushman confirm the 'threatened egotism'[18] theory:

> The highest levels of aggression were exhibited by narcissists who had been insulted. Moreover, this aggression was directed only toward the source of the insult. Narcissists were not made generally aggressive by the insult, as shown by their lack of aggression toward an innocent third person. [...] Such aggression defends the favorable self-image and discourages others from questioning it, and people who are strongly invested in sustaining a favorable image may be especially prone toward such violence. It can operate at either the group or the individual level. [...] [T]he violent response to threatened egotism may characterize individuals (or groups) who have both a strong emotional investment in being superior to others and a deep concern with having this favorable self-image validated by others. Narcissism, rather than high self-esteem per se, is the predisposing factor for this [...] path to violence.[19]

This description fits Filbert closely, who felt insulted by having his commitment to the Nazi regime called into question. The discrepancy cannot be overlooked, however, between the target of the aggression in the results of the Bushman/Baumeister studies and Filbert's own reaction: he did not direct his aggression 'toward the source of the insult' but precisely 'toward an innocent third person'. This can again be explained with reference to the twin factors of ideology and egotism: Filbert's ideological commitment to Nazism allowed him to perceive – or, more accurately, substitute – an innocent third party, namely the Jews, as the ultimate source of the insult, whilst his careerism persuaded him that the only way to put his career back on track and not lose favour with his superiors was to demonstrate ever greater commitment to the cause. Bushman and Baumeister furthermore regard it as 'plausible that narcissists perceive social life as a series of struggles for dominance, and so they may attack others regardless of direct threat, simply as a means of establishing themselves in a superior position by conquering or

intimidating other individuals'.[20] In Filbert's case, narcissism con-
verged with ideological conviction and careerism to form an explosive
mix that resulted in the radical pursuit first and foremost of Soviet Jews,
the alleged pillars of the Jewish–Bolshevik system.

The victim complex described earlier also informed Filbert's post-war
mindset. Significantly, Henry V. Dicks recognised that Filbert 'felt
uniquely singled out'.[21] This victim mentality was evident throughout
Filbert's trial, during his imprisonment (as Dicks's conclusions illustrate) and indeed subsequent to his release (as demonstrated by the
footage from *Notre Nazi*). To this end, he utilised first and foremost the
fate of his elder brother Otto, who served a prison term, was incarcerated in a concentration camp, spent time in a penal battalion and,
ultimately, failed to survive the war, leaving his wife without a husband
and his three sons without a father. The appalling fate of his brother
became a constant and decisive factor in Filbert's post-war portrayal of
himself as a victim.

The appropriation of victim status by perpetrators is a rather wide-
spread phenomenon. As the historian Timothy Snyder concludes,
'No major war or act of mass killing in the twentieth century began
without the aggressors or perpetrators first claiming innocence and
victimhood.'[22] In the mindset of the Holocaust perpetrators, they –
and their families back home in Greater Germany – were the victims of a
global Jewish conspiracy, which was responsible for unleashing the
Second World War. This is clearly demonstrated by letters sent home
from the killing fields of the East, one of which will be quoted here for
illustrative purposes. The police official Walter Mattner from Vienna
wrote to his wife on 5 October 1941 regarding the massacres in the
Belarusian city of Mogilev:

When the first truckloads [of victims] arrived my hand slightly trembled when
shooting, but one gets used to this. When the tenth truck arrived I already aimed
calmly and shot assuredly at the many women, children and infants. Bearing in
mind that I also have two infants at home, with whom these hordes would do the
same, if not ten times worse. The death we gave them was a nice, quick death
compared with the hellish torture of thousands upon thousands in the dungeons
of the GPU. Infants flew in a wide arc through the air and we shot them down still
in flight, before they fell into the pit and into the water. Let's get rid of this brood
that has plunged all of Europe into war and is still stirring things up in America.
[. . .] I am actually already looking ahead, and many say here that [after] we return
home, then it will be the turn of our own Jews.[23]

The ingredient that made it possible for Filbert to portray himself as a
victim, both to himself and to others, even *after the war* was, as we have

seen, first and foremost the persecution and death of his own brother at the hands of the very regime that Filbert himself so loyally and fanatically served. If ideology and egotism are the main ingredients in explaining why Filbert became an enthusiastic genocidal perpetrator, it was the fate of his brother Otto that served as the pretext of a mass murderer, long after the war and the Holocaust had ended.

Notes

Introduction

1. Boris Barth, *Genozid. Völkermord im 20. Jahrhundert: Geschichte, Theorien, Kontroversen* (Munich: C. H. Beck, 2006), p. 55. Large sections of this book do, however, deal with someone who suffered and died at the hands of the Nazis (though he was not a victim of the Holocaust): Alfred Filbert's elder brother, Otto.
2. Timothy Snyder, *Bloodlands: Europe between Hitler and Stalin* (New York: Basic Books, 2010), p. 400.
3. Dieter Pohl, *Holocaust. Die Ursachen, das Geschehen, die Folgen* (Freiburg im Breisgau: Herder, 2000), p. 124; Wendy Lower, *Hitler's Furies: German Women in the Nazi Killing Fields* (Boston, MA: Houghton Mifflin Harcourt, 2013), p. 244, n. 154. This figure is limited to those involved in the *killing* of Jews and does not include other, related crimes, such as theft. For a total of 'more than 500,000 people' with functions in the 'machinery of annihilation' see Konrad Kwiet, 'Rassenpolitik und Völkermord', in Wolfgang Benz, Hermann Graml and Hermann Weiß, eds., *Enzyklopädie des Nationalsozialismus* (Munich: dtv, 2001 [1997]), pp. 50–65, here p. 62. On the involvement of women in Nazi genocide see Lower, *Hitler's Furies*.
4. See especially Ulrich Herbert, *Best. Biographische Studien über Radikalismus, Weltanschauung und Vernunft, 1903–1989* (Bonn: Dietz, 1996); Ian Kershaw, *Hitler 1889–1936: Hubris* (London: Allen Lane, 1998); Ian Kershaw, *Hitler 1936–1945: Nemesis* (London: Allen Lane, 2000); Ernst Piper, *Alfred Rosenberg. Hitlers Chefideologe* (Munich: Blessing, 2005); Peter Longerich, *Heinrich Himmler. Biographie* (Munich: Siedler, 2008); Eleanor Hancock, *Ernst Röhm: Hitler's SA Chief of Staff* (Basingstoke: Palgrave Macmillan, 2008); Peter Longerich, *Goebbels. Biographie* (Munich: Siedler, 2010); Robert Gerwarth, *Hitler's Hangman: The Life of Heydrich* (New Haven, CT/ London: Yale University Press, 2011).
5. Longerich, *Heinrich Himmler*; Gerwarth, *Hitler's Hangman*; Andreas Seeger, *Gestapo-Müller. Die Karriere eines Schreibtischtäters* (Berlin: Metropol, 1996).
6. Berndt Rieger, *Creator of Nazi Death Camps: The Life of Odilo Globocnik* (London/Portland, OR: Vallentine Mitchell, 2007); Heinz Schneppen, *Walther Rauff. Organisator der Gaswagenmorde: Eine Biographie* (Berlin: Metropol, 2011); Claudia Steur, *Theodor Dannecker: Ein Funktionär der 'Endlösung'* (Essen: Klartext, 1997).

7. Ulrich Herbert nonetheless poses the same questions on personality and motivation in relation to Otto Ohlendorf 'and the other leading men of the Einsatzgruppen' as he does in relation to Best. See Herbert, *Best*, pp. 14–15 (quote: p. 14).

8. Thomas Kühne, 'Der nationalsozialistische Vernichtungskrieg und die "ganz normalen" Deutschen: Forschungsprobleme und Forschungstendenzen der Gesellschaftsgeschichte des Zweiten Weltkrieges. Erster Teil', *Archiv für Sozialgeschichte*, Vol. 39 (1999), pp. 580–662, here p. 618. See also Klaus-Michael Mallmann, '"Mensch, ich feiere heut' den tausendsten Genickschuß". Die Sicherheitspolizei und die Shoah in Westgalizien', in Gerhard Paul, ed., *Täter der Shoah. Fanatische Nationalsozialisten oder ganz normale Deutsche?* (Göttingen: Wallstein, 2002), pp. 109–136, here pp. 112–113.

9. Jörn Hasenclever, *Wehrmacht und Besatzungspolitik. Die Befehlshaber der rückwärtigen Heeresgebiete 1941–1943* (Paderborn: Schöningh, 2010), p. 33. For the best overviews of research on Holocaust perpetrators see Kühne, 'Der nationalsozialistische Vernichtungskrieg', pp. 580–662; Gerhard Paul, 'Von Psychopathen, Technokraten des Terrors und "ganz gewöhnlichen Deutschen". Die Täter der Shoah im Spiegel der Forschung', in Paul, ed., *Täter der Shoah*, pp. 13–90. On recent trends see Peter Klein, 'Die Wannsee-Konferenz als Echo auf die gefallene Entscheidung zur Ermordung der europäischen Juden', in Norbert Kampe and Peter Klein, eds., *Die Wannsee-Konferenz am 20. Januar 1942. Dokumente, Forschungsstand, Kontroversen* (Cologne/Weimar/Vienna: Böhlau, 2013), pp. 182–201, here pp. 182–188.

10. Michael Wildt, *Generation des Unbedingten. Das Führungskorps des Reichssicherheitshauptamtes* (Hamburg: Hamburger Edition, 2002). Wildt's book was heavily influenced by the earlier Herbert, *Best*, and Jens Banach, *Heydrichs Elite. Das Führerkorps der Sicherheitspolizei und des SD 1936–1945* (Paderborn: Schöningh, 1998).

11. Ronald Smelser and Enrico Syring, eds., *Die SS: Elite unter dem Totenkopf. 30 Lebensläufe* (Paderborn: Schöningh, 2000); Klaus-Michael Mallmann and Gerhard Paul, eds., *Karrieren der Gewalt. Nationalsozialistische Täterbiographien* (Darmstadt: Wissenschaftliche Buchgesellschaft, 2004). The average length of the biographical sketches contained in these two works is only 14 and 10 pages, respectively.

12. Hasenclever, *Wehrmacht und Besatzungspolitik*, pp. 33–34.

13. As noted by Wolfram Wette, *Karl Jäger. Mörder der litauischen Juden* (Frankfurt am Main: Fischer Taschenbuch, 2011), p. 22.

14. Paul, 'Von Psychopathen, Technokraten des Terrors und "ganz gewöhnlichen Deutschen"', p. 51.

15. Helmut Krausnick, 'Die Einsatzgruppen vom Anschluß Österreichs bis zum Feldzug gegen die Sowjetunion. Entwicklung und Verhältnis zur Wehrmacht', in Helmut Krausnick and Hans-Heinrich Wilhelm, *Die Truppe des Weltanschauungskrieges: Die Einsatzgruppen der Sicherheitspolizei und des SD 1938 – 1942* (Stuttgart: Deutsche Verlags-Anstalt, 1981), pp. 11–278, here p. 148.

16. Lutz Hachmeister, *Der Gegnerforscher. Die Karriere des SS-Führers Franz Alfred Six* (Munich: C. H. Beck, 1998); Ronald Rathert, *Verbrechen und Verschwörung. Arthur Nebe, der Kripochef des Dritten Reiches* (Münster: LIT, 2001); Wette, *Karl Jäger*. Thilo Figaj is currently working on a biography of the second chief of Einsatzgruppe A, Heinz Jost. See also Hilary Earl, *The Nuremberg SS-Einsatzgruppen Trial, 1945–1958: Atrocity, Law, and History* (Cambridge: Cambridge University Press, 2009), which constitutes the first in-depth examination of proceedings against 24 officers of the Einsatzgruppen at the ninth of the twelve Subsequent Nuremberg Trials.

17. Rathert, *Verbrechen und Verschwörung*, p. 118. See also pp. 220–222 ('Archivmaterial').

18. The same applies to Otto Ohlendorf, head of Office III (SD Domestic) and the subject of an unpublished doctoral thesis: Alexander Stollhof, 'SS-Gruppenführer und Generalleutnant der Polizei Otto Ohlendorf – Eine biographische Skizze', unpublished doctoral thesis, Vienna, 1993.

19. See the back cover of Wette, *Karl Jäger: 'Die erste Biographie eines NS-Direkttäters "vor Ort".'*

20. See the reviews by Ruth Bettina Birn, 'Zeitgeschichte und Zeitgeist', *Einsicht 06. Bulletin des Fritz Bauer Instituts*, Vol. 3 (autumn 2011), p. 70, and Klaus Richter, *Zeitschrift für Ostmitteleuropa-Forschung*, Vol. 63, No. 3 (2014), pp. 482–483.

21. Christian Gerlach, *Kalkulierte Morde. Die deutsche Wirtschafts-und Vernichtungspolitik in Weißrußland 1941 bis 1944* (Hamburg: Hamburger Edition, 1999), p. 185.

22. On Eichmann see David Cesarani, *Eichmann: His Life and Crimes* (London: William Heinemann, 2004). Like Eichmann, Filbert joined the SS and the NSDAP in 1932. See Chapter 2 of this study and Annette Weinke, 'Der Eichmann-Prozess, Hannah Arendts "Eichmann in Jerusalem" und die Semantik des industrialisierten Massenmords', in Martin Cüppers, Jürgen Matthäus and Andrej Angrick, eds., *Naziverbrechen. Täter, Taten, Bewältigungsversuche* (Darmstadt: Wissenschaftliche Buchgesellschaft, 2013), pp. 289–302, here p. 291.

23. See now Alex J. Kay, 'Transition to Genocide, July 1941: Einsatzkommando 9 and the Annihilation of Soviet Jewry', *Holocaust and Genocide Studies*, Vol. 27, No. 3 (winter 2013), pp. 411–442.

24. See now Alex J. Kay, 'Brothers – The SS Mass Murderer and the Concentration Camp Inmate', *Tr@nsit online*, 8 August 2013: http://www .iwm.at/read-listen-watch/transit-online/brothers-the-ss-mass-murderer-an d-the-concentration-camp-inmate/ [last accessed on 10 August 2013]; Alex J. Kay, 'Ungleiche Brüder. Der SS-Massenmörder und der KZ-Häftling', *Einsicht 10. Bulletin des Fritz Bauer Instituts*, Vol. 5 (autumn 2013), pp. 49–55. In this context, reference should be made to Karl Rahm, a colleague of Adolf Eichmann in the Central Office for Jewish Emigration (*Zentralstelle für jüdische Auswanderung*) in Vienna and from February 1944 commandant of Theresienstadt ghetto, whose brother was sentenced to eight years in prison for oppositional activity as a Communist. Unlike Otto Filbert, however, Franz Rahm survived the war and was thereupon released from Dachau

concentration camp. See Jan Björn Potthast, *Das Jüdische Zentralmuseum der SS in Prag. Gegnerforschung und Völkermord im Nationalsozialismus* (Frankfurt am Main/New York: Campus, 2002), p. 83.

25. See Chapter 7 of this study.
26. See Chapter 10 of this study; *Wundkanal – Hinrichtung für vier Stimmen* (Germany/France: Quasar Film/Reass Films, 1984); and *Notre Nazi*, directed by Robert Kramer (France/Germany: Reass Films/Quasar Film, 1984).
27. See Kay, 'Brothers'; Kay, 'Ungleiche Brüder'. There is now a scholarly article, also written by the author, on the activities of Einsatzkommando 9 under Filbert's leadership (though the article is not a biographical study as such): Kay, 'Transition to Genocide, July 1941'.
28. Wildt, *Generation des Unbedingten*, passim. The error was corrected neither in the revised edition of *Generation des Unbedingten* (2003) nor in its English-language translation: Michael Wildt, *An Uncompromising Generation: The Nazi Leadership of the Reich Security Main Office*, translated from German by Tom Lampert (Madison, WI: University of Wisconsin Press, 2009).
29. Andrej Angrick, *Besatzungspolitik und Massenmord: Die Einsatzgruppe D in der südlichen Sowjetunion 1941–1943* (Hamburg: Hamburger Edition, 2003), pp. 76, fn. 132, and 100; Ernst Klee, *Das Personenlexikon zum Dritten Reich. Wer war was vor und nach 1945*, rev. ed. (Frankfurt am Main: Fischer Taschenbuch, 2005 [2003]), p. 150; Florian Altenhöner, 'Heinz Jost und das Amt III des SD-Hauptamtes: Ein MI5-Bericht aus dem Jahr 1945', *Journal for Intelligence, Propaganda and Security Studies*, Vol. 2, No. 2 (2008), pp. 55–76, here pp. 57 and 72, n. 12; *Die Verfolgung und Ermordung der europäischen Juden durch das nationalsozialistische Deutschland 1933–1945. Band 7, Sowjetunion mit annektierten Gebieten I: Besetzte sowjetische Gebiete unter deutscher Militärverwaltung, Baltikum und Transnistrien*, compiled by Bert Hoppe and Hildrun Glass (Munich: Oldenbourg, 2011), pp. 44, 196, 222 and 286; Andreas Schmiedecker, 'Fassungslose Geschichtsschreibung. Geschichtliche und biografische (De)Konstruktionen bei Thomas Harlan', in Thomas Marchart, Stefanie Schmitt and Stefan Suppanschitz, eds., *reflexiv. Geschichte denken*, SYN. Magazin für Theater-, Film–und Medienwissenschaft, Vol. 2 (Berlin/Münster/Vienna/Zürich/London: LIT, 2011), pp. 69–83, here pp. 74–75; Thilo Figaj, 'Die blutige Karriere des Heinz Jost', *Darmstädter Echo*, 23 March 2012, pp. 16–17, here p. 17. Hilary Earl omits Filbert entirely from her list of Einsatzkommando chiefs deployed in the Soviet Union between 1941 and 1944/45. See Earl, *The Nuremberg SS-Einsatzgruppen Trial*, Table 7, p. 143.
30. Landesarchiv Berlin (hereafter LArch Berlin), B Rep. 058, Nr. 7218, fol. 31, 'Betr.: Ausübung des Rechts der Begnadigung in der Strafsache gegen Albert [*sic*] Filbert – Senatsbeschluß Nr. 2805/74 vom 21. Mai 1974', Der Regierende Bürgermeister von Berlin, Senatskanzlei, signed Kuba, 21 May 1974; LArch Berlin, B Rep. 058, Nr. 7218, fol. 79, Letter (from the Public Prosecutor in Berlin?) to the director of Tegel Prison 'Betrifft: Strafgefangenen Albert [*sic*] Filbert hier: Unterbrechung der Strafvollstreckung wegen Vollzug[s]untauglichkeit gemäß §§ 45 und 46 Strafvollstreckungsanordnung', 3 P (K) Ks 1/62, 5 June 1975; LArch

Berlin, B Rep. 058, Nr. 7218, fol. 80, Letter (from the Public Prosecutor in Berlin?) to Albert [sic] Filbert, 3 P (K) Ks 1/62, signed Redlich (Rechtspfleger), 5 June 1975.

31. See, for example, '27facher Mörder überführt', *BZ am Abend*, 25 July 1959, in LArch Berlin, B Rep. 058, Nr. 5199, fol. 2; 'Massenmörder in Brandts Schoß', *Berliner Zeitung*, 26 July 1959, in ibid.; 'Die Mörder sind noch unter uns', *Die Andere Zeitung*, 5 August 1959, in Bundesarchiv Zwischenarchiv Dahlwitz-Hoppegarten (hereafter BArch D-H), Dok/P 12569.

32. LArch Berlin, B Rep. 058, Nr. 7166–7247, Fall Filbert AZ 3 P (K) Ks 1/62.

33. On the advantages and disadvantages to the historian of using documents from legal proceedings against Nazi perpetrators, see Gerlach, *Kalkulierte Morde*, pp. 28–33.

34. See Chapter 8 of this study.

35. Transcripts of hearings were composed not by the defendants/witnesses themselves but by transcript writers on the basis of oral statements. Thus, the language used in the written transcripts is, strictly speaking, that of the transcript writers (see Gerlach, *Kalkulierte Morde*, p. 30, fn. 76). Having said that, the defendants/witnesses had the opportunity to check and, if required, to amend the text of the transcripts, which they often did. Thus, the final version (and wording) of the transcripts was approved by the defendants/witnesses. On the potential usefulness of post-war testimony given by perpetrators, using the example of Adolf Eichmann, see Christopher R. Browning, 'Perpetrator Testimony: Another Look at Adolf Eichmann', in Christopher R. Browning, *Collected Memories: Holocaust History and Postwar Testimony* (Madison, WI: University of Wisconsin Press, 2003), pp. 3–36 and 87–95.

36. Bundesarchiv Außenstelle Ludwigsburg (hereafter BArch Ludwigsburg), B 162; Staatsarchiv Hamburg (hereafter StArch Hamburg), 213–12; Staatsarchiv München (hereafter StArch München), Staatsanwaltschaften, 32970/5.

37. Bundesarchiv Berlin-Lichterfelde (hereafter BArch Berlin), R 58/214 – R 58/219; Bundesarchiv-Militärarchiv, Freiburg im Breisgau (hereafter BArch-MA), RH 26–403; Der Bundesbeauftragte für die Unterlagen des Staatssicherheitsdienstes der ehemaligen Deutschen Demokratischen Republik, Archiv der Zentralstelle, Berlin (hereafter BStU), MfS, HA IX/11. On the so-called 'Nazi Archives' (*NS-Archiv*) of the Ministry for State Security see Dagmar Unverhau, *Das 'NS-Archiv' des Ministeriums für Staatssicherheit. Stationen einer Entwicklung*, 2nd rev. ed. (Münster: LIT, 2004 [1998]).

38. Especially BArch Berlin, R 58/825 and R 58/826.

39. Hessisches Staatsarchiv Darmstadt (hereafter HStAD), G 21 B, Personalakte Nr. 2862, Filbert, Alfred; Universitätsarchiv Gießen, Promotionen und Dissertationen an der Universität Gießen von 1894 bis 1945, Jur. Prom. Nr. 775, Promotionsakte Alfred Filbert (hereafter UniA GI, Juristische Promotionsakten Nr. 775); Universitätsarchiv Heidelberg (hereafter UAH), StudA, Filbert, Alfred (1929).

40. International Tracing Services Archives, Bad Arolsen (hereafter ITS Archives), 1.1.5. Konzentrationslager Buchenwald; Archiv der

Gedenkstätte Buchenwald, Weimar, Sammlungsbestand des Archivs der Gedenkstätte Buchenwald: Buchenwald-Archiv; Instytut Pamięci Narodowej, Warsaw (hereafter IPN, Warsaw), IPN GK 127/34 KL BUCHENWALD. On the ITS see Karsten Kühnel, 'Archivierung beim Internationalen Suchdienst in Bad Arolsen', *Archivnachrichten aus Hessen*, Vol. 9, No. 1 (2009), pp. 25–28.

41. Einwohnermeldearchiv der Stadt Bad Gandersheim.
42. Written notification from Lars Hoffmann, Beauftragter für Öffentlichkeitsarbeit der Justizvollzugsanstalt Tegel, 10 September 2012.
43. The fruits of this interview are presented in Henry V. Dicks, *Licensed Mass Murder: A Socio-Psychological Study of Some S.S. Killers* (New York: Basic Books, 1972), ch. 9.
44. See *Notre Nazi*, passim.
45. Interview with Alfred Filbert's nephew, Peter Filbert, Weinheim, 29 August 2013; interview with Ursula Langmann, Paris, 25 June 2013; interview with Robert Kramer's widow, Erika Kramer, Paris, 6 April 2013; interview with Holocaust survivor and former Soviet partisan Fania Brancovskaya, Rudniki Forest, near Vilnius, 29 May 2012.
46. Written notifications from Dieter Filbert, Berlin, 17 and 31 March 2013 and 21 November 2014; written notification from Ralph Filbert's wife, Erika Filbert, Media, PA, 29 July 2013.
47. Written notification from Dieter Filbert, Berlin, 21 November 2014.
48. From the Archives of the Russian Research and Educational Holocaust Centre in Moscow, as well as copies of Soviet judicial investigation documents and survivor testimony consulted in the Ludwigsburg branch of the German Federal Archives and in the Yad Vashem Archives, Jerusalem.
49. Søren Kierkegaard, *Papers and Journals: A Selection*, translated from Danish by Alastair Hannay (London: Penguin, 1996), p. 161.
50. Pierre Bourdieu, 'L'illusion biographique', in Pierre Bourdieu, *Raisons pratiques. Sur la théorie de l'action* (Paris: Éd. du Seuil, 1994), pp. 81–89, here pp. 81–82.
51. Ibid., p. 82.
52. Ibid., p. 88.
53. Of the four Einsatzgruppen deployed in the occupied Soviet territories, comprehensive studies have been written on Einsatzgruppen A and D, including their respective sub-commandos: Hans-Heinrich Wilhelm, 'Die Einsatzgruppe A der Sicherheitspolizei und des SD 1941/42 – Eine exemplarische Studie', in Krausnick and Wilhelm, *Die Truppe des Weltanschauungskrieges*, pp. 279–643; Angrick, *Besatzungspolitik und Massenmord*. Short portrayals of each of the four Einsatzgruppen can be found in Peter Klein, ed., *Die Einsatzgruppen in der besetzten Sowjetunion 1941/42. Die Tätigkeits–und Lageberichte des Chefs der Sicherheitspolizei und des SD* (Berlin: Edition Hentrich, 1997), here pp. 29–110. For detailed collective studies of the Einsatzgruppen see Krausnick, 'Die Einsatzgruppen'; Richard Rhodes, *Masters of Death: The SS-Einsatzgruppen and the Invention of the Holocaust* (New York: Alfred A. Knopf, 2002).

Einsatzgruppen B and C and their respective commandos constitute research desiderata.

1   'I went to school with quite a number of Jewish co-religionists and never knew hatred for Jews'

1. Archiv des Standesamtes Darmstadt, Heiratsregister Darmstadt, Nr. 491, Heiratsurkunde Peter Filbert und Christiane Kühner; BArch Berlin, VBS 283/6010010064, 'SS-Ahnentafel von Dr. Filbert, Karl Wilhelm Alfred', 18 January 1937; HStAD, H 13 Darmstadt, Nr. 1291/25, 'Strafsache gegen Dr. Alfred Filbert wegen Mordes', Landgericht Berlin, 14 January 1960, p. 2.
2. HStAD, G 21 B, Personalakte Nr. 2862, 'Fragebogen zur Durchführung des Gesetzes zur Wiederherstellung des Berufsbeamtentums vom 7. April 1933'; BArch Berlin, VBS 283/6010010064, 'SS-Ahnentafel von Dr. Filbert, Karl Wilhelm Alfred', 18 January 1937.
3. HStAD, Ztg 169, 'Leibgardisten in Darmstadt. Zum Treffen des ältesten deutschen Infanterie-Regiments in seiner alten Garnisonstadt', *Darmstädter Tagblatt*, 29/30 May 1954. On the history of the regiment see Rolf von Wenz zu Niederlahnstein, Heinrich Henß and Otto Abt, *Dreihundert Jahre Leibgarde Regiment: Blätter der Erinnerung an die ruhmvolle Vergangenheit des Leibgarde-Infanterie-Regiments (1. Großherzoglich Hessisches) Nr. 115* (Darmstadt: Kichler, 1929).
4. Archiv des Standesamtes Darmstadt, Geburtenregister Darmstadt, Nr. 1169, Geburtsurkunde Karl Wilhelm Alfred Filbert; LArch Berlin, B Rep. 058, Nr. 7166, fols. 28–31R, Hearing of Dr Alfred Filbert, 25 February 1959, here fol. 29; UniA GI, Juristische Promotionsakten Nr. 775, 'Urteil des Schwurgerichts beim Landgericht Berlin 3 P (K) Ks 1/62, vom 22. Juni 1962', fols. 37–159 (hereafter UniA GI, 'Urteil Landgericht Berlin vom 22. Juni 1962'), here fols. 39–40, reprinted in slightly edited form in: *Justiz und NS-Verbrechen. Sammlung deutscher Strafurteile wegen nationalsozialistischer Tötungsverbrechen 1945–1966*, Vol. XVIII, ed. Irene Sagel-Grande, H. H. Fuchs and C. F. Rüter (Amsterdam: University Press Amsterdam, 1978), No. 540, pp. 601–651.
5. Stadtarchiv Mannheim – Institut für Stadtgeschichte, Meldekarte Adolf Hille. I am grateful to Manfred Kielhorn for providing me with a copy of this document. Dr Henry V. Dicks, a British psychiatrist and psychoanalyst who interviewed Filbert at length in July 1969 whilst the latter was serving his life sentence in a West Berlin prison, devotes an entire chapter to Filbert: Chapter 9, 'The Lawyer Turns Hangman', pp. 204–229. Although Dicks refers to the interviewee throughout as 'PF', it is clear from the information provided that it is Alfred Filbert. According to what Filbert told Dicks, he had an elder brother and a younger sister (see Dicks, *Licensed Mass Murder*, p. 220). The register of births in Darmstadt contains entries for only Otto and Alfred Filbert (written notification from Jürgen Holler, Standesamt Darmstadt, 9 June 2010). The register of births for Worms, where the family moved to in 1911, does not contain an entry for a child named 'Filbert' for the

years 1910–1920 (written notification from Dagmar Lerch, Standesamt Worms, 21 September 2010).

6. Archiv des Standesamtes Darmstadt, Heiratsregister Darmstadt, Nr. 491, Heiratsurkunde Peter Filbert und Christiane Kühner; HStAD, G 21 B, Personalakte Nr. 2862, 'Fragebogen zur Durchführung des Gesetzes zur Wiederherstellung des Berufsbeamtentums vom 7. April 1933'.

7. Archiv des Standesamtes Darmstadt, Geburtenregister Darmstadt, Nr. 666, Geburtsurkunde Otto Filbert.

8. HStAD, H 13 Darmstadt, Nr. 1291/25, 'Strafsache gegen Dr. Alfred Filbert wegen Mordes', 14 January 1960, p. 2.

9. UniA GI, 'Urteil Landgericht Berlin vom 22. Juni 1962', fol. 40; Dicks, *Licensed Mass Murder*, p. 209.

10. Dicks, *Licensed Mass Murder*, p. 209.

11. HStAD, H 13 Darmstadt, Nr. 1291/25, 'Strafsache gegen Dr. Alfred Filbert wegen Mordes', 14 January 1960, p. 2. UniA GI, 'Urteil Landgericht Berlin vom 22. Juni 1962', fol. 40.

12. HStAD, H 13 Darmstadt, Nr. 1291/25, 'Strafsache gegen Dr. Alfred Filbert wegen Mordes', 14 January 1960, p. 2; BArch Berlin, VBS 286/6400010138, SSO-Akte Dr. Alfred Filbert, 'Lebenslauf', signed Dr Alfred Filbert, 27 January 1937; UniA GI, 'Urteil Landgericht Berlin vom 22. Juni 1962', fol. 40; UniA GI, Juristische Promotionsakten Nr. 775, 'Lebenslauf (des Gerichtsref. Alfred Filbert)', n.d., fol. 180. The then Oberrealschule Worms is today the Gauß-Gymnasium Worms. The Gauß-Gymnasium is no longer in possession of any school records relating to Filbert (written notification from G. Potthoff, Gauß-Gymnasium, 2 August 2010). The Commerzbank declined to allow me access to records relating to Filbert for undefined 'reasons of confidentiality' (written notification from Group Human Resources, Commerzbank, 3 September 2010). The Commerzbank subsequently informed me that a personnel file and other records relating to Filbert no longer exist (written notification from Group Human Resources, Commerzbank, 9 September 2010, and Dr Detlef Krause, Historisches Archiv der Commerzbank, 10 September 2010).

13. UniA GI, 'Urteil Landgericht Berlin vom 22. Juni 1962', fol. 40.

14. Dicks, *Licensed Mass Murder*, pp. 209 and 220 (quote: p. 209).

15. Interview with Alfred Filbert's nephew, Peter Filbert, Weinheim, 29 August 2013.

16. Dicks, *Licensed Mass Murder*, p. 220 and the discussion on pp. 222–228.

17. Lower, *Hitler's Furies*, p. 160.

18. In Robert Kramer's documentary film *Notre Nazi*, 01:21:45 – 01:21:48: *'Wir haben als Kinder uns sehr geliebt.'*

19. UniA GI, Juristische Promotionsakten Nr. 775, fols. 23–27, Letter from Alfred Filbert to the Justus Liebig University 'Betr.: Aberkennung der Doktor-Würde', 2 March 1964, here fol. 24.

20. See 'List or Manifest of Alien Passengers for the United States Immigration Officer at Port of Arrival. S.S. "Columbus", Passengers sailing from Bremen, April 8th, 1926, arriving at Port of New York, Apr[il] 17, 1926', List 3, No. 23, at: Ancestry.com. *New York, Passenger Lists, 1820–1957* [database on-

line]. Provo, UT, USA: Ancestry.com Operations, Inc., 2010 [last accessed on 18 February 2013].

21. See 'List or Manifest of Alien Passengers for the United States Immigration Officer at Port of Arrival. S.S. "Bremen", Passengers sailing from Bremen, June 13th, 1926, arriving at Port of New York, Jun[e] 24, 1926', List 4, No. 1, at: Ancestry.com. *New York, Passenger Lists, 1820–1957* [database on-line]. Provo, UT, USA: Ancestry.com Operations, Inc., 2010 [last accessed on 25 February 2013].

22. LArch Berlin, B Rep. 058, Nr. 7168, fols. 39–45R, Hearing of the accused Dr Alfred Filbert in the criminal case against Dr Alfred Filbert for murder, Landgericht Berlin, 14 January 1960, here fol. 43: '*Ich habe meine Jugendzeit in Worms/Rhein verbracht, einer Stadt mit einer größeren jüdischen Gemeinde, mit Familien, die seit Jahrhunderten dort lebten. Viele waren mir bekannt. Ich ging mit einer ganzen Anzahl jüdischer Glaubensgenossen zur Schule und habe einen Hass gegen Juden nie gekannt. Ich war oftmals in meiner Tanzstundenzeit bei jüdischen Familien eingeladen und mein Bruder, der ein Jahr älter war wie ich, verkehrte früher in jüdischen Familien.*'

23. Michael Mann, 'Were the Perpetrators of Genocide "Ordinary Men" or "Real Nazis"? Results from Fifteen Hundred Biographies', *Holocaust and Genocide Studies*, Vol. 14, No. 3 (winter 2000), pp. 331–366, here p. 348. An exception here, like Filbert, is Theodor Dannecker, Adolf Eichmann's specialist for Jewish affairs in Paris, whose first girlfriend – Lisbeth Stern – was Jewish. See Steur, *Theodor Dannecker*, pp. 15 and 151.

24. BArch Berlin, VBS 283/6010010064, 'R. u. S.-Fragebogen, Dr. Filbert, Alfred, V. B. Nr. 47318', signed Dr Filbert, 11 January 1937; HStAD, H 13 Darmstadt, Nr. 1291/25, 'Strafsache gegen Dr. Alfred Filbert wegen Mordes', 14 January 1960, p. 2. On the occupation of the Rhineland see Margaret Pawley, *The Watch on the Rhine: The Military Occupation of the Rhineland, 1918–1930* (London/New York: I. B. Tauris, 2007). On the 1923/24 crisis in general see Heinrich August Winkler, *Weimar 1918–1933. Die Geschichte der ersten deutschen Demokratie* (Munich: C. H. Beck, 1993), pp. 186–243. For a contemporary's viewpoint see Sebastian Haffner, *Geschichte eines Deutschen. Die Erinnerungen 1914–1933* (Munich: dtv, 2002), pp. 54–68. In 1929 the Deutsche Bank, the *Disconto-Gesellschaft*, the *Rheinische Kreditbank* and the *A. Schaaffhausen'scher Bankverein* merged to form the *Deutsche und Disconto-Bank* (DeDi-Bank). From 1937 onwards, this was known simply as the Deutsche Bank. The Deutsche Bank declined to allow me access to records relating to Filbert (written notification from Jenny Kempkes, Deutsche Bank, 1 September 2010).

25. Mann, 'Were the Perpetrators of Genocide "Ordinary Men" or "Real Nazis"?', pp. 343–344 and 346 (quote: p. 343).

26. HStAD, H 13 Darmstadt, Nr. 1291/25, 'Strafsache gegen Dr. Alfred Filbert wegen Mordes', 14 January 1960, p. 2.

27. HStAD, G 21 B, Personalakte Nr. 2862, 'Bescheinigung', Handelsinstitut Lust-Dickescheid, 9 January 1934, and 'Zeugnis', Handelsinstitut Lust-Dickescheid, Worms am Rhein, 19 January 1934; LArch Berlin, B Rep.

058, Nr. 7168, fols. 39–45R, Hearing of the accused Dr Alfred Filbert, 14 January 1960, here fols. 42R–43 and 44R.
28. HStAD, H 13 Darmstadt, Nr. 1291/25, 'Strafsache gegen Dr. Alfred Filbert wegen Mordes', 14 January 1960, pp. 2–3; UniA GI, 'Urteil Landgericht Berlin vom 22. Juni 1962', fol. 40; HStAD, G 21 B, Personalakte Nr. 2862, 'Bericht der juristischen Prüfungskommission an der Landes-Universität', 20 December 1933. The then Oberrealschule Mainz is today the Gutenberg-Gymnasium Mainz. The school records from that period are now kept in the Stadtarchiv Mainz (Record Group 202). As Filbert was an external examination candidate, however, no school pupil card (Schülerkarte) for school-leavers exists for him in the municipal administrative files (Record Group 70) for 1927 (written notification from Dr Frank Teske, Stadtarchiv Mainz, 8 September 2010).
29. HStAD, G 21 B, Personalakte Nr. 2862, 'Auszug aus dem Reifezeugnis', Mainz, 28 March 1927.
30. UniA GI, 'Urteil Landgericht Berlin vom 22. Juni 1962', fol. 40; HStAD, H 13 Darmstadt, Nr. 1291/25, 'Strafsache gegen Dr. Alfred Filbert wegen Mordes', 14 January 1960, p. 3.
31. See Mann, 'Were the Perpetrators of Genocide "Ordinary Men" or "Real Nazis"?', pp. 341–342 (quote: p. 341).
32. UniA GI, Matrikelakten des Studierendensekretariats, Stud. Mat. Nr. 5493, fol. 1. Filbert received the registration number 205.
33. HStAD, G 21 B, Personalakte Nr. 2862, 'Bericht der juristischen Prüfungskommission an der Landes-Universität', 20 December 1933; UniA GI, Juristische Promotionsakten Nr. 775, 'Lebenslauf (des Gerichtsref. Alfred Filbert)', n.d., fol. 180; UAH, StudA, Filbert, Alfred (1929), 'Anmeldung zur Immatrikulation an der Universität Heidelberg'.
34. Archiv des Standesamtes Darmstadt, Heiratsregister Darmstadt, Nr. 491, Heiratsurkunde Peter Filbert und Christiane Kühner; HStAD, G 21 B, Personalakte Nr. 2862, 'Fragebogen zur Durchführung des Gesetzes zur Wiederherstellung des Berufsbeamtentums vom 7. April 1933'.
35. LArch Berlin, B Rep. 058, Nr. 7166, fols. 28–31R, Hearing of Dr Alfred Filbert, 25 February 1959, here fol. 29; HStAD, H 13 Darmstadt, Nr. 1291/25, 'Strafsache gegen Dr. Alfred Filbert wegen Mordes', 14 January 1960, p. 3.
36. Written notification from Dr Carsten Lind, Archiv der Philipps-Universität Marburg, 8 March 2011.
37. UAH, StudA, Filbert, Alfred (1929), 'Anmeldung zur Immatrikulation an der Universität Heidelberg'. Filbert received the registration number 1565.
38. Eike Wolgast, 'Die Studierenden', in Wolfgang U. Eckart, Volker Sellin and Eike Wolgast, eds., Die Universität Heidelberg im Nationalsozialismus (Heidelberg: Springer, 2006), pp. 57–94, here pp. 58–59. On the Law Faculty see Dorothee Mußgnug, 'Die Juristische Fakultät', in Eckart, Sellin and Wolgast, eds., Die Universität Heidelberg im Nationalsozialismus, pp. 261–317.

39. UAH, StudA, Schleyer, Hanns Martin (1937), 'Anmeldung zur Immatrikulation an der Universität Heidelberg'. Schleyer received the registration number 503.
40. On Schleyer see Lutz Hachmeister, *Schleyer. Eine deutsche Geschichte*, rev. paperback ed. (Munich: C. H. Beck, 2007 [2004]).
41. *Personenbestand der Hessischen Ludwigs-Universität zu Giessen. Sommersemester 1927* (Giessen: Münchow'sche Universitäts-Druckerei Otto Kindt, 1927), pp. 44 (for Filbert) and 50 (for Jost).
42. HStAD, G 21 B, Personalakte Nr. 3415, 'Bericht der juristischen Prüfungskommission an der Landes-Universität', 24 May 1927. Jost spent seven semesters at the University of Giessen and one semester at the University of Munich. On Jost see HStAD, G 21 B, Personalakte Nr. 3415; Michael Wildt, *Generation des Unbedingten. Das Führungskorps des Reichssicherheitshauptamtes*, rev. ed. (Hamburg: Hamburger Edition, 2003), pp. 938–939; Earl, *The Nuremberg SS-Einsatzgruppen Trial*, pp. 156–158.
43. *Personenbestand der Hessischen Ludwigs-Universität zu Giessen. Sommersemester 1927*, pp. 44 and 50.
44. UniA GI, 'Urteil Landgericht Berlin vom 22. Juni 1962', fol. 40. See also HStAD, H 13 Darmstadt, Nr. 1291/25, 'Strafsache gegen Dr. Alfred Filbert wegen Mordes', 14 January 1960, p. 4.
45. *Personenbestand der Hessischen Ludwigs-Universität zu Giessen. Wintersemester 1927/28* (Giessen: Münchow'sche Universitäts-Druckerei Otto Kindt, 1928), p. 45; *Personenbestand der Hessischen Ludwigs-Universität zu Giessen. Sommersemester 1928* (Giessen: Münchow'sche Universitäts-Druckerei Otto Kindt, 1928), p. 52; *Personenbestand der Hessischen Ludwigs-Universität zu Giessen. Wintersemester 1928/29* (Giessen: Münchow'sche Universitäts-Druckerei Otto Kindt, 1928), p. 52; *Personenbestand der Hessischen Ludwigs-Universität zu Giessen. Winter-Semester 1929/30* (Giessen: Münchowsche Universitäts-Druckerei Otto Kindt, 1929), p. 54.
46. HStAD, G 21 B, Personalakte Nr. 2862, 'Bericht der juristischen Prüfungskommission an der Landes-Universität', 20 December 1933; HStAD, G 21 B, Personalakte Nr. 2862, 'Bescheinigung', 20 December 1933. For a list of the lectures and tutorials Filbert attended during the ten semesters of his undergraduate university studies see HStAD, G 21 B, Personalakte Nr. 2862.
47. HStAD, G 21 B, Personalakte Nr. 3415, 'Bericht der juristischen Prüfungskommission an der Landes-Universität', 24 May 1927.
48. UniA GI, Juristische Promotionsakten Nr. 775, 'Lebenslauf (des Gerichtsref. Alfred Filbert)', n.d., fol. 180.
49. BArch Berlin, VBS 283/6010010064, 'R. u. S.-Fragebogen, Dr. Filbert, Alfred, V. B. Nr. 47318', 11 January 1937: *'[...] habe ich schon vor meinem Eintritt in die Partei die Bewegung unterstützt.'*
50. UniA GI, Juristische Promotionsakten Nr. 775, 'Betr. Befreiung vom grossen Latinum, zwecks Zulassung zur Promotion an der Landesuniversität Giessen', 4 December 1934, fol. 170, and 'Lebenslauf (des Gerichtsref. Alfred Filbert)', n.d., fol. 180.
51. In *Notre Nazi*, 00:08:47 – 00:08:54.

52. UAH, StudA, Filbert, Alfred (1929), 'Erkennungskarte'.
53. Hans Schneider and Georg Lehnert, *Die Gießener Burschenschaft 1814 bis 1936. Sonderdruck aus den Burschenschafterlisten, Band 2* (Görlitz: Verlag für Sippenforschung und Wappenkunde C. A. Starke, 1942), p. 128. In Robert Kramer's documentary film *Notre Nazi*, Filbert explains how he obtained his facial scars: 00:04:52 – 00:05:14, 00:05:58 – 00:06:44 and 00:07:50 – 00:08:30. Hanns Martin Schleyer also bore scars as a result of his fencing activity as a member of the corporation Corps Suevia, of which he was a member from 1933 to 1935 and again from 1958 till his death in 1977 (see Hachmeister, *Schleyer*, p. 105). Schleyer joined the SS on 30 June 1933 and belonged to the SS-Sturm 2/I/32. See UAH, StudA, Schleyer, Hanns Martin (1937), 'Deutsche Studentenschaft' card. On Schleyer's position and activities in the Corps Suevia and the NSDStB see Norbert Giovannini, *Zwischen Republik und Faschismus. Heidelberger Studentinnen und Studenten 1918–1945* (Weinheim: Deutscher Studien Verlag, 1990), pp. 212–213. The *Burschenschaften* still exist today.
54. Schneider and Lehnert, *Die Gießener Burschenschaft 1814 bis 1936*, p. 128. On the history of the Alemannia see Carl Walbrach, ed., *Geschichte der Giessener Burschenschaft Alemannia 1861–1961* (Giessen: Selbstverlag der G. B. Alemannia, 1961).
55. *Matrikel des Corps Hassia Giessen zu Mainz 1815–1985* (Mainz: Selbstverlag des Verbandes der Alten Herren des Corps Hassia Gießen zu Mainz, 1985), p. 464. On the history of the Corps Hassia-Gießen see *Geschichte des Corps Hassia Giessen zu Mainz 1815–1965* (Mainz: Selbstverlag des Verbandes der Alten Herren des Corps Hassia Gießen zu Mainz, 1965).
56. Ulrich Herbert, '"Generation der Sachlichkeit". Die völkische Studentenbewegung der frühen zwanziger Jahre in Deutschland', in Frank Bajohr, Werner Johe and Uwe Lohalm, eds., *Zivilisation und Barbarei: Die widersprüchlichen Potentiale der Moderne* (Hamburg: Christians, 1991), pp. 115–144, here pp. 121–122, 125, 130–132 and 136–137.
57. Ibid., p. 138.
58. E. Günther Gründel, *Die Sendung der Jungen Generation. Versuch einer umfassenden revolutionären Sinndeutung der Krise* (Munich: C. H. Beck, 1932), pp. 23–24, 31–42 and 59–61. At his 1961 trial in Jerusalem, Adolf Eichmann also used the term 'revaluation of values' to refer to the transformation prescribed by the Nazi state. See Klaus Bölling, 'Das Pflichtgefühl eines Mörders', *Süddeutsche Zeitung*, 5 April 2011, p. 2. On the members of the front generation see also the discussion in Tony Judt, with Timothy Snyder, *Thinking the Twentieth Century* (London: Heinemann, 2012), pp. 161–163.
59. This is reflected, for example, in Kershaw, *Hitler 1889–1936*, pp. 1–69; Herbert, *Best*, pp. 42–100. Not all biographers of National Socialist perpetrators take this view, however. A case in point is Piper, *Alfred Rosenberg*. On a total of less than eleven pages, including notes, the author summarises the first twenty-five years – very nearly half – of Rosenberg's life. This must be considered less than comprehensive in any biography, but particularly so in one of its length (831 pages). Piper makes no mention of the available source material having prevented a more in-depth analysis, and the reader is left to

assume that the author was not particularly interested in Rosenberg's childhood or youth, an assumption expressly confirmed by Piper in his response to a question during the presentation of the book on 27 October 2005 at the Zentrum für Zeithistorische Forschung in Potsdam. See Alex J. Kay, Review of Ernst Piper, *Alfred Rosenberg. Hitlers Chefideologe* (Munich: Blessing, 2005), in: *University of Sussex Journal of Contemporary History*, No. 10 (spring 2006).

60. Gründel, *Die Sendung der Jungen Generation*, pp. 81–85: '*Wir suchen nicht so sehr die besten Ansichten als die besten Methoden*' (p. 85).

61. Haffner, *Geschichte eines Deutschen*, pp. 22–24: '*Die eigentliche Generation des Nazismus aber sind die in der Dekade 1900 bis 1910 Geborenen, die den Krieg, ganz ungestört von seiner Tatsächlichkeit, als großes Spiel erlebt haben*' (p. 23).

62. See Herbert, '"Generation der Sachlichkeit"'. See also Wildt, *Generation des Unbedingten* ['unconditional generation']. The title of the English translation of Wildt's book diverges slightly from the German original: Wildt, *An Uncompromising Generation*.

63. Peter Suhrkamp, 'Söhne ohne Väter und Lehrer. Die Situation der bürgerlichen Jugend', *Die Neue Rundschau*, Vol. 43, No. 5 (May 1932), pp. 681–696, here pp. 687–688: '*Sie sind die Unruhigsten, die Unklarsten und die Abenteuerlichsten. [...] Das Bezeichnendste an ihnen ist ihr Mangel an Humanität, ihre Achtlosigkeit gegen das Menschliche. [...] Sie sind die schärfsten Gegner des Liberalismus.*'

64. Earl, *The Nuremberg SS-Einsatzgruppen Trial*, pp. 105–106, 112 and 134.

65. Dicks, *Licensed Mass Murder*, p. 223. For the date of the interview see ibid., p. 208.

66. For more on this see Chapter 2.

2   'In terms of his character he is irreproachable in every respect'

1. BArch Berlin, VBS 286/6400010138, SSO-Akte Dr. Alfred Filbert; UniA GI, Juristische Promotionsakten Nr. 775, 'Dienstleistungszeugnis', 15 December 1934, fol. 166. See also HStAD, G 21 B, Personalakte Nr. 2862, 'Betreffend: Gesuch des Referendars S.S. Mann Alfred Filbert zu Worms um Einstellung in die politische Polizei', Ministerialabteilung Ia (Polizei) des Hessischen Staatsministeriums, 13 March 1934; BArch Berlin, VBS 286/6400010138, SSO-Akte Dr. Alfred Filbert, 'Lebenslauf!', 27 January 1937.

2. BArch Berlin, VBS 286/6400010138, SSO-Akte Dr. Alfred Filbert; BArch Berlin, VBS 286/6400010138, SSO-Akte Dr. Alfred Filbert, 'Personal-Bericht des Dr. Alfred Filbert', signed SS-Oberführer [Rudolf] Fumy, Amtschef III, 1 March 1938; HStAD, G 21 B, Personalakte Nr. 2862, 'Fragebogen zur Durchführung des Gesetzes zur Wiederherstellung des Berufsbeamtentums vom 7. April 1933', signed Alfred Filbert; UniA GI, Juristische Promotionsakten Nr. 775, 'Dienstleistungszeugnis', 15 December 1934, fol. 166.

3. Either on 28 August (see BArch Berlin, R 2/12150, fols. 115–116R, 'Vorschlag zur Ernennung des Referendars Dr. Filbert zum Regierungsrat', I C (a) 1 a Nr. 1263/40, n.d. [5 June 1940], here fol. 116R) or on 1 September (see BArch Berlin, MF-OK-32/E0045, fol. 1819; BArch Berlin, VBS 286/ 6400010138, SSO-Akte Dr. Alfred Filbert, 'Fragebogen zur Ergänzung bzw. Berichtigung der Führerkartei und der Dienstaltersliste', signed Dr Alfred Filbert, 10 August 1937). See also BArch Berlin, VBS 286/6400010138, SSO-Akte Dr. Alfred Filbert, 'Lebenslauf!', 27 January 1937 ('August 1932'); HStAD, G 21 B, Personalakte Nr. 2862, 'Fragebogen zur Durchführung des Gesetzes zur Wiederherstellung des Berufsbeamtentums vom 7. April 1933', signed Alfred Filbert ('August 1932'). According to the biographical information provided in the 1962 judgement at Filbert's trial in Berlin, he first joined the SS in 'late summer' 1932 and the NSDAP 'straight after' (see UniA GI, 'Urteil Landgericht Berlin vom 22. Juni 1962', fol. 40). In a statement made in court in 1960, Filbert erroneously claimed to have joined both the Nazi Party and the SS in October 1932 (see HStAD, H 13 Darmstadt, Nr. 1291/25, 'Strafsache gegen Dr. Alfred Filbert wegen Mordes', 14 January 1960, p. 3).

4. BArch Berlin, MF-OK-32/E0045, fol. 1819; BArch Berlin, VBS 286/ 6400010138, SSO-Akte Dr. Alfred Filbert, 'Fragebogen zur Ergänzung bzw. Berichtigung der Führerkartei und der Dienstaltersliste', signed Dr Alfred Filbert, 10 August 1937; BArch Berlin, VBS 286/6400010138, SSO-Akte Dr. Alfred Filbert, 'Personal-Bericht des Dr. Alfred Filbert', 1 March 1938; BArch Berlin, R 2/12150, fols. 115–116R, 'Vorschlag zur Ernennung des Referendars Dr. Filbert zum Regierungsrat', n.d. [5 June 1940], here fol. 116R.

5. See the photograph in HStAD, R 4, Nr. 29813 / 24 A, 'Worms am Rhein, 1932 Juni 12 / Rede Adolf Hitlers (1889–1945) im Wormser Fußballstadion Wormatia vor 30.000 Zuhörern / Blick von der Ulmenallee (Rudi-Stephan-Allee) auf Alzeyer Str.'.

6. UniA GI, Juristische Promotionsakten Nr. 775, 'Dienstleistungszeugnis', 15 December 1934, fol. 166: *'Während dieser Zeit hat er seinen Dienst jederzeit freudig und zur Zufriedenheit seiner sämtlichen Vorgesetzten ausgeführt. Insbesondere wird lobend angeführt, dass er sich während der Hauptkampfzeit im ehemals roten Worms im Jahre 1932 bis zur Machtübernahme als SS-Angehöriger restlos bewährt hat. Er war allzeit ein guter Kamerad.'*

7. UniA GI, Juristische Promotionsakten Nr. 775, 'Dienstleistungszeugnis', 15 December 1934, fol. 166; BArch Berlin, VBS 286/6400010138, SSO-Akte Dr. Alfred Filbert, 'Lebenslauf!', 27 January 1937.

8. HStAD, G 21 B, Personalakte Nr. 2862, Letter to SS-Mann Alfred Filbert from the commander of SS-Sturm 4/II/33, 19 October 1933.

9. On the Enabling Act see Dieter Deiseroth, 'Die Legalitäts-Legende. Vom Reichstagsbrand zum NS-Regime', *Blätter für deutsche und internationale Politik*, Vol. 53, No. 2 (February 2008), pp. 91–102.

10. HStAD, G 21 B, Personalakte Nr. 2862, 'Betrifft: Urlaubsgesuch des Referendars Alfred Filbert in Worms', signed Neuroth, 22 May 1934; HStAD, G 21 B, Personalakte Nr. 2862, 'Zeugnis', signed by the supervising

judge at the Amtsgericht Worms, Dr. Lemser, 3 November 1934. See also BArch Berlin, VBS 286/6400010138, SSO-Akte Dr. Alfred Filbert, 'Beurteilung', signed SS-Oberführer [Rudolf] Fumy, Amtschef III, 1 March 1938.

11. BArch Berlin, NS 48/19, 'Dienstleistungszeugnis der S.S. Sportschule Waldlager Fürth über den SA-Mann Kratzer, Friedrich', 10/III/41 S., 11 July 1934. This is one of only three surviving certificates in the German Federal Archives in Berlin. Judging from the date of the certificate, the course participant attended the SS sports school in Fürth at the same time as Filbert. The Stadtarchiv Fürth does not possess any records on participants of courses at the school (written notification from Ronald Langer, Stadtarchiv und Stadtmuseum, Stadt Fürth, 23 August 2012).

12. BArch Berlin, VBS 286/6400010138, SSO-Akte Dr. Alfred Filbert, 'Beurteilung', 1 March 1938.

13. HStAD, G 21 B, Personalakte Nr. 2862, 'Zeugnis', 3 November 1934. For Filbert's attendance of the autumn parade in Nuremberg on 2 September see BArch Berlin, VBS 286/6400010138, SSO-Akte Dr. Alfred Filbert, 'SS-Stammrollen-Auszug des Filbert, Alfred', 15 February 1937.

14. HStAD, G 21 B, Personalakte Nr. 2862, 'Betr.: Den Referendar Alfred Filbert beim Amtsgericht Worms', Ministerialabteilung 1c (Justiz) des Hessischen Staatsministeriums, 7 February 1934; HStAD, G 21 B, Personalakte Nr. 2862, 'Betreffend: Gesuch des Referendars S.S. Mann Alfred Filbert zu Worms um Einstellung in die politische Polizei', Ministerialabteilung 1a (Polizei) des Hessischen Staatsministeriums, 13 March 1934.

15. HStAD, G 21 B, Personalakte Nr. 2862, 'Gesuch des Referendars SS. Mann Alfred Filbert zu Worms um Einstellung in die politische Polizei', 21 March 1934.

16. HStAD, G 21 B, Personalakte Nr. 2862, 'Betr.: Referendar SS-Mann Alfred Filbert zu Worms Schr. v. 21.3. P.A. II/6524 um Einstellung in die politische Polizei', Nationalsozialistische Deutsche Arbeiterpartei Gau Hessen-Nassau, 11 May 1934: *'Gegen die nationale Zuverlässigkeit des Genannten bestehen keine Bedenken.'*

17. UniA GI, 'Urteil Landgericht Berlin vom 22. Juni 1962', fol. 40. See also HStAD, H 13 Darmstadt, Nr. 1291/25, 'Strafsache gegen Dr. Alfred Filbert wegen Mordes', 14 January 1960, p. 4. Michael Wildt states that Filbert and Jost first met in Worms, though not when or in which context: Wildt, *Generation des Unbedingten*, p. 396.

18. BArch Berlin, R 2/12150, 'Vorschlag zur Ernennung des Oberregierungsrats Jost zum Generalmajor der Polizei', Reichsminister des Innern, Pol. SIC (a) 1 a Nr. 1098/40, signed [Wilhelm] Frick, n.d., fols. 133–135, here fol. 134; BArch Berlin, R 601/1813, '[SA-]Führer-Fragebogen', signed Heinz Jost, 30 November 1933; Horst-Gerhard Dehmel, *Die Geschichte der Wormser Polizei* (Guntersblum: Horst-Gerhard Dehmel, 1997), p. 41.

19. Thorsten J. Querg, 'Spionage und Terror – Das Amt VI des Reichssicherheitshauptamtes 1939–1945', unpublished doctoral thesis, Freie Universität Berlin, 1997, p. 165. Jost became head of Office III

(Counterintelligence) of the SD on 2 September 1936. See ibid., pp. 157–158.

20. HStAD, G 21 B, Personalakte Nr. 2862, 'Betr.: Vorbereitungsdienst des Ger. Ref. Alfred Filbert aus Worms am Rh. Heinrichstr. 8. jetzt Berlin Wilhelmstr. 102', signed Dr. Alfred Filbert, 2 January 1936; BArch Berlin, VBS 286/6400010138, SSO-Akte Dr. Alfred Filbert, 'Lebenslauf', 27 January 1937; BArch Berlin, R 2/12150, fols. 114–114R, Letter of recommendation from Dr [Werner] Best to the Reichsminister der Finanzen, Pol. SIC (a) 1 a Nr. 1263/40, 5 June 1940, here fol. 114; BArch Berlin, R 2/12150, fols. 115–116R, 'Vorschlag zur Ernennung des Referendars Dr. Filbert zum Regierungsrat', n.d. [5 June 1940], here fol. 116.

21. See Alfred Filbert, *Kann das Ablehnungsrecht des Konkursverwalters des Vorbehaltsverkäufers mit der Anwartschaft des Käufers auf den Eigentumserwerb ausgeräumt werden?* (Gießen: Buchdruckerei Meyer, 1935), Dissertation zur Erlangung der Doktorwürde der Juristischen Fakultät der Hessischen Ludwigs-Universität zu Gießen, p. 21 ('Lebenslauf'), in UniA GI, Juristische Promotionsakten Nr. 775.

22. HStAD, G 21 B, Personalakte Nr. 2862, 'Betr.: Die Fakultätsprüfung des Rechtskandidaten Alfred Filbert aus Worms und dessen Gesuch um Zulassung zum Vorbereitungsdienst', Hessisches Staatsministerium, 23 January 1934.

23. HStAD, G 21 B, Personalakte Nr. 2862, 'Betreffend: Den Referendar Alfred Filbert, geb. am 8. Sept. 1905 zu Worms', Hessisches Amtsgericht Worms, 29 January 1934.

24. HStAD, G 21 B, Personalakte Nr. 2862, 'Betreffend: den Referendar Alfred Filbert aus Worms', Hessisches Amtsgericht Worms, 18 October 1934.

25. For Filbert's certificate from the local court in Worms see HStAD, G 21 B, Personalakte Nr. 2862, 'Zeugnis', 3 November 1934.

26. HStAD, G 21 B, Personalakte Nr. 2862, 'Betr. Vorbereitungsdienst des Referendars Filbert, Worms', 15 November 1934.

27. HStAD, G 21 B, Personalakte Nr. 2862, 'Betreffend: Den Vorbereitungsdienst des Referendars Alfred Filbert aus Worms', Präsident des Oberlandesgerichts, 30 October 1934.

28. HStAD, G 21 B, Personalakte Nr. 2862, 'Betr. Beurlaubung aus dem Vorbereitungsdienst des Ger. Ref. Alfred Filbert aus Worms, zur Zeit am Amtsgericht Alzey', 27 October 1934: *'Da ich von dem Herrn Staatsminister die Zusicherung erhalten habe, dass ich in nächster Zeit Verwendung im Polizeidienst finden werde, und meine Einberufung jeden Tag erfolgen kann, bitte ich um meine Beurlaubung aus dem Vorbereitungsdienst, damit ich in der Zeit bis zu meiner Einberufung die Doktorprüfung an der Universität Gießen ablegen kann. Ich bitte unter Berücksichtigung meiner besonderen Lage meinem Gesuch stattzugeben.'*

29. HStAD, G 21 B, Personalakte Nr. 2862, 'Betr.: Vorbereitungsdienst des Ger. Ref. Alfred Filbert aus Worms am Rh. Heinrichstr. 8. jetzt Berlin Wilhelmstr. 102', 2 January 1936; BArch Berlin, VBS 286/6400010138, SSO-Akte Dr. Alfred Filbert, 'Lebenslauf', 27 January 1937.

30. See the certificate, dated 27 February 1935, in UniA GI, Juristische Promotionsakten Nr. 775, fols. 181, 182 and 183.

31. Filbert, *Kann das Ablehnungsrecht*, in UniA GI, Juristische Promotionsakten Nr. 775. Filbert's doctoral thesis was printed in 170 copies, of which 125 copies were submitted to the library of the University of Giessen on 21 March (see ibid., fols. 161 and 162, 'Formular II zu Nr. J. F. 133/34').

32. Christian Bülte, 'Erich Bley', in Mathias Schmoeckel, ed., *Die Juristen der Universität Bonn im 'Dritten Reich'* (Cologne: Böhlau, 2004), pp. 48–79, here pp. 50, 53 and 66.

33. Nockemann, born 1903, was active as a 20-year-old student against separatists in the Rhineland. He later became head of Office II (Administration) in the Reich Security Main Office. On Nockemann see Wildt, *Generation des Unbedingten*, pp. 185–189.

34. Christian Ingrao, *Croire et détruire: Les intellectuels dans la machine de guerre SS* (n.pl. [Paris]: Fayard, 2010), p. 80.

35. HStAD, H 13 Darmstadt, Nr. 1291/25, 'Strafsache gegen Dr. Alfred Filbert wegen Mordes', 14 January 1960, p. 3; Dicks, *Licensed Mass Murder*, pp. 209–210.

36. HStAD, H 13 Darmstadt, Nr. 1291/25, 'Strafsache gegen Dr. Alfred Filbert wegen Mordes', 14 January 1960, p. 4.

37. HStAD, G 21 B, Personalakte Nr. 2862, 'Betr.: Vorbereitungsdienst des Ger. Ref. Alfred Filbert aus Worms am Rh. Heinrichstr. 8. jetzt Berlin Wilhelmstr. 102', 2 January 1936.

38. HStAD, G 21 B, Personalakte Nr. 2862, 'Betreffend: Den Vorbereitungsdienst des Referendars Dr. Alfred Filbert', 9 January 1936.

39. HStAD, G 21 B, Personalakte Nr. 2862, Letter from [Hans] Tesmer to the Kammergerichtspräsident in Berlin, 25 March 1936. Tesmer signed here 'on behalf of' the deputy chief of the Prussian Gestapo, that is, Reinhard Heydrich. In summer 1941, Tesmer was appointed Chief of Military Administration attached to the commander of the rear area of Army Group Centre, precisely where Filbert was deployed as chief of Einsatzkommando 9. On Tesmer see Gerlach, *Kalkulierte Morde*, esp. pp. 136–137.

40. HStAD, G 21 B, Personalakte Nr. 2862, 'Zeugnis', signed [Hans] Tesmer, 17 November 1936; HStAD, G 21 B, Personalakte Nr. 2862, Letter from [Hans] Tesmer to the Oberlandesgerichtspräsident in Darmstadt, 7 December 1936; BArch Berlin, VBS 286/6400010138, SSO-Akte Dr. Alfred Filbert, 'Lebenslauf!', 27 January 1937.

41. HStAD, G 21 B, Personalakte Nr. 2862, 'Zeugnis', signed [Hans] Tesmer, 17 November 1936.

42. Ibid.: '*Dr. Filbert wurde in allen wichtigen Arbeitsgebieten der Geheimen Staatspolizei gründlich unterwiesen. Die ihm übertragenen Arbeiten erledigte er sorgfältig und geschickt. In der Beurteilung politischer Zusammenhänge zeigte er einen klaren Blick und ein gutes Verständnis. Seine Neigung und Eignung für die Aufgabengebiete der Politischen Polizei traten bei ihm in begrüßenswerter Weise in Erscheinung. Dr. Filbert verfügt über ein sicheres und gewandtes Auftreten, das besonders in seinem mündlichen Vortrag zum Ausdruck kam. Sein Verhalten den Mitarbeitern gegenüber zeugte von Kameradschaftssinn. Seine Berichtsentwürfe waren flüssig und gut durchdacht. Charakterlich in jeder Hinsicht einwandfrei, verspricht er ein tüchtiger höherer Verwaltungsbeamter zu werden. Seine Führung in und außer Dienst war tadelfrei.*'

43. HStAD, G 21 B, Personalakte Nr. 2862, Letter from Kammergerichtsrat Dr Wernecke to Alfred Filbert, 13 June 1936.

44. On the training in the camp in Jüterbog see Haffner, *Geschichte eines Deutschen*, pp. 252–290. Hanns Kerrl was Reich Commissioner for the Prussian Ministry of Justice from 1933 to 1935.

45. HStAD, G 21 B, Personalakte Nr. 2862, 'Betr. Den Vorbereitungsdienst des Referendars Alfred Filbert', 26 September 1936.

46. BArch Berlin, VBS 286/6400010138, SSO-Akte Dr. Alfred Filbert, 'Personal-Bericht des Dr. Alfred Filbert', 1 March 1938.

47. HStAD, G 21 B, Personalakte Nr. 2862, 'Betreffend: Vorbereitungsdienst des Referendars Alfred Filbert', 2 October 1936.

48. HStAD, G 21 B, Personalakte Nr. 2862, 'Betr.: Filbert, Alfred, Referendar', 10 May 1937; HStAD, G 21 B, Personalakte Nr. 2862, 'Betreffend: Den Vorbereitungsdienst des Referendars Dr. Alfred Filbert', 12 May 1937.

49. HStAD, G 21 B, Personalakte Nr. 2862, 'Betr.: Vorbereitungsdienst des Referendars Dr. Alfred Filbert, Berlin', 1 October 1937; HStAD, G 21 B, Personalakte Nr. 2862, Letter from the Oberlandesgerichtspräsident to Dr Alfred Filbert, 8 October 1937.

50. HStAD, G 21 B, Personalakte Nr. 2862, 'Betr.: Vorbereitungsdienst des Gerichtsreferendars Dr. Alfred Filbert', 14 November 1938.

51. HStAD, G 21 B, Personalakte Nr. 2862, 'Betr. Den Referendar Dr. Alfred Filbert', 18 November 1938.

52. Mann, 'Were the Perpetrators of Genocide "Ordinary Men" or "Real Nazis"?', p. 351.

53. Ibid., pp. 350–351 and 359 (quote).

54. Ibid., pp. 340–342 (quote: pp. 341–342).

55. Archiv des Instituts für Zeitgeschichte, Munich (hereafter IfZ-Archiv), ZS-429/II, fols. 2–71, 'Interrogation Report No. 15', Interrogation Section, Third US Army, 9 July 1945, here fol. 25. On the 'foreign intelligence mission' of the SD see George C. Browder, *Hitler's Enforcers: The Gestapo and the SS Security Service in the Nazi Revolution* (New York/Oxford: Oxford University Press, 1996), pp. 197–209.

56. Browder, *Hitler's Enforcers*, pp. 204–205.

57. Katrin Paehler, 'Making Intelligence Nazi: The SD, Foreign Intelligence, and Ideology', revised doctoral thesis, 2014, pp. 184–188. I am grateful to Katrin Paehler for providing me with a copy of her book manuscript prior to publication.

58. HStAD, G 21 B, Personalakte Nr. 2862, 'Betr.: Vorbereitungsdienst des Gerichtsreferendars Dr. Alfred Filbert', 14 November 1938. According to an MI5 report from July 1945, Heinz Jost was also in the Sudetenland during this period, specifically between 1 and 15 October 1938. See Altenhöner, 'Heinz Jost und das Amt III', p. 65.

59. On the German occupation of the Sudetenland see Volker Zimmermann, *Die Sudetendeutschen im NS-Staat. Politik und Stimmung der Bevölkerung im Reichsgau Sudetenland (1938–1945)* (Essen: Klartext, 1999).

60. See Nuremberg Document (hereafter Nbg. Doc.) 509-USSR, 'Meldung. Betr.: Einsatz des S. D. im Falle CSR', III 225 g.Rs., 29 June 1938,

reproduced in: International Military Tribunal, ed., *Der Prozess gegen die Hauptkriegsverbrecher vor dem Internationalen Militärgerichtshof, Nürnberg, 14. November 1945 – 1. Oktober 1946* (hereafter *IMG*), Vol. 39 (Nuremberg: Sekretariat des Gerichtshofs, 1949), pp. 536–551, here pp. 536–543. See also Krausnick, 'Die Einsatzgruppen', pp. 21–22.

61. Paehler, 'Making Intelligence Nazi', p. 198; Altenhöner, 'Heinz Jost und das Amt III', p. 74, n. 59.

62. Nbg. Doc. 509-USSR, reproduced in: *IMG*, Vol. 39, p. 537.

63. BArch Berlin, VBS 286/6400010138, SSO-Akte Dr. Alfred Filbert.

64. On the German invasion of Poland see Jochen Böhler, *Auftakt zum Vernichtungskrieg. Die Wehrmacht in Polen 1939* (Frankfurt am Main: Fischer Taschenbuch, 2006).

65. LArch Berlin, B Rep. 057–01, Nr. 1017, fols. 153–156, Statement by the prisoner Alfred Filbert, Tegel Prison, 1 Js 12/65 (RSHA), 22 September 1966, here fol. 153. See also StArch Hamburg, 213–12, Nr. 33, Bd. 16, fols. 7563–7572, 'Protokoll in der gerichtlichen Voruntersuchung gegen Bruno Streckenbach', signed Alfred Filbert, 23 September 1971, here fol. 7570.

66. For the minutes of the three meetings see BArch Berlin, R 58/825, 'Vermerk: Amtschefbesprechung am 7. 9. 1939', Stabskanzlei, I 11 Rf. / Fh., 8 September 1939, fols. 1–3; BArch Berlin, R 58/825, 'Vermerk: Betrifft: Amtschefbesprechung am 12. Sept. 1939', Stabskanzlei, I 11 Rf. / Fh., 13 September 1939, fols. 7–9; BArch Berlin, R 58/825, 'Betrifft: Amtschefbesprechung am 19. 9. 39.', Stabskanzlei, I 11 Rf. / Fh., 21 September 1939, fols. 14–17.

67. BArch Berlin, R 58/825, 'Betrifft: Amtschefbesprechung am 19. 9. 39.', Stabskanzlei, I 11 Rf. / Fh., 21. September 1939, fols. 14–17, here fol. 14: '*C [Chef] sagte dem SS-Obersturmbannführer Dr. Filbert in eindeutiger Weise, daß die Auslandsberichte schlecht seien und erheblich umgestellt werden müßten. In der vorliegenden Form seien sie eine schlechte Zusammenstellung von Zeitungs–und Rundfunkmeldungen ausländischer Sender. Er verlangt eine Aktivierung der Arbeit und wünscht nur Meldungen, die durch unmittelbare Nachrichtentätigkeit angefallen sind.*' Filbert is missing from the list of participants (see fol. 14), but the minutes make it quite clear that he attended the meeting.

68. For the minutes of the meeting see BArch Berlin, R 58/825, 'Vermerk: Amtschef und Einsatzgruppenleiterbesprechung.', Stabskanzlei, I 11 Rf./ Fh., 27 September 1939, fols. 26–30.

69. BArch Berlin, R 58/825, 'Vermerk: Amtschef und Einsatzgruppenleiterbesprechung.', Stabskanzlei, I 11 Rf./Fh., 27 September 1939, fols. 26–30, here fol. 29: '*1.) Juden so schnell wie möglich in die Städte, 2.) Juden aus dem Reich nach Polen, 3.) die restlichen 30.000 Zigeuner auch nach Polen, 4.) systematische Ausschickung der Juden aus den deutschen Gebieten mit Güterzügen.*'

70. See LArch Berlin, B Rep. 057–01, Nr. 1017, fols. 153–156, Statement by the prisoner Alfred Filbert, Tegel Prison, 1 Js 12/65 (RSHA), 22 September 1966, here fol. 154.

71. BArch   Berlin,   R   58/825,   'Vermerk: Amtschef   und Einsatzgruppenleiterbesprechung.', Stabskanzlei, I 11 Rf./Fh., 27 September 1939, fols. 26–30, here fol. 26.

72. For the minutes of the two meetings see BArch Berlin, R 58/825, 'Vermerk: Amtschefbesprechung am 8. 9. 39:', Stabskanzlei, I 11 Rf./Fh., 9 September 1939, fols. 5–5R; BArch Berlin, R 58/825, 'Vermerk: Amtschefbesprechung am 14. 9. 1939.', Stabskanzlei, I 11 Rf./Fh., 15 September 1939, fols. 10–12.

73. BArch Berlin, R 58/825, 'Betrifft: Amtschefbesprechung am 29. 9. 1939.', Reichssicherheitshauptamt, Amt I/I 11 Rf./Fh., 2 October 1939, fols. 36–37, here fol. 36. Katrin Paehler points out that Jost was absent from the meeting on 19 September due to him still being on Einsatzgruppen duty in Poland: Paehler, 'Making Intelligence Nazi', p. 172.

74. BArch Berlin, R 58/825, 'Vermerk: Betrifft: Amtschefbesprechung', Stabskanzlei, I 11 Rf./Fh., 28 September 1939, fols. 34–35, here fol. 34.

75. Ibid., here fol. 35.

76. BArch Berlin, R 58/826, fols. 297–298, 'Betrifft: Die Zusammenfassung der zentralen Ämter der Sicherheitspolizei und des SD.', Reichsführer SS und Chef der Deutschen Polizei, S-V 1 Nr. 719/39 – 151 –, signed H[einrich]. Himmler, 27 September 1939, here fols. 297–298R. On the establishment of the RSHA see Hachmeister, *Der Gegnerforscher*, pp. 207–214; Wildt, *Generation des Unbedingten*, pp. 276–282.

77. Hachmeister, *Der Gegnerforscher*, p. 203.

78. Querg, 'Spionage und Terror', p. 167.

79. BArch D-H, ZR 537, A. 6, 'Betr.: Geschäftsverteilungsplan des Amtes VI', VI H Fi/Sc. 23798/39, signed SS-Sturmbannführer Finke, 19 December 1939, fols. 1–14, here fol. 2.

80. BArch Berlin, R 58/840, fols. 210–221R, 'Geschäftsverteilungsplan des Reichssicherheitshauptamtes (Stand vom 1.2.1940)', Chef der Sicherheitspolizei und des SD., I HB 147/40, 1 February 1940, here fol. 220; BArch Berlin, R 58/840, fols. 230–236, 'Planstellenbesetzung des Amts VI des Reichssicherheitshauptamtes', Amtschef VI, n.d., here fol. 231. See also IfZ-Archiv, ZS-429/II, fols. 2–71, 'Interrogation Report No. 15', 9 July 1945, here fols. 29 and 31.

81. HStAD, H 13 Darmstadt, Nr. 1291/25, 'Strafsache gegen Dr. Alfred Filbert wegen Mordes', 14 January 1960, p. 4.

82. BArch Berlin, R 58/240, fols. 246–293R, 'Geschäftsverteilungsplan des Reichssicherheitshauptamtes. Stand: 1.3.1941', Chef der Sicherheitspolizei und des SD, II A 1 (I B 1) 92 IX/40–154 – 2 -, 1 March 1941, here fol. 283.

83. Wildt, *Generation des Unbedingten*, pp. 391–392. Contrast with IfZ-Archiv, ZS-429/I, fols. 3–7, 'Eidesstattliche Versicherung', signed Dr [Wilhelm] Hoettl [*sic*], here fol. 3.

84. Wildt, *Generation des Unbedingten*, p. 395; IfZ-Archiv, ZS-429/II, fols. 2–71, 'Interrogation Report No. 15', here fol. 28.

85. Quoted in Querg, 'Spionage und Terror', p. 165: *'Er hat sich auf seinen sehr tüchtigen Stabsführer verlassen, den Dr. Filbert, der hat das damalige Amt III weitgehend in der Hand gehabt.'* On Höttl see Norman J. W. Goda, 'The Nazi Peddler: Wilhelm Höttl and Allied Intelligence', in Richard Breitman,

Norman J. W. Goda, Timothy Naftali and Robert Wolfe, *U.S. Intelligence and the Nazis* (Cambridge/New York: Cambridge University Press, 2005), pp. 265–292.

86. IfZ-Archiv, ZS-429/II, fols. 2–71, 'Interrogation Report No. 15', 9 July 1945, here fol. 29.
87. Ibid., here fol. 25.

3   'Pity that the scoundrel didn't perish'

1. BArch Berlin, VBS 286/6400010138, SSO-Akte Dr. Alfred Filbert.
2. Ibid.
3. Ibid., 'Beurteilung', 1 March 1938: '*SS-Hauptsturmführer Dr. Filbert leitet mit grosser Umsicht und Tatkraft die Hauptabteilung III 22. Die Hauptabteilung III 22 ist unter seiner Leitung vorbildlich ausgebaut worden. Seine Kenntnisse und Leistungen stehen weit über dem Durchschnitt. In Anbetracht der Dienststellung als Hauptabteilungsleiter und der vorbildlichen Leistungen wird die Beförderung zum SS-Sturmbannführer vorgeschlagen.*'
4. BArch Berlin, VBS 286/6400010138, SSO-Akte Dr. Alfred Filbert.
5. Ibid.; UniA GI, 'Urteil Landgericht Berlin vom 22. Juni 1962', fol. 42.
6. Einwohnermeldearchiv der Stadt Bad Gandersheim, Meldekarte Käthe Filbert. I am grateful to Manfred Kielhorn for providing me with a copy of this document. See also BArch Berlin, VBS 283/6010010064, 'R. u. S.-Fragebogen', V. B. Nr. 47318, signed Käthe Bernicke, 12 January 1937; BArch Berlin, VBS 286/6400010138, SSO-Akte Dr. Alfred Filbert.
7. Einwohnermeldearchiv der Stadt Bad Gandersheim, Meldekarte Käthe Filbert.
8. Ibid. See also BArch Berlin, VBS 286/6400010138, 'Meldung an die SS-Personalkartei', 2 March 1940.
9. BArch Berlin, VBS 286/6400010138, SSO-Akte Dr. Alfred Filbert. See also Dicks, *Licensed Mass Murder*, p. 210.
10. Dicks, *Licensed Mass Murder*, p. 210.
11. BArch Berlin, VBS 283/6010010064, 'Fragebogen!, V.B.Nr. 47 318, Ortsgruppenleiter der NSDAP. Menteroda', 17 January 1937; BArch Berlin, VBS 283/6010010064, 'R. u. S.-Fragebogen, Bernicke, Käthe', 12 January 1937.
12. On Grawitz see Klee, *Das Personenlexikon zum Dritten Reich*, p. 198.
13. BArch Berlin, MF-OK-32/E0045, fol. 1835. His membership number was 2,290,035. See also Dicks, *Licensed Mass Murder*, p. 216. Filbert later claimed that *both* his parents had joined the Party shortly *before* the Nazi takeover of power. See HStAD, H 13 Darmstadt, Nr. 1291/25, 'Strafsache gegen Dr. Alfred Filbert wegen Mordes', 14 January 1960, p. 6.
14. BArch Berlin, VBS 283/6010010064, 'Fragebogen!, V.B.Nr. 47 318, Ortsgruppenleiter der NSDAP. Menteroda', 17 January 1937.
15. See *Notre Nazi*, 01:20:13 – 01:20:19.
16. Otto Filbert had married Wilhelmina Filbert, née Koskamp, in Philadelphia in 1933. Their marriage licence number was 623250. See 'Philadelphia, Pennsylvania, Marriage Index, 1885–1951', Digital GSU Number:

4141695, at: Ancestry.com. *Philadelphia, Pennsylvania, Marriage Index, 1885–1951* [database on-line]. Provo, UT, USA: Ancestry.com Operations, Inc., 2011 [last accessed on 18 February 2013].

17. Written notification from Ralph Filbert's wife, Erika Filbert, Media, PA, 29 July 2013.

18. HStAD, H 13 Darmstadt, Nr. 1291/25, 'Strafsache gegen Dr. Alfred Filbert wegen Mordes', 14 January 1960, p. 6. See also Dicks, *Licensed Mass Murder*, p. 211. Otto Filbert's residence abroad since 1926 is confirmed in ITS Archives, 1.1.5.3 KZ Buchenwald–individuelle Unterlage, Effektenkarte– (Doc. ID # 5856615, reverse).

19. HStAD, H 13 Darmstadt, Nr. 1291/25, 'Strafsache gegen Dr. Alfred Filbert wegen Mordes', 14 January 1960, pp. 6–7.

20. Ibid., p. 7: '*Schade, daß der Lump nicht ums Leben gekommen ist*'. On the failed assassination attempt see Lothar Gruchmann, ed., *Autobiographie eines Attentäters: Johann Georg Elser. Aussage zum Sprengstoffanschlag im Bürgerbräukeller, München, am 8. November 1939* (Stuttgart: Deutsche Verlags-Anstalt, 1970); Anton Hoch, 'Das Attentat auf Hitler im Münchner Bürgerbräukeller 1939', *Vierteljahrshefte für Zeitgeschichte*, Vol. 17, No. 4 (October 1969), pp. 383–413.

21. ITS Archives, 1.1.5.3 KZ Buchenwald–individuelle Unterlage, Häftlingspersonalbogen–(Doc. ID # 5856618).

22. Ibid. See also HStAD, H 13 Darmstadt, Nr. 1291/25, 'Strafsache gegen Dr. Alfred Filbert wegen Mordes', 14 January 1960, p. 7 (here '3-year prison sentence').

23. 'Gesetz gegen heimtückische Angriffe auf Staat und Partei und zum Schutz der Parteiunifromen. Vom 20. Dezember 1934', in *Reichsgesetzblatt*, 1934, Part I, 20 December 1934, pp. 1269–1271, specifically §2 (1).

24. Interview with Otto Filbert's son, Peter Filbert, Weinheim, 29 August 2013.

25. On Himmler's leadership style and his disciplining of SS officers see Longerich, *Heinrich Himmler*, pp. 309–364.

26. HStAD, H 13 Darmstadt, Nr. 1291/25, 'Strafsache gegen Dr. Alfred Filbert wegen Mordes', 14 January 1960, pp. 7–8. See also Dicks, *Licensed Mass Murder*, p. 211; *Notre Nazi*, 01:21:09 – 01:21:13. The relevant files of Dessau Prison no longer exist. An examination of the collections of the Dessau State Ministry, the Dessau Public Prosecutor's Office, the Bernburg Prison and the Coswig Prison failed to yield any results (written notification from Thomas Brünnler, Landeshauptarchiv Sachsen-Anhalt, Abteilung Dessau, 27 August 2010).

27. LArch Berlin, B Rep. 058, Nr. 7179, fols. 244–244R, Hearing of Paul Lehn, n.d. [20 February 1961], here fol. 244.

28. Wildt, *Generation des Unbedingten*, p. 397.

29. For example Arthur Nebe (Einsatzgruppe B), promoted to SS-Gruppenführer on 9 November 1941; Walter Blume (Sonderkommando 7a), promoted to SS-Standartenführer in September 1941; and Erwin Schulz (Einsatzkommando 5), promoted to SS-Oberführer on 9 November 1941. See Rathert, *Verbrechen und Verschwörung*, p. 129; Peter Witte, Michael Wildt, Martina Voigt, Dieter Pohl, Peter Klein, Christian Gerlach, Christoph

Dieckmann and Andrej Angrick, eds., *Der Dienstkalender Heinrich Himmlers 1941/42* (Hamburg: Christians, 1999), p. 254, entry for 5 November 1941; Andrej Angrick, Klaus-Michael Mallmann, Jürgen Matthäus and Martin Cüppers, eds., *Deutsche Besatzungsherrschaft in der UdSSR 1941–1945. Dokumente der Einsatzgruppen in der Sowjetunion* (Darmstadt: Wissenschaftliche Buchgesellschaft, 2013), p. 62, n. 1; Wildt, *Generation des Unbedingten*, p. 578. Otto Ohlendorf was also promoted to SS-Oberführer on 9 November 1941, though he continued to serve as head of Einsatzgruppe D until June of the following year (see Krausnick, 'Die Einsatzgruppen', p. 145, fn. 198).

30. On the Memel Medal see Klaus Jäger, 'Die "Medaille zur Erinnerung an die Heimkehr des Memellandes"', *Orden und Ehrenzeichen*, Vol. 2, No. 6 (April 2000), pp. 2–5.

31. BArch Berlin, VBS 286/6400010138, 'Meldung an die SS-Personalkartei', 30 March 1940.

32. BArch Berlin, R 2/12150, fols. 114–114R, Letter of recommendation from Dr [Werner] Best to the Reich Minister of Finance, Pol. SIC (a) 1 a Nr. 1263/ 40, 5 June 1940.

33. On the attempts of the Security Police and the SD to make use of the civil service in order to achieve their personnel goals see Banach, *Heydrichs Elite*, pp. 239–258.

34. BArch Berlin, R 2/12150, fols. 114–114R, Letter of recommendation from Dr [Werner] Best to the Reich Minister of Finance, Pol. SIC (a) 1 a Nr. 1263/ 40, 5 June 1940, here fol. 114R: '*Durch seine reichen Erfahrungen im Auslandsnachrichtendienst und seine zahlreichen persönlichen Verbindungen zum Ausland ist die Mitarbeit des Dr. Filbert in staatspolizeilicher Hinsicht von unschätzbarem Wert. Es besteht daher ein dringendes dienstliches Interesse an seiner Übernahme in das Beamtenverhältnis.*'

35. BArch Berlin, R 2/12150, fols. 114–114R, Letter of recommendation from Dr [Werner] Best to the Reich Minister of Finance, Pol. SIC (a) 1 a Nr. 1263/ 40, 5 June 1940, here fol. 114.

36. BArch Berlin, R 2/12150, fol. 123, Letter to the Reich Minister of the Interior, [?] December 1940.

37. See BArch Berlin, VBS 286/6400010138, SSO-Akte Dr. Alfred Filbert.

38. Herbert, *Best*, p. 233. On Best's switch to the Wehrmacht in France see ibid., pp. 254–255.

39. Later Office VII.

40. Hachmeister, *Der Gegnerforscher*, pp. 216–217.

41. HStAD, H 13 Darmstadt, Nr. 1291/25, 'Strafsache gegen Dr. Alfred Filbert wegen Mordes', 14 January 1960, p. 10; Dicks, *Licensed Mass Murder*, p. 211.

42. BArch Berlin, VBS 286/6400010138, SSO-Akte Dr. Alfred Filbert, 'Betr.: SS-Ostubaf. d. Allg.-SS Dr. Alfred Filbert, geb. 8.9.05', IIa/ 31.7.40./ Kü., 31 July 1940.

43. See Alex J. Kay, *Exploitation, Resettlement, Mass Murder: Political and Economic Planning for German Occupation Policy in the Soviet Union, 1940–1941* (New York/Oxford: Berghahn, 2006), pp. 26–46, esp. pp. 27–34.

44. Rossiiskii Gosudarstvennyi Voennyi Arkhiv [Russian State Military Archives], Moscow, 500/3/795, fols. 16–21, 'Aktenvermerk', signed [Reinhard] Heydrich, 26 March 1941, here fol. 20: '*10.) Bezüglich der Lösung der Judenfrage berichtete ich kurz dem Reichsmarschall und legte ihm meinen Entwurf vor, den er mit einer Änderung bezüglich der Zuständigkeit Rosenbergs zustimmte und Wiedervorlage befahl. 11.) Der Reichsmarschall sprach mich u.a. darauf an, dass bei einem Einsatz in Russland wir eine ganz kurze, 3–4seitige Unterrichtung vorbereiten sollten, die die Truppe mitbekommen könne, über die Gefährlichkeit der GPU-Organisation, der Polit-Kommissare, Juden usw., damit sie wisse, wen sie praktisch an die Wand zu stellen habe.*' The GPU (*Gosudarstvennoe Politicheskoe Upravlenie*, or State Political Administration) was the designation for the Soviet secret police between 1922 and 1934.
45. See Klein, ed., *Die Einsatzgruppen*, Doc. 2, 'Aktennotiz für Himmler über eine Unterredung Heydrichs mit Göring am 26.3.1941', pp. 367–368, here p. 368.
46. See Kay, *Exploitation, Resettlement, Mass Murder*, pp. 68–95.
47. Götz Aly, *"Endlösung". Völkerverschiebung und der Mord an den europäischen Juden* (Frankfurt am Main: S. Fischer, 1995), pp. 271–272; Kay, *Exploitation, Resettlement, Mass Murder*, p. 109.
48. StArch Hamburg, 213–12, Nr. 33, Bd. 16, fols. 7563–7572, 'Protokoll in der gerichtlichen Voruntersuchung gegen Bruno Streckenbach', 23 September 1971, here fol. 7564. On the credibility of Filbert's testimony concerning this meeting see Angrick, *Besatzungspolitik und Massenmord*, p. 76, fn. 132.
49. HStAD, H 13 Darmstadt, Nr. 1291/25, 'Strafsache gegen Dr. Alfred Filbert wegen Mordes', 14 January 1960, p. 10; StArch Hamburg, 213–12, Nr. 33, Bd. 16, fols. 7563–7572, 'Protokoll in der gerichtlichen Voruntersuchung gegen Bruno Streckenbach', 23 September 1971, here fol. 7564.
50. A meeting with some of the Einsatzgruppen personnel for the Polish campaign took place in Heydrich's private apartment on 5 July 1939. See Klaus-Michael Mallmann, Jochen Böhler and Jürgen Matthäus, *Einsatzgruppen in Polen. Darstellung und Dokumentation* (Darmstadt: Wissenschaftliche Buchgesellschaft, 2008), pp. 116–117, 'Dok. 1) Vermerk SD-Hauptamt II 12 v. 8.7.1939'.
51. StArch München, Staatsanwaltschaften, 32970/5, fols. 966–970, Transcript of hearing of Dr Alfred Filbert, 9 June 1959, here fol. 966R; HStAD, H 13 Darmstadt, Nr. 1291/25, 'Strafsache gegen Dr. Alfred Filbert wegen Mordes', 14 January 1960, pp. 10–11 (quote); StArch Hamburg, 213–12, Nr. 33, Bd. 16, fols. 7563–7572, 'Protokoll in der gerichtlichen Voruntersuchung gegen Bruno Streckenbach', 23 September 1971, here fol. 7564 (quote).
52. StArch München, Staatsanwaltschaften, 32970/5, fols. 966–970, Transcript of hearing of Dr Alfred Filbert, 9 June 1959, here fol. 966R (here no mention is made of Nebe); StArch Hamburg, 213–12, Nr. 33, Bd. 16, fols. 7563–7572, 'Protokoll in der gerichtlichen Voruntersuchung gegen Bruno Streckenbach', 23 September 1971, here fol. 7565.
53. BArch Berlin, VBS 286/6400010138, SSO-Akte Dr. Alfred Filbert, 'Meldung an die SS-Personalkartei', 9 June 1941.

54. StArch Hamburg, 213–12, Nr. 33, Bd. 16, fols. 7563–7572, 'Protokoll in der gerichtlichen Voruntersuchung gegen Bruno Streckenbach', 23 September 1971, here fol. 7565.

55. BArch Ludwigsburg, B 162/4113, Hearing of the witness Dr Walter Blume, Criminal Police in Soest, StA Flensburg 2 Js 467/65, 3 March 1966, fols. 1535–1541, here fol. 1537.

56. Krausnick, 'Die Einsatzgruppen', pp. 143 and 161, fn. 289; Gerlach, *Kalkulierte Morde*, pp. 631–632.

57. LArch Berlin, B Rep. 058, Nr. 7171, fols. 260–263, Hearing of the witness Eduard Holste in the criminal case against Dr Alfred Filbert and Gerhard Schneider for murder, Landgericht Berlin, 19 May 1960, here fol. 261R; BArch Ludwigsburg, B 162/4133, fols. 1580–1585, Hearing of the witness Alfred Filbert, StA Flensburg 2 Js 467/65, 22 February 1966, here fol. 1582; BArch Ludwigsburg, B 162/4113, fols. 1485–1503, Hearing of the accused Ernst Ehlers, 2 Js 467/65, 12 May 1966, here fols. 1488–1489.

58. StArch München, Staatsanwaltschaften, 32970/5, fols. 966–970, Transcript of hearing of Dr Alfred Filbert, 9 June 1959, here fol. 966R. On the personnel of the Einsatzgruppen see Klaus-Michael Mallmann, 'Die Türöffner der "Endlösung". Zur Genesis des Genozids', in Gerhard Paul and Klaus-Michael Mallmann, eds., *Die Gestapo im Zweiten Weltkrieg. 'Heimatfront' und besetztes Europa* (Darmstadt: Wissenschaftliche Buchgesellschaft, 2000), pp. 437–463, here pp. 456–463.

59. See Mallmann, Böhler and Matthäus, *Einsatzgruppen in Polen*, pp. 20–21.

60. Ralf Ogorreck, *Die Einsatzgruppen und die "Genesis der Endlösung"* (Berlin: Metropol, 1996), pp. 56–58. On the assembly of the Einsatzgruppen see Krausnick, 'Die Einsatzgruppen', pp. 141–150; Angrick, *Besatzungspolitik und Massenmord*, pp. 74–98.

61. See Krausnick, 'Die Einsatzgruppen', p. 143.

62. HStAD, G 21 B, Personalakte Nr. 2862, Letter from Bruno Streckenbach to the Oberlandesgerichtspräsident in Darmstadt, 16 June 1941.

63. LArch Berlin, B Rep. 058, Nr. 7168, fols. 39–45R, Hearing of the accused Dr Alfred Filbert, 14 January 1960, here fol. 44R; StArch Hamburg, 213–12, Nr. 33, Bd. 16, fols. 7563–7572, 'Protokoll in der gerichtlichen Voruntersuchung gegen Bruno Streckenbach', 23 September 1971, here fol. 7565.

64. On 18 August 1939, on Berlin's Prinz-Albrecht-Straße a discussion took place that was hosted by Himmler and Heydrich and attended by all those designated as Einsatzgruppen and Einsatzkommando chiefs for the Polish campaign. See Mallmann, Böhler and Matthäus, *Einsatzgruppen in Polen*, pp. 55–56.

65. LArch Berlin, B Rep. 058, Nr. 7178, fols. 82–86R, Hearing of the accused Wilhelm Greiffenberger in the criminal case against Dr Filbert et al. for murder, Landgericht Berlin, 21 October 1960, here fol. 86. See also BArch Berlin, R 70 Sowjetunion/32, fols. 11–12, Teletype message from Heydrich to the four Einsatzgruppen chiefs, 29 June 1941, here fol. 11, where Heydrich refers to his 'verbal remarks already made on 17.VI in Berlin' (*meine bereits am 17.VI. in Berlin gemachten mündlichen Ausführungen*). On the Prinz-Albrecht-

Palais as the location of Heydrich's address see *Trials of War Criminals before the Nuernberg Military Tribunals under Control Council Law No. 10, Nuernberg, October 1946–April 1949: Volume IV* (Washington, DC: US Government Printing Office, n.d. [1950]), Affidavit of Erwin Schulz, 26 May 1947, pp. 135–138, here p. 136, and Affidavit of Walter Blume, 29 June 1947, pp. 139–140, here p. 140.

66. See StArch München, Staatsanwaltschaften, 32970/5, fols. 966–970, Transcript of hearing of Dr Alfred Filbert, 9 June 1959, here fol. 967; LArch Berlin, B Rep. 058, Nr. 7178, fols. 82–86R, Hearing of the accused Wilhelm Greiffenberger, 21 October 1960, here fol. 86.

67. See, also for the following, the discussion in Kay, 'Transition to Genocide, July 1941', pp. 413–416; Christoph Dieckmann, *Deutsche Besatzungspolitik in Litauen 1941–1944*, Vol. 1 (Göttingen: Wallstein, 2011), pp. 394–401. For a divergent view regarding Heydrich's comments on 17 June, see Ogorreck, *Die Einsatzgruppen*, pp. 96–99.

68. As posited by Helmut Krausnick, 'Hitler und die Befehle an die Einsatzgruppen im Sommer 1941', in Eberhard Jäckel and Jürgen Rohwer, eds., *Der Mord an den Juden im Zweiten Weltkrieg: Entschlussbildung und Verwirklichung* (Stuttgart: Deutsche Verlags-Anstalt, 1985), pp. 88–106, and Ronald Headland, 'The *Einsatzgruppen*: The Question of their Initial Operations', *Holocaust and Genocide Studies*, Vol. 4, No. 4 (1989), pp. 401–412. Also, more recently, Wolfgang Curilla, *Die deutsche Ordnungspolizei und der Holocaust im Baltikum und in Weißrußland 1941–1944* (Paderborn: Schöningh, 2006), pp. 86–123, esp. pp. 107 and 123.

69. Mallmann, 'Die Türöffner der "Endlösung"', p. 448.

70. Christian Streit, 'Ostkrieg, Antibolschewismus und "Endlösung"', *Geschichte und Gesellschaft*, Vol. 19 (1991), pp. 242–255, here pp. 244–245; Peter Longerich, *Politik der Vernichtung. Eine Gesamtdarstellung der nationalsozialistischen Judenverfolgung* (Munich: Piper, 1998), p. 315; Wette, *Karl Jäger*, p. 49. For a contrasting view, to the effect that the SS directives, 'both written and verbal [...] were likely more extreme in substance' than those of the Wehrmacht, see Headland, 'The *Einsatzgruppen*', p. 402. On discrepancies between the written orders (also known to the Wehrmacht) and the verbal orders issued to the Einsatzgruppen in the Polish campaign, see Mallmann, Böhler and Matthäus, *Einsatzgruppen in Polen*, pp. 57–59.

71. For the text of the so-called Commissar Order see BArch-MA, RW 4/v. 578, fols. 41–44, 'Richtlinien für die Behandlung politischer Kommissare', 6 June 1941. For the text of the so-called Jurisdiction Decree Barbarossa, see Nbg. Doc. 050–C, 'Erlass über die Ausübung der Kriegsgerichtsbarkeit im Gebiet "Barbarossa" und über besondere Massnahmen der Truppe', 13 May 1941, reproduced in: *IMG*, Vol. 34 (Nuremberg: Sekretariat des Gerichtshofs, 1949), pp. 249–255. For the text of the Guidelines for the Conduct of the Troops in Russia see BArch-MA, RH 22/12, fols. 114–115, 'Richtlinien für das Verhalten der Truppe in Rußland', n.d. [19 May 1941].

72. BArch Berlin, R 70 Sowjetunion/32, fols. 4–10, 'Als Geheime Reichssache', signed [Reinhard] Heydrich, 2 July 1941, here fols. 6–7.

73. Ibid.: '[. . .] alle [. . .] sonstigen radikalen Elemente (Saboteure, Propagandeure, Heckenschützen, Attentäter, Hetzer usw.)'.

4 'So, we've finished off the first Jews'

1. Klaus-Michael Mallmann, 'Menschenjagd und Massenmord. Das neue Instrument der Einsatzgruppen und –kommandos 1938–1945', in Paul and Mallmann, eds., *Die Gestapo im Zweiten Weltkrieg*, pp. 291–316, here p. 304.
2. This number includes the 134 members of the 2nd company of Reserve Police Battalion 9, who were assigned to EG B in Warsaw and divided between the group staff and EKs 8 and 9. The overall breakdown by sub-unit was as follows: group staff: 71; SK 7a: 93; SK 7b: 91; EK 8: 214; and EK 9: 186. See BStU, MfS, HA IX/11 ZUV, Nr. 9, Bd. 31, fols. 3–17, 'Tätigkeitsbericht für die Zeit vom 23.6.1941 bis 13.7.1941', Einsatzgruppe B, signed [Arthur] Nebe, 14 July 1941, here fol. 11; BArch-MA, RH 22/224, fols. 107–108, 'Anlage zum Korpsbefehl Nr. 18 vom 24.6.41', here fol. 108.
3. See Krausnick, 'Die Einsatzgruppen', p. 145. Initially, the unit that became Einsatzgruppe B was known as Einsatzgruppe C, and vice versa. On 11 July an alteration in the respective designation occurred 'for organisational reasons'. The designation of the subordinated commandos, on the other hand, remained the same 'for technical reasons'. See BArch Berlin, R 58/214, fols. 123–129, 'Ereignismeldung UdSSR Nr. 19', Chef der Sicherheitspolizei und des SD, 11 July 1941, here fol. 123. To avoid confusion, the unit will be referred to here throughout with the letter 'B'. A comprehensive study of Einsatzgruppe B is yet to be written. For a brief overview see Christian Gerlach, 'Die Einsatzgruppe B 1941/42', in Klein, ed., *Die Einsatzgruppen*, pp. 52–70.
4. See BArch-MA, RH 22/12, fols. 37b–37d, 'Betr.: Regelung des Einsatzes der Sicherheitspolizei und des SD im Verbande des Heeres', Oberkommando des Heeres, Gen. St. d. H./Gen. Qu., Az. Abt. Kriegsverwaltung, Nr. II/2101/41 geh., signed [Walther] von Brauchitsch, 28 April 1941, here fol. 37b: '*führende Emigranten, Saboteure, Terroristen usw.*'. Although the order differentiates between the tasks to be carried out, it does not differentiate between Sonderkommandos and Einsatzkommandos as such. The Sonderkommandos were later occasionally referred to as Vorkommandos, that is, 'advance commandos', because they operated further forward than the Einsatzkommandos. See BStU, MfS, HA IX/11 ZUV, Nr. 9, Bd. 31, fols. 34–44, 'Polizeilicher Tätigkeitsbericht für die Zeit vom 17. bis 23. August 1941 zum Vortrag bei der Heeresgruppe Mitte', Einsatzgruppe B, 25 August 1941, here fols. 37–38. See also HStAD, Q 61 Nr. 188, Testimony of the witness Bruno Streckenbach during the trial against Boettig, Landgericht Darmstadt, 25 March 1969. On the respective personnel strengths of EG B's Einsatzkommandos and Sonderkommandos see BArch-MA, RH 22/12, fol. 128, 'Kriegsgliederung der den Höh. SS–und Pol.Führern bei den Befehlshabern des rückw. Heeresgebiets unterstehenden Einsatzkräfte der Sicherheitspolizei und des SD', Gen. Qu. Abt. K. Verw. Nr. II/807/41 g.K.,

Anlage 3, 14 June 1941; BArch-MA, RH 22/224, fols. 107–108, 'Anlage zum
Korpsbefehl Nr. 18 vom 24.6.41', here fol. 108.

5. Whilst some of the commandos departed from Düben and Bad
Schmiedeberg, EK 9 departed from Pretzsch. See StArch Hamburg, 213–
12, Nr. 33, Bd. 16, fols. 7563–7572, 'Protokoll in der gerichtlichen
Voruntersuchung gegen Bruno Streckenbach', 23 September 1971, here
fol. 7565; UniA GI, 'Urteil Landgericht Berlin vom 22. Juni 1962', fol. 66.

6. BStU, MfS, HA IX/11 ZUV, Nr. 9, Bd. 31, fols. 3–17, 'Tätigkeitsbericht für
die Zeit vom 23.6.1941 bis 13.7.1941', here fol. 11; BArch-MA, RH 22/224,
fols. 107–108, 'Anlage zum Korpsbefehl Nr. 18 vom 24.6.41', here fol. 108;
UniA GI, 'Urteil Landgericht Berlin vom 22. Juni 1962', fol. 68. The drivers
had been conscripted and then assigned by the employment office to the
Gestapo or the SD (see Mallmann, 'Menschenjagd und Massenmord', p.
304). Each of the EGs was assigned a company from Reserve Police Battalion
9. See Alexandr Kruglov, 'Sekretnoye delo imperii. Massovoye unichtozheniye mirnogo naseleniya zonderkomandami SD na vremenno okkupirovannoi territorii SSSR v 1941–1944 gg. (dokumenty i materialy)', unpublished
manuscript, 2011, pp. 16–17. I am grateful to Alexandr Kruglov for providing me with a copy of the introduction and foreword to his as yet unpublished
collection of Einsatzgruppen documents.

7. UniA GI, 'Urteil Landgericht Berlin vom 22. Juni 1962', fol. 65. For an
overview of the activities of EK 9 between June 1941 and autumn 1943,
though with the main focus on the police platoon assigned to it, see Curilla,
Die deutsche Ordnungspolizei und der Holocaust, pp. 410–425.

8. BArch-MA, RH 22/224, fols. 107–108, 'Anlage zum Korpsbefehl Nr. 18
vom 24.6.41', here fol. 108; BStU, MfS, HA IX/11 ZUV, Nr. 9, Bd. 31, fols.
3–17, 'Tätigkeitsbericht für die Zeit vom 23.6.1941 bis 13.7.1941', here fol.
12. For similar figures see BArch Ludwigsburg, B 162/2400, fols. 9–13,
Hearing of Dr Alfred Filbert, 11 May 1959, here fol. 12.

9. BArch-MA, RH 22/224, fols. 107–108, 'Anlage zum Korpsbefehl Nr. 18
vom 24.6.41', here fol. 108.

10. LArch Berlin, B Rep. 058, Nr. 7178, fols. 82–86R, Hearing of the accused
Wilhelm Greiffenberger, 21 October 1960, here fol. 84R; UniA GI, 'Urteil
Landgericht Berlin vom 22. Juni 1962', fol. 65. In 1962, the court mistakenly
concluded that the Gestapo and the Criminal Police were unified in one
'police section', probably for the reason that Schneider headed both
Sections IV and V.

11. Gerlach, 'Die Einsatzgruppe B 1941/42', p. 63; Wolfgang Scheffler, 'Die
Einsatzgruppe A 1941/42', in Klein, ed., *Die Einsatzgruppen*, pp. 29–51, here
p. 44. See also BArch Ludwigsburg, B 162/4133, fols. 1580–1585, Hearing
of the witness Alfred Filbert, 22 February 1966, here fol. 1582.

12. LArch Berlin, B Rep. 058, Nr. 7178, fols. 82–86R, Hearing of the accused
Wilhelm Greiffenberger, 21 October 1960, here fol. 84R; LArch Berlin, B
Rep. 058, Nr. 7178, fols. 87–91R, Hearing of the accused Wilhelm
Greiffenberger in the criminal case against Dr Alfred Filbert et al.,
Landgericht Berlin, 24 October 1960, here fol. 91R; UniA GI, 'Urteil
Landgericht Berlin vom 22. Juni 1962', fols. 65–66. On the EM see Klaus-

Michael Mallmann, Andrej Angrick, Jürgen Matthäus and Martin Cüppers, eds., *Die "Ereignismeldungen UdSSR" 1941. Dokumente der Einsatzgruppen in der Sowjetunion* (Darmstadt: Wissenschaftliche Buchgesellschaft, 2011), esp. pp. 7–38; Hans-Heinrich Wilhelm, 'Die Einsatzgruppe A der Sicherheitspolizei und des SD 1941/42 – Eine exemplarische Studie', in Krausnick and Wilhelm, *Die Truppe des Weltanschauungskrieges*, pp. 279–643, here pp. 333–347; Krausnick and Wilhelm, *Die Truppe des Weltanschauungskrieges*, pp. 649–652; Alex J. Kay, 'Nicht nur Erschießungsmeldungen', *Einsicht 07. Bulletin des Fritz Bauer Instituts*, Vol. 4 (spring 2012), p. 64.

13. See Ronald Headland, *Messages of Murder: A Study of the Reports of the Einsatzgruppen of the Security Police and the Security Service, 1941–1943* (Rutherford: Fairleigh Dickinson University Press, 1992), pp. 38–40. A decade and a half ago, Klaus-Michael Mallmann noted that the sub-commando chiefs had been completely overlooked in the historiography (see Mallmann, 'Die Türöffner der "Endlösung"', p. 459). This assessment still holds true.

14. LArch Berlin, B Rep. 058, Nr. 7178, fols. 82–86R, Hearing of the accused Wilhelm Greiffenberger, 21 October 1960, here fol. 82R; BArch Ludwigsburg, B 162/2401, fols. 23–32, 'Urteil und Urteilsbegründung im SS-Prozeß Filbert u.a. Vorsitzender: Kammergerichtsrat Meyer', n.d. [22 June 1962], here fol. 26R.

15. LArch Berlin, B Rep. 058, Nr. 7174, fols. 91–113, Hearing of the accused Wilhelm Greiffenberger, Polizeipräsident in Berlin, 29 June 1960, here fols. 91–94 and 100–101; LArch Berlin, B Rep. 058, Nr. 7178, fols. 82–86R, Hearing of the accused Wilhelm Greiffenberger, 21 October 1960, here fols. 84–85R. Greiffenberger joined the NSDAP at the turn of the year 1931/32 and the SS in summer 1932. See LArch Berlin, B Rep. 058, Nr. 7174, fols. 91–94, Hearing of the accused Wilhelm Greiffenberger, 29 June 1960, here fol. 94. On Greiffenberger see also the copies of his SSO and RuSHA files (with photographs) in LArch Berlin, B Rep. 058, Nr. 7175, fols. 3–13; UniA GI, 'Urteil Landgericht Berlin vom 22. Juni 1962', fols. 37 and 53–56.

16. LArch Berlin, B Rep. 058, Nr. 7178, fols. 87–91R, Hearing of the accused Wilhelm Greiffenberger, 24 October 1960, here fol. 91; UniA GI, 'Urteil Landgericht Berlin vom 22. Juni 1962', fols. 44 and 47–48. On Schneider see ibid., fols. 37 and 44–50; LArch Berlin, B Rep. 058, Nr. 7171, fols. 3–11 and 12–18, Hearing of the accused Gerhard Schneider in the criminal case against Dr Alfred Filbert et al. for murder, Landgericht Berlin, 4 and 7 March 1960.

17. LArch Berlin, B Rep. 058, Nr. 7166, fols. 102–109, Hearing of Richard W., 22 April 1959, here fol. 109.

18. LArch Berlin, B Rep. 058, Nr. 7178, fols. 82–86R, Hearing of the accused Wilhelm Greiffenberger, 21 October 1960, here fol. 84R.

19. LArch Berlin, B Rep. 058, Nr. 7171, fols. 12–18, Hearing of the accused Gerhard Schneider, 7 March 1960, here fol. 16R.

20. Hearing of Gerhard Schneider, Hanover, 6 July 1965, cited in Uwe Ruprecht, 'SS-Mann 52729. Ein ganz gewöhnlicher deutscher Verbrecher',

unpublished manuscript, 2003. I am grateful to Uwe Ruprecht for providing me with a copy of his as yet unpublished manuscript.

21. LArch Berlin, B Rep. 058, Nr. 7171, fols. 256–259R, Hearing of the witness Heinrich Tunnat in the criminal case against Dr Alfred Filbert and Gerhard Schneider for murder, Landgericht Berlin, 17 May 1960, here fol. 257; BArch Ludwigsburg, B 162/20580, fols. 77–88, Hearing of the accused Heinrich Tunnat in the criminal case against Dr Alfred Filbert et al. for murder, Landgericht Berlin, 3 July 1961, here fol. 83; LArch Berlin, B Rep. 058, Nr. 7171, fols. 52–56R, Hearing of the accused Gerhard Schneider in the criminal case against Dr Alfred Filbert and Gerhard Schneider for murder, Landgericht Berlin, 14 March 1960, here fol. 56R; BArch Ludwigsburg, B 162/4114, fols. 1756–1758, Hearing of Heinrich Karl Walter Tunnat, Criminal Police in Oldenburg, StA Flensburg 2 Js 467/65 and StA Kiel 2 Js 762/63, 6 September 1965, here fol. 1756; UniA GI, 'Urteil Landgericht Berlin vom 22. Juni 1962', fols. 58 and 66. On Tunnat see ibid., fols. 38 and 57–59. There was some confusion during hearings of former commando members regarding Tunnat's name. For 'Donath' see LArch Berlin, B Rep. 058, Nr. 7166, fols. 9–12, 'Vernehmungsprotokoll', signed Richard Neubert, 22 January 1959, here fol. 9R; StArch München, Staatsanwaltschaften, 32970/5, fols. 966–970, Transcript of hearing of Dr Alfred Filbert, 9 June 1959, here fol. 969R; LArch Berlin, B Rep. 058, Nr. 7171, fols. 12–18, Hearing of the accused Gerhard Schneider, 7 March 1960, here fol. 18. For 'Donald' see LArch Berlin, B Rep. 058, Nr. 7171, fols. 266–270R, Hearing of the witness Karl Rath in the criminal case against Dr Alfred Filbert and Gerhard Schneider for murder, Landgericht Berlin, 23 May 1960, here fol. 269.
22. BArch Ludwigsburg, B 162/20580, fols. 11–29, Hearing of the accused Wilhelm Greiffenberger, I 4 – KJ 1, 30 June 1960, here fols. 15–16; LArch Berlin, B Rep. 058, Nr. 7178, fols. 87–91R, Hearing of the accused Wilhelm Greiffenberger, 24 October 1960, here fol. 91; BArch Ludwigsburg, B 162/20580, fols. 77–88, Hearing of the accused Heinrich Tunnat, 3 July 1961, here fol. 84.
23. BArch Ludwigsburg, B 162/20580, fols. 11–29, Hearing of the accused Wilhelm Greiffenberger, 30 June 1960, here fol. 17.
24. LArch Berlin, B Rep. 058, Nr. 7178, fols. 87–91R, Hearing of the accused Wilhelm Greiffenberger, 24 October 1960, here fol. 91.
25. UniA GI, 'Urteil Landgericht Berlin vom 22. Juni 1962', fol. 66.
26. BStU, MfS, HA IX/11 ZUV, Nr. 9, Bd. 31, fols. 3–17, 'Tätigkeitsbericht für die Zeit vom 23.6.1941 bis 13.7.1941', here fols. 3–4; BArch-MA, RH 22/224, fols. 109–109R, 'Korpsbefehl Nr. 19', Befehlshaber des rückw. Heeres-Gebietes 102, Ia Br. B. Nr. 300/41 geh., 27 June 1941, here fol. 109; BArch Berlin, R 58/214, fols. 102–117, 'Ereignismeldung UdSSR Nr. 17', Chef der Sicherheitspolizei und des SD, 9 July 1941, here fols. 103–104; UniA GI, 'Urteil Landgericht Berlin vom 22. Juni 1962', fol. 68, according to which Einsatzkommando 9 did not depart from Pretzsch until 26 or 27 June; LArch Berlin, B Rep. 058, Nr. 7166, fols. 9–12, 'Vernehmungsprotokoll', signed

Richard Neubert, 22 January 1959, here fol. 9R. On Neubert see Wolfgang
Zaehle, '"Die Sühne kommt spät". Nachtrag zum Prozeß EK 9', *Die Andere
Zeitung*, 5 July 1962, p. 5, in Archiv der Vereinigung der Verfolgten des
Naziregimes – Bund der Antifaschistinnen und Antifaschisten (VVN-BdA
Bundesvereinigung, Berlin (hereafter Archiv der VVN-BdA
Bundesvereinigung), Dossier Alfred Filbert. On the assignment of EK 9 to
the 403rd Security Division see BArch-MA, RH 26–403/4a, 'Zusätze zum
Einsatzbefehl Ia 142/41 g.Kdos. v. 16.6.41', Sicherungs-Division 403, Ia
318/41 g., 1 July 1941.

27. LArch Berlin, B Rep. 058, Nr. 7167, fols. 53–57, Hearing of Richard
Neubert, 26 August 1959, here fols. 56; LArch Berlin, B Rep. 058, Nr.
7178, fols. 87–91R, Hearing of the accused Wilhelm Greiffenberger, 24
October 1960, here fol. 88; LArch Berlin, B Rep. 058, Nr. 7171, fols. 12–
18, Hearing of the accused Gerhard Schneider, 7 March 1960, here fol. 18.
28. LArch Berlin, B Rep. 058, Nr. 7178, fols. 87–91R, Hearing of the accused
Wilhelm Greiffenberger, 24 October 1960, here fol. 88R; LArch Berlin, B
Rep. 058, Nr. 7174, fols. 91–113, Hearing of the accused Wilhelm
Greiffenberger, 29 June 1960, here fol. 98. See also UniA GI, 'Urteil
Landgericht Berlin vom 22. Juni 1962', fol. 68.
29. LArch Berlin, B Rep. 058, Nr. 7178, fols. 87–91R, Hearing of the accused
Wilhelm Greiffenberger, 24 October 1960, here fol. 88R; BArch
Ludwigsburg, B 162/20580, fols. 77–88, Hearing of the accused Heinrich
Tunnat, 3 July 1961, here fol. 88. See also UniA GI, 'Urteil Landgericht
Berlin vom 22. Juni 1962', fols. 68–69.
30. BArch Ludwigsburg, B 162/3633, fols. 7574–7581, 'Protokoll in der gericht-
lichen Voruntersuchung gegen Bruno Streckenbach', signed Wilhelm
Greiffenberger, Landgericht Hamburg, 1 October 1971, here fol. 7577.
31. BArch Ludwigsburg, B 162/20862, fols. 2–3, Notes by the Chief Public
Prosecutor on testimony given by Gustav Wolters on 5 June 1962, 3 P (K)
Ks 1/62, 28 May 1964, here fol. 2; LArch Berlin, B Rep. 058, Nr. 3059, fols.
62–71, Hearing of the witness Walter T., I 1 – KJ 1, 20 February 1964, here
fols. 62–62R. I am grateful to Martin Holler for drawing my attention to the
latter testimony. On Gustav Wolters see Uwe Ruprecht, 'Ein offenes
Geheimnis', *Jungle World*, No. 20, 7 May 2003. On the mandate of the
Einsatzgruppen regarding the mass murder of Soviet Jewry see especially
(in chronological order) the essays by Krausnick, 'Hitler und die Befehle an
die Einsatzgruppen', and Alfred Streim, 'Zur Eröffnung des allgemeinen
Judenvernichtungsbefehls gegenüber den Einsatzgruppen' (pp. 107–119),
in Jäckel and Rohwer, eds., *Der Mord an den Juden im Zweiten Weltkrieg*;
Christopher R. Browning, *Fateful Months: Essays on the Emergence of the
Final Solution* (New York/London: Holmes & Meier, 1985), pp. 8–38;
Headland, 'The *Einsatzgruppen*'; Ogorreck, *Die Einsatzgruppen*; Gerlach,
Kalkulierte Morde, pp. 628–646; Peter Longerich, *Der ungeschriebene Befehl:
Hitler und der Weg zur "Endlösung"* (Munich: Piper, 2001), pp. 97–109;
Wildt, *Generation des Unbedingten*, pp. 553–561; Curilla, *Die deutsche
Ordnungspolizei und der Holocaust*, pp. 86–123; Dieckmann, *Deutsche*

Besatzungspolitik in Litauen, Vol. 1, pp. 391–401; Kay, 'Transition to Genocide, July 1941'.

32. BArch-MA, RH 26–403/2, 'Kriegstagebuch der Sich. Div. 403', entry for 30 June 1941, fols. 26R–27; BArch Berlin, R 58/214, fols. 45–50, 'Ereignismeldung UdSSR Nr. 9', Chef der Sicherheitspolizei und des SD, 1 July 1941, here fol. 48; LArch Berlin, B Rep. 058, Nr. 7178, fols. 87–91R, Hearing of the accused Wilhelm Greiffenberger, 24 October 1960, here fols. 89–89R; LArch Berlin, B Rep. 058, Nr. 7178, fols. 92–97R, Hearing of the accused Wilhelm Greiffenberger in the criminal case against Dr Filbert et al., Landgericht Berlin, 25 October 1960, here fol. 92R; LArch Berlin, B Rep. 058, Nr. 7174, fols. 91–113, Hearing of the accused Wilhelm Greiffenberger, 29 June 1960, here fol. 99. See also UniA GI, 'Urteil Landgericht Berlin vom 22. Juni 1962', fol. 69, where the date is given as 1 July.

33. UniA GI, 'Urteil Landgericht Berlin vom 22. Juni 1962', fol. 69; BArch Ludwigsburg, B 162/3922, fols. 434–478, 'Anklageschrift', Indictment against Kurt Schulz-Isenbeck for acting as an accessory to the murder of at least 90 people on 5 July 1941 in Lida, Staatsanwaltschaft Dortmund, 45 Js 15/62, 45 Js 15/62, 30 June 1970, here fol. 460; LArch Berlin, B Rep. 058, Nr. 7174, fols. 91–113, Hearing of the accused Wilhelm Greiffenberger, 29 June 1960, here fol. 99; LArch Berlin, B Rep. 058, Nr. 7178, fols. 87–91R, Hearing of the accused Wilhelm Greiffenberger, 24 October 1960, here fols. 90–90R; BStU, MfS, HA IX/11 ZUV, Nr. 9, Bd. 31, fols. 3–17, 'Tätigkeitsbericht für die Zeit vom 23.6.1941 bis 13.7.1941', here fol. 6; BArch Berlin, R 58/214, fols. 51–56, 'Ereignismeldung UdSSR Nr. 10', Chef der Sicherheitspolizei und des SD, 2 July 1941, here fol. 55; BArch Berlin, R 58/214, fols. 57–65, 'Ereignismeldung UdSSR Nr. 11', Chef der Sicherheitspolizei und des SD, 3 July 1941, here fol. 62. Haupt was already dead at the time of Filbert's trial. See BArch Ludwigsburg, B 162/2401, fols. 23–32, 'Urteil und Urteilsbegründung im SS-Prozeß Filbert', n.d. [22 June 1962], here fol. 27.

34. Gerlach, *Kalkulierte Morde*, p. 511. See also ibid., p. 512.

35. BArch Ludwigsburg, B 162/3922, fols. 434–478, 'Anklageschrift', Indictment against Kurt Schulz-Isenbeck for acting as an accessory to the murder of at least 90 people on 5 July 1941 in Lida, Staatsanwaltschaft Dortmund, 45 Js 15/62, 30 June 1970, here fols. 460–461; BArch Ludwigsburg, B 162/3921, fols. 349–357, Hearing of the witness Felix U., 45 Js 15/62, 25 August 1966, here fol. 352; UniA GI, 'Urteil Landgericht Berlin vom 22. Juni 1962', fols. 69–70.

36. BArch Ludwigsburg, B 162/3921, fols. 349–357, Hearing of the witness Felix U., 25 August 1966, here fols. 352–353.

37. BArch Ludwigsburg, B 162/3922, fols. 434–478, 'Anklageschrift', Indictment against Kurt Schulz-Isenbeck, Staatsanwaltschaft Dortmund, 30 June 1970, here fol. 460; BArch Ludwigsburg, B 162/3921, fols. 349–357, Hearing of the witness Felix U., 25 August 1966, here fol. 350. On the Commissar Order see Felix Römer, *Der Kommissarbefehl: Wehrmacht und NS-Verbrechen an der Ostfront 1941/42* (Paderborn: Schöningh, 2008); Felix Römer, 'The Wehrmacht in the War of Ideologies: The Army and Hitler's Criminal Orders on the Eastern Front', in Alex J. Kay, Jeff

Rutherford and David Stahel, eds., *Nazi Policy on the Eastern Front, 1941: Total War, Genocide, and Radicalization* (Rochester, NY: University of Rochester Press, 2012), pp. 73–100.

38. 'Befehl Nr. 3', Chef der Sicherheitspolizei und des SD, 1 July 1941, reproduced in: Klein, ed., *Die Einsatzgruppen*, pp. 321–322, here p. 321: '[...] kein Angehöriger der SP und des SD in diesem Ort.' Both Gerlach, *Kalkulierte Morde*', p. 544, and Longerich, *Der ungeschriebene Befehl*, p. 101, date Himmler and Heydrich's presence in Grodno to 30 June, although Heydrich explicitly states in his order that he accompanied Himmler there on 1 July. According to Himmler's appointments diary, he visited Grodno on 30 June and returned the same evening; no mention is made of Heydrich (see Witte et al., eds., *Der Dienstkalender Heinrich Himmlers 1941/42*, p. 181, entry for 30 June).

39. BArch Berlin, R 58/214, fols. 139–153, 'Ereignismeldung UdSSR Nr. 21', Chef der Sicherheitspolizei und des SD, 13 July 1941, here fol. 151 (both quotes). In a later report, Nebe also emphasised – presumably in response to Heydrich's rebuke – that a sub-commando had been sent to Grodno and Lida for 30 June (see BStU, MfS, HA IX/11 ZUV, Nr. 9, Bd. 31, fols. 3–17, 'Tätigkeitsbericht für die Zeit vom 23.6.1941 bis 13.7.1941', here fol. 6). Himmler and Heydrich visited Grodno again on 11 July (see Witte et al., eds., *Der Dienstkalender Heinrich Himmlers 1941/42*, p. 183, entry for 11 July).

40. BStU, MfS, HA IX/11 ZUV, Nr. 9, Bd. 31, fols. 3–17, 'Tätigkeitsbericht für die Zeit vom 23.6.1941 bis 13.7.1941', here fol. 6. See also UniA GI, 'Urteil Landgericht Berlin vom 22. Juni 1962', fol. 69, where the date is given as 2 July.

41. See Herman Kruk, *The Last Days of the Jerusalem of Lithuania: Chronicles from the Vilna Ghetto and the Camps, 1939–1944*, edited and with an introduction by Benjamin Harshav, translated from Yiddish by Barbara Harshav (New Haven, CT/London: YIVO Institute for Jewish Research/Yale University Press, 2002); Saul Friedländer, *The Years of Extermination: Nazi Germany and the Jews, 1939–1945* (New York: HarperCollins, 2007), pp. 219–220.

42. See Hearing of the witness Abra[ha]m Su[t]zkever, 27 February 1946, in: *IMG*, Vol. 8 (Nuremberg: Sekretariat des Gerichtshofs, 1947), pp. 333–340, here p. 334; Benjamin Harshav, 'Introduction: Herman Kruk's Holocaust Writings', in Kruk, *The Last Days of the Jerusalem of Lithuania*, pp. xxi–lii, here p. xxvi.

43. NKVD = *Narodnyy Komissariat Vnutrennikh Del* (People's Commissariat for Internal Affairs). As in Vilnius, the Einsatzkommandos and Sonderkommandos occupied the NKVD offices in a series of seized cities, including Brest, Kaunas, L'viv, Siauliai, Grodno, Smolensk, Vinnytsia, Vileyka and Velizh. See BArch Berlin, R 58/214, fols. 3–8, 'Sammelmeldung "UdSSR" Nr. 1', signed [Heinrich] Müller, 23 June 1941, here fol. 3; ibid., fols. 39–44, 'Ereignismeldung UdSSR Nr. 8', Chef der Sicherheitspolizei und des SD, 30 June 1941, here fol. 40; ibid., fols. 45–50, 'Ereignismeldung UdSSR Nr. 9', 1 July 1941, here fol. 46; ibid., fols. 57–65, 'Ereignismeldung UdSSR Nr. 11', 3 July 1941, here fol. 61; ibid., fols. 74–79, 'Ereignismeldung UdSSR Nr. 13', Chef der Sicherheitspolizei und des SD, 5 July 1941, here fols. 77–78; BArch Berlin, R 58/215, fols.

48–65, 'Ereignismeldung UdSSR Nr. 34', Chef der Sicherheitspolizei und
des SD, 26 July 1941, here fol. 58; ibid., fols. 222–245, 'Ereignismeldung
UdSSR Nr. 47', Chef der Sicherheitspolizei und des SD, 9 August 1941, here
fol. 228; ibid., fols. 259–270, 'Ereignismeldung UdSSR Nr. 50', Chef der
Sicherheitspolizei und des SD, 12 August 1941, here fol. 266; BArch Berlin,
R 58/216, fols. 215–246, 'Ereignismeldung UdSSR Nr. 67', Chef der
Sicherheitspolizei und des SD, 29 August 1941, here fol. 239. In an order
dated 4 July, Heydrich had instructed the Einsatzgruppen to seize NKVD
buildings before the arrival of the Wehrmacht's counterintelligence troops
(see 'Befehl Nr. 6', Chef der Sicherheitspolizei und des SD, 4 July 1941,
reproduced in: Klein, ed., *Die Einsatzgruppen*, pp. 329–330, here p. 330). In
fact, this had already been happening since the very first day of the campaign.
44. LArch Berlin, B Rep. 058, Nr. 7171, fols. 19–23, Hearing of the accused
Gerhard Schneider in the criminal case against Dr Alfred Filbert et al. for
murder, Landgericht Berlin, 10 March 1960, here fol. 119R; LArch Berlin, B
Rep. 058, Nr. 7166, fols. 102–109, Hearing of Richard W., 22 April 1959,
here fol. 105; BArch Ludwigsburg, B 162/3921, fols. 261–263, Hearing of
Fritz S., Landeskriminalamt Baden-Württemberg – Sonderkommission –
Zentrale Stelle, 18 July 1959, here fol. 262.
45. LArch Berlin, B Rep. 058, Nr. 7166, fols. 102–109, Hearing of Richard W.,
22 April 1959, here fol. 105; UniA GI, 'Urteil Landgericht Berlin vom 22.
Juni 1962', fol. 121.
46. BArch Berlin, R 58/214, fols. 102–117, 'Ereignismeldung UdSSR Nr. 17', 9
July 1941, here fols. 114–115; BArch Berlin, R 58/214, fols. 139–153,
'Ereignismeldung UdSSR Nr. 21', 13 July 1941, here fol. 148; BArch
Berlin, R 58/215, fols. 156–188, 'Ereignismeldung UdSSR Nr. 43', Chef
der Sicherheitspolizei und des SD, 5 August 1941, here fol. 171.
47. Sonderkommando 7a under SS-Obersturmbannführer Dr Walter Blume was
in Vilnius from 27 June to 2 July carrying out 'Security Police tasks'. See
BStU, MfS, HA IX/11 ZUV, Nr. 9, Bd. 31, fols. 3–17, 'Tätigkeitsbericht für
die Zeit vom 23.6.1941 bis 13.7.1941', here fol. 5. See also BArch Berlin, R
58/214, fols. 51–56, 'Ereignismeldung UdSSR Nr. 10', 2 July 1941, here fols.
54–55; BArch Berlin, R 58/214, fols. 57–65, 'Ereignismeldung UdSSR Nr.
11', 3 July 1941, here fol. 62. The first units of the German Army had
marched into the city at daybreak on 24 June. See Grigorij Schur, *Die Juden
von Wilna: Die Aufzeichungen des Grigorij Schur*, ed. Wladimir Porudominskij,
translated from Russian by Jochen Hellbeck (Munich: dtv, 1999 [1997]),
p. 37.
48. UniA GI, 'Urteil Landgericht Berlin vom 22. Juni 1962', fol. 71; Dieckmann,
Deutsche Besatzungspolitik in Litauen, Vol. 1, pp. 354 and 360. On
Schauschütz see Dieckmann, *Deutsche Besatzungspolitik in Litauen*, Vol. 1,
pp. 296 and 355.
49. BArch Berlin, R 58/214, fols. 139–153, 'Ereignismeldung UdSSR Nr.
21', 13 July 1941, here fol. 147: *'Der litauische Ordnungsdienst, der nach
Auflösung der litauischen politischen Polizei dem Einsatzkommando unterstellt
worden ist, wurde angewiesen, sich an der Liquidierungen der Juden zu beteili-
gen. Hierfür wurden 150 litauische Beamte abgestellt, die die Juden festnehmen*

und sie in Konzentrationslager schaffen, wo sie noch am gleichen Tage der Sonderbehandlung unterzogen werden. Diese Arbeit hat jetzt begonnen, und so werden laufend täglich nunmehr etwa 500 Juden u. a. Saboteure liquidiert.'

50. BArch Berlin, R 58/214, fols. 139–153, 'Ereignismeldung UdSSR Nr. 21', 13 July 1941, here fol. 147; Dieckmann, *Deutsche Besatzungspolitik in Litauen,* Vol. 1, pp. 354–355.

51. UniA GI, 'Urteil Landgericht Berlin vom 22. Juni 1962', fol. 71. See also BArch Berlin, R 58/215, fols. 156–188, 'Ereignismeldung UdSSR Nr. 43', 5 August 1941, here fol. 171. On the availability of voluntary shooters among locals in Lithuania and elsewhere and its influence in the switchover to genocide against Soviet Jewry see Dovid Katz, 'Review Article. Detonation of the Holocaust in 1941: A Tale of Two Books', *East European Jewish Affairs,* Vol. 41, No. 3 (December 2011), pp. 207–221, here pp. 210–212.

52. BArch Berlin, R 58/214, fols. 102–117, 'Ereignismeldung UdSSR Nr. 17', 9 July 1941, here fol. 115.

53. LArch Berlin, B Rep. 058, Nr. 7166, fols. 102–109, Hearing of Richard W., 22 April 1959, here fol. 106: *'So, die ersten Juden hätten wir erledigt.'* See also LArch Berlin, B Rep. 058, Nr. 7168, fols. 81–85, Hearing of the witness Richard W. in the criminal case against Dr Alfred Filbert for murder, Landgericht Berlin, 28 January 1960, here fol. 82R.

54. LArch Berlin, B Rep. 058, Nr. 7166, fols. 102–109, Hearing of Richard W., 22 April 1959, here fol. 106. On sadism as a reason for performing violent acts see Roy F. Baumeister and W. Keith Campbell, 'The Intrinsic Appeal of Evil: Sadism, Sensational Thrills, and Threatened Egotism', *Personality and Social Psychology Review,* Vol. 3, No. 3 (1999), pp. 210–221, here pp. 211–215. The authors conclude, however, that sadistic pleasure generally emerges only gradually. Filbert's orderly described him as a sadist, however, already after the *first* shooting operation Filbert led personally.

55. BStU, MfS, HA IX/11 ZUV, Nr. 9, Bd. 31, fols. 3–17, 'Tätigkeitsbericht für die Zeit vom 23.6.1941 bis 13.7.1941', here fol. 6. See also BArch Berlin, R 58/214, fols. 74–79, 'Ereignismeldung UdSSR Nr. 13', 5 July 1941, here fol. 78. The district court in Berlin concluded that the sub-commando had rejoined the rest of EK 9 in Vilnius 'around 5 July' (see UniA GI, 'Urteil Landgericht Berlin vom 22. Juni 1962', fol. 70).

56. BArch Berlin, R 58/214, fols. 139–153, 'Ereignismeldung UdSSR Nr. 21', 13 July 1941, here fol. 147.

57. BStU, RHE 4/85 SU, Bd. 7, fols. 172–175, 'Abt. III (Polizeiliche Angelegenheiten)', Einsatzgruppe B, n.d. [18 July 1941], here fol. 173; LArch Berlin, B Rep. 058, Nr. 7168, fols. 75–80R, Hearing of the witness Karl B. in the criminal case against Dr Alfred Filbert for murder, Landgericht Berlin, 26 January 1960, here fol. 76; LArch Berlin, B Rep. 058, Nr. 7167, fols. 23–26, Transcript of hearing of Wilhelm W., 2 March 1959, here fol. 24; UniA GI, 'Urteil Landgericht Berlin vom 22. Juni 1962', fol. 73. See also BArch Berlin, R 58/214, fols. 180–196, 'Ereignismeldung UdSSR Nr. 24', Chef der Sicherheitspolizei und des SD, 16 July 1941, here fol. 186, which makes it clear that this shooting took place in addition to those being carried out on a daily basis outside the city. Although the court put the number of

victims of this shooting at 'at least 20' (fols. 74 and 76), a series of participants in the operation estimated it to be 'ca. 50–60 male persons' (Wilhelm W.), 'ca. 60 – 80' (Wilhelm S.), '60–80 Jews' (Paul N.), or 'around 80 men' (Gerhard Schneider): see LArch Berlin, B Rep 058, Nr. 7167, fols. 15–21, Hearing of Wilhelm W., 15 May 1959, here fol. 18; LArch Berlin, B Rep. 058, Nr. 7166, fols. 218–226, Hearing of Wilhelm S., 11 May 1959, here fol. 223; LArch Berlin, B Rep. 058, Nr. 7171, fols. 148–151R, Hearing of the witness Paul N. in the criminal case against Dr Alfred Filbert and Gerhard Schneider for murder, Landgericht Berlin, 5 April 1960, here fol. 149R; LArch Berlin, B Rep. 058, Nr. 7171, fols. 19–23, Hearing of the accused Gerhard Schneider, 7 March 1960, here fol. 22. The staff of the 403rd Security Division put the number at '300 Jews': see BArch-MA, RH 26–403/4a, 'Bericht über die Tätigkeit des Div.Stabes in Wilna', n.d. [14 July 1941]. In a report to Army Group Centre, EG B – citing a report submitted by EK 9 – put the number of those 'apprehended and, following the confiscation of their property, shot' (*festgenommen und nach Beschlagnahme ihres Vermögens erschossen*) at '408 Jews'. As it was concluded at Filbert's trial that not all those who were arrested were then actually shot (see UniA GI, 'Urteil Landgericht Berlin vom 22. Juni 1962', fol. 74), it seems safe to opt for a *conservative* estimate of 300 Jewish dead.

58. LArch Berlin, B Rep. 058, Nr. 7166, fols. 218–226, Hearing of Wilhelm S., 11 May 1959, here fol. 223; LArch Berlin, B Rep 058, Nr. 7167, fols. 15–21, Hearing of Wilhelm W., 15 May 1959, here fol. 18; UniA GI, 'Urteil Landgericht Berlin vom 22. Juni 1962', fols. 73–76.

59. BArch-MA, RH 26–403/4a, 'Bericht über die Tätigkeit des Div.Stabes in Wilna', n.d. [14 July 1941]; Dieckmann, *Deutsche Besatzungspolitik in Litauen*, Vol. 1, pp. 356 and 358, fn. 285. Dieter Pohl misdates the report of the staff of the 403rd Security Division to August. See Dieter Pohl, *Die Herrschaft der Wehrmacht: Deutsche Militärbesatzung in der Sowjetunion, 1941–1944* (Munich: Oldenbourg, 2008), p. 157, fn. 40.

60. LArch Berlin, B Rep. 058, Nr. 7167, fols. 77–87, Hearing of Otto H., 1 P Js 198/59 K, Generalstaatsanwalt beim Landgericht, 5 March 1959, here fols. 80–81; LArch Berlin, B Rep. 058, Nr. 7166, fols. 163–170, Hearing of Richard Neubert, 4 May 1959, here fols. 165–166; UniA GI, 'Urteil Landgericht Berlin vom 22. Juni 1962', fol. 75.

61. LArch Berlin, B Rep. 058, Nr. 7166, fols. 13–18R, Transcript of hearing of Karl B., 24 February 1959, here fol. 14R: *'Was ist da los mit den Schießbudenfiguren. Da brauchen Sie nicht so zu zittern!'* See also UniA GI, 'Urteil Landgericht Berlin vom 22. Juni 1962', fols. 75–76.

62. LArch Berlin, B Rep. 058, Nr. 7166, fols. 13–18R, Transcript of hearing of Karl B., 24 February 1959, here fols. 14–14R; LArch Berlin, B Rep. 058, Nr. 7167, fols. 77–87, Hearing of Otto H., 1 P Js 198/59 K, Generalstaatsanwalt beim Landgericht, 5 March 1959, here fols. 80–81; LArch Berlin, B Rep. 058, Nr. 7166, fols. 218–226, Hearing of Wilhelm S., 11 May 1959, here fol. 223; UniA GI, 'Urteil Landgericht Berlin vom 22. Juni 1962', fol. 75.

63. LArch Berlin, B Rep. 058, Nr. 7166, fols. 176–186, Hearing of Dr Alfred Filbert, 12 May 1959, here fol. 178; UniA GI, 'Urteil Landgericht Berlin vom

22. Juni 1962', fol. 104; 'Filbert: Ich selbst schoß vorbei. Zweiter Tag im
Prozeß gegen das Einsatzkommando IX in Berlin', *Augsburger Allgemeine*,
17 May 1962.

64. UniA GI, 'Urteil Landgericht Berlin vom 22. Juni 1962', fols. 104–105.

65. Earl, *The Nuremberg SS-Einsatzgruppen Trial*, pp. 103 and 120: 'there is no
evidence that any of the *Einsatzgruppenführer* actually executed people
personally'.

66. StArch München, Staatsanwaltschaften, 32970/5, fols. 966–970, Transcript
of hearing of Dr Alfred Filbert, 9 June 1959, here fol. 967; LArch Berlin, B
Rep. 058, Nr. 7168, fols. 39–45R, Hearing of the accused Dr Alfred Filbert,
14 January 1960, here fol. 44R; StArch Hamburg, 213–12, Nr. 33, Bd. 16,
fols. 7563–7572, 'Protokoll in der gerichtlichen Voruntersuchung gegen
Bruno Streckenbach', 23 September 1971, here fol. 7572. Kurt Werner, a
driver in Sonderkommando 4a, testified in 1968 that an order was issued by
SS-Standartenführer Paul Blobel, the commander of SK 4a, to the effect that
all members of the commando had to actively take part in larger executions.
See *Babi Jar – Das vergessene Massaker*, dir. Christine Rütten and Lutz
Rentner (Germany: Hessischer Rundfunk, 2012). Georg Heuser, head of
the Gestapo in occupied Minsk, also testified at his trial in Koblenz that an
order 'from above' had stipulated that every member of his commando shoot
at least once. See Dietrich Strothmann, 'Die gehorsamen Mörder. Das
Heuser-Verfahren in Koblenz – Porträt eines Prozesses', *Die Zeit*, 7 June
1963, p. 4. The head of Einsatzkommando 8, SS-Sturmbannführer Dr
Otto Bradfisch, denied after the war that there had been such an order. See
'LG München I vom 21.7.1961, 22 Ks 1/61', reprinted in: *Justiz und NS-
Verbrechen*, Vol. XVII, ed. Irene Sagel-Grande, H. H. Fuchs and C. F. Rüter
(Amsterdam: University Press Amsterdam, 1977), No. 519, pp. 661–708,
here p. 694.

67. LArch Berlin, B Rep. 058, Nr. 7166, fols. 176–186, Hearing of Dr Alfred
Filbert, 12 May 1959, here fol. 178; StArch München, Staatsanwaltschaften,
32970/5, fols. 966–970, Transcript of hearing of Dr Alfred Filbert, 9 June
1959, here fol. 967. During these interrogations Filbert described the events
of mid-July as 'this first assignment' (*diesem ersten Einsatz*) and 'the first
[shooting] operation in Vilnius', respectively.

68. LArch Berlin, B Rep. 058, Nr. 7166, fols. 135–153, 'Vernehmungs-
Niederschrift' of Paul Dinter, 1a Js 1522/58, 3 April 1959, here fols.
143–145; 'LG München I vom 21.7.1961, 22 Ks 1/61', reprinted in:
Justiz und NS-Verbrechen, Vol. XVII, ed. Sagel-Grande, Fuchs and
Rüter, No. 519, pp. 661–708, here pp. 672, 674–675, 692 and 694.
Bradfisch participated actively in shooting operations directed against
both men and women. On Bradfisch see Peter Klein, 'Der Mordgehilfe:
Schuld und Sühne des Dr. Otto Bradfisch', in Klaus-Michael Mallmann
and Andrej Angrick, eds., *Die Gestapo nach 1945. Karrieren, Konflikte,
Konstruktionen* (Darmstadt: Wissenschaftliche Buchgesellschaft, 2009),
pp. 221–234.

69. For post-war statements to the effect that Karl Jäger, head of EK 3 of EG A,
also participated actively in shooting operations, see Wette, *Karl Jäger*,

p. 107. Bruno Müller, second head of SK 11b of EG D, personally shot a Jewish mother and her two-year-old child with his pistol, declaring: 'You must die in order that we can live' (*Ihr mußt sterben, damit wir leben können*). See Mallmann, 'Die Türöffner der "Endlösung"', pp. 449–450; Angrick, *Besatzungspolitik und Massenmord*, p. 188. Even the Higher SS and Police Leader for Russia South, SS-Obergruppenführer Friedrich Jeckeln, shot and killed a Jewish man after he, Jeckeln, had finished addressing members of the 8th Regiment of the 1st SS Infantry Brigade, who had just carried out a massacre of Jews in Starokonstantinov. See Martin Cüppers, *Wegbereiter der Shoah. Die Waffen-SS, der Kommandostab Reichsführer-SS und die Judenvernichtung 1939 – 1945* (Darmstadt: Wissenschaftliche Buchgesellschaft, 2005), pp. 167–168. On commando chiefs killing with their own hands see also Ingrao, *Croire et détruire*, pp. 332–336 and 449.

70. Yitzhak Arad, *Ghetto in Flames: The Struggle and Destruction of the Jews of Vilna in the Holocaust* (Jerusalem: Yad Vashem, 1980), pp. 77–78: '*Thus Filbert turned each individual in his unit into accomplices in crime*' (p. 78). On the importance of group conformity and peer pressure in the killing process see Christopher R. Browning, *Ordinary Men: Reserve Police Battalion 101 and the Final Solution in Poland*, exp. ed. (London: Penguin, 1998 [1992]), pp. 174–175, 184–186 and 189; Harald Welzer, *Täter. Wie aus ganz normalen Menschen Massenmörder werden* (Frankfurt am Main: S. Fischer, 2005), pp. 82–91.

71. BArch-MA, RH 26–403/4a, 'Bericht über die Tätigkeit des Div.Stabes in Wilna', n.d. [14 July 1941]: '*Geheime Feldpolizei und Sicherheitsdienst (SD) wirken zusammen bei der Bekämpfung jüdischer Übergriffe. Sämtliche Juden sind durch Abzeichen gekennzeichnet. Eine grosse Zahl von Erschiessungen hat bereits stattgefunden. Ich habe mit dem sehr loyalen Führer des SD, Obersturmbannführer Dr. Filbert, vereinbart, dass diese Erschiessungen möglichst unauffällig stattfinden und der Truppe verborgen bleiben.*'

72. BArch-MA, RH 26–403/4a, 'Bericht über die Tätigkeit des Div.Stabes in Wilna', n.d. [14 July 1941]; BArch-MA, RH 26–403/4a, 'Tätigkeitsbericht. I c / Juli 1941', n.d.

73. This term was used by Filbert. See LArch Berlin, B Rep. 058, Nr. 7187, fols. 83–91, Hearing of the accused Heinrich Tunnat in the criminal case against Dr Filbert et al. for murder, Landgericht Berlin, 4 July 1961, here fol. 89.

74. UniA GI, 'Urteil Landgericht Berlin vom 22. Juni 1962', fol. 76.

75. BStU, RHE 4/85 SU, Bd. 7, fols. 172–175, 'Abt. III (Polizeiliche Angelegenheiten)', Einsatzgruppe B, n.d. [18 July 1941], here fol. 173. This document has been dated to 20 July by Angrick et al., eds., *Deutsche Besatzungsherrschaft in der UdSSR*, doc. 24, pp. 73–75, here p. 73. This is presumably because the earliest sets of initials at the top of the document are from 20 July. However, there are two sets of initials dated 18 July at the *bottom* of the document. This means that the document must date from no later than 18 July. Its contents cover the period up to and including 16 July.

76. UniA GI, 'Urteil Landgericht Berlin vom 22. Juni 1962', fols. 76–77; Dieckmann, *Deutsche Besatzungspolitik in Litauen*, Vol. 1, pp. 356 and 360.

77. UniA GI, 'Urteil Landgericht Berlin vom 22. Juni 1962', fols. 71–72.
78. Kazimierz Sakowicz, *Ponary Diary, 1941–1943: A Bystander's Account of a Mass Murder* (New Haven, CT/London: Yale University Press, 2005), ed. Yitzhak Arad, translated from Polish by Yad Vashem, pp. 11–14, entries for 11 and 23 July. Sakowicz began keeping his diary on 11 July. The entries for 11 and 23 July also contain information referring to events that happened after these respective dates because Sakowicz sometimes returned to an entry and added new information. See Sakowicz, *Ponary Diary*, Note on the Text. On Sakowicz see Rachel Margolis, 'Foreword', in Sakowicz, *Ponary Diary*, pp. vii–xii, here pp. ix–x. The original calendar from Sakowicz's diary for November 1941 can be found in the Valstybinis Vilniaus Gaono Žydų Muziejus, Holokausto ekspozicija, Žaliasis namas [Vilna Gaon State Jewish Museum, Holocaust Exhibition, Green House], Vilnius.
79. LArch Berlin, B Rep. 058, Nr. 7167, Transcripts of hearings of the following members of the 96th Infantry Division: Hans G. (fols. 150–161, 29 May 1959, and fol. 162, 5 June 1959); Ernst L. (fols. 164–172, 4 June 1959); Paul S. (fols. 173–182, 4 June 1959); Josef G. (fols. 183–192, 5 June 1959); Otto Schroff (fols. 193–194, 29 June 1959, and fols. 195–202, 5 June 1959); Fritz H. (fols. 203–212, 5 June 1959); Friedrich M. (fols. 213–218, 6 June 1959); Georg H. (fols. 219–224, 6 June 1959); Alex P. (fols. 225–235, 18 June 1959, and fols. 236–237, 29 June 1959); Johann I. (fols. 238–245, 19 June 1959); Joseph B. (fols. 246–252, 19 June 1959); Werner H. (fols. 253–262, 21 July 1959). See also UniA GI, 'Urteil Landgericht Berlin vom 22. Juni 1962', fol. 73.
80. See LArch Berlin, B Rep. 058, Nr. 7167, Transcript of hearing of Otto Schroff, fols. 195–202, 5 June 1959. At the end of August, Heydrich requested the Einsatzgruppen chiefs, wherever possible, to prevent 'the gathering of spectators at mass executions, even if it concerns Wehrmacht officers' (*bei Massen-Exekutionen das Ansammeln von Zuschauern, auch wenn es sich um Wehrmachtsoffiziere handelt*). See 'Funkspruch Reichssicherheitshauptamt Amtschef IV an Einsatzgruppen', 30 August 1941, reproduced in: Angrick et al., eds., *Deutsche Besatzungsherrschaft in der UdSSR*, doc. 49, p. 117.
81. Interview with Holocaust survivor and former Soviet partisan Fania Brancovskaya, Rudniki Forest, near Vilnius, 29 May 2012. I am grateful to Gudrun Schroeter for her assistance in arranging this interview. On armed Jewish resistance in Lithuania see Christoph Dieckmann, 'Bewaffnete jüdische Untergrund–und Widerstandsbewegungen. Litauen 1941–1944', *Einsicht 09. Bulletin des Fritz Bauer Instituts*, Vol. 5 (spring 2013), pp. 28–34.
82. Kruk, *The Last Days of the Jerusalem of Lithuania*, p. 66, entry for 20 July [1941] ('What is happening in Ponar?').
83. BStU, RHE 4/85 SU, Bd. 7, fols. 172–175, 'Abt. III (Polizeiliche Angelegenheiten)', Einsatzgruppe B, n.d. [18 July 1941], here fol. 173.
84. BStU, MfS, HA IX/11 ZUV, Nr. 9, Bd. 31, fols. 3–17, 'Tätigkeitsbericht für die Zeit vom 23.6.1941 bis 13.7.1941', here fol. 6; BArch Berlin, R 58/214, fols. 180–196, 'Ereignismeldung UdSSR Nr. 24', 16 July 1941, here fol. 186.

85. Dieckmann, *Deutsche Besatzungspolitik in Litauen*, Vol. 1, p. 341, fn. 190. See also BArch Berlin, R 58/215, fols. 2–15, 'Ereignismeldung UdSSR Nr. 31', Chef der Sicherheitspolizei und des SD, 23 July 1941, here fol. 6.

86. BArch Berlin, R 58/214, fols. 139–153, 'Ereignismeldung UdSSR Nr. 21', 13 July 1941, here fol. 152.

87. BStU, MfS, HA IX/11 ZUV, Nr. 9, Bd. 31, fols. 3–17, 'Tätigkeitsbericht für die Zeit vom 23.6.1941 bis 13.7.1941', here fols. 8–10: '*[. . .] habe ich erreicht, daß die Tätigkeit meiner Einsatzgruppe von sämtlichen Wehrmachtstellen in jeder Weise anerkannt und gefördert wird*' (fol. 8).

88. BArch-MA, RH 26–403/2, 'Kriegstagebuch der Sich. Div. 403', entry for 23 July 1941, fol. 40.

89. UniA GI, 'Urteil Landgericht Berlin vom 22. Juni 1962', fol. 77. Greiffenberger testified that the commando had shot 'in total around 5,000 people' during its three-week stay in Vilnius (see 'Filbert schwer belastet', *Augsburger Allgemeine*, 18 May 1962). The figure of 'around 5,000 by the end of July 1941' also in Dieckmann, *Deutsche Besatzungspolitik in Litauen*, Vol. 1, p. 360. By contrast, Peter Longerich assumes that as many as 10,000 people were killed by EK 9 and the Lithuanians during the course of July (see Longerich, *Politik der Vernichtung*, p. 333).

90. LArch Berlin, B Rep. 058, Nr. 7178, fols. 92–97RR, Hearing of the accused Wilhelm Greiffenberger, 25 October 1960, here fol. 94R; LArch Berlin, B Rep. 058, Nr. 7189, fols. 124–132R, Hearing of the accused Gerhard Schneider in the criminal case against Dr Filbert et al. for murder, Landgericht Berlin, 26 September 1961, here fol. 131. See also BArch Berlin, R 58/215, fols. 2–15, 'Ereignismeldung UdSSR Nr. 31', 23 July 1941, here fol. 6.

91. 'Tätigkeits–und Lagebericht Nr. 2 der Einsatzgruppen der Sicherheitspolizei und des SD in der UdSSR (Berichtszeit v. 29.7.–14.8.1941)', Chef der Sicherheitspolizei und des SD, n.d., reproduced in: Klein, ed., *Die Einsatzgruppen*, pp. 134–152, here p. 137; BArch Berlin, R 58/215, fols. 259–270, 'Ereignismeldung UdSSR Nr. 50', 12 August 1941, here fol. 266; BArch Ludwigsburg, B 162/30134, fols. 259–260, 'AKT', Report of the Extraordinary State Commission in Ashmyany, 24 May 1945, here fol. 259 (shooting of 573 'peaceful residents of the city of Oshmyany' [*mirnykh zhitelei goroda Oshmyany*] dated to 3 and 4 July). See also Curilla, *Die deutsche Ordnungspolizei und der Holocaust*, p. 416.

92. Speculation to this effect in Gerlach, *Kalkulierte Morde*, p. 553, fn. 312. See also the testimony in BArch Ludwigsburg, B 162/20580, fols. 224–226, 'Protokol Doprosa', hearing of the Belarusian witness Elenu Iosifovnu D. before the senior investigating judge of the Investigative Department, Committee for State Security (KGB), Belarusian Soviet Republic, 27 September 1965, here fol. 226; BArch Ludwigsburg, B 162/20580, fols. 227–229, 'Protokol Doprosa', hearing of the Polish witness Frantsa Kazimirovicha D. before the senior investigating judge of the Investigative Department, Committee for State Security (KGB), Belarusian Soviet Republic, 27 September 1965, here fol. 228.

93. BArch Berlin, R 58/215, fols. 48–65, 'Ereignismeldung UdSSR Nr. 34', 26 July 1941, here fol. 59.

5   'In Vileyka, the Jews had to be liquidated in their entirety'

1. BArch Berlin, R 58/215, fols. 48–65, 'Ereignismeldung UdSSR Nr. 34', 26 July 1941, here fol. 60; BArch-MA, RH 26–102/9, War diary enclosure No. 348, '102. ID Div. Befehl', 25 July 1941.
2. Kay, 'Transition to Genocide, July 1941', pp. 415–416. On the other commandos see Longerich, *Politik der Vernichtung*, pp. 321–351. On events in Lithuania see also Dieckmann, *Deutsche Besatzungspolitik in Litauen*, Vol. 1, pp. 313–379, and Dieckmann, 'Der Krieg und die Ermordung der litauischen Juden', in Ulrich Herbert, ed., *Nationalsozialistische Vernichtungspolitik 1939–1945: Neue Forschungen und Kontroversen* (Frankfurt am Main: Fischer Taschenbuch, 1998), pp. 292–329, here pp. 295–300. On Belarus see also Gerlach, *Kalkulierte Morde*, pp. 536–555.
3. According to Gerhard Schneider's post-war testimony, Filbert passed on the new orders the day before the first shooting operation in Vileyka, which took place on 30 July. See the testimony in LArch Berlin, B Rep. 058, Nr. 7166, fols. 305–310, Hearing of Gerhard Schneider, 12 June 1959, here fol. 306; LArch Berlin, B Rep. 058, Nr. 7171, fols. 24–30R, Hearing of the accused Gerhard Schneider, 11 March 1960, here fol. 25R. For the date see also Kay, 'Transition to Genocide, July 1941', pp. 424 and 426.
4. See the congruent post-war testimony in LArch Berlin, B Rep. 058, Nr. 7171, fols. 69–74, 'Stenogramm-Übertragung des Vernehmungsprotokolls vom 10. Februar 1960', Oberstaatsanwalt beim Landgericht Bremen, signed [Gerhard] Schneider, 10 February 1960, here fol. 71; LArch Berlin, B Rep. 058, Nr. 7171, fols. 24–30R, Hearing of the accused Gerhard Schneider in the criminal case against Dr Alfred Filbert et al. for murder, Landgericht Berlin, 11 March 1960, here fols. 25–25R; LArch Berlin, B Rep. 058, Nr. 7174, fols. 95–113, Hearing of the accused Wilhelm Greiffenberger, 30 June 1960, here fol. 105; LArch Berlin, B Rep. 058, Nr. 7178, fols. 92–97R, Hearing of the accused Wilhelm Greiffenberger, 25 October 1960, here fol. 95; LArch Berlin, B Rep. 058, Nr. 7189, fols. 124–132R, Hearing of the accused Gerhard Schneider, 26 September 1961, here fol. 131R. For a comprehensive discussion of the nature, timing and conveyance of these new orders, see Kay, 'Transition to Genocide, July 1941', pp. 420–423 and 426–429.
5. LArch Berlin, B Rep. 058, Nr. 7171, fols. 24–30R, Hearing of the accused Gerhard Schneider, 11 March 1960, here fols. 25–25R; LArch Berlin, B Rep. 058, Nr. 7174, fols. 95–113, Hearing of the accused Wilhelm Greiffenberger, 30 June 1960, here fol. 105; LArch Berlin, B Rep. 058, Nr. 7178, fols. 92–97R, Hearing of the accused Wilhelm Greiffenberger, 25 October 1960, here fol. 95; LArch Berlin, B Rep. 058, Nr. 7189, fols. 124–132R, Hearing of the accused Gerhard Schneider, 26 September 1961, here fol. 131R.

6. LArch Berlin, B Rep. 058, Nr. 7171, fols. 24–30R, Hearing of the accused Gerhard Schneider, 11 March 1960, here fols. 25–25R: '*Wir waren von Wilna kommend gerade in Wilejka eingetroffen, als Dr. Filbert von einer Kommandoführerbesprechung in einem anderen Ort zurückkommend, eine Führerbesprechung anordnete. Man spürte ihm an, daß er selbst aufgeregt, verbittert und sehr ernst war. Er teilte uns nun mit, daß er von einer Kommandoführerbesprechung komme, bei der Heydrich entweder selbst anwesend gewesen sein muss, oder aber neue Befehle Heydrichs bekanntgegeben wurden. Auf dieser Besprechung habe er sich jedenfalls einiges sagen lassen müssen. So sei das Ek. 9 bei Heydrich besonders dadurch unangenehm aufgefallen, weil es eine viel zu geringe Aktivität bei der Erfüllung des Erschießungsbefehls entwickelt hatte. Da außerdem die Einbeziehung von Frauen und Kindern in die Erschießungsaktion befohlen worden sei, käme er jetzt einfach nicht mehr darum herum, den verstärkten Einsatz seines Kommandos anzuordnen.*'

7. LArch Berlin, B Rep. 058, Nr. 7178, fols. 92–97R, Hearing of the accused Wilhelm Greiffenberger, 25 October 1960, here fol. 95: '*Wir waren erst einige Tage in Wilejka, als Filbert im engeren Führerkreise eine Dienstbesprechung abhielt. Ich meine, daß außer Filbert und mir bei dieser Besprechung Schneider und Klein zugegen waren. Im Verlaufe dieser Dienstbesprechung eröffnete Filbert uns, daß er von höherer Stelle den Befehl erhalten hätte, künftig hin auch jüdische Frauen und Kinder mit zu erschießen. Außerdem wies Filbert bei dieser Gelegenheit darauf hin, daß höheren Ortes die gemeldeten Erschießungsziffern als zu niedrig beanstandet worden waren.*'

8. LArch Berlin, B Rep. 058, Nr. 7171, fols. 230–234R, Hearing of the witness Andreas von Amburger in the criminal case against Dr Alfred Filbert and Gerhard Schneider for murder, Landgericht Berlin, 11 May 1960, here fols. 232–232R; BArch Berlin, R 58/216, fols. 279–315, 'Ereignismeldung UdSSR Nr. 73', Chef der Sicherheitspolizei und des SD, 4 September 1941, here fols. 309–310 [as of 20 August]. This fact was already noted at Filbert's trial in 1962 (see UniA GI, 'Urteil Landgericht Berlin vom 22. Juni 1962', fol. 78).

9. LArch Berlin, B Rep. 058, Nr. 7166, fols. 71–76, Hearing of Andreas von Amburger, 1 April 1959, here fol. 74: '*[...] in der Einsatzgruppe B war allgemein bekannt, daß das EK 9 besonders rigoros bei der Liquidierung der jüdischen Bevölkerung vorgegangen ist.*' See also LArch Berlin, B Rep. 058, Nr. 7171, fols. 230–234R, Hearing of the witness Andreas von Amburger, 11 May 1960, here fols. 232–232R. On Andreas von Amburger see Klee, *Das Personenlexikon zum Dritten Reich*, p. 15.

10. On Tunnat's misgivings in respect of the youth of some of the Waffen SS men subordinated to him see LArch Berlin, B Rep. 058, Nr. 7171, fols. 256–259R, Hearing of the witness Heinrich Tunnat, 17 May 1960, here fol. 258R. On Schneider's objections to the inclusion of women and children in the shooting operations see also LArch Berlin, B Rep. 058, Nr. 7178, fols. 92–97R, Hearing of the accused Wilhelm Greiffenberger, 25 October 1960, here fol. 95. Greiffenberger's testimony regarding the objections voiced by Schneider contradicts the assertion that neither Filbert nor any other member of the commando could recall such an incident, as made by Christina

Ullrich, 'Ich fühl' mich nicht als Mörder'. Die Integration von NS-Tätern in die Nachkriegsgesellschaft (Darmstadt: Wissenschaftliche Buchgesellschaft, 2011), pp. 186–187.

11. LArch Berlin, B Rep. 058, Nr. 7166, fols. 305–310, Hearing of Gerhard Schneider, 12 June 1959, here fol. 306: '[. . .] auf der entweder Heydrich selbst anwesend war oder auf der ein direkter Befehl Heydrichs übermittelt wurde.' See also the similar formulation quoted earlier in LArch Berlin, B Rep. 058, Nr. 7171, fols. 24–30R, Hearing of the accused Gerhard Schneider, 11 March 1960, here fol. 25.

12. LArch Berlin, B Rep. 058, Nr. 7178, fols. 87–91R, Hearing of the accused Wilhelm Greiffenberger, 24 October 1960, here fol. 90R: 'Mit der Einsatzgruppe B hatten wir Funkverbindung. Einige Male war Filbert auf Befehl zu Besprechungen beim Gruppenstab. [. . .] Das RSHA. Berlin hat sich meines Wissens in der Frage der Judenerschießungen in späterer Zeit, als wir in Wilejka lagen, ein einziges Mal eingeschaltet, als es um die Frage ging, künftig hin auch Frauen und Kinder zu erschießen.'

13. Gerwarth, Hitler's Hangman, pp. 196–197. The assumption that Filbert had travelled back to Berlin to see Heydrich can be found in Gerlach, Kalkulierte Morde, p. 546.

14. See Witte et al., eds., Der Dienstkalender Heinrich Himmlers 1941/42, pp. 200 and 203, entries for 1 and 2 September 1941.

15. UniA GI, 'Urteil Landgericht Berlin vom 22. Juni 1962', fol. 76.

16. See the discussion in Kay, 'Transition to Genocide, July 1941', pp. 420–424 and p. 430.

17. UniA GI, 'Urteil Landgericht Berlin vom 22. Juni 1962', fols. 78–79.

18. BArch Ludwigsburg, B 162/30135, fols. 450–453, 'Protokol oprosa', hand-written transcript of hearing of the witness Mark Moeyseevich Ya. (Jewish survivor and resident of Vileyka), 30 March 1945, here fol. 450 [I am grateful to Vadim Morochek for his assistance in deciphering this hand-written transcript]; Gerlach, Kalkulierte Morde, pp. 545–546 ('400 people'); I. E. Yelenskaya and Ye. S. Rozenblat, 'Viléyka', in I. A. Al'tman, ed., Kholokost na territorii SSSR: Entsiklopediya (Moscow: ROSSPEN, 2009), pp. 155–156, here p. 155 ('ca. 400 Jews, incl. women and children'); Leonid Smilovitskii [Smilovitsky], Katastrofa evreev v Belorussii, 1941–1944 gg. (Tel Aviv: Biblioteka Matveia Chernogo, 2000), p. 165 ('up to 350 people'). The court in Berlin put the number of victims at 'at least 40', including three women (see UniA GI, 'Urteil Landgericht Berlin vom 22. Juni 1962', fols. 78–79).

19. LArch Berlin, B Rep. 058, Nr. 7178, fols. 92–97R, Hearing of the accused Wilhelm Greiffenberger, 25 October 1960, here fols. 96RR–97R; UniA GI, 'Urteil Landgericht Berlin vom 22. Juni 1962', fols. 79–81. Curilla makes no mention of children as victims of this mass shooting (see Curilla, Die deutsche Ordnungspolizei und der Holocaust, p. 416).

20. LArch Berlin, B Rep. 058, Nr. 7166, fols. 155–162R, Transcript of hearing of Alfred Weitenhagen, 16 April 1959, here fol. 156R.

21. LArch Berlin, B Rep. 058, Nr. 7178, fols. 98–102, Hearing of the accused Wilhelm Greiffenberger in the criminal case against Dr Filbert et al. for

murder, Landgericht Berlin, 27 October 1960, here fol. 99: '*[. . .] sämtliche in Wilejka ansässig gewesenen Juden [. . .].*' Before the Second World War, there had been 710 Jewish inhabitants of Vileyka (see Smilovitskii, *Katastrofa evreev v Belorussii*, p. 167).

22. 'Tätigkeits–und   Lagebericht   Nr.   2   der   Einsatzgruppen   der Sicherheitspolizei und des SD in der UdSSR (Berichtszeit v. 29.7.– 14.8.1941)', reproduced in: Klein, ed., *Die Einsatzgruppen*, pp. 134–152, here p. 136: '*In Wilejka musste die gesamte Judenschaft liquidiert werden.*' Contrast with BArch Berlin, R 58/215, fols. 259–270, 'Ereignismeldung UdSSR Nr. 50', 12 August 1941, here fol. 266: 'the male Jews in their entirety' (*die gesamte männliche Judenschaft*). Peter Longerich wrongly attributes these killings to Sonderkommando 7a, although it is clear from the report period covered by Activity and Situation Report (*Tätigkeits–und Lagebericht*, or TuLB) No. 2 that the killings must have been carried out by EK 9. See Longerich, *Politik der Vernichtung*, pp. 335 and 374. The correct interpretation can be found in Gerlach, *Kalkulierte Morde*, p. 545, and Mallmann et al., eds., *Die "Ereignismeldungen UdSSR" 1941*, p. 282, fn. 2.

23. BStU, MfS, HA IX/11 ZUV, Nr. 9, Bd. 31, fols. 3–17, 'Tätigkeitsbericht für die Zeit vom 23.6.1941 bis 13.7.1941', here fol. 5; BArch Ludwigsburg, B 162/30135, fols. 450–453, 'Protokol oprosa', handwritten transcript of hearing of the witness Mark Moeyseevich Ya., 30 March 1945, here fol. 451; Gerlach, *Kalkulierte Morde*, pp. 545–546; Yelenskaya and Rozenblat, 'Viléyka', p. 155 ('140 men'); Smilovitskii, *Katastrofa evreev v Belorussii*, p. 165.

24. LArch Berlin, B Rep. 058, Nr. 7171, fols. 239–247, Transcript of hearing of Alfred Weitenhagen in the criminal case against Dr Alfred Filbert and Gerhard Schneider for murder, Landgericht Berlin, 13 May 1960, here fol. 244: '*Ich kann nur sagen, dass die Situation im Kommando 9 ab Wilejka eine andere war als zuvor. Seit unserem Aufenthalt in Wilejka wurden in zunehmendem Maße kleine Teilkommandos zu mir unbekannten Sonderaufgaben von dem Hauptkommando Filbert unter Leitung der verschiedenen SS–und SD-Führer abgezogen, sodass das Stammkommando sich immer weiter verringerte.*'

25. BArch Berlin, R 58/215, fols. 156–188, 'Ereignismeldung UdSSR Nr. 43', 5 August 1941, here fol. 166.

26. For the term see Kay, 'Transition to Genocide, July 1941', esp. pp. 420–429.

27. See ibid., pp. 424–426 and 430, where the thesis was first presented that Filbert was the earliest of the commando chiefs to receive and implement the order to expand the murder of Soviet Jews to include women and children, thus initiating genocide. See also the literature cited in fn. 31 in Chapter 4. In light of the fact that EK 9 had already carried out no fewer than two shooting operations targeting children by the time EK 3 of EG A began killing children, it is difficult to concur with Jürgen Matthäus that the massacres by EK 3 in Rokiškis on 15 August marked 'a caesura in the history of the Holocaust', as opposed to the massacres by EK 9 in Vileyka on 30 July

or in Surazh on 12 August. See Christopher R. Browning, with contributions by Jürgen Matthäus, *The Origins of the Final Solution: The Evolution of Nazi Jewish Policy, September 1939 – March 1942* (Lincoln, NE: University of Nebraska Press, 2004), p. 283. Although EK 3 had killed Jewish women in small but increasing numbers from the first half of July onwards (reaching triple figures for the first time on 13 August), the commando did not include any children in their massacres until 15–16 August in Rokiškis, as Alfred Streim noted as early as 1984 (see Streim, 'Zur Eröffnung des allgemeinen Judenvernichtungsbefehls gegenüber den Einsatzgruppen', pp. 113–114). For the EK 3 statistics see 'Gesamtaufstellung der im Bereich des EK. 3 bis zum 1. Dez. 1941 durchgeführten Exekutionen' [*Jäger-Bericht*], signed [Karl] Jäger, 1 December 1941, reproduced in: Wette, *Karl Jäger*, pp. 237–245.

28. LArch Berlin, B Rep. 058, Nr. 7178, fols. 98–102, Hearing of the accused Wilhelm Greiffenberger, 27 October 1960, here fol. 98R.

29. UniA GI, 'Urteil Landgericht Berlin vom 22. Juni 1962', fols. 81–82.

30. Ibid., fols. 82–83. On the use of tracer ammunition see Zaehle, '"Die Sühne kommt spät"', in Archiv der VVN-BdA Bundesvereinigung, Dossier Alfred Filbert; 'Hohe Zuchthausstrafen im Einsatzkommando-Prozeß. Lebenslänglich für den ehemaligen SS-Offizier Alfred Filbert – Aberkennung der bürgerlichen Ehrenrechte auf Lebenszeit', *Augsburger Allgemeine*, 23 June 1962. The use of tracer ammunition is also mentioned in the film *Wundkanal*, 00:31:55 – 00:32:08.

31. Gerlach, *Kalkulierte Morde*, p. 526, fn. 141. See also Hasenclever, *Wehrmacht und Besatzungspolitik*, pp. 470–471; Il'ya Al'tman, Zhertvy nenavisti. Kholokost v SSSR 1941 – 1945 gg. (Moscow: Fond Kovcheg, 2002), p. 88. Filbert later testified that the 'Jew camp' (*Judenlager*) already existed when EK 9 arrived in Vitebsk and 'could only have been set up by the German Wehrmacht' (*konnte dieses Lager nur von der Deutschen Wehrmacht eingerichtet worden sein*). See LArch Berlin, B Rep. 058, Nr. 7166, fols. 187–194, Hearing of Dr Alfred Filbert, 13 May 1959, here fol. 193. Similar testimony in LArch Berlin, B Rep. 058, Nr. 7168, fols. 61–66R, Hearing of the accused Dr Alfred Filbert in the criminal case against Dr Alfred Filbert for murder, Landgericht Berlin, 22 January 1960, here fol. 63R; LArch Berlin, B Rep. 058, Nr. 7172, fols. 4–6R, Hearing of the accused Dr Alfred Filbert in the criminal case against Dr Alfred Filbert and Gerhard Schneider for murder, Landgericht Berlin, 14 June 1960, here fol. 4R. Greiffenberger also testified that the ghetto had already been there when EK 9 arrived in Vitebsk. See LArch Berlin, B Rep. 058, Nr. 7174, fols. 91–113, Hearing of the accused Wilhelm Greiffenberger, 29 June 1960, here fol. 106.

32. UniA GI, 'Urteil Landgericht Berlin vom 22. Juni 1962', fol. 83. The Jewish population of Vitebsk in 1939 had been 37,095. See Mordechai Altshuler, ed., *Distribution of the Jewish Population of the USSR 1939* (Jerusalem: Centre for Research and Documentation of East European Jewry, 1993), p. 39.

33. BArch Berlin, R 58/215, fols. 259–270, 'Ereignismeldung UdSSR Nr. 50', 12 August 1941, here fol. 266: '*27 Juden wurden öffentlich erschossen, weil sie sich weigerten, zur Arbeit zu gehen.*' The figure of 27 is incorrectly reproduced as '97' in the printed edition of the Incident Reports: see Mallmann et al., eds., *Die "Ereignismeldungen UdSSR" 1941*, p. 279. See also 'Tätigkeits–und Lagebericht Nr. 2 der Einsatzgruppen der Sicherheitspolizei und des SD in der UdSSR (Berichtszeit v. 29.7.–14.8.1941)', reproduced in: Klein, ed., *Die Einsatzgruppen*, pp. 134–152, here p. 137.

34. UniA GI, 'Urteil Landgericht Berlin vom 22. Juni 1962', fol. 84. The court recognised 'at least two shooting operations with at least 100 victims apiece'.

35. LArch Berlin, B Rep. 058, Nr. 7166, fols. 13–18R, Transcript of hearing of Karl B., 24 February 1959, here fols. 15R–16R.

36. BArch Berlin, R 58/216, fols. 215–246, 'Ereignismeldung UdSSR Nr. 67', 29 August 1941, here fol. 239.

37. Krausnick, 'Die Einsatzgruppen', p. 183.

38. BArch Berlin, R 58/215, fols. 156–188, 'Ereignismeldung UdSSR Nr. 43', 5 August 1941, here fol. 172.

39. BStU, MfS, HA IX/11 ZUV, Nr. 9, Bd. 31, fols. 27–33, 'Polizeilicher Lagebericht für die Zeit vom 9. bis 16. August 1941 zum Vortrag bei der Heeresgruppe Mitte', Einsatzgruppe B, 19 August 1941, here fols. 29–30; BArch Berlin, R 58/216, fols. 215–246, 'Ereignismeldung UdSSR Nr. 67', 29 August 1941, here fol. 235. See also BStU, RHE 4/85 SU, Bd. 7, fols. 181–187, Letter from Army Group Command Centre with enclosure 'II. Polizeiliche Tätigkeit' (excerpt from a report by Einsatzgruppe B), 14 August 1941, here fol. 182.

40. BStU, MfS, HA IX/11 ZUV, Nr. 9, Bd. 31, fols. 34–44, 'Polizeilicher Tätigkeitsbericht für die Zeit vom 17. bis 23. August 1941 zum Vortrag bei der Heeresgruppe Mitte', here fol. 39.

41. Ibid., fols. 39–40.

42. UniA GI, 'Urteil Landgericht Berlin vom 22. Juni 1962', fols. 84–86; LArch Berlin, B Rep. 058, Nr. 7166, fols. 155–162R, Transcript of hearing of Alfred Weitenhagen, 16 April 1959, here fol. 157; LArch Berlin, B Rep. 058, Nr. 7166, fols. 163–170, Hearing of Richard Neubert, 4 May 1959, here fol. 168. Although the court put the death toll at 'at least 200' (fol. 85), Alfred Weitenhagen believed that the number of those shot 'could have been 5 – 600' (*es können 5 – 600 gewesen sein*). Wolfgang Curilla interprets these two figures as the number of victims of *two* separate shooting operations (see Curilla, *Die deutsche Ordnungspolizei und der Holocaust*, pp. 420–421). Leonid Smilovitsky puts the number of those killed at 'over 700 people' (see Smilovitskii, *Katastrofa evreev v Belorussii*, p. 192). The Jewish population of Surazh in 1939 had been 451 (see Al'tman, ed., *Kholokost na territorii SSSR*, p. 957) or 461 (see Altshuler, ed., *Distribution of the Jewish Population of the USSR 1939*, p. 40; Smilovitskii, *Katastrofa evreev v Belorussii*, p. 193).

43. LArch Berlin, B Rep. 058, Nr. 7166, fols. 155–162R, Transcript of hearing of Alfred Weitenhagen, 16 April 1959, here fol. 157: '[. . .] *Kinder jeden Alters.*' See also '"Es war Sadismus". Erschütternde Aussagen im

Einsatzkkommando-Prozeß', *Allgemeine Wochenzeitung der Juden in Deutschland*, 8 June 1962, p. 2. Other former policemen also referred to the victims of the mass shootings as 'delinquents' when testifying at Filbert's trial. See LArch Berlin, B Rep. 058, Nr. 7166, fols. 13–18R, Transcript of hearing of Karl B., 24 February 1959, here fol. 14R; LArch Berlin, B Rep. 058, Nr. 7166, Bl. 218–226, Hearing of the witness Wilhelm S., 11 May 1959, here fol. 223; Hearing of the witness Gustav Wolters, Stade, 24 October 1961, cited in Ruprecht, 'SS-Mann 52729'.

44. See Kay, 'Transition to Genocide, July 1941', p. 426.
45. UniA GI, 'Urteil Landgericht Berlin vom 22. Juni 1962', fols. 48 and 86.
46. The town of Lepel is located directly on the road eastwards from Vileyka, roughly halfway to Vitebsk. The timing would fit, as the advance of EK 9 from Vileyka to Vitebsk took place at the beginning of August. A ghetto had been established in Lepel at the end of July, presumably by the Wehrmacht, which had occupied the town on 8 July. See G. Vinnitsa, 'Lepel', in Al'tman, ed., *Kholokost na territorii SSSR*, p. 521. Lepel was not mentioned explicitly during Filbert's trial, perhaps because no one was able to recall the name of the town. According to other sources, EK 9 murdered a political commissar from the prison camp in Lepel in August and 23 Roma there the following month, in September (see later paragraphs for details).
47. UniA GI, 'Urteil Landgericht Berlin vom 22. Juni 1962', fols. 86–87. See also Curilla, *Die deutsche Ordnungspolizei und der Holocaust*, pp. 418–419. This massacre is discussed in Robert Kramer's *Notre Nazi*, 01:35:06 – 01:37:58, where Thomas Harlan states that two of the designated victims managed to escape. The date of this massacre is given in the film as 20 August.
48. BStU, MfS, HA IX/11 ZUV, Nr. 9, Bd. 31, fols. 45–55, 'Polizeilicher Tätigkeitsbericht für die Zeit vom 24. – 31. August 1941 zum Vortrag bei der Heeresgruppe Mitte', Einsatzgruppe B, 3 September 1941, here fol. 53: '*Mit Rücksicht auf seine politische Gefährlichkeit wurde er der Sonderbehandlung unterzogen.*'
49. BStU, MfS, HA IX/11 ZUV, Nr. 9, Bd. 31, fols. 34–44, 'Polizeilicher Tätigkeitsbericht für die Zeit vom 17. bis 23. August 1941 zum Vortrag bei der Heeresgruppe Mitte', here fol. 43; BArch Berlin, R 58/216, fols. 279–315, 'Ereignismeldung UdSSR Nr. 73', 4 September 1941, here fol. 308. In the entry for Vitebsk in Eberhard Jäckel, Peter Longerich and Julius H. Schoeps, eds., *Enzyklopädie des Holocaust. Die Verfolgung und Ermordung der europäischen Juden, Band III: Q–Z* (Munich/Zürich: Piper, 1995), p. 1609, the figure of 397 becomes '4,397'. On the civilian internment camps set up by the Wehrmacht see Gerlach, *Kalkulierte Morde*, pp. 503–514.
50. BStU, MfS, HA IX/11 ZUV, Nr. 9, Bd. 31, fols. 34–44, 'Polizeilicher Tätigkeitsbericht für die Zeit vom 17. bis 23. August 1941 zum Vortrag bei der Heeresgruppe Mitte', here fol. 42; BArch Berlin, R 58/216, fols. 279–315, 'Ereignismeldung UdSSR Nr. 73', 4 September 1941, here fol. 306; 'Tätigkeits–und Lagebericht Nr. 4 der Einsatzgruppen der Sicherheitspolizei und des SD in der UdSSR (Berichtszeit

v. 1.9.–15.9.1941)', Chef der Sicherheitspolizei und des SD, n.d., reproduced in: Klein, ed., *Die Einsatzgruppen*, pp. 180–198, here p. 184.
51. BStU, MfS, HA IX/11 ZUV, Nr. 9, Bd. 31, fols. 34–44, 'Polizeilicher
Tätigkeitsbericht für die Zeit vom 17. bis 23. August 1941 zum Vortrag
bei der Heeresgruppe Mitte', here fol. 42.
52. Ibid.; BArch Berlin, R 58/216, fols. 279–315, 'Ereignismeldung UdSSR Nr.
73', 4 September 1941, here fol. 307; 'Tätigkeits–und Lagebericht Nr. 4 der
Einsatzgruppen der Sicherheitspolizei und des SD in der UdSSR
(Berichtszeit v. 1.9.–15.9.1941)', reproduced in: Klein, ed., *Die
Einsatzgruppen*, pp. 180–198, here p. 184.
53. BStU, MfS, HA IX/11 ZUV, Nr. 9, Bd. 31, fols. 45–55, 'Polizeilicher
Tätigkeitsbericht für die Zeit vom 24. – 31. August 1941 zum Vortrag bei
der Heeresgruppe Mitte', here fol. 52. EK 9 was already in Polatsk before
the end of August and not from the beginning of September, as Christian
Gerlach claims (see Gerlach, *Kalkulierte Morde*, p. 601). The staff of the
403rd Security Division arrived in Polatsk on 29 August (see BArch-MA,
RH 26–403/2, 'Kriegstagebuch der Sich. Div. 403', entry for 29 August
1941, fol. 61R).
54. BArch Ludwigsburg, B 162/3921, fols. 146–151, Hearing of Siegfried S., 16
December 1965, here fol. 147.
55. Gerlach, *Kalkulierte Morde*, pp. 380 and 421.
56. Wila Orbach, 'The Destruction of the Jews in the Nazi-Occupied
Territories of the USSR', *Soviet Jewish Affairs*, Vol. 6, No. 2 (1976), pp.
14–51, here pp. 21 and 33. The Jewish population of Polatsk in 1939 had
been 6,464. See Altshuler, ed., *Distribution of the Jewish Population of the
USSR*, p. 39.
57. 'Massovoye istreblenie mirnykh grazhdan i voennoplennykh', Chairman of
the Polatsk Regional (*oblast*) Extraordinary State Commission, n.d. [after 9
May 1945], reproduced in: Z. I. Beluga et al., eds., *Prestupleniya nemetsko-
fashistskikh okkupantov v Belorussii 1941 – 1944* (Minsk: Izdatel'stvo
"Belarus", 1965), doc. 135 (pp. 296–304), here p. 300; Gerlach, 'Die
Einsatzgruppe B 1941/42', p. 58; Gerlach, *Kalkulierte Morde*, p. 568;
Orbach, 'The Destruction of the Jews', p. 45.
58. BArch Ludwigsburg, B 162/3921, fols. 146–151, Hearing of Siegfried S., 16
December 1965, here fol. 148. It is unclear whether this was the same
massacre as that in August with an unknown number of victims including
women and children.
59. BStU, MfS, HA IX/11 ZUV, Nr. 9, Bd. 31, fols. 45–55, 'Polizeilicher
Tätigkeitsbericht für die Zeit vom 24. – 31. August 1941 zum Vortrag bei
der Heeresgruppe Mitte', here fols. 52–53.
60. Ibid., fol. 55. On the housing of Jews in ghettos see Dan Michman, *The
Emergence of Jewish Ghettos during the Holocaust*, translated from Hebrew by
Lenn J. Schramm (Cambridge/New York: Cambridge University Press,
2011), esp. ch. 10, pp. 102–121; Gustavo Corni, *I ghetti di Hitler: Voci da
una società sotto assedio 1939–1944* (Bologna: il Mulino, 2001).

61. See Gert Robel, 'Sowjetunion', in Wolfgang Benz, ed., *Dimension des Völkermords. Die Zahl der jüdischen Opfer des Nationalsozialismus* (Munich: Oldenbourg, 1991), pp. 499–560, here p. 533.

62. Orbach, 'The Destruction of the Jews', p. 32. The Jewish population of Haradok in 1939 had been 1,584. See Altshuler, ed., *Distribution of the Jewish Population of the USSR*, p. 39. Infantry Regiment 406 of the 403rd Security Division arrived in Haradok on 29 August. See BArch-MA, RH 26–403/2, 'Kriegstagebuch der Sich. Div. 403', entry for 29 August 1941, fol. 61R.

63. Gerlach, *Kalkulierte Morde*, p. 538; Al'tman, Zhertvy nenavisti, p. 88; Orbach, 'The Destruction of the Jews', p. 38. See also BStU, RHE 4/85 SU, Bd. 7, fols. 181–187, Letter from Army Group Command Centre with enclosure 'II. Polizeiliche Tätigkeit' (excerpt from a report by Einsatzgruppe B), 14 August 1941, here fols. 184–185.

64. BArch Berlin, R 58/217, fols. 254–299, 'Ereignismeldung UdSSR Nr. 92', Chef der Sicherheitspolizei und des SD, 23 September 1941, here fols. 283–284. Curilla incorrectly concludes that the four Soviet soldiers were also killed by EK 9 (see Curilla, *Die deutsche Ordnungspolizei und der Holocaust*, p. 421).

65. BArch Berlin, R 58/217, fols. 254–299, 'Ereignismeldung UdSSR Nr. 92', Chef der Sicherheitspolizei und des SD, 23 September 1941, here fols. 284–285.

66. BArch-MA, RH 26–403/4a, 'Tätigkeitsbericht. I c / September 1941', n.d.

67. National Archives and Records Administration, College Park, MA (hereafter NARA), RG 242, T-501, Roll 1, 'Tagesmeldung', Befehlshaber des rückw. Heeres-Gebietes Mitte Ia, 2 September 1941. I am grateful to Jörn Hasenclever for placing this microfilm at my disposal.

68. BArch-MA, RH 26–403/4a, 'Tätigkeitsbericht. I c / September 1941', n.d.

69. BArch Ludwigsburg, B 162/21177, fols. 27–29, Hearing of the witness Alfred Filbert, 348 Gs 24/65, 15 February 1965, here fol. 28; BArch Ludwigsburg, B 162/21177, fols. 34–35, Hearing of the witness Heinrich Tunnat, 28 Gs 197/65, 16 March 1965, here fol. 35; BArch Ludwigsburg, B 162/4114, fols. 1756–1758, Hearing of Heinrich Karl Walter Tunnat, Criminal Police in Oldenburg, StA Flensburg 2 Js 467/65 and StA Kiel 2 Js 762/63, 6 September 1965, here fol. 1757.

70. LArch Berlin, B Rep. 058, Nr. 7186, fols. 187–196, Hearing of Felix U., 11 April 1961, here fol. 190; LArch Berlin, B Rep. 058, Nr. 7187, fols. 94–101, Hearing of the accused Heinrich Tunnat in the criminal case against Dr Filbert et al. for murder, Landgericht Berlin, 6 July 1961, here fol. 97R; LArch Berlin, B Rep. 058, Nr. 7178, fols. 98–102, Hearing of the accused Wilhelm Greiffenberger, 27 October 1960, here fol. 99R; UniA GI, 'Urteil Landgericht Berlin vom 22. Juni 1962', fols. 87–88.

71. BStU, MfS, HA IX/11 ZUV, Nr. 9, Bd. 31, fols. 34–44, 'Polizeilicher Tätigkeitsbericht für die Zeit vom 17. bis 23. August 1941 zum Vortrag bei der Heeresgruppe Mitte', here fol. 44. The Jewish population of Nevel in

1939 had been 3,178. See Altshuler, ed., *Distribution of the Jewish Population of the USSR*, p. 33.

72. 'Tätigkeits–und Lagebericht Nr. 4 der Einsatzgruppen der Sicherheitspolizei und des SD in der UdSSR (Berichtszeit v. 1.9.–15.9.1941)', reproduced in: Klein, ed., *Die Einsatzgruppen*, pp. 180–198, here p. 184.

73. For more details on the destruction of the Nevel ghetto and Tunnat's role in leading the operation see the statement by Tunnat's driver in LArch Berlin, B Rep. 058, Nr. 7186, fols. 197–207, Hearing of Felix U., 12 April 1961, here fols. 199–201. See also UniA GI, 'Urteil Landgericht Berlin vom 22. Juni 1962', fols. 88–90. Although the court cited the number of victims as 'at least 100' (fol. 90), both EM 92 from 23 September and the RSHA's Activity and Situation Report for the second half of September put the number of victims considerably higher, at 640. See BArch Berlin, R 58/217, fols. 254–299, 'Ereignismeldung UdSSR Nr. 92', 23 September 1941, here fol. 291; BArch Berlin, R 70 Sowjetunion/31, fols. 1–33, 'Tätigkeits–und Lagebericht Nr. 5 der Einsatzgruppen der Sicherheitspolizei und des SD in der UdSSR. (Berichtszeit vom 15.–30.9.1941)', n.d., here fol. 13. The Nevel District (*raion*) Extraordinary State Commission put the number of victims at 'more than 800 people, women, children and old men' (*bolee 800 chelovek, zhenshchin, detey i starikov*), whilst Aleksandra Bolotnikova, a Russian witness born in 1920, put the figure as high as 1,800. See Yad Vashem Archives, Jerusalem, JM/19924, 'AKT', 21 December 1944, and testimony of Aleksandra Bolotnikova from 12 November 1944.

74. UniA GI, 'Urteil Landgericht Berlin vom 22. Juni 1962', fols. 56 and 90–91; LArch Berlin, B Rep. 058, Nr. 7174, fols. 114–121, Hearing of the accused Wilhelm Greiffenberger, Polizeipräsident in Berlin, 1 July 1960, here fol. 119.

75. BArch Berlin, R 58/217, fols. 254–299, 'Ereignismeldung UdSSR Nr. 92', 23 September 1941, here fol. 291; BArch Berlin, R 70 Sowjetunion/31, fols. 1–33, 'Tätigkeits–und Lagebericht Nr. 5 der Einsatzgruppen der Sicherheitspolizei und des SD in der UdSSR. (Berichtszeit vom 15.–30.9.1941)', here fol. 13. See also LArch Berlin, B Rep. 058, Nr. 7184, fols. 107–118, Hearing of the accused Karl Rath, 8 April 1960, here fols. 114–115.

76. BArch Berlin, R 58/217, fols. 254–299, 'Ereignismeldung UdSSR Nr. 92', 23 September 1941, here fol. 291: '*Die Aktion wurde lediglich von einem Führer und 12 Männern durchgeführt.*' On Rath see 'Urteil des Schwurgerichts beim Landgericht Berlin (500) 3 P (K) Ks 1/65, vom 6. Mai 1966', reprinted in: *Justiz und NS-Verbrechen. Sammlung deutscher Strafurteile wegen nationalsozialistischer Tötungsverbrechen 1945–1999*, Vol. XXIII, ed. C. F. Ruter and D. W. de Mildt (Maarssen: APA – Holland University Press, 1998), No. 630, pp. 507–532, here pp. 509–510; Ullrich, '*Ich fühl' mich nicht als Mörder*', pp. 263–264.

77. See Daniel Romanovsky, 'Ianovichi', in United States Holocaust Memorial Museum, *Encyclopedia of Camps and Ghettos, 1933–1945, Volume II: Ghettos in German-Occupied Eastern Europe, Part B*, ed. Martin Dean (Bloomington, IN/Indianapolis, IN: Indiana University Press, 2012), pp. 1679–1680, here

p. 1679. On sexual crimes committed by German soldiers in the occupied Soviet territories see the ground-breaking Regina Mühlhäuser, *Eroberungen. Sexuelle Gewalttaten und intime Beziehungen deutscher Soldaten in der Sowjetunion 1941 – 1945* (Hamburg: Hamburger Edition, 2010).

78. BArch Berlin, R 58/217, fols. 254–299, 'Ereignismeldung UdSSR Nr. 92', 23 September 1941, fol. 291.
79. BArch Berlin, R 58/216, fols. 279–315, 'Ereignismeldung UdSSR Nr. 73', 4 September 1941, here fol. 306. NKGB = *Narodnyy Komissariat Gosudarstvennoi Bezopasnosti* (People's Commissariat for State Security). The RSHA's Activity and Situation Report for the first half of September, by contrast, cited the considerably lower number of 14 Jews shot 'as informants and political functionaries'. See 'Tätigkeits–und Lagebericht Nr. 4 der Einsatzgruppen der Sicherheitspolizei und des SD in der UdSSR (Berichtszeit v. 1.9.–15.9.1941)', reproduced in: Klein, ed., *Die Einsatzgruppen*, pp. 180–198, here p. 184. For the date see BStU, MfS, HA IX/11 ZUV, Nr. 9, Bd. 31, fols. 34–44, 'Polizeilicher Tätigkeitsbericht für die Zeit vom 17. bis 23. August 1941 zum Vortrag bei der Heeresgruppe Mitte', here fol. 42. The same wording – 'NKGB informants and political functionaries' – is also used here, though no figure is cited.
80. See Gerlach, *Kalkulierte Morde*, p. 569.
81. This point is made in Klein, ed., *Die Einsatzgruppen*, p. 221, n. 2.
82. BArch Berlin, R 58/217, fols. 254–299, 'Ereignismeldung UdSSR Nr. 92', 23 September 1941, here fol. 292: '[. . .] *weil sie die Landbevölkerung terrorisiert und zahlreiche Diebstähle ausgeführt hatten.*' See also Klein, ed., *Die Einsatzgruppen*, p. 221, n. 2. Helmut Krausnick attributes the shooting to EK 8 (see Krausnick, 'Die Einsatzgruppen', p. 236).
83. BArch Berlin, R 58/217, fols. 254–299, 'Ereignismeldung UdSSR Nr. 92', 23 September 1941, here fol. 292; BArch Berlin, R 70 Sowjetunion/31, fols. 1–33, 'Tätigkeits–und Lagebericht Nr. 5 der Einsatzgruppen der Sicherheitspolizei und des SD in der UdSSR. (Berichtszeit vom 15.–30.9.1941)', here fol. 12.
84. LArch Berlin, B Rep. 058, Nr. 7168, fols. 52–55, Hearing of the accused Dr Alfred Filbert in the criminal case against Dr Alfred Filbert for murder, Landgericht Berlin, 19 January 1960, here fol. 53. On the genocide of Soviet Roma see Martin Holler, *Der nationalsozialistische Völkermord an den Roma in der besetzten Sowjetunion (1941–1944)* (Heidelberg: Dokumentations–und Kulturzentrum Deutscher Sinti und Roma, 2009); Wolfgang Wippermann, 'Nur eine Fußnote? Die Verfolgung der sowjetischen Roma: Historiographie, Motive, Verlauf', in Klaus Meyer and Wolfgang Wippermann, eds., *Gegen das Vergessen: Der Vernichtungskrieg gegen die Sowjetunion, 1941–1945* (Frankfurt am Main: Haag u. Herchen, 1992), pp. 75–90; Martin Holler, 'Extending the Genocidal Program: Did Otto Ohlendorf Initiate the Systematic Extermination of Soviet "Gypsies"?', in Kay et al., eds., *Nazi Policy on the Eastern Front*, pp. 267–288.
85. BArch Berlin, R 70 Sowjetunion/32, fols. 4–10, 'Als Geheime Reichssache', signed [Reinhard] Heydrich, 2 July 1941.

86. BArch Berlin, R 58/272, fols. 46–58, 'Einsatzbefehl Nr. 8, Betr.: Richtlinien für die in die Stalags und Dulags abzustellenden Kommandos des Chefs der Sicherheitspolizei und des SD', 21 B/41 g Rs. IV A 1 c, Chef der Sicherheitspolizei und des SD, 17 July 1941.

87. BArch Berlin, R 58/217, fols. 254–299, 'Ereignismeldung UdSSR Nr. 92', Chef der Sicherheitspolizei und des SD, 23 September 1941, here fols. 290–291 and 293.

88. BArch Berlin, R 58/218, fols. 104–130, 'Ereignismeldung UdSSR Nr. 108', Chef der Sicherheitspolizei und des SD, 9 October 1941, here fols. 115 and 120–121.

89. Ibid., fols. 120–121.

90. BArch Berlin, R 58/218, fols. 284–297, 'Ereignismeldung UdSSR Nr. 123', Chef der Sicherheitspolizei und des SD, 24 October 1941, here fols. 295–297.

91. BArch Berlin, R 58/218, fols. 299–305, 'Ereignismeldung UdSSR Nr. 124', Chef der Sicherheitspolizei und des SD, 25 October 1941, here fol. 305: '[...] die durch Verbreitung von Gerüchten Unruhe in die Bevölkerung getragen hatten.'

92. BArch-MA, RS 4/932, fols. 197–212, 'Betr.: Tätigkeitsbericht für die Zeit vom 3.–10.10.1941', SS-Kav.-Rgt. 2, Ia, Bo./Schr., 10 October 1941, here fols. 197–198. According to this report, the regiment's command post during the report period was in Haradok (fol. 198). On the SS Cavalry Regiment 2 see Cüppers, Wegbereiter der Shoah.

93. BArch Berlin, R 58/218, fols. 299–305, 'Ereignismeldung UdSSR Nr. 124', 25 October 1941, here fols. 304–305.

94. See Klein, ed., Die Einsatzgruppen, p. 221, n. 3; Gerlach, Kalkulierte Morde, pp. 585–586. On the TuLB see Peter Klein, 'Einleitung', in Klein, ed., Die Einsatzgruppen, pp. 9–28, here pp. 9–11; Krausnick and Wilhelm, Die Truppe des Weltanschauungskrieges, pp. 649–654; Krausnick, 'Die Einsatzgruppen', p. 165.

95. Gerlach, Kalkulierte Morde, p. 596.

96. Hasenclever, Wehrmacht und Besatzungspolitik, p. 504.

97. Arkhiv Rossiyskogo Nauchno–Prosvetitel'nogo Tsentra Kholokost [Archives of the Russian Research and Educational Holocaust Centre], Moscow, Letter from Sofiya Ratner, 6 and 8 September 1941: 'Dorogiye detki! Marusen'ka, Amochka, Viten'ka, Ninochka, proshchayte! Umirayu. Chto my tut perezhivayem v getto ne poddayetsya opisaniyu. Luchshe umeret'. [...] Dorogiye, lyubimyye, beskonechno lyubimyye. Proshchayte. Zhivy li Vy vse i etogo ne znayu. Nichego my ne znayem, chto krugom delayetsya otretsany ot vsego mira. My zdes' s tetey Faney plyus, konechno, vse ostavsheysya v Vitebske yevreystvo. Proshchayte zhe yeshche raz, dorogiye. Kak tyazhelo rasstavat'sya s Vami navsegda. Beskonechno lyubyashchaya Vas mama. 6 / IX 41 g. My yeshche zhivy. Nashe get[t]o ovobyat [sic] provolokoy. My obrecheny na golodnuyu smert'. 8 / IX 41 g.' I am grateful to Il'ya Al'tman for providing me with a copy of this letter and to Vadim Morochek for his assistance in deciphering the handwriting.

98. See Gerlach, *Kalkulierte Morde*; Kay, *Exploitation, Resettlement, Mass Murder*; Wigbert Benz, *Der Hungerplan im 'Unternehmen Barbarossa' 1941* (Berlin: Wissenschaftlicher Verlag Berlin, 2011); Alex J. Kay, "'The Purpose of the Russian Campaign is the Decimation of the Slavic Population by Thirty Million": The Radicalization of German Food Policy in early 1941', in Kay et al., eds., *Nazi Policy on the Eastern Front*, pp. 101–129.
99. Friedländer, *The Years of Extermination*, p. 208.
100. On Soviet prisoners of war see Christian Streit, Keine Kameraden: Die Wehrmacht und die sowjetischen Kriegsgefangenen 1941–1945, 4th rev. ed. (Bonn: Dietz, 1997 [1978]). On Leningrad see Jörg Ganzenmüller, Das belagerte Leningrad 1941–1944: Die Stadt in den Strategien von Angreifern und Verteidigern (Paderborn: Schöningh, 2005). On Kharkiv see Norbert Kunz, 'Das Beispiel Charkow: Eine Stadtbevölkerung als Opfer der deutschen Hungerstrategie 1941/42,' in Christian Hartmann, Johannes Hürter and Ulrike Jureit, eds., Verbrechen der Wehrmacht: Bilanz einer Debatte (Munich: C. H. Beck, 2005), pp. 136–144.
101. LArch Berlin, B Rep. 058, Nr. 7178, fols. 103–110R, Hearing of the accused Wilhelm Greiffenberger in the criminal case against Dr Filbert et al. for murder, Landgericht Berlin, 31 October 1960, here fol. 104R: '*Der Anblick, der sich uns in diesem Keller bot, war furchtbar. In diesem Raum lagen etwa 10 zu Skeletten abgemagerte Juden, die zum Teil infolge des Hungers inzwischen verstorben waren, andere mit dicken Bäuchen und Geschwüren herum.*'
102. LArch Berlin, B Rep. 058, Nr. 7171, fols. 297–300R, Hearing of the witness Bodo Struck in the criminal case against Dr Alfred Filbert and Gerhard Schneider for murder, Landgericht Berlin, 9 June 1960, here fol. 299; LArch Berlin, B Rep. 058, Nr. 7174, fols. 91–113, Hearing of the accused Wilhelm Greiffenberger, 29 June 1960, here fol. 107.
103. BArch Berlin, R 58/218, fols. 299–305, 'Ereignismeldung UdSSR Nr. 124', 25 October 1941, here fol. 304; BArch Berlin, R 70 Sowjetunion/31, fols. 36–72, 'Tätigkeits–und Lagebericht Nr. 6 der Einsatzgruppen der Sicherheitspolizei und des SD in der UdSSR. (Berichtszeit vom 1. – 31.10.1941.)', n.d., here fol. 51; LArch Berlin, B Rep. 058, Nr. 7178, fols. 103–110R, Hearing of the accused Wilhelm Greiffenberger, 31 October 1960, here fol. 108.
104. LArch Berlin, B Rep. 058, Nr. 7178, fols. 103–110R, Hearing of the accused Wilhelm Greiffenberger, 31 October 1960, here fols. 105–108; UniA GI, 'Urteil Landgericht Berlin vom 22. Juni 1962', fols. 91–92; HStAD, Ztg 136, 'Hauptaufgabe: Judenerschießungen. SS-Offizier bekam Schreikrämpfe nach Kindermord', *Darmstädter Echo*, 18 May 1962, p. 2.
105. UniA GI, 'Urteil Landgericht Berlin vom 22. Juni 1962', fol. 93: '*Und so etwas will ein SS-Führer sein. Den sollte man mit einer entsprechenden Beurteilung gleich wieder nach Hause schicken.*' See also LArch Berlin, B Rep. 058, Nr. 7178, fols. 103–110R, Hearing of the accused Wilhelm Greiffenberger, 31 October 1960, here fol. 107R; HStAD, Ztg 136, 'Hauptaufgabe: Judenerschießungen', *Darmstädter Echo*, 18 May 1962, p.

2. On children as victims of the massacres see Gerlach, *Kalkulierte Morde*, pp. 1074–1092; Welzer, *Täter*, pp. 173–188.
106. UniA GI, 'Urteil Landgericht Berlin vom 22. Juni 1962', fols. 92–94; '"Es war Sadismus". Erschütternde Aussagen im Einsatzkkommando-Prozeß', *Allgemeine Wochenzeitung der Juden in Deutschland*, 8 June 1962, p. 2. On the consumption of alcohol during massacres see Edward B. Westermann, 'Stone Cold Killers or Drunk with Murder? Alcohol and Atrocity in the Holocaust', unpublished manuscript, 2014; Browning, *Ordinary Men*, pp. 81–82; Stephan Lehnstaedt, 'The Minsk Experience: German Occupiers and Everyday Life in the Capital of Belarus', in Kay et al., eds., *Nazi Policy on the Eastern Front*, pp. 240–266, here pp. 253–255.
107. 'Merkblatt für die Führer der Einsatzgruppen und Einsatzkommandos der Sicherheitspolizei und des SD für den Einsatz "Barbarossa"', n.d. [before 22 June 1941], reproduced in: Angrick et al., eds., *Deutsche Besatzungsherrschaft in der UdSSR*, doc. 4, pp. 30–33, here p. 32.
108. Following post-war denazification, Struck was briefly head of the Hanover Criminal Police. On Struck see UniA GI, 'Urteil Landgericht Berlin vom 22. Juni 1962', fols. 50–53; LArch Berlin, B Rep. 058, Nr. 7166, fols. 83–89, Hearing of Bodo Struck, 3 April 1959; LArch Berlin, B Rep. 058, Nr. 7171, fols. 201–207, Hearing of Bodo Struck, 5 April 1960; 'Ex-Nazis Sentenced', *AJR Information*, Vol. 17, No. 8, August 1962, p. 5. During his deployment with EK 9, Struck wore the uniform of an SS-Hauptsturmführer, although he was not a member of the SS. See LArch Berlin, B Rep. 058, Nr. 7166, fol. 84 and Nr. 7171, fol. 203; BArch Ludwigsburg, B 162/2401, fols. 23–32, 'Urteil und Urteilsbegründung im SS-Prozeß Filbert', n.d. [22 June 1962], here fols. 27 and 31.
109. LArch Berlin, B Rep. 058, Nr. 7174, fols. 23–35, Hearing of the witness Hugo G., 30 May 1960, here fols. 31–32; LArch Berlin, B Rep. 058, Nr. 7174, fols. 131–135, Written statement by Wilhelm Greiffenberger to the Generalstaatsanwaltschaft beim Landgericht Berlin, 'Betr. Akt.Z. 3 P (K) JS 82/60', 4 July 1960, here fol. 132.
110. UniA GI, 'Urteil Landgericht Berlin vom 22. Juni 1962', fols. 93–94.
111. See Hasenclever, Wehrmacht und Besatzungspolitik, p. 504.
112. Ibid., pp. 351, 362–364, 498–499, 519 and 521–522. On von Schenckendorff's role in the annihilation of Soviet Jewry see ibid., pp. 474–522. The programme of the anti-partisan warfare seminar, the list of participants and the text of von Schenckendorff's opening remarks can all be found in BArch-MA, WF-03/13302, 'Tagesordnung für den Kursus "Bekämpfung von Partisanen" v. 24.–26.9.41', Befehlshaber des rückw. Heeres-Gebietes Mitte, Ia, H. Qu., 23 September 1941; 'Teilnehmer-Verzeichnis am Partisanen-Lehrgang vom 24.–26.9.1941', Befehlshaber des rückw. Heeres-Gebietes Mitte, IIa, H. Qu., 23 September 1941; and 'Einleitungsworte zum Partisanen-Bekämpfungs-Lehrgang', K. H. Qu., signed *General der Infanterie* von Schenckendorff, 24 September 1941.
113. Quoted in Miroslav Kárný, Jaroslava Milotová and Margita Kárná, eds., *Deutsche Politik im "Protektorat Böhmen und Mähren" unter Reinhard*

Heydrich 1941–1942: Eine Dokumentation (Berlin: Metropol, 1997), doc. 106, p. 283.

114. BArch Berlin, R 58/219, fols. 328–337, 'Ereignismeldung UdSSR Nr. 148', Chef der Sicherheitspolizei und des SD, 19 December 1941, here fol. 337 ('altogether 4,090 Jews of both genders'); Gerlach, *Kalkulierte Morde*, pp. 595 and 597 ('between 4,000 and 8,000 Jews'); The National Archives, Kew (hereafter TNA, Kew), WO 208/4139, S.R.M. 1024, 'S. R. Report', 15 November 1944 ('about 5,000 people'); Al'tman, *Zhertvy nenavisti*, p. 88. As Christian Gerlach correctly points out, the figure of 'roughly 3,000' (*etwa 3000*) mentioned in EM 124 was cited *in anticipation* of the end result of the mass slaughter still in the process of being carried out at the time of reporting. See BArch Berlin, R 58/218, fols. 299–305, 'Ereignismeldung UdSSR Nr. 124', 25 October 1941, here fol. 304; Gerlach, *Kalkulierte Morde*, p. 597, fn. 558.

115. Daniel Romanovsky, 'Vitebsk', in United States Holocaust Memorial Museum, *Encyclopedia of Camps and Ghettos, 1933–1945, Volume II, Part B*, pp. 1745–1748, here p. 1747. See also Orbach, 'The Destruction of the Jews', p. 50; Gerlach, *Kalkulierte Morde*, p. 597, fn. 558. According to other sources, the Jews were shot at the Vitba River and their corpses thrown into the water (see Jäckel, Longerich and Schoeps, eds., *Enzyklopädie des Holocaust. Band III: Q–Z*, p. 1609).

116. See *Die Verfolgung und Ermordung der europäischen Juden. Band 7*, p. 285, fn. 2.

117. Gerlach, *Kalkulierte Morde*, pp. 569 and 597.

118. LArch Berlin, B Rep. 058, Nr. 7174, fols. 91–113, Hearing of the accused Wilhelm Greiffenberger, 29 June 1960, here fol. 110.

119. TNA, Kew, WO 208/4139, S.R.M. 1024, 'S. R. Report', 15 November 1944: *Faller: Ich habe in Russland erlebt, schon mehrmals, wie sie Juden umlegen da. Das war wirklich grauenhaft. Zuerst, bevor die so weit waren, dass sie erschossen wurden, mussten sie sich dann ausziehen usw., sind die vorher so geknüppelt worden, das sah man dann nachher, wie sie sich den Oberkörper entblössten. Die haben so breite Streifen, so dick aufgeschwollen, zentimeterdick aufgeschwollen, also ganz blutunterlaufene Striefen, kreuz und quer, überall, das war fürchterlich. Die haben sich abführen lassen, sind überall hingegangen, wo sie hin mussten, wo sie hinverwiesen wurden. Aber da auf dem Weg dahin sind die geknüppelt worden bis dort hinaus. Ich habe die SS gesehen, wie … die Ärmel aufgekrempelt hier, dann den Prügel in die Hand, das war nicht von schlechten Eltern, und immer "gib ihm", immer drauf, auf alle Männer. Einer, der war über achtzig, weit über achtzig, fast an neunzig 'ran, der konnte kaum laufen, den haben sie gejagt, der ist vornübergefallen, ist liegen geblieben, und haben den geschlagen da. Da sind zwei andere Männer, auch so alte Säcke, haben den noch mit hochgenommen, haben ihn weggetragen, mit so einem Bart, furchtbar alter Kerl schon, die haben den fast totgeschlagen. Der jüngste, der erschossen wurde, war dreizehn und der älteste war etwas über neunzig. 21 J: Und auch Frauen und Mädchen? Faller: Alles. Ein Lager, da ist eine Krankheit drin ausgebrochen, weil, die Leute konnten sich nicht pflegen, nichts. Nichts zu fressen gekriegt, gar nichts. Da ist natürlich Krankheit ausgebrochen usw., da haben sie*

das ganze Lager mit MGs zusammengeschossen, wurden einfach zusammenge-
knallt, in Vitebsk. 5000 Mann ungefähr. Frauen, Männer, Kind und Kegel,
alles. 21 J: Wann war das? Faller*: '41 war das. Da sind wir nachher weggekom-*
men.' The translation in the main text is the author's own because the
contemporary translation enclosed with the original German text is in places
only an approximation of that text.

120. LArch Berlin, B Rep. 058, Nr. 7178, fols. 111–116R, Hearing of the
   accused Wilhelm Greiffenberger in the criminal case against Dr Filbert et
   al. for murder, Landgericht Berlin, 3 November 1960, here fol. 113R; UniA
   GI, 'Urteil Landgericht Berlin vom 22. Juni 1962', fol. 95.
121. LArch Berlin, B Rep. 058, Nr. 7178, fols. 111–116R, Hearing of the
   accused Wilhelm Greiffenberger, 3 November 1960, here fol. 113R.
122. UniA GI, 'Urteil Landgericht Berlin vom 22. Juni 1962', fol. 95. See also
   BArch Berlin, R 58/218, fols. 319–323, 'Ereignismeldung UdSSR Nr. 126',
   Chef der Sicherheitspolizei und des SD, 29 October 1941, here fol. 321,
   where Schäfer is listed as the head of Einsatzkommando 9 with his headquarters in Vyazma as of 21 October.
123. LArch Berlin, B Rep. 058, Nr. 7178, fols. 92–97R, Hearing of the accused
   Wilhelm Greiffenberger, 25 October 1960, here fol. 94: *'In Wilna ließ Filbert*
   ein Fotoalbum über den Vormarsch und den Einsatz des Ek 9 mit den Fotografien
   sämtlicher Führer und des ganzen Kommandos anlegen und mit weißer Schrift
   beschriften. Ich kann heute nicht mehr sagen, ob Filbert in dieses Album auch
   Aufnahmen von Judenerschießungen einkleben ließ. Daß Filbert derartige Szenen
   von Judenerschießungen aufnehmen ließ, ist mir bekannt. Dieses Album war
   meines Wissens in Wilna noch nicht fertiggestellt worden; vielmehr war es so,
   daß Filbert das Album nach Fertigstellung dem Obergruppenführer Heydrich zu
   einem festlichen Anlass, wahrscheinlich zu einem Geburtstag, von Witebsk aus
   übergeben wollte. Ich vermute, daß Filbert, als er später von Witebsk
   zurückbeordert wurde, dieses Buch mitnahm und Heydrich persönlich
   überreichte.' Christian Gerlach already drew attention to the existence of
   this photo album, though he speculated that Filbert may have presented it to
   Heydrich on the occasion of his probable trip to Berlin at the end of July (see
   Gerlach, *Kalkulierte Morde,* p. 546).
124. BArch Berlin, R 58/218, fols. 307–315, 'Ereignismeldung UdSSR Nr. 125',
   Chef der Sicherheitspolizei und des SD, 26 October 1941, here fol. 310.
125. LArch Berlin, B Rep. 058, Nr. 7166, fols. 176–186, Hearing of Dr Alfred
   Filbert, 12 May 1959, here fol. 185; 'Angeklagter: Damit werde ich mein
   Leben lang nicht fertig. Russische Lehrerinnen mußten sich entkleiden,
   bevor sie erschossen wurden – "Wir hatten üble Leute im
   Einsatzkommando"', *Augsburger Allgemeine,* 23 May 1962; BArch
   Ludwigsburg, B 162/3633, fols. 7709–7716, Hearing of the accused Karl
   Schulz, Landgericht Bremen, 6 Js 3/60, 11 July 1960, here fol. 7712; UniA
   GI, 'Urteil Landgericht Berlin vom 22. Juni 1962', fols. 97–98.
126. Erich Naumann, successor to Nebe as chief of EG B.
127. LArch Berlin, B Rep. 058, Nr. 7171, fols. 260–263, Hearing of the witness
   Eduard Holste, 19 May 1960, here fol. 262: *'Ich habe niemals Zweifel an der*
   Richtigkeit der uns gemeldeten Zahlen gehabt. Ich habe auch niemals davon

gehört, daß von den Kommandoführern Erschießungszahlen willkürlich erhöht wurden. Ich selbst habe niemals eine Erhöhung der Ziffern über die Erschießungen vorgenommen und bin auch niemals von Nebe oder Naumann oder einem anderen angewiesen worden, die von den Kommandos gemeldeten Ziffern "aufzufrisieren".' For similar comments by his predecessor Ernst Ehlers see LArch Berlin, B Rep. 058, Nr. 7179, fols. 178–181, Hearing of the witness Ernst Ehlers in the criminal case against Dr Filbert et al. for murder, Landgericht Berlin, 26 January 1962, here fol. 180.

128. LArch Berlin, B Rep. 058, Nr. 7178, fols. 111–116R, Hearing of the accused Wilhelm Greiffenberger, 3 November 1960, here fol. 115: '*Wenn Filbert höhere Zahlen gemeldet hätte als tatsächlich Juden erschossen wurden, hätte ich es grundsätzlich erfahren. Es ist mir nie zu Ohren gekommen, daß Filbert Schneider oder einen anderen Sachbearbeiter vom Referat IV veranlasst hat, unrichtige Erschießungsziffern zu melden.*'

129. A point made by Gerlach, *Kalkulierte Morde*, p. 28, fn. 64.

130. LArch Berlin, B Rep. 058, Nr. 7171, fols. 271–278, Hearing of the witness Dr Otto Bradfisch in the criminal case against Dr Alfred Filbert and Gerhard Schneider for murder, Landgericht Berlin, 25 May 1960, here fol. 276: '*Die von meinem Kommando abgegebenen Zahlmeldungen dürfen stimmen [. . .].*'

131. Robel, 'Sowjetunion', pp. 542–543; Gerlach, *Kalkulierte Morde*, p. 27, fn. 64. For a contrasting view see Longerich, *Politik der Vernichtung*, p. 323.

132. 'Schwurgericht Berlin: Befehlsnotstand lag nicht vor. Zuchthausstrafen im Prozeß gegen die Einsatzgruppe [*sic*] 9', *Stuttgarter Zeitung*, 23 June 1962; Zaehle, '"Die Sühne kommt spät"', in *Archiv der VVN-BdA Bundesvereinigung*, Dossier Alfred Filbert. See also Uwe Ruprecht, 'Für eine Schachtel Zigaretten', *Die Gazette. Das politische Kulturmagazin*, 15 March 2003.

133. BArch Berlin, R 58/218, fols. 104–130, 'Ereignismeldung UdSSR Nr. 108', Chef der Sicherheitspolizei und des SD, 9 October 1941, here fol. 123.

134. A point made by Gerlach, *Kalkulierte Morde*, p. 639, fn. 752.

135. BArch-MA, RH 26–403/4a, 'Tätigkeitsbericht. I c / Juli 1941', n.d.

136. Ibid., 'Tätigkeitsbericht. I c / August 1941', n.d.

137. Ibid., 'Tätigkeitsbericht. I c / September 1941', n.d.

138. Ibid., 'Tätigkeitsbericht. I c / Oktober 1941', n.d.

139. Felix Römer describes the division's implementation of the Commissar Order as 'exemplary'. See Römer, *Der Kommissarbefehl*, pp. 359–360 (quote: p. 360).

140. See BArch-MA, RW 4/v. 578, fols. 41–44, 'Richtlinien für die Behandlung politischer Kommissare', 6 June 1941, here fols. 42–44 (both quotes fol. 44).

141. See BArch-MA, RH 26–403/4a, 'Tätigkeitsbericht. I c / Juli 1941', n.d.

142. LArch Berlin, B Rep. 058, Nr. 7178, fols. 111–116R, Hearing of the accused Wilhelm Greiffenberger, 3 November 1960, here fol. 113R; UniA GI, 'Urteil Landgericht Berlin vom 22. Juni 1962', fols. 43 and 95.

143. On Nebe's return to Berlin see Gerlach, *Kalkulierte Morde*, pp. 641–642.

144. LArch Berlin, B Rep. 058, Nr. 7166, fols. 269–271, Hearing of Dr Alfred Filbert, 1 June 1959, here fol. 271; UniA GI, 'Urteil Landgericht Berlin vom 22. Juni 1962', fol. 105; LArch Berlin, B Rep. 058, Nr. 7179, fols. 244–244R, Hearing of Paul Lehn, n.d. [20 February 1961], here fol. 244R. Lehn testified as a witness at Filbert's trial (see UniA GI, 'Urteil Landgericht Berlin vom 22. Juni 1962', fol. 96).

145. UniA GI, 'Urteil Landgericht Berlin vom 22. Juni 1962', fols. 105–106. In considering the evidence, the court noted Filbert's 'zeal in the implementation of the shooting order' (*Eifer in der Ausführung des Erschießungsbefehls*). See UniA GI, 'Urteil Landgericht Berlin vom 22. Juni 1962', fol. 103.

146. Dicks, *Licensed Mass Murder*, pp. 212–214.

147. Rhodes, *Masters of Death*, p. 228. On the documented breakdown of Erich von dem Bach-Zelewski, Higher SS and Police Leader for Central Russia, in March 1942 see Longerich, *Heinrich Himmler*, pp. 344–346.

148. Gerlach, *Kalkulierte Morde*, pp. 641–642; Rathert, *Verbrechen und Verschwörung*, p. 116; Hachmeister, *Der Gegnerforscher*, p. 238.

149. UniA GI, 'Urteil Landgericht Berlin vom 22. Juni 1962', fol. 43; LArch Berlin, B Rep. 058, Nr. 7171, fols. 297–300R, Hearing of the witness Bodo Struck, 9 June 1960, here fols. 300–300R.

150. UniA GI, 'Urteil Landgericht Berlin vom 22. Juni 1962', fols. 100–101. See also LArch Berlin, B Rep. 058, Nr. 7171, fols. 297–300R, Hearing of the witness Bodo Struck, 9 June 1960, here fol. 299.

151. UniA GI, 'Urteil Landgericht Berlin vom 22. Juni 1962', fol. 102; LArch Berlin, B Rep. 058, Nr. 7166, fols. 9–12, 'Vernehmungsprotokoll', signed Richard Neubert, 22 January 1959, here fol. 11. See also the evidence cited earlier.

152. LArch Berlin, B Rep. 058, Nr. 7174, fols. 114–121, Hearing of the accused Wilhelm Greiffenberger, Polizeipräsident in Berlin, 1 July 1960, here fol. 121: '*Ich möchte Filbert dagegen als rabiaten und rücksichtslosen Kommandoführer bezeichnen, der nur sein Weiterkommen im Auge hatte und daher rigoros für die Judenerschiessungen eintrat.*'

153. UniA GI, 'Urteil Landgericht Berlin vom 22. Juni 1962', fol. 106: '*[...] eindeutig ergeben, daß Dr. Filbert bestrebt gewesen ist, möglichst alle Juden erschiessen zu lassen, deren er habhaft werden konnte, und dass er sich den Juden gegenüber unmenschlich verhalten hat.*'

6   'Was it thinkable that I, a jurist and a soldier, would do such a thing?'

1. Querg, 'Spionage und Terror', p. 223.

2. Figaj, 'Die blutige Karriere des Heinz Jost', p. 16.

3. IfZ-Archiv, ZS-429/II, fols. 2–71, 'Interrogation Report No. 15', 9 July 1945, here fol. 29. The internal SS investigation file is lost (see Figaj, 'Die blutige Karriere des Heinz Jost', p. 17). In fact, the files of the Main Office SS Court (*Hauptamt SS-Gericht*), which was based in Munich, as well as those of the individual SS and Police Courts, appear to be almost entirely lost. See the 'Vorläufige Vorbemerkung' in the finding aid for record group NS 7 (*SS–und*

Polizeigerichtsbarkeit) in the Bundesarchiv Berlin-Lichterfelde. See also Bianca Vieregge, *Die Gerichtsbarkeit einer "Elite". Nationalsozialistische Rechtsprechung am Beispiel der SS–und Polizei-Gerichtsbarkeit* (Baden-Baden: Nomos Verlagsgesellschaft, 2002), esp. p. 5.

4. LArch Berlin, B Rep. 058, Nr. 7166, fols. 194–206, Hearing of Dr Alfred Filbert, 14 May 1959, here fol. 198; StArch Hamburg, 213–12, Nr. 33, Bd. 16, fols. 7563–7572, 'Protokoll in der gerichtlichen Voruntersuchung gegen Bruno Streckenbach', 23 September 1971, here fol. 7568 (quote); LArch Berlin, B Rep. 058, Nr. 7179, fols. 241–243, Hearing of the witness Heinz Jost in the criminal case against Dr Alfred Filbert et al. for murder, Landgericht Berlin, 20 February 1961, here fol. 242R. See also Dicks, *Licensed Mass Murder*, pp. 212–213. Richard Rhodes states that the 60,000 Reich marks had been 'confiscated from his victims', namely the Soviet Jews murdered by EK 9 (see Rhodes, *Masters of Death*, p. 223). Although Rhodes' source for his passages on Filbert is Henry V. Dicks, Dicks makes no mention of where Filbert had – or was supposed to have – obtained the 60,000 Reich marks. In a post-war hearing, Heinz Jost referred to the sum in question as intelligence funds returned from abroad (see LArch Berlin, B Rep. 058, Nr. 7179, fols. 241–243, Hearing of the witness Heinz Jost, 20 February 1961, here fol. 242R).

5. LArch Berlin, B Rep. 058, Nr. 7166, fols. 194–206, Hearing of Dr Alfred Filbert, 14 May 1959, here fol. 198.

6. LArch Berlin, B Rep. 058, Nr. 7166, fols. 77–81, Hearing of Karl Schulz, 2 May 1960, here fol. 81. On the purchase of the villa see Henning Schröder and Hans H. Lembke, *Nikolassee. Häuser und Bewohner der Villenkolonie* (Berlin: H. Schröder, 2008), p. 195. Michael Wildt suggests that Karl Schulz, formerly Nebe's adjutant, had confused Filbert with Jost, who had acquired a Jewish-owned property in Berlin-Wannsee in March 1940 (see Wildt, *Generation des Unbedingten*, p. 397, fn. 335). There is no reason to question Schulz's testimony, however, since Filbert had also acquired a Jewish-owned property in Berlin-Wannsee.

7. UniA GI, Juristische Promotionsakten Nr. 775, fols. 23–27, Letter from Alfred Filbert to the Justus Liebig University 'Betr.: Aberkennung der Doktor-Würde', 2 March 1964, here fol. 25; StArch Hamburg, 213–12, Nr. 33, Bd. 16, fols. 7563–7572, 'Protokoll in der gerichtlichen Voruntersuchung gegen Bruno Streckenbach', 23 September 1971, here fols. 7568 and 7572.

8. Dicks, *Licensed Mass Murder*, p. 213. See also StArch Hamburg, 213–12, Nr. 33, Bd. 16, fols. 7563–7572, 'Protokoll in der gerichtlichen Voruntersuchung gegen Bruno Streckenbach', 23 September 1971, here fol. 7568.

9. See Gitta Sereny, *Am Abgrund: Gespräche mit dem Henker. Franz Stangl und die Morde von Treblinka*, translated from English by Helmut Röhrling, rev. ed. (Munich: Piper, 1995 [1974]), p. 197.

10. Quoted in Welzer, *Täter*, p. 67: '[. . .] *daß ich einen Diebstahl nie begangen hätte. Ich weiß, daß man so etwas nicht tun darf. In der schlechten Zeit war ich Verkäuferin und ich hätte damals leicht Gelegenheit gehabt. Aber so etwas habe*

ich nie getan, weil ich einfach wußte, das darf man nicht tun. Schon als Kind hatte ich gelernt: Du darfst nicht stehlen.'

11. Ibid.: *'Wenn mir vorgehalten wird, ob ich auf einen entsprechenden Befehl hin einen Diebstahl ausgeführt hätte, so sage ich hierzu, daß ich das nicht getan hätte. Die Verabreichung von Medikamenten und sei es auch zum Zwecke der Tötung von Geisteskranken gewesen, sah ich allerdings als eine mir obliegende Dienstpflicht an, die ich nicht verweigern durfte.'*

12. See Frank Bajohr, *Parvenüs und Profiteure. Korruption in der NS-Zeit* (Frankfurt am Main: S. Fischer, 2001).

13. Ibid., pp. 105–120.

14. Ibid., pp. 95–96.

15. Nbg. Doc. 050–C, 'Rede des Reichsführer-SS bei der SS-Gruppenführertagung in Posen am 4. Oktober 1943', reproduced in: *IMG*, Vol. 29 (Nuremberg: Sekretariat des Gerichtshofs, 1948), pp. 110–173, here p. 146: *'Wir hatten das moralische Recht, wir hatten die Pflicht gegenüber unserem Volk, dieses Volk, das uns umbringen wollte, umzubringen. Wir haben aber nicht das Recht, uns auch nur mit einem Pelz, mit einer Uhr, mit einer Mark, mit einer Zigarette oder mit sonst etwas zu bereichern.'*

16. See Alex J. Kay, 'Death Threat in the Reichstag, June 13, 1929: Nazi Parliamentary Practice and the Fate of Ernst Heilmann', *German Studies Review*, Vol. 35, No. 1 (February 2012), pp. 19–32, here p. 25. For more on the Koch affair see Jens Banach, *Heydrichs Elite. Das Führerkorps der Sicherheitspolizei und des SD 1936–1945*, 3rd rev. ed. (Paderborn: Schöningh, 2002 [1998]), pp. 168–173.

17. Mallmann, '"Mensch, ich feiere heut' den tausendsten Genickschuß"', pp. 122–124 and 126–127 (quote: p. 122).

18. BArch Berlin, R 58/240, fols. 88–88R, 'Betrifft: Verhütung von Korruptionen innerhalb der Sicherheitspolizei und des SD.', V C 2 Nr. 1583/40, signed [Reinhard] Heydrich, 22 December 1940: *'Sollte ich erfahren, daß Angehörige der Sicherheitspolizei und des SD. Vorteile irgendwelcher Art entgegengenommen oder gefordert haben, so werde ich mit den schärfsten Mitteln gegen die Betreffenden vorgehen.'*

19. BArch Berlin, R 58/240, fols. 143–144, 'Betrifft: Bearbeitung von Korruptionsfällen bei der Wehrmacht, bei Behörden und Körperschaften öffentlichen Rechts, bei der NSDAP, deren Gliederungen und den angeschlossenen Verbänden.', signed [Reinhard] Heydrich, 12 August 1941.

20. Hartmut Jäckel, *Menschen in Berlin. Das letzte Telefonbuch der alten Reichshauptstadt 1941* (Stuttgart/Munich: Deutsche Verlags-Anstalt, 2000), pp. 12–13.

21. Ibid., p. 133.

22. Schröder and Lembke, *Nikolassee*, p. 195.

23. Ibid.

24. Written notification from Henning Schröder, Berlin-Nikolassee, 10 March 2013.

25. Schröder and Lembke, *Nikolassee*, p. 195.

26. Dicks, *Licensed Mass Murder*, pp. 224–225. On the alleged nervous breakdown see ibid., pp. 212–214. See also the discussion in Chapter 5.
27. See Wildt, *Generation des Unbedingten*, pp. 399–400.
28. LArch Berlin, B Rep. 058, Nr. 7179, fols. 241–243, Hearing of the witness Heinz Jost, 20 February 1961, here fol. 242R: *'Tatsächlich war das Geld auf Heller und Pfennig vorhanden, was auch Heydrich bekannt war, ohne daß dieser jedoch Gelegenheit nahm diese Frage zu Gunsten von Filbert oder von mir zu klären.'*
29. LArch Berlin, B Rep. 058, Nr. 7166, fols. 28–31R, Hearing of Dr Alfred Filbert, 25 February 1959, here fol. 30R; Dicks, *Licensed Mass Murder*, p. 213.
30. LArch Berlin, B Rep. 058, Nr. 7166, fols. 194–206, Hearing of Dr Alfred Filbert, 14 May 1959, here fol. 198; LArch Berlin, B Rep. 058, Nr. 5199, fols. 22–26, Hearing of Dr Alfred Filbert, 3 March 1960, here fol. 23; UniA GI, Juristische Promotionsakten Nr. 775, fols. 23–27, Letter from Alfred Filbert to the Justus Liebig University 'Betr.: Aberkennung der Doktor-Würde', 2 March 1964, here fol. 25; StArch Hamburg, 213–12, Nr. 33, Bd. 16, fols. 7563–7572, 'Protokoll in der gerichtlichen Voruntersuchung gegen Bruno Streckenbach', 23 September 1971, here fols. 7568 and 7571.
31. Dicks, *Licensed Mass Murder*, p. 213.
32. See BArch Berlin, VBS 286/6400010138, SSO-Akte Dr. Alfred Filbert. Michael Wildt nevertheless inexplicably cites Filbert's SSO file as his main source for the allegations against Filbert as well as his two-year suspension (see Wildt, *Generation des Unbedingten*, p. 397, fn. 335).
33. LArch Berlin, B Rep. 058, Nr. 7166, fols. 28–31R, Hearing of Dr Alfred Filbert, 25 February 1959, here fol. 30R; LArch Berlin, B Rep. 058, Nr. 7166, fols. 194–206, Hearing of Dr Alfred Filbert, 14 May 1959, here fol. 198; LArch Berlin, B Rep. 058, Nr. 5199, fols. 22–26, Hearing of Dr Alfred Filbert, 3 March 1960, here fol. 23.
34. LArch Berlin, B Rep. 058, Nr. 7166, fols. 77–81, Hearing of Karl Schulz, 2 April 1959, here fol. 81.
35. This assumption can also be found in Dicks, *Licensed Mass Murder*, p. 214.
36. BArch Berlin, R 58/240, fols. 218–219, 'Betrifft: Gruppe V Wi', signed [Arthur] Nebe, 4 July 1944: *'Zwecks einheitlicher Zusammenfassung aller Dienststellen zur Bekämpfung der Wirtschaftskriminalität [. . .]'* (fol. 218). See also LArch Berlin, B Rep. 058, Nr. 7166, fols. 28–31R, Hearing of Dr Alfred Filbert, 25 February 1959, here fol. 30R; IfZ-Archiv, ZS-429/II, fols. 2–71, 'Interrogation Report No. 15', 9 July 1945, here fol. 66. Contrary to Karl Schulz's post-war testimony, Department V B 2 was not expanded to *become* Group V Wi. Instead, Department V B 2 continued to exist and retained its focus on fraud (see BArch Berlin, R 58/240, fols. 218–219, 'Betrifft: Gruppe V Wi', signed [Arthur] Nebe, 4 July 1940, here fol. 218R).
37. Dicks, *Licensed Mass Murder*, p. 220.
38. LArch Berlin, B Rep. 058, Nr. 7166, fols. 28–31R, Hearing of Dr Alfred Filbert, 25 February 1959, here fol. 30R; LArch Berlin, B Rep. 058, Nr. 7166, fols. 77–81, Hearing of Karl Schulz, 2 April 1959, here fol. 81; TNA, Kew, FO 1050/312, 'Report on R[e]ich[s]sicherheitshauptamt', 2 July 1945,

signed Major J. Timmerman, p. 2. Contrary to Filbert's post-war testimony, Group V B was not responsible for 'Capital Offences'. Capital Offences fell to Department I *within* Group V B. The confusion may have arisen because Lobbes, whom Filbert replaced, had been head of Department V B I (Capital Offences) – as well as deputy head of Group V B – before being promoted to head Group V B (Operations). Contrast BArch Berlin, R 58/240, fols. 246–293R, 'Geschäftsverteilungsplan des Reichssicherheitshauptamtes. Stand: 1.3.1941', 1 March 1941, here fol. 277R, with BArch Berlin, R 58/240, fols. 303–349, 'Geschäftsverteilungsplan des Reichssicherheitshauptamtes. Stand 1.10.1943', here fol. 330.

39. LArch Berlin, B Rep. 057–01, Nr. 1017, fols. 157–159, Statement by the prisoner Alfred Filbert, Tegel Prison, 1 Js 4/65 (RSHA), 24 August 1966, here fol. 158.

40. Wildt, *Generation des Unbedingten*, p. 708, fn. 338.

41. BArch Berlin, VBS 286/6400010138, SSO-Akte Dr. Alfred Filbert, 'Aktennotiz', I 2 a, Mü, 22 November 1944.

42. LArch Berlin, B Rep. 058, Nr. 7166, fols. 77–81, Hearing of Karl Schulz, 2 April 1959, here fol. 81.

43. LArch Berlin, B Rep. 058, Nr. 5199, fols. 22–26, Hearing of Dr Alfred Filbert, 3 March 1960, here fols. 23–24.

44. Banach, *Heydrichs Elite*, p. 171.

45. ITS Archives, 1.1.5.3 KZ Buchenwald–individuelle Unterlage, Häftlingspersonalbogen–(Doc. ID # 5856618).

46. See Henriette Harris, 'Die menschenfeindlichen Potenziale', *Die Tageszeitung*, 7 May 2014, p. 15 (interview with the director of the Buchenwald Memorial Foundation, Volkhard Knigge).

47. ITS Archives, 1.1.5.3 KZ Buchenwald–individuelle Unterlage-, 'Häftlings-Personal-Karte' (Doc. ID # 5856617); Archiv der Gedenkstätte Buchenwald, Weimar (hereafter BwA), Häftlingsnummernkartei 29092; BwA, 'Neuzugänge vom 6. Dez. 1943', Politische Abteilung, 6 December 1943; BwA, 'Nachtrag zur Veränderungsmeldung vom 6. Dezember 1943', 9 December 1943. I am grateful to Sabine Stein for providing me with a copy of the last three documents.

48. IPN, Warsaw, IPN GK 127/34, 'Verlegung am 13.12.43'. I am grateful to Władysław Bułhak for providing me with a copy of this document.

49. Robert Leibbrand, *Buchenwald. Ein Tatsachenbericht zur Geschichte der deutschen Widerstandsbewegung* (Stuttgart: Europa, n.d. [1945]), p. 36.

50. Ibid., p. 51.

51. LArch Berlin, B Rep. 058, Nr. 7168, fols. 39–45R, Hearing of the accused Dr Alfred Filbert, 14 January 1960, here fol. 42R.

52. ITS Archives, 1.1.5.1 KZ Buchenwald–Veränderungsmeldung-, 'Veränderungsmeldung', K.L. Buchenwald, 20 October 1944 (Doc. ID # 5283701).

53. On the Fritz Sauckel Works see Studienkreis Deutscher Widerstand 1933–1945, ed., *Heimatgeschichtlicher Wegweiser zu Stätten des Widerstandes und der Verfolgung 1933–1945, Band 8: Thüringen* (Frankfurt am Main: VAS, 2003), pp. 346–347.

54. ITS Archives, 1.1.5.1 KZ Buchenwald, 'Namentliche Liste. Betr.: Einsatz bei der Formation Dirlewanger', 21 November 1944 (Doc. ID # 5343397); ITS Archives, 1.1.5.1 KZ Buchenwald–Veränderungsmeldung-, 'Veränderungsmeldung', K.L. Buchenwald, 28 November 1944 (Doc. ID # 5283886).

55. ITS Archives, 1.1.5.3 KZ Buchenwald–individuelle Unterlage, Effektenkarte–(Doc. ID # 5856615, reverse).

56. Hellmuth Auerbach, 'Die Einheit Dirlewanger', *Vierteljahrshefte für Zeitgeschichte*, Vol. 10, No. 3 (July 1962), pp. 250–263, here p. 250. On Oskar Dirlewanger see Knut Stang, 'Dr. Oskar Dirlewanger – Protagonist der Terrorkriegsführung', in Mallmann and Paul, eds., *Karrieren der Gewalt*, pp. 66–75; Hans-Peter Klausch, *Antifaschisten in SS-Uniform. Schicksal und Widerstand der deutschen politschen KZ-Häftlinge, Zuchthaus–und Wehrmachtsgefangenen in der SS-Sonderformation Dirlewanger* (Bremen: Edition Temmen, 1993), pp. 35–45; Auerbach, 'Die Einheit Dirlewanger', pp. 250–252.

57. Stang, 'Dr. Oskar Dirlewanger', p. 66.

58. Auerbach, 'Die Einheit Dirlewanger', pp. 253–254. See also BArch-MA, RS 3–36/10, fol. 89, 'Aktenvermerk. Betr.: Rücksprache mit SS-Brigadeführer Klücks [sic] am heutigen Tage', SS-Obersturmbannführer Dr Dirlewanger, 8 June 1943.

59. Hellmuth Auerbach, 'Konzentrationslagerhäftlinge im Fronteinsatz', in Wolfgang Benz, ed., *Miscellanea. Festschrift für Helmut Krausnick zum 75. Geburtstag* (Stuttgart: Deutsche Verlags-Anstalt, 1980), pp. 63–83, here p. 68; Klausch, *Antifaschisten in SS-Uniform*, p. 140.

60. Auerbach, 'Die Einheit Dirlewanger', p. 257. The standard work on the deployment of political inmates of concentration camps in the Dirlewanger formation is Klausch, *Antifaschisten in SS-Uniform*.

61. BArch Berlin, NS 3/401, fols. 2–2R, 'Betr.: Vorschlag des SS-Stubaf.' Zill', signed SS-Oberführer [Dr Oskar] Dirlewanger, 7 October 1944, here fol. 2.

62. Stang, 'Dr. Oskar Dirlewanger', p. 72; Auerbach, 'Die Einheit Dirlewanger', pp. 257–258; Rolf Michaelis, ed., *Erinnerungen an das SS-Sonderkommando "Dirlewanger"* (Berlin: Michaelis, 2008), p. 76.

63. 'Vergebliche Werbung für die SS. Bericht des ehemaligen deutschen Häftlings Walter Bartel aus dem Jahr 1945', reproduced in: Nationale Mahn–und Gedenkstätte Buchenwald, ed., *Buchenwald. Mahnung und Verpflichtung. Dokumente und Berichte*, 4th rev. ed. ([East] Berlin: VEB Deutscher Verlag der Wissenschaften, 1983 [1960]), pp. 481–483, here pp. 482–483; Leibbrand, *Buchenwald. Ein Tatsachenbericht*, p. 51.

64. For the figure and the quote see Eugen Kogon, *Der SS-Staat. Das System der deutschen Konzentrationslager*, 5th exp. ed. (n.pl.: Europäische Verlagsanstalt, 1959 [1946]), p. 323.

65. Auerbach, 'Konzentrationslagerhäftlinge im Fronteinsatz', pp. 74–75; Rolf Michaelis, *Die SS-Sturmbrigade 'Dirlewanger'. Vom Warschauer Aufstand bis zum Kessel von Halbe* (Dresden: Winkelried, 2006), p. 62.

66. Auerbach, 'Konzentrationslagerhäftlinge im Fronteinsatz', p. 63.

67. Auerbach, 'Die Einheit Dirlewanger', pp. 259–260. The 'liquidation' of political prisoners is mentioned in Michaelis, ed., *Erinnerungen*, p. 76.
68. See Gerlach, *Kalkulierte Morde*, pp. 217, 899–902, 928 and 958; Christian Ingrao, *Les chasseurs noirs: La brigade Dirlewanger* (n.pl. [Paris]: Perrin, 2006), p. 50.
69. Włodzimierz Borodziej, *Der Warschauer Aufstand 1944* (Frankfurt am Main: S. Fischer, 2001), pp. 119–120.
70. Ibid., pp. 122–124; Snyder, *Bloodlands*, pp. 303–305.
71. See Borodziej, *Der Warschauer Aufstand*, pp. 202–208; Snyder, *Bloodlands*, pp. 308–309.
72. Auerbach, 'Konzentrationslagerhäftlinge im Fronteinsatz', p. 67.
73. Auerbach, 'Die Einheit Dirlewanger', pp. 258 and 261.
74. Klausch, *Antifaschisten in SS-Uniform*, pp. 194–195 and 257.
75. Ibid., p. 262. See also Auerbach, 'Die Einheit Dirlewanger', pp. 259 and 261; Auerbach, 'Konzentrationslagerhäftlinge im Fronteinsatz', pp. 78–80; Krisztián Ungváry, *Battle for Budapest: 100 Days in World War II*, translated from Hungarian by Ladislaus Löb (London/New York: I. B. Tauris, 2011 [1998]), pp. 21–22. For a total figure of 'approximately 600' (*etwa 600*) former concentration camp inmates who deserted to the Red Army see Michaelis, ed., *Erinnerungen*, p. 79.
76. Klausch, *Antifaschisten in SS-Uniform*, pp. 262–263.
77. Auerbach, 'Die Einheit Dirlewanger', pp. 261–262.
78. BArch-MA, RS 3–36/12, fols. 1–3, 'Führerbefehl zur Aufstockung der SS-Brigade "Dirlewanger" zu einer Division (Fernspruch)', signed Brigadier Gehlen, 14 February 1945.
79. For example by Wildt, *Generation des Unbedingten*, p. 397.
80. 'Beschluß für Todeserklärung', 2 II 57/51, Amtsgericht Bottrop, 15 October 1951.
81. Written notification from Ralph Filbert's wife, Erika Filbert, Media, PA, 29 July 2013; interview with Otto Filbert's son, Peter Filbert, Weinheim, 29 August 2013.
82. LArch Berlin, B Rep. 058, Nr. 7168, fols. 39–45R, Hearing of the accused Dr Alfred Filbert, 14 January 1960, here fol. 42R; telephonic notification from Ralph Filbert's wife, Erika Filbert, Media, PA, 12 June 2013; interview with Otto Filbert's son, Peter Filbert, Weinheim, 29 August 2013.
83. See Chapters 8, 9 and 10 of this study. For further discussion of Filbert's victim mentality, see the final chapter, 'Concluding Thoughts'.
84. TNA, Kew, FO 1050/312, 'Report on R[e]ich[s]sicherheitshauptamt', 2 July 1945, p. 4; Stephan Linck, *Der Ordnung verpflichtet: Deutsche Polizei 1933–1949: Der Fall Flensburg* (Paderborn: Schöningh, 2000), p. 148.
85. Linck, *Der Ordnung verpflichtet*, pp. 148–149; Carsten Dams and Michael Stolle, *Die Gestapo. Herrschaft und Terror im Dritten Reich*, 3rd rev. ed. (Munich: C. H. Beck, 2012 [2008]), p. 172.
86. TNA, Kew, FO 1050/312, 'Report on R[e]ich[s]sicherheitshauptamt' Linck, 2 July 1945, p. 2. I am grateful to Felix Römer for providing me with a copy of this document.
87. Ibid.

7   'My son, who has not yet returned home from the war'

1. LArch Berlin, B Rep. 058, Nr. 7166, fols. 28–32R, Hearing of Dr Alfred
   Filbert, 25 February 1959, here fol. 31. On Filbert's submergence see also
   TNA, Kew, FO 1050/312, 'Report on R[e]ich[s]sicherheitshauptamt', 2 July
   1945, p. 2.
2. On the murder of Germans by loyal representatives of the regime during the
   final weeks of the war, see the excellent essay by Andrej Angrick, 'Abendrot
   des Dritten Reichs – oder vom somnambulen Kannibalismus eines Regimes
   im Untergang', in Cüppers et al., eds., *Naziverbrechen*, pp. 117–131.
3. LArch Berlin, B Rep. 058, Nr. 7166, fols. 28–32R, Hearing of Dr Alfred
   Filbert, 25 February 1959, here fol. 31. Filbert actually stated: 'I returned to
   Bad Gandersheim' (*ging ich nach Bad Gandersheim zurück*). This would
   indicate that he had already been in Bad Gandersheim previously.
4. Einwohnermeldearchiv der Stadt Bad Gandersheim, Meldeliste Heckenbeck
   – Hilprechtshausen 1945, Eintrag-Nr. 86. I am grateful to Manfred Kielhorn
   for providing me with a copy of the relevant excerpt.
5. LArch Berlin, B Rep. 058, Nr. 7168, fols. 46–51R, Hearing of the accused
   Dr Alfred Filbert in the criminal case against Dr Alfred Filbert for murder,
   Landgericht Berlin, 18 January 1960, here fol. 48R. Former head of EK 8,
   Otto Bradfisch, was released from Allied captivity at the end of the war on the
   basis of fake identification papers. See Gerhard Paul, 'Zwischen Selbstmord,
   Illegalität und neuer Karriere. Ehemalige Gestapo-Bedienstete im
   Nachkriegsdeutschland', in Gerhard Paul and Klaus-Michael Mallmann,
   eds., *Die Gestapo – Mythos und Realität* (Darmstadt: Wissenschaftliche
   Buchgesellschaft, 1995), pp. 529–547, here p. 535.
6. 'Einsatzkommando-Prozeß in Berlin. Dr. Filbert: Heydrich entließ mich
   nicht – Murren im Zuhörerraum bei Selbstbemitleidung des Angeklagten',
   Augsburger Allgemeine, 15 May 1962.
7. NARA, RG 319, Investigative Records Repository (hereafter IRR), File D
   158813.
8. Einwohnermeldearchiv der Stadt Bad Gandersheim, Meldekarte Käthe
   Filbert. According to her local registration card, prior to moving to Bad
   Gandersheim Käthe Filbert had lived in Menteroda, which is situated a few
   kilometres north of Volkenroda.
9. Written notification from Manfred Kielhorn, Pressesprecher/
   Öffentlichkeitsarbeit, Stadt Bad Gandersheim, 21 November 2011. See
   also LArch Berlin, B Rep. 058, Nr. 7168, fols. 46–51R, Hearing of the
   accused Dr Alfred Filbert, 18 January 1960, here fol. 48R.
10. LArch Berlin, B Rep. 058, Nr. 7168, fols. 46–51R, Hearing of the accused
    Dr Alfred Filbert, 18 January 1960, here fol. 49.
11. Ibid., fol. 49: '[...] da aber seine Tätigkeit infolge der damaligen Lage ziemlich
    lahmgelegt war, beschäftigte ich mich zunächst an seinem damaligen Wohnsitz,
    dem Rittergut Hilprechtshausen in der Nähe von Bad Gandersheim. Wir beabsich-
    tigten [...] eine Siedlung zu errichten und Holzwerkstätten zu errichten, wo
    Flüchtlinge angesiedelt werden sollten. Um mich selbst darauf vorzubereiten, habe
    ich in der verhältnismäßig kleinen Werkstatt, die sich auf dem Rittergut befand, als
    Bank–und Maschinentischler gearbeitet. Wir bauten dann die Firma Leinetal auf,*

eine Möbelfabrik, mit einer entsprechenden Siedlung. Ich übernahm unter einem Geschäftsführer die kaufmännische, insbesondere die finanzielle Leitung.'

12. Written notification from Manfred Kielhorn, Pressesprecher/ Öffentlichkeitsarbeit, Stadt Bad Gandersheim, 21 November 2011.

13. Filbert's eldest son, Dieter, was not aware of any prior relationship between his father and Heinrich Pferdmenges (written notification from Dieter Filbert, Berlin, 31 March 2013).

14. Einwohnermeldearchiv der Stadt Bad Gandersheim, Meldeliste Heckenbeck – Hilprechtshausen 1945, 'Evakuierte und Flüchtlinge von 1945'. I am grateful to Manfred Kielhorn for providing me with a copy of the relevant page.

15. Interview with Henning Pferdmenges, grandson of Heinrich Pferdmenges, 7 March 2013. Heinrich Pferdmenges died on 22 September 1947. See Friedrich Richter, 'Tuchfabrik Hinrichssegen in Workallen, Gemeinde Bolitten bei Liebstadt', *Mohrunger Heimatkreis-Nachrichten*, Vol. 33, No. 102 (Easter 2004), pp. 54–57, here p. 56. According to the biographical information on its author provided in this article, Friedrich Richter, born 1913, had worked in the East Prussia department of the Reich Economics Ministry in Berlin from May 1939 onwards and was the private secretary of Heinrich Pferdmenges from 15 June 1946 to 31 October 1947, during which time he lived at the Hilprechtshausen manor (see ibid., p. 57).

16. Written notification from Manfred Kielhorn, Pressesprecher/ Öffentlichkeitsarbeit, Stadt Bad Gandersheim, 28 February 2012.

17. Berliot von Mende and Erling von Mende, 'Ein Bürokrat der mittleren Ebene', unpublished manuscript, 2013. I am grateful to Erling von Mende, Berlin, for providing me with a copy of this text. I am also grateful to Manfred Kielhorn, Bad Gandersheim, for drawing my attention to Gerhard von Mende's period of residence at the Hilprechtshausen manor.

18. Kay, *Exploitation, Resettlement, Mass Murder*, p. 19.

19. Von Mende and von Mende, 'Ein Bürokrat der mittleren Ebene'.

20. Written notification from Erling von Mende, Berlin, 26 June 2013.

21. Einwohnermeldearchiv der Stadt Bad Gandersheim, Meldeliste Heckenbeck – Hilprechtshausen 1949, Eintrag-Nr. 588; Familienkarte Dr. Alfred Selbert. I am grateful to Manfred Kielhorn for providing me with a copy of the relevant excerpts.

22. Standesamt Worms, Sterbeeintrag 427/1949, Sterbeurkunde Christiane Filbert, geb. Kühner, 22 July 1949. During a hearing on the day of his arrest in 1959 Filbert incorrectly dated the death of his mother to 1947 (see LArch Berlin, B Rep. 058, Nr. 7166, fols. 28–31R, Hearing of Dr Alfred Filbert, 25 February 1959, here fol. 28R).

23. Einwohnermeldearchiv der Stadt Bad Gandersheim, Familienkarte Dr. Alfred Selbert. I am grateful to Manfred Kielhorn for providing me with a copy of the relevant excerpt. It was thus not until 1951 that Filbert reassumed his real name, and not 1950, as claimed by Wildt, *Generation des Unbedingten*, p. 819.

24. Written notification from Dieter Filbert, Berlin, 17 March 2013.

25. Stadtarchiv Mannheim – Institut für Stadtgeschichte, Meldekarte Dr. Alfred Filbert; Stadtarchiv Mannheim – Institut für Stadtgeschichte, Meldekarte

Adolf Hille. I am grateful to Manfred Kielhorn for providing me with a copy of these documents.

26. Interview with Peter Filbert, Weinheim, 29 August 2013.
27. As postulated by Wildt, *Generation des Unbedingten*, p. 819.
28. 'Gesetz über die Gewährung von Straffreiheit. Vom 31. Dezember 1949', in *Bundesgesetzblatt*, 1949, No. 9, 31 December 1949, pp. 37–38. The content of § 2(2) demonstrates that this amnesty did not relate 'alone to imposed prison sentences of up to six months', as claimed by Herbert, *Best*, p. 439.
29. 'Gesetz über die Gewährung von Straffreiheit. Vom 31. Dezember 1949', p. 38, § 10. See also Norbert Frei, *Vergangenheitspolitik. Die Anfänge der Bundesrepublik und die NS-Vergangenheit*, rev. ed. (Munich: C. H. Beck, 2012 [1996]), pp. 17–19. In his discussion of the Law on the Granting of Impunity from Prosecution, no mention of this aspect is made by Andreas Eichmüller, *Keine Generalamnestie. Die Strafverfolgung von NS-Verbrechen in der frühen Bundesrepublik* (Munich: Oldenbourg, 2012), pp. 36–42.
30. On the sentence revisions see Earl, *The Nuremberg SS-Einsatzgruppen Trial*, pp. 277–287.
31. Bernhard Baatz, former Commander of the Security Police and the SD in Estonia, also resurfaced in the wake of the McCloy amnesty (see Paul, 'Zwischen Selbstmord, Illegalität und neuer Karriere', pp. 536–537).
32. Stadtarchiv Mannheim – Institut für Stadtgeschichte, Meldekarte Dr. Alfred Filbert.
33. Einwohnermeldearchiv der Stadt Hannover, Meldekarte Dr. Alfred Filbert. I am grateful to Manfred Kielhorn for providing me with a copy of this document.
34. 'Beschluß für Todeserklärung', 2 II 57/51, Amtsgericht Bottrop, 15 October 1951; written notification from the Deutsche Dienststelle für die Benachrichtigung der nächsten Angehörigen von Gefallenen der ehemaligen deutschen Wehrmacht (WASt), Berlin, 13 January 2012.
35. ITS Archives, 1.1.5.3 KZ Buchenwald–individuelle Unterlage-, 'Häftlings-Personal-Karte' (Doc. ID # 5856617); ITS Archives, 1.1.5.3 KZ Buchenwald–individuelle Unterlage, Effektenkarte–(Doc. ID # 5856615).
36. Written notification from the Deutsche Dienststelle für die Benachrichtigung der nächsten Angehörigen von Gefallenen der ehemaligen deutschen Wehrmacht (WASt), Berlin, 13 January 2012.
37. LArch Berlin, B Rep. 058, Nr. 7166, fols. 28–32R, Hearing of Dr Alfred Filbert, 25 February 1959, here fol. 31.
38. Written notification from Christa Bischof, Bürgeramt Mitte, Hannover, 3 January 2012. I am grateful to Manfred Kielhorn for passing on this information.
39. Written notification from Manfred Kielhorn, Pressesprecher/Öffentlichkeitsarbeit, Stadt Bad Gandersheim, 9 January 2012.
40. Einwohnermeldearchiv der Stadt Bad Gandersheim, Meldekarte Käthe Filbert.

41. Written notifications from Manfred Kielhorn, Pressesprecher/ Öffentlichkeitsarbeit, Stadt Bad Gandersheim, 21 November 2011 and 28 February 2012.
42. Manfred Kielhorn draws this conclusion based on his research (written notification from Manfred Kielhorn, Pressesprecher/Öffentlichkeitsarbeit, Stadt Bad Gandersheim, 28 February 2012).
43. Einwohnermeldearchiv der Stadt Bad Gandersheim, Meldekarte Käthe Filbert.
44. Written notification from Dieter Filbert, Berlin, 17 March 2013.
45. Ullrich, '*Ich fühl' mich nicht als Mörder*', pp. 154 and 270. It is unclear why Ullrich abbreviates Schneider's name to 'Gerhard S.' throughout her study, evidently in an attempt to anonymise him. This is in spite of his conviction in 1966, which was confirmed as legally binding later the same year, and which Ullrich herself notes (p. 270). She furthermore uses the full name of five of the nineteen Nazi perpetrators she examines in her book.
46. Ibid., p. 307, n. 473.
47. Wildt, *Generation des Unbedingten*, pp. 769–770; Patrick Wagner, *Volksgemeinschaft ohne Verbrecher: Konzeptionen und Praxis der Kriminalpolizei in der Zeit der Weimarer Republik und des Nationalsozialismus* (Hamburg: Christians, 1996), pp. 11 and 307.
48. Quoted in Wagner, *Volksgemeinschaft ohne Verbrecher*, p. 307: '*[. . .] vor allem beruflich dankbar, d.h. befriedrigend [. . .].*'
49. LArch Berlin, B Rep. 058, Nr. 7166, fols. 28–32R, Hearing of Dr Alfred Filbert, 25 February 1959, here fol. 31. In August 1959, half a year after Filbert's arrest, a newspaper article referred to him as the manager of the Berlin branch of the 'Bank für Binnenschifffahrt', Hanover (see 'Die Mörder sind noch unter uns. Schleppende Ermittlungen der Berliner Staatsanwaltschaft gegen ehemalige Angehörige des berüchtigten Polizeibataillons 9', *Die Andere Zeitung*, 5 August 1959, in BArch D-H, Dok/P 12569). In 1968, the *Bank für Binnenschiffahrt* rebranded itself the *Bank für Schiffahrt, Handel und Gewerbe*. See Norbert Fiks, *1869–1994. 125 Jahre Ostfriesische Volksbank – ein geschichtlicher Abriß* (Leer: MaYa-Ebooks, 2002 [1994]), p. 40. Following a merger in 1991, the *Bank für Schiffahrt* (BfS), Hanover, became a subsidiary of the *Ostfriesische Volksbank*. According to the *Ostfriesische Volksbank*, no records exist on Alfred Filbert and it can thus neither be confirmed nor denied that Filbert actually worked for the *Bank für Binnenschifffahrt* (telephonic notification from Gregor Klusmann, Personalabteilung, Ostfriesische Volksbank, 5 December 2011).
50. LArch Berlin, B Rep. 058, Nr. 7166, fols. 27–27R, 'Vermerk', 1 4 – K 1 2, signed Gilch, KM, 26 February 1959, here fol. 27R.
51. LArch Berlin, B Rep. 058, Nr. 7168, fols. 46–51R, Hearing of the accused Dr Alfred Filbert, 18 January 1960, here fol. 49R. The *Braunschweig-Hannoversche Hypothekenbank* was the subject of a merger in 1996 and ceased to exist as an independent entity thereafter. The bank's personnel files were thus destroyed (written notification from Bernhard Loh, Vorstandssekretariat/ Recht, Berlin-Hannoversche Hypothekenbank AG, 19 October 2011).

52. Written notification from Christa Bischof, Bürgeramt Mitte, Hanover, 30 December 2011. I am grateful to Manfred Kielhorn for passing on this information.
53. LArch Berlin, B Rep. 058, Nr. 7168, fols. 46–51R, Hearing of the accused Dr Alfred Filbert, 18 January 1960, here fol. 50.
54. UniA GI, Matrikelakten des Studierendensekretariats, Stud. Mat. Nr. 5493, fol. 2, Letter from Peter Filbert to the Hessische Ludwigs-Universität Giessen, 30 March 1951.
55. Standesamt Worms, Sterbeeintrag 845/1956, Sterbeurkunde Peter Filbert, 31 December 1956. During a hearing on the day of his arrest in 1959, Filbert incorrectly dated the death of his father to 1957 (see LArch Berlin, B Rep. 058, Nr. 7166, fols. 28–31R, Hearing of Dr Alfred Filbert, 25 February 1959, here fol. 28R).
56. *Thomas Harlan – Extrasplitter*, dir. Christoph Hübner (Germany: Christoph Hübner Filmproduktion, 2007), 01:10:42–01:10:55.
57. James F. Siekmeier, *The Bolivian Revolution and the United States, 1952 to the Present* (University Park, PA: The Pennsylvania State University Press, 2011), pp. 39–41; Cole Blasier, 'The United States and the Revolution', in James M. Malloy and Richard Thorn, eds., *Beyond the Revolution: Bolivia since 1952* (Pittsburgh, PA: University of Pittsburgh Press, 1971), pp. 53–109, here pp. 100–101.
58. Christopher Simpson, *Blowback: America's Recruitment of Nazis and its Effects on the Cold War* (London: Weidenfeld & Nicolson, 1988), pp. 187–190; Peter Hammerschmidt, '"Daß V-43 118 SS-Hauptsturmführer war, schließt nicht aus, ihn als Quelle zu verwenden". Der Bundesnachrichtendienst und sein Agent Klaus Barbie', *Zeitschrift für Geschichtswissenschaft*, Vol. 59, No. 4 (2011), pp. 333–348, here pp. 333 and 338.
59. *Nazi War Crimes and Japanese Imperial Government Records Interagency Working Group: Final Report to the United States Congress*, April 2007, p. 45, 'Table 3. CIA declassification summary (number of pages)': https://www.archives.gov/iwg/reports/final-report-2007.pdf [last accessed on 3 November 2015]. On the CIA's response to the Disclosure Act see ibid., pp. 45–50.
60. 'The CIA and Nazi War Criminals: National Security Archive Posts Secret CIA History Released Under Nazi War Crimes Disclosure Act', in *National Security Archive Electronic Briefing Book*, No. 146, ed. Tamara Feinstein, 4 February 2005: http://www2.gwu.edu/~nsarchiv/NSAEBB/NSAEBB146/ [last accessed on 3 November 2015].
61. Timothy Naftali, 'Reinhard Gehlen and the United States', in Richard Breitman, Norman J. W. Goda, Timothy Naftali and Robert Wolfe, *U.S. Intelligence and the Nazis* (Cambridge/New York: Cambridge University Press, 2005), pp. 375–418, here pp. 383–384.
62. Written notification from Michele Meeks, Information and Privacy Coordinator, Central Intelligence Agency, 16 May 2012.
63. Written notification from Michele Meeks, Executive Secretary, Agency Release Panel, Central Intelligence Agency, 26 September 2012.
64. Written notification from Michele Meeks, Information and Privacy Coordinator, Central Intelligence Agency, 25 January 2013; written

notification from Michele Meeks, Executive Secretary, Agency Release Panel, Central Intelligence Agency, 26 September 2012 (quote).

65. NARA, RG 319, IRR, File D 158813 and File XE 158813. The files are in fact duplicates.

8   'A trial of this magnitude has never previously taken place before a German court'

1. On the killings perpetrated by the Einsatzkommando Tilsit see Dieckmann, *Deutsche Besatzungspolitik in Litauen*, Vol. 1, pp. 379–391; idem, 'Der Krieg und die Ermordung der litauischen Juden', pp. 292–300.

2. Annette Weinke, *Eine Gesellschaft ermittelt gegen sich selbst. Die Geschichte der Zentralen Stelle Ludwigsburg 1958–2008* (Darmstadt: Wissenschaftliche Buchgesellschaft, 2008), pp. 10–29.

3. *Thomas Harlan – Extrasplitter*, 01:11:11–01:11:24.

4. 'Die Mörder sind noch unter uns. Schleppende Ermittlungen der Berliner Staatsanwaltschaft gegen ehemalige Angehörige des berüchtigten Polizeibataillons 9', *Die Andere Zeitung*, 5 August 1959, in BArch D-H, Dok/P 12569.

5. 'Befehlsnotstand anerkannt. Verfahren gegen Polizisten eingestellt – Voruntersuchungen gegen SS-Führer', *Berliner Allgemeine Wochenzeitung der Juden in Deutschland*, 12 February 1960, p. 1, in BArch D-H, Dok/P 12569.

6. Written notification from Dieter Filbert, Berlin, 17 March 2013.

7. LArch Berlin, B Rep. 058, Nr. 7166, fols. 27–27R, 'Vermerk', 26 February 1959, here fol. 27R.

8. Ibid.

9. For the transcript of the hearing see LArch Berlin, B Rep. 058, Nr. 7166, fols. 28–31R, Hearing of Dr Alfred Filbert, 25 February 1959.

10. LArch Berlin, B Rep. 058, Nr. 7166, fol. 1, 'Strafanzeige', Polizeipräsident in Berlin, 26 February 1959.

11. LArch Berlin, B Rep. 058, Nr. 7166, fol. 44, 'Aufnahmemitteilung', Untersuchungshaftanstalt Moabit.

12. LArch Berlin, B Rep. 058, Nr. 7167, fol. 5, 'Strafprozeßvollmacht', 1 4 – K 1 2, signed Dr Alfred Filbert, 1 June 1959.

13. For the transcripts of the hearings see LArch Berlin, B Rep. 058, Nr. 7166.

14. LArch Berlin, B Rep. 058, Nr. 5199, fol. 1, 'Strafanzeige', Polizeipräsident in Berlin, 18 August 1959. In his memoirs, published a year after Filbert was sentenced, Ronge staggeringly makes no mention of his infamous client. See Paul Ronge, *Im Namen der Gerechtigkeit. Erinnerungen eines Strafverteidigers* (Munich: Kindler, 1963).

15. LArch Berlin, B Rep. 058, Nr. 7167, fol. 10, Letter from Dr Paul Ronge to the Staatsanwaltschaft Berlin, 19 June 1959: '[. . .] *bestehen ernstliche Bedenken wegen des Gesundheitszustandes meines Mandanten, der bekanntlich an einer Lungentuberkulose leidet.*'

16. LArch Berlin, B Rep. 058, Nr. 7167, fols. 39–39R, 'Betr.: Untersuchungshäftling Dr. Alfred Filbert, geb. 8.9.05, Gef.B.Nr. 216/59', signed Dr Bottke, 26 June 1959.
17. LArch Berlin, B Rep. 058, Nr. 7178, fol. 35, Jugendstrafanstalt Plötzensee, Zugangsliste Nr. 216/59, An die Staatsanwaltschaft bei dem Landgericht Berlin, 20 July 1960.
18. LArch Berlin, B Rep. 058, Nr. 7166, fol. 227, 'Bericht!', I 4 – K 1 2, 26 May 1959.
19. LArch Berlin, B Rep. 058, Nr. 7167, fol. 38, 'Vermerk', I 4 – K I 2, signed Brucker, KOM, 14 July 1959.
20. LArch Berlin, B Rep. 058, Nr. 7168, fols. 26–30, 'Antrag der Generalstaatsanwalt bei dem Landgericht Berlin vom 19. Dezember 1959 an den Untersuchungsrichter bei dem Landgericht Berlin'.
21. LArch Berlin, B Rep. 058, Nr. 7168, fols. 31–31R, 'Verfügung des Untersuchungsrichters I bei dem Landgericht [Berlin]', 1 P Js 287/59, 28 December 1959: 'Er wird beschuldigt in der Zeit vom Juli 1941 bis April 1942 in Russland, Litauen und Polen, im Mittelabschnitt des rückwärtigen Heeresgebietes [...] gemeinschaftlich mit anderen [...] durch mehrere selbständige Handlungen aus niedrigen Beweggründen, heimtückisch und grausam eine bisher unbestimmte Anzahl von Menschen, meist jüdischen Glaubens, getötet bzw. durch andere, ihm unterstelle Personen töten gelassen zu haben [...].'
22. LArch Berlin, B Rep. 058, Nr. 5199, fol. 1, 'Strafanzeige', Polizeipräsident in Berlin, 18 August 1959.
23. '27facher Mörder überführt', BZ am Abend, 25 July 1959, in LArch Berlin, B Rep. 058, Nr. 5199, fol. 2. See also 'Die Mörder sind noch unter uns', Die Andere Zeitung, 5 August 1959, in BArch D-H, Dok/P 12569.
24. LArch Berlin, B Rep. 058, Nr. 5199, fols. 22–26, Hearing of Dr Alfred Filbert, 3 March 1960, here fols. 23–24.
25. LArch Berlin, B Rep. 058, Nr. 5199, fol. 1, 'Strafanzeige', 18 August 1959.
26. LArch Berlin, B Rep. 058, Nr. 7191, fols. 48–112, 'Schwurgerichtsanklage', Generalstaatsanwalt beim Landgericht an das Landgericht Berlin, 21 November 1961, here fols. 49–49R: 'I. der Angeschuldigte Dr. Filbert in der Zeit von Anfang Juli bis zum 20. Oktober 1941 im Raume von Wilna, Grodno, Lida, Wilejka, Molodeczno, Newel und Witebsk gemeinschaftlich mit Hitler, Himmler, Heydrich u.A. handelnd in mindestens 11.000 Fällen mit Überlegung aus niedrigen Beweggründen, heimtückisch und grausam Menschen getötet bzw. deren Tötung durch Untergebene veranlaßt zu haben.'
27. UniA GI, 'Urteil Landgericht Berlin vom 22. Juni 1962', fol. 38. See also LArch Berlin, B Rep. 058, Nr. 7196, fols. 1–2, 'Verhandlungsplan in der Strafsache gegen Filbert u. a.', n.d., which only lists sixteen days (not 18 May, 20 and 22 June but instead 6 June) and was evidently drawn up prior to the trial.
28. 'Größter Judenmordprozeß in Berlin. Die Angeklagten nach dem Krieg in leitenden Stellungen tätig', Augsburger Allgemeine, 11 May 1962: 'Ein Prozeß dieses Umfangs hat bisher vor keinem deutschen Gericht stattgefunden.'
29. 'Hohe Zuchthausstrafen im Einsatzkommando-Prozeß', Augsburger Allgemeine, 23 June 1962.

30. Ibid.; 'Revision von Filbert verworfen', *Der Tagesspiegel*, Berlin, 10 April 1963, in Archiv der VVN-BdA Bundesvereinigung, Dossier Alfred Filbert. A total of 111 witnesses had been summoned (see 'Größter Judenmordprozeß in Berlin', *Augsburger Allgemeine*, 11 May 1962; 'Angeklagter: Damit werde ich mein Leben lang nicht fertig', *Augsburger Allgemeine*, 23 May 1962).

31. UniA GI, 'Urteil Landgericht Berlin vom 22. Juni 1962', fol. 96; LArch Berlin, B Rep. 058, Nr. 7196, fols. 1–2, 'Verhandlungsplan in der Strafsache gegen Filbert u. a.', n.d.

32. 'Einsatzkommando-Prozeß in Berlin', *Augsburger Allgemeine*, 15 May 1962.

33. 'Angeklagter: Damit werde ich mein Leben lang nicht fertig', *Augsburger Allgemeine*, 23 May 1962.

34. UniA GI, 'Urteil Landgericht Berlin vom 22. Juni 1962', fol. 99.

35. H 13 Darmstadt, Nr. 1291/25, 'Strafsache gegen Dr. Alfred Filbert wegen Mordes', 14 January 1960, p. 12.

36. See the comprehensive discussions of the post-war testimonies regarding the so-called 'Führer order' in Ogorreck, *Die Einsatzgruppen*, pp. 47–109, and Earl, *The Nuremberg SS-Einsatzgruppen Trial*, pp. 182–210, and the summary in Browning, *The Origins of the Final Solution*, pp. 226–227.

37. Browning, *The Origins of the Final Solution*, p. 227.

38. Mallmann, 'Die Türöffner der "Endlösung"', p. 448.

39. UniA GI, 'Urteil Landgericht Berlin vom 22. Juni 1962', fols. 98–99 and 106 (quote): '[. . .] weil er bei Befehlsverweigerung um Leib oder Leben hätte fürchten müssen.'

40. See 'Hohe Zuchthausstrafen', *Augsburger Allgemeine*, 23 June 1962; Herbert Jäger, *Verbrechen unter totalitärer Herrschaft. Studien zur nationalsozialistischen Gewaltkriminalität* (Olten/Freiburg im Breisgau: Walter-Verlag, 1967), pp. 158–159; Adalbert Rückerl, *NS-Verbrechen vor Gericht. Versuch einer Vergangenheitsbewältigung*, 2nd rev. ed. (Heidelberg: C. F. Müller, 1984 [1982]), pp. 281–286; Eberhard Jäckel, 'Einfach ein schlechtes Buch', in Julius H. Schoeps, ed., *Ein Volk von Mördern? Die Dokumentation zur Goldhagen-Kontroverse um die Rolle der Deutschen im Holocaust* (Hamburg: Hoffmann & Campe, 1996), pp. 187–192, here p. 188; Gerlach, *Kalkulierte Morde*, pp. 31, fn. 82, and 1111; Cüppers, *Wegbereiter der Shoah*, p. 110.

41. UniA GI, 'Urteil Landgericht Berlin vom 22. Juni 1962', fol. 56. See also 'Filbert schwer belastet', *Augsburger Allgemeine*, 18 May 1962. Greiffenberger was subsequently arrested on 29 June 1960 (see LArch Berlin, B Rep. 058, Nr. 7174, fol. 90, 'Vermerk', I 4 – IK 1, 18 July 1960).

42. UniA GI, 'Urteil Landgericht Berlin vom 22. Juni 1962', fol. 116: *'Der Angeklagte Greiffenberger ist geständig. Er hat sich von seiner ersten Vernehmung an nach der Überzeugung des Schwurgerichts ehrlich bemüht, offen mitzuteilen, was er von den damaligen Vorgängen noch in Erinnerung hatte, und Erinnerungsfehler zu korrigieren.'* See also 'Angeklagter: Damit werde ich mein Leben lang nicht fertig', *Augsburger Allgemeine*, 23 May 1962.

43. BArch Ludwigsburg, B 162/2401, fols. 23–32, 'Urteil und Urteilsbegründung im SS-Prozeß Filbert', n.d. [22 June 1962], here fol. 30R.

44. 'Hauptaufgabe: Judenerschießungen. Erdrückende Aussagen im Berliner Einsatzkommandoprozeß', *Stuttgarter Nachrichten*, 18 May 1962; HStAD, Ztg 136, 'Hauptaufgabe: Judenerschießungen. SS-Offizier bekam Schreikrämpfe nach Kindermord', *Darmstädter Echo*, 18 May 1962, p. 2: '*Wir reden hier, als wenn es sich um den Verkauf von Fleisch handelte. Es klingt alles so nüchtern. Die Last und Verantwortung, die wir tragen, kann aber niemand von uns nehmen.*' I am grateful to Clemens Uhlig for providing me with a copy of the second article. See also Dicks, *Licensed Mass Murder*, p. 207.
45. HStAD, Ztg 136, 'Hauptaufgabe: Judenerschießungen', *Darmstädter Echo*, 18 May 1962, p. 2.
46. See ibid.
47. I am grateful to Clemens Uhlig for this information.
48. On the trial and execution of Adolf Eichmann see Cesarani, *Eichmann*, Ch. 8.
49. Norbert Frei, *Karrieren im Zwielicht: Hitlers Elite nach 1945* (Frankfurt/New York: Campus, 2001), p. 280.
50. 'Karrieren mit braunem Schatten. Dr. Georg Fleischmann, geb. 14. Juli 1906 in Kolberg', in *"Befehl ist Befehl"? Eine Ausstellung über die Polizei in der NS-Zeit mit Schwerpunkt auf dem Gebiet des heutigen Rheinland-Pfalz*, Arbeitsgruppe "Polizei im NS-Staat" beim Ministerium des Innern und für Sport Rheinland-Pfalz, January 2004.
51. 'Zeuge streckt Schwurhand zum Hitlergruß. Hauptangeklagter Filbert als "strenger und rigoroser Führer" geschildert', *Augsburger Allgemeine*, 25 May 1962; Dietrich Strothmann, 'Kriminelle Kriminalisten? Gestern SS-Sturmbannführer – heute Polizeidirektor', *Die Zeit*, 8 June 1962.
52. BArch Ludwigsburg, B 162/2401, fols. 23–32, 'Urteil und Urteilsbegründung im SS-Prozeß Filbert', n.d. [22 June 1962], here fol. 29R. Slightly different wording in Zaehle, '"Die Sühne kommt spät"', in Archiv der VVN-BdA Bundesvereinigung, Dossier Alfred Filbert.
53. 'Staatsräson vor Recht. Moabiter Richter: Naziverbrecher werden geschont', *Berliner Zeitung*, 23 June 1962, p. 2: '*Er sitzt hier im Haus und gehörte eigentlich auch auf die Anklagebank.*'
54. 'Schwurgericht Berlin: Befehlsnotstand lag nicht vor. Zuchthausstrafen im Prozeß gegen die Einsatzgruppe [sic] 9', *Stuttgarter Zeitung*, 23 June 1962; Zaehle, '"Die Sühne kommt spät"', in Archiv der VVN-BdA Bundesvereinigung, Dossier Alfred Filbert (here 'at least 15,000').
55. UniA GI, 'Urteil Landgericht Berlin vom 22. Juni 1962', fols. 120–121: '*Dr. Filbert hat in einer Reihe von Einzelfällen gezeigt, dass sein Handeln und seine Entschlüsse von Judenhass bestimmt waren. So hat er Angehörigen seines Einsatzkommandos die Unterhaltung mit jüdischen Arbeitskräften verboten, die die Unterkunftsräume des Kommandos in Wilna und Witebsk säuberten. Er hat beanstandet, dass solchen jüdischen Arbeitskräften Kaffee oder Tee aus Beständen des Kommandos ausgeschenkt wurde, und sich darüber empört geäussert, dass den Juden auch noch Trinkgefässe zur Verfügung gestellt wurden, die auch von Angehörigen des Kommandos benutzt wurden.*' On the story about the tea and coffee, which was cited by more than one member of EK 9, see also Ruprecht, 'SS-Mann 52729'. On the story about the drinking vessels see also Dicks, *Licensed Mass Murder*, p. 208.

56. For the sentences see UniA GI, 'Urteil Landgericht Berlin vom 22. Juni 1962', fols. 38–39 and 146–158.
57. For the nineteen-page text of the judgement and the reasons given for the sentences see BArch Ludwigsburg, B 162/2401, fols. 23–32, 'Urteil und Urteilsbegründung im SS-Prozeß Filbert', n.d. [22 June 1962], here fol. 30.
58. See Dicks, *Licensed Mass Murder*, p. 208.
59. LArch Berlin, B Rep. 058, Nr. 7196, fol. 240, Letter from Dr Ronge to the Landgericht Berlin, 23 June 1962.
60. 'Revision von Filbert verworfen', *Der Tagesspiegel*, Berlin, 10 April 1963, in Archiv der VVN-BdA Bundesvereinigung, Dossier Alfred Filbert; 'Lebenslang Zuchthaus für Filbert jetzt rechtskräftig', *Frankfurter Rundschau*, 11 April 1963, in Archiv der VVN-BdA Bundesvereinigung, Dossier Alfred Filbert. For the text of the Federal Supreme Court resolution see BArch Ludwigsburg, B 162/14138, 'Urteil BGH 5 StR 22/63 v. 9.4.63'.

9   'A limited, lower middle class, status-and-promotion seeking philistine'

1. UniA GI, Juristische Promotionsakten Nr. 775, fol. 30, Letter from Generalstaatsanwalt beim Landgericht to Rektor der Justus Liebig-Universität 'Betrifft: Alfred Filbert, geboren am 8. Mai [*sic*] 1905', 11 February 1964.
2. See Pieter Spierenburg, *The Prison Experience: Disciplinary Institutions and Their Inmates in Early Modern Europe* (New Brunswick, NJ/London: Rutgers University Press, 1991), pp. 41–68. On incarceration in early modern and modern Europe see also the essays in Pieter Spierenburg, ed., *The Emergence of Carceral Institutions: Prisons, Galleys and Lunatic Asylums 1550–1900* (Rotterdam: Erasmus Universiteit, 1984).
3. 'Erstes Gesetz zur Reform des Strafrechts (1. StrRG). Vom 25. Juni 1969', in *Bundesgesetzblatt*, 1969, No. 52, 30 June 1969, pp. 645–682, here esp. p. 651, Erster Abschnitt, Artikel 1, 25.a), and p. 677, Fünfter Abschnitt, Artikel 86, (1).
4. Ibid., p. 679, Fünfter Abschnitt, Artikel 99.
5. Ibid., p. 680, Fünfter Abschnitt, Artikel 105, 2.
6. UniA GI, Juristische Promotionsakten Nr. 775, fol. 32, 'Protokoll über die Sitzung des Ausschusses über die Entziehung akademischer Grade an der Justus Liebig-Universität Giessen am 15. Januar 1964'. See also UniA GI, Juristische Promotionsakten Nr. 775, fol. 31, Letter from Rektor der Justus Liebig-Universität to Generalstaatsanwalt beim Landgericht, 6 February 1964.
7. See UniA GI, Juristische Promotionsakten Nr. 775, fol. 6, Letter from Kanzler der Justus Liebig-Universität Giessen to Verwaltungsgericht Darmstadt, 'Betr.: Entziehung des Doktorgrades des Dr. jur. des Alfred Karl Wilhelm Filbert, geb. 8. 9. 1905 in Darmstadt, wohnhaft Berlin 27, Seidelstr. 39', 15 October 1964.

8. UniA GI, Juristische Promotionsakten Nr. 775, fols. 23–27, Letter from Alfred Filbert to the Justus Liebig University 'Betr.: Aberkennung der Doktor-Würde', 2 March 1964.
9. Ibid., fol. 26: *'Ich muß leider auch darauf hinweisen, dass Herr Kammergerichtsrat Meyer, Vorsitzender des Schwurgerichts Jude ist und seine Familie in der Hitlerzeit sehr zu leiden hatte. Ob ein Richter in einem solchen Fall objektiv entscheiden kann, oder befangen ist überlasse ich der Universität.'*
10. Diether Dehnicke, 'Karlheinz Meyer – Leben und Werk', in Klaus Geppert and Diether Dehnicke, eds., *Gedächtnisschrift für Karlheinz Meyer* (Berlin/ New York: De Gruyter, 1990), pp. 1–3, here p. 1.
11. UniA GI, Juristische Promotionsakten Nr. 775, fols. 9–11, 'Widerspruchsbescheid', Justus Liebig-Universität, 14 July 1964.
12. '"Jeder mußte mindestens einmal mitschießen"', *Der Tagesspiegel*, 26 March 1966, in BArch D-H, Dok/P 12569. For the judgement see 'Urteil des Schwurgerichts beim Landgericht Berlin (500) 3 P (K) Ks 1/65, vom 6. Mai 1966', reprinted in: *Justiz und NS-Verbrechen*, Vol. XXIII, ed. Ruter and de Mildt, No. 630, pp. 507–532.
13. LArch Berlin, B Rep. 058, Nr. 7187, fols. 25–26R, 'Übertragung des Protokolls vom 1. März 1961 (Stenogramm)', Hearing of the accused Wilhelm Wiebens, Generalstaatsanwalt bei dem Landgericht Berlin, 1 March 1961, here fol. 25.
14. 'Urteil des Schwurgerichts beim Landgericht Berlin (500) 3 P (K) Ks 1/65, vom 6. Mai 1966', reprinted in: *Justiz und NS-Verbrechen*, Vol. XXIII, ed. Ruter and de Mildt, No. 630, pp. 507–508 and 522–524.
15. Ibid., pp. 515–516 and 523–524 (quote: p. 524).
16. LArch Berlin, B Rep. 057–01, Nr. 1017, fols. 168–169, 'Vermerk. Auszugsweise Abschrift', 1 Js 12/65 (RSHA), signed Public Prosecutor Filipiak, 18 January 1968, here fols. 168–169.
17. On the intended RSHA trials and preliminary proceedings against former members of the RSHA between 1963 and 1969 see Annette Weinke, 'Amnestie für Schreibtischtäter. Das verhinderte Verfahren gegen die Bediensteten des Reichssicherheitshauptamtes', in Mallmann and Angrick, eds., *Die Gestapo nach 1945*, pp. 200–220; Wildt, *Generation des Unbedingten*, pp. 823–838.
18. See 'Befehl Nr. 39/67', 23 December 1967, reproduced in: Unverhau, *Das "NS-Archiv" des Ministeriums für Staatssicherheit*, Doc. 2, pp. 198–200.
19. See BStU, MfS, HA IX/11, RHE 75/68, fols. 90–91, 'Information: Anfrage Nr. 656/68', 3 April 1969; BStU, MfS, HA IX/11, AV 1/80, Bd. 5, fols. 92–94, Notes, n.d., here fol. 92: *'Anfrage des KfS Nr. 656/68 zur Untersuchung des Todes der Leiterin der Witebsker antifaschistischen Widerstandsbewegung; beteiligt SS-Ostubaf. Filbert'.*
20. BStU, MfS, HA IX/11, RHE 75/68, fols. 90–91, 'Information: Anfrage Nr. 656/68', 3 April 1969, here fol. 90.
21. For the results of the interview see Dicks, *Licensed Mass Murder*, pp. 204–229. For the date of the interview see ibid., p. 208.
22. Ibid., pp. 208–209 and 221.

23. Interview with Alfred Filbert's nephew, Peter Filbert, Weinheim, 29 August 2013; Dicks, *Licensed Mass Murder*, p. 222.
24. See John Russell, 'Art View: In Search of the Real Thing', *New York Times*, 1 December 1985.
25. Dicks, *Licensed Mass Murder*, p. 222.
26. Ibid., pp. 211–213 and 219.
27. Ibid., pp. 219–220.
28. This is how Dicks refers to Filbert throughout.
29. Dicks, *Licensed Mass Murder*, p. 222.
30. Ibid., pp. 222–223.
31. Ibid., p. 218.
32. He thus commanded EK 8 for just over nine months and not, as Filbert claimed, two-and-a-half years (see Dicks, *Licensed Mass Murder*, p. 218).
33. 'LG München I vom 21.7.1961, 22 Ks 1/61', reprinted in: *Justiz und NS-Verbrechen*, Vol. XVII, ed. Sagel-Grande, Fuchs and Rüter, No. 519, pp. 661–708, here p. 661. See also Weinke, *Eine Gesellschaft ermittelt gegen sich selbst*, p. 65.
34. 'LG München I vom 21.7.1961, 22 Ks 1/61', reprinted in: *Justiz und NS-Verbrechen*, Vol. XVII, ed. Sagel-Grande, Fuchs and Rüter, No. 519, pp. 661–708, here p. 661. See also Klein, 'Der Mordgehilfe', pp. 224–225.
35. See Falko Kruse, 'Zweierlei Maß für NS-Täter? Über die Tendenzen schichtenspezifischer Privilegierungen in Urteilen gegen nationalsozialistische Gewaltverbrecher', *Kritische Justiz: Vierteljahresschrift für Recht und Politik*, Vol. 11, No. 3 (1978), pp. 236–253, here pp. 252–253. See also Jäger, *Verbrechen unter totalitärer Herrschaft*, pp. 21 and 77, who differentiates between 'acts of excess' (*Exzeßtaten*), 'acts of initiative' (*Initiativtaten*) and 'acts committed under orders' (*Befehlstaten*).
36. 'LG Hannover vom 18.11.1963, 2 Ks 1/63', reprinted in: *Justiz und NS-Verbrechen*, Vol. XIX, ed. Irene Sagel-Grande, H. H. Fuchs and C. F. Rüter (Amsterdam: University Press Amsterdam, 1978), No. 557, pp. 489–555, here pp. 553–554. See also Klein, 'Der Mordgehilfe', pp. 222–223 and 226–227.
37. Wildt, *Generation des Unbedingten*, p. 817. The other three were Rudolf Seidel (one year), Dr Albert Widmann (five years plus six-and-a-half years) and Erich Ehrlinger (12 years, though the verdict was never confirmed as legally binding). On the post-war prosecution of senior members of the RSHA see Ibid., pp. 814–838.
38. Dicks, *Licensed Mass Murder*, pp. 213 and 215.
39. LArch Berlin, B Rep. 058, Nr. 7218, fol. 16, 'Betr.: Ausübung des Rechts der Begnadigung in der Strafsache gegen Alfred Filbert – Senatsbeschluß Nr. 2300/70 vom 17. Februar 1970', Der Regierende Bürgermeister von Berlin, Senatskanzlei, signed Burghause, 17 February 1970. That same year, Filbert's eldest son, Dieter, completed his doctoral thesis in electrical engineering at the Technical University in Berlin. See the biographical information at: http://onlinelibrary.wiley.com/doi/10.1002/etep.4450050407/ abstract [last accessed on 21 May 2014].

40. LArch Berlin, B Rep. 058, Nr. 7208, 'Beschluß', (508) 3 P (K) (Ks 1/62 (106/72)[)], 1 November 1973.
41. LArch Berlin, B Rep. 058, Nr. 7218, fol. 31, 'Betr.: Ausübung des Rechts der Begnadigung in der Strafsache gegen Albert [sic] Filbert – Senatsbeschluß Nr. 2805/74 vom 21. Mai 1974', Der Regierende Bürgermeister von Berlin, Senatskanzlei, signed Kuba, 21 May 1974.
42. LArch Berlin, B Rep. 058, Nr. 7208, fol. 81, 'Pressemitteilung Nr. 45/75, Betrifft: Strafunterbrechung für Dr. Filbert', Justizpressestelle, 5 June 1975. See also 'Früherer SS-Führer frei', Frankfurter Rundschau, 6 June 1975, in Archiv der VVN-BdA Bundesvereinigung, Dossier Alfred Filbert; 'Früherer SS-Führer entlassen', Frankfurter Allgemeine Zeitung, 7 June 1975. The year of release is incorrectly given as 1977 by Bert Rebhandl, 'Aus der Generation der Unbedingten', Frankfurter Allgemeine Zeitung, 26 October 2010, and in 'Immensee in Wilna', Der Spiegel, No. 38, 17 September 1984, pp. 210–211, here p. 211.
43. See LArch Berlin, B Rep. 058, Nr. 7218, fol. 77, Letter from Alfred Filbert to the Public Prosecutor's Office attached to the Regional Court in Berlin, 26 May 1975. See also Thomas Harlan – Extrasplitter, 01:29:19 – 1:29:22; Jean-Pierre Stephan, Thomas Harlan. Das Gesicht Deines Feindes: Ein deutsches Leben (Frankfurt am Main: Eichborn, 2007), p. 172.
44. LArch Berlin, B Rep. 005, Nr. 584/1, fols. 76–78, 'Gutachtliche Stellungnahme über Herrn Dr. [sic] Alfred Filbert, geb. 8.9.05', Dr Horst Plattner, specialist for eye disease, to Filbert's social care worker in Tegel Prison, 10 October 1974, here fol. 77.
45. LArch Berlin, B Rep. 005, Nr. 584/1, fol. 75, 'Betr.: Strafgef. Filbert, Alfred, geb. 8.9.1905. Bezug: Fachärztliche Stellungnahme.', Dr Ladeburg, specialist for eye disease, to the director of Tegel Prison, 15 May 1975.
46. LArch Berlin, B Rep. 058, Nr. 7218, fol. 41, 'Betr.: Den Strafgefangenen Alfred Filbert; hier: Antrag auf Strafunterbrechung gem. Nrn. 45/46 StVollstrO', 23 January 1975: 'Die Führung des Gefangenen während der bisherigen Strafhaft hat zu Klagen niemals Anlaß gegeben; sein Verhalten gegenüber Anstaltsbediensteten war stets einwandfrei. [...] Ich beantrage daher, die Vollstreckung der Freiheitsstrafe gegen den Strafgefangenen Filbert wegen Vollzugsuntauglichkeit gemäß §§ 45, 46 StVollstrO zu unterbrechen.'
47. LArch Berlin, B Rep. 005, Nr. 584/1, fol. 75, 'Betr.: Strafgef. Filbert, Alfred, geb. 8.9.1905', 15 May 1975: 'Es muss deshalb nochmals mit Nachdruck darauf hingewiesen werden, dass dem Pat. unter den gegebenen Umständen den [sic] baldige Erblindung droht.'
48. LArch Berlin, B Rep. 058, Nr. 7218, fol. 81, 'Entlassungsmitteilung', Letter from Tegel Prison to the Public Prosecutor's Office in Berlin, 5 June 1975.
49. Stephan, Thomas Harlan, p. 172.
50. Telephonic notification from the director of the JVA Stuttgart, Ltd. Regierungsdirektorin Regina Grimm, 5 September 2012.
51. Written notification from Ulrike Leuchtweis, Staatsarchiv Ludwigsburg, 21 September 2012.

52. Stephan, *Thomas Harlan*, pp. 172–173: '*Und wir haben ihn nach dem Tod von Ulrike Meinhof gefragt und ihn gebeten zu sagen und zu zeigen, was er von ihrem Tod wußte und wie sich Ulrike Meinhof das Leben genommen hatte. Seltsamerweise wußte er alles, was man wissen muß, und er sprach sogar wie ein Mitwisser, denn er verweigerte sich in einem bestimmten Moment und sagte: "Dazu möchte ich mich nicht äußern", als hütete er ein Geheimnis, obwohl er, soweit wir wußten, mit dem Tod von Ulrike Meinhof nichts zu tun hatte und also nichts zu verschweigen, und so konnten wir ihn, mit seiner Hilfe, mit dem Tod von Ulrike Meinhof in Verbindung bringen.*'

53. 'Interview mit Thomas Harlan. Von Noël Simsolo', in Internationales Forum des jungen Films / Freunde der deutschen Kinemathek, ed., *15. internationales Forum des jungen Films, Berlin 1985. 35. Internationale Filmfestspiele Berlin. Nr. 9: Wundkanal (Execution a Quatre Voix): Hinrichtung für Vier Stimmen* (Berlin: Internationales Forum des jungen Films, 1985), pp. 2–4, here p. 3: '*Filbert [...] war nicht wirklich Mörder in Stammheim; er hat lediglich eine Art Guru-Funktion gehabt unter seinen alten Kameraden.*'

54. LArch Berlin, B Rep. 058, Nr. 7218, fol. 13, 'Aufnahmemitteilung', Vollzugskrankenhaus Hohenasperg, 15 July 1969; LArch Berlin, B Rep. 058, Nr. 7218, fol. 12, 'Mitteilung über eine Veränderung der Unterbringung', Vollzugskrankenhaus Hohenasperg, 18 July 1969.

10   'A chess game of egos'

1. Written notification from Dieter Filbert, Berlin, 17 March 2013.
2. See the correspondence in BStU, MfS, HA IX/11, AK 3101/83, 'Überprüfung zur Person Fillbert [*sic*], wohnhaft: Westberlin [*sic*]', Bezirksverwaltung für Staatssicherheit Rostock, Abteilung II, II/1138/83 A, 2 June 1983, fol. 3, and 'Auskunftsersuchen vom 02.06.1983, 1138/83 A, eck-sto', Ministerrat der Deutschen Demokratischen Republik, Ministerium für Staatssicherheit, Hauptabteilung IX/11, gei-br/3377/83, 28 July 1983, fols. 1–2.
3. BStU, MfS, HA IX/11, AK 3101/83, 'Überprüfung zur Person Fillbert [*sic*], wohnhaft: Westberlin [*sic*]', Bezirksverwaltung für Staatssicherheit Rostock, Abteilung II, 2 June 1983, fol. 3.
4. BStU, MfS, HA IX/11, AK 3101/83, fol. 5, Memorandum, 28 July 1983.
5. Hachmeister, *Der Gegnerforscher*, pp. 224 (with photo) and 372, n. 69.
6. *Wundkanal*, 01:38:34. The film was viewed by the author on the DVD released jointly in 2009 by the Filmmuseum München and the Goethe-Institut München as volume 49 in the series *Edition Filmmuseum*.
7. Jean-Pierre Stephan, 'Fritz Bauers Briefe an Thomas Harlan. Eine deutsche Freundschaft', *Einsicht 09. Bulletin des Fritz Bauer Instituts*, Vol. 5 (spring 2013), pp. 36–44, here p. 36.
8. 'Interview mit Thomas Harlan. Von Noël Simsolo', in Internationales Forum des jungen Films / Freunde der deutschen Kinemathek, ed., *15. internationales Forum des jungen Films, Berlin 1985. 35. Internationale Filmfestspiele Berlin. Nr. 9: Wundkanal (Execution a Quatre Voix):*

Hinrichtung für Vier Stimmen (Berlin: Internationales Forum des jungen Films, 1985), pp. 2–4, here p. 3: '*Der Film ist eine Arbeit über den Plural, ich fange lediglich mit meinem Vater an [. . .].*' See also *Notre Nazi*, 00:06:45 – 00:07:50. The film was viewed by the author on the DVD released jointly in 2009 by the Filmmuseum München and the Goethe-Institut München as volume 49 in the series *Edition Filmmuseum*.

9. Stephan, *Thomas Harlan*, p. 170. On Geschonneck see F.-B. Habel, ed., *Lexikon Schauspieler in der DDR* (Berlin: Neues Leben, 2009), pp. 117–119.

10. Written notification from Ulrich Adomat, Berlin, 18 September 2013. Adomat was the accountant of the production firm Quasar Film at the time *Wundkanal* was made and was present during the entire shoot.

11. Thomas Heise, 'Das Projekt "Wundkanal"', *Der Freitag*, 23 February 2010.

12. See the closing credits of *Wundkanal*, 01:42:06.

13. Written notification from Heike Geschonneck, Berlin, 11 April 2013. On the *Zentrale Stelle* see Weinke, *Eine Gesellschaft ermittelt gegen sich selbst*.

14. See LArch Berlin, B Rep. 058, Nr. 7189, fol. 49, Letter from Thomas Harlan, c/o Smolinska, Smolna 13, Warszawa, POLSKA, to the Generalstaatsanwalt beim Landgericht Berlin, AZ: 3 P (K) Js 45/60, 26 April 1961.

15. Stephan, *Thomas Harlan*, pp. 171–172: '*[. . .] er war gerührt über den Besuch eines Harlan-Sohns, eines Sohnes des großen Trösters, und es war an dem ersten Tag unserer Bekanntschaft schon klar, daß er bereit war zu sprechen; ob zu spielen, das konnte niemand wissen. Und später auch dauerte es zwei Wochen, bevor wir merkten, daß er angebissen hatte und Schauspieler werden wollte; es war an dem Tag, an dem wir in der Wüste stehen mit ihm und er bereit ist, die Pistole zu halten, wie sie Andreas Baader gehalten haben soll an seinen Nacken, aber nicht gehalten haben konnte.*' Parts of Veit Harlan's wartime film *Immensee* (1943) are shown in *Wundkanal* and Dr S. watches it with a captivated smile on his face. His kidnappers also briefly question Dr S. about the film.

16. Stefan Aust, *Der Baader-Meinhof-Komplex*, exp. and rev. ed. (Hoffmann und Campe: Hamburg, 1997 [1985]), pp. 651–652; Stephan, *Thomas Harlan*, pp. 166 and 174–175.

17. *Wundkanal*, 00:05:28.

18. Stephan, *Thomas Harlan*, p. 166.

19. Ibid., pp. 174–175 (quote: p. 175); *Thomas Harlan – Extrasplitter*, 01:16:12 – 01:16:34. See also Robert Kramer's questions as one of the interrogators in *Wundkanal*, 00:24:51 – 00:24:59: '*Why did the prisoners then kill themselves? Why? Answer: to prove that they had been murdered, right?*'.

20. See *Thomas Harlan – Extrasplitter*, 01:32:39 – 01:32:44.

21. Stephan, *Thomas Harlan*, p. 170.

22. See the closing credits of *Wundkanal*, 01:42:06. See also Stephan, *Thomas Harlan*, p. 170.

23. Written notification from Ursula Langmann, Paris, 15 May 2013; written notification from Danièle Brey, Paris, 9 April 2013; written notification from Heike Geschonneck, Berlin, 11 April 2013.

24. Written notification from Ursula Langmann, Paris, 15 May 2013. The duration of the shoot is incorrectly given as three weeks in 'Immensee in Wilna', p. 210.
25. Pierre Joffroy, 'Les faussaires de la mort', *Libération*, 30 November 1983. Pierre Joffroy receives special thanks in the closing credits of *Wundkanal* (01:41:50).
26. Written notification from Ursula Langmann, Paris, 12 March 2013.
27. Written notification from Ursula Langmann, Paris, 14 April 2013: '*Kein Unwohlsein, nicht das geringste Schuldgefühl … Das hatte in seinen Augen mit ihm und seiner Geschichte überhaupt nichts zu tun.*'
28. On Feltrinelli see Stephan, *Thomas Harlan*, pp. 123–125.
29. Ibid., pp. 96–97: '*Die Wahrheit, die man nicht mehr verbergen muß, hat die größte Wucht*' (quote: p. 96).
30. *Wundkanal*, 00:04:16.
31. See *Mitteilungen der Forschungs–und Arbeitsgruppe 'Geschichte des BND'*, ed. Bundesnachrichtendienst, special issue 'Kassationen von Personalakten im Bestand des BND-Archivs', 22 December 2011.
32. According to the BND, there is no record of Filbert in the BND Archives (written notification from Dr Andreas Elbach, Leiter der Arbeitsgruppe Archiv, Bundesnachrichtendiesnt, Pullach, 4 January 2013; written notification from Ulrich Utis, Leiter der Arbeitsgruppe Archiv, Bundesnachrichtendienst, Berlin, 19 April 2012). According to Germany's domestic intelligence agency, the Federal Office for the Protection of the Constitution (*Bundesamt für Verfassungsschutz*, or BfV), there is no record of Filbert in the BfV Archives (written notifications from Laura Kempers, Bundesamt für Verfassungsschutz, Cologne, 9 January 2013 and 10 April 2012).
33. See *Wundkanal*, 00:04:27. See also Andreas Schmiedecker, 'Fassungslose Geschichtsschreibung. Geschichtliche und biografische (De)Konstruktionen bei Thomas Harlan', in Thomas Marchart, Stefanie Schmitt and Stefan Suppanschitz, eds., *reflexiv. Geschichte denken*, SYN. Magazin für Theater-, Film–und Medienwissenschaft, Vol. 2 (Berlin/Münster/Vienna/Zürich/London: LIT, 2011), pp. 69–83, here p. 74. It is tempting to speculate that the character of 'Colonel Humphrey Ian Donald Calleigh' may be a reference to Second Lieutenant William Laws Calley, who was sentenced to life imprisonment for his role in the My Lai massacre of 16 March 1968 during the Vietnam War (though the sentence was subsequently commuted to 20 and then 10 years imprisonment, and Calley was in fact released after only three-and-a-half years under house arrest).
34. Paul Werner was head of Group A in the Reich Criminal Police Office (Office V of the RSHA) and Nebe's deputy. After the war he held a senior position in the Interior Ministry of the federal state of Baden-Württemberg. The city of Stuttgart is located in Baden-Württemberg. In *Wundkanal* he is referred to as being responsible for the construction of the secure wing of Stammheim Prison that housed the RAF leadership. On Werner see Wildt, *Generation des Unbedingten*, pp. 314–316.
35. *Wundkanal*, 00:04:57.

36. The corresponding passage can be found in UniA GI, 'Urteil Landgericht Berlin vom 22. Juni 1962', fols. 91–92.
37. *Wundkanal*, 00:57:09 – 00:57:40: '*Ja, was sage ich denn dazu? Da wäre ja allerhand zu sagen dazu.*'
38. See Schmiedecker, 'Fassungslose Geschichtsschreibung', p. 75. Schmiedecker correctly points out that the name 'Albert Filbert' is not used at all during the film, but incorrectly claims that this is the name of the 'real person' (see Schmiedecker, 'Fassungslose Geschichtsschreibung', pp. 74–75 and 81).
39. Internationales Forum des jungen Films / Freunde der deutschen Kinemathek, ed., *15. internationales Forum des jungen Films, Berlin 1985*, p. 1.
40. Ibid., p. 8.
41. Interview with Robert Kramer's widow, Erika Kramer, Paris, 6 April 2013. I am very grateful to Erika for her time and her candour.
42. *Notre Nazi*, 00:03:26 – 00:03:35; Ulrich Greiner, 'Über den Tod hinaus: Liebe und Haß. Die 41. Filmfestspiele von Venedig', *Die Zeit*, 14 September 1984, p. 52; Jonas Engelmann, 'Sauvater, du Land, du Un, du Tier', *Jungle World*, 18 February 2010; Bert Rebhandl, 'Aus der Generation der Unbedingten', *Frankfurter Allgemeine Zeitung*, 26 October 2010.
43. *Thomas Harlan – Extrasplitter*, 01:18:50 – 01:19:29. See also Christoph Schneider, 'Täterarbeit', *Einsicht 03. Bulletin des Fritz Bauer Instituts*, Vol. 2 (spring 2010), p. 82.
44. *Thomas Harlan – Extrasplitter*, 01:20:38 – 01:23:43 and 01:29:25 – 01:30:17 (quote 01:23:29 – 01:23:31). See also Stephan, *Thomas Harlan*, p. 172.
45. *Thomas Harlan – Extrasplitter*, 01:22:58 – 01:23:03: '*Er wartete fiebernd darauf, am nächsten Tag wieder geschminkt zu werden.*'
46. Written notification from Ursula Langmann, Paris, 4 September 2013. Harlan later referred erroneously to a 'Mercedes with a uniformed chauffeur' (*Mercedes mit einem Chauffeur in Uniform*). See *Thomas Harlan – Extrasplitter*, 01:22:45 – 01:22:47.
47. See *Notre Nazi*, 00:55:49 – 00:59:31.
48. Interview with Robert Kramer's widow, Erika Kramer, Paris, 6 April 2013.
49. See Stephan, *Thomas Harlan*, p. 173.
50. Ekkehard Knörrer [*sic*], 'Der Täter im Spiegelkabinett', *Die Tageszeitung*, 10 December 2009.
51. Stephan, *Thomas Harlan*, p. 179. The moment it happens can be seen in *Notre Nazi*, 01:42:51–01:43:00.
52. Written notification from Ursula Langmann, Paris, 12 March 2013.
53. Interview with Ursula Langmann, Paris, 25 June 2013. I am very grateful to Ursula for generously giving of her time and for the effort she took to recall the events of thirty years before.
54. See Chapter 5.
55. Thomas Harlan in *Notre Nazi*, 01:34:41 – 01:35:04: '*[. . .] ce barbare, qui est resté un barbare. Il n'est pas que vous trouvez [sic] devant un homme. C'est le reste, la dépouille mortelle de quelqu'un qui n'existe plus, et qui n'a jamais existé, qui n'a même pas existé comme enfant. C'est un des pires des [sic] individus que la terre a*

vu, qui a le malheur de ne pas le savoir.' I am grateful to Ursula Langmann and Martin Holler for their assistance in transcribing this passage from the film.

56. See *Notre Nazi*, 01:35:06–01:45:05: *'Mein Bruder war in Buchenwald und er ist tot'* (quote 01:42:05–01:42:09). According to Robert Kramer's widow, Erika, the six men were in fact spontaneously 'scooped up and brought in' that same day, in order that Harlan could shoot this scene with the Jewish men (interview with Erika Kramer, Paris, 6 April 2013). Ursula Langmann confirms that Thomas Harlan had the spontaneous idea during the shoot, though she insists that – whatever the recruitment process may have been – the men were *genuine* Holocaust survivors (interview with Ursula Langmann, Paris, 25 June 2013).

57. *Notre Nazi*, 01:31:09–01:31:29: *'Ich habe durch meinen Bruder, durch diese Aussage, musste ich 18* [sic] *Jahre sitzen. Ich habe meine Augen dabei verloren, verlorene Ehre, Nervenbelastung. Ja, danke schön!'*

58. Ibid., 01:33:46–01:33:52.

59. Ibid., 01:33:14–01:33:27: *'[. . .] schuldig sind an einem der größten Verbrechen, die gegen die Menschheit möglich sind.'* According to his widow Erika, Robert Kramer was 'playing himself' here (interview with Erika Kramer, Paris, 6 April 2013).

60. *Notre Nazi*, 01:18:58–01:23:16 (quote 01:20:03–01:20:09): *'Ich habe natürlich schwer darunter gelitten.'*

61. M. Scott Peck, *The Road Less Travelled*, 25th Anniversary Edition (Rider: London, 2003 [1978]), pp. 163–167 (quote: p. 165).

62. Dicks, Licensed Mass Murder, p. 251.

63. Stephan, *Thomas Harlan*, p. 179.

64. Interview with Erika Kramer, Paris, 6 April 2013.

65. 'Interview mit Thomas Harlan. Von Noël Simsolo', p. 3.

66. Stephan, *Thomas Harlan*, p. 178: *'Ein Film, der* Wundkanal *die Maske abreißt.* Wundkanal *ist ein Film über die Schuld, und* Nôtre Nazi *ist ein zweiter Film über die Schuld. Der Film über die Schuld geht in den Film über die Entstehung der Schuld über. Diese neu entstandene Schuld, von der* Nôtre Nazi *handelt, war unsere Schuld. Es war kein Wunder, daß diese Selbstentblößung durch das Publikum bestraft werden mußte über kurz oder lang.'*

67. Stephan, *Thomas Harlan*, pp. 178 and 180.

68. Thomas Harlan, 'Das Gesicht des Feindes', in Stefan Drössler and Michael Farin, eds., *Thomas Harlan. Wundkanal* (Munich: Filmmuseum München/Goethe-Institut München, 2009) [12-page booklet accompanying the DVD].

69. 'Interview mit Thomas Harlan. Von Noël Simsolo', p. 3: *'Hier wird ein Großvater entführt, nicht ein Vater, und verhört und gequält. Und der Großvater ist sympathisch; die Enkel können nicht leiden, daß ein gestandener Ahne – auch wenn er viel auf dem Kerbholz hat – in diesem Alter zum zweiten Mal Verfolgungen ausgesetzt wird; ihnen schaudert bei der Einkreisung eines Familienoberhauptes und seiner Ausfragung nach 40-Jahre alten Morden und Selbstmorden; ganz besonders, wenn sie dann Robert Kramers* Unser Nazi, *sehen, den Spiegelfilm von* WUNDKANAL: *hier legen wir uns selbst bloß und zeigen, wie Verfolger*

rasch die Eigenschaften des Verfolgten annehmen, wir werden ekelhaft, vor allem ich selbst. [. . .] Unser Nazi, das bin dann ich selbst.'

70. Written notification from Manfred Hobsch, *Zitty*, Berlin, 8 June 2013.
71. Written notification from Danièle Brey, Paris, 9 April 2013.
72. Greiner, 'Über den Tod hinaus'; 'Immensee in Wilna'.
73. See 'Interview mit Thomas Harlan. Von Noël Simsolo', p. 4.
74. *Notre Nazi*, 01:45:56–01:46:35.
75. Standesamt Wilmersdorf von Berlin, Sterbeeintrag 1391/1990, Sterbeurkunde Alfred Filbert, Beglaubigte Abschrift aus dem Sterbebuch, 3 August 1990. I am grateful to Dieter Filbert for providing me with a copy of this document. Incorrect date of death (30 July) in Klee, *Das Personenlexikon zum Dritten Reich*, p. 150; 'Biografie Alfred (Albert) Filbert', in Drössler and Farin, eds., *Thomas Harlan. Wundkanal*.
76. Obituary in *WAZ Bottrop*, 12 September 1984, p. 122/13.
77. Written notification from Dieter Filbert, Berlin, 21 November 2014.
78. See *Notre Nazi*, 00:14:22–00:14:38.
79. Written notification from Dieter Filbert, Berlin, 17 March 2013; written notification from Ralph Filbert's wife, Erika Filbert, Media, PA, 29 July 2013.
80. Written notification from Erika Filbert, Media, PA, 29 July 2013.
81. See 'Ralph Filbert. Obituary', *The Daily Times*, 26 February 2014.
82. Interview with Peter Filbert, Weinheim, 29 August 2013.

Concluding thoughts

1. *Notre Nazi*, 00:09:05–00:09:10: *'Aber die Aktiven, die waren alle Nationalsozialisten.'*
2. Mann, 'Were the Perpetrators of Genocide "Ordinary Men" or "Real Nazis"?', pp. 332–333. The other categories of 'ordinary people' for which Filbert might qualify are: *'bigoted* killers' and *'fearful or compliant* killers' (see discussion below).
3. Dicks, *Licensed Mass Murder*, p. 222.
4. LArch Berlin, B Rep. 058, Nr. 7174, fols. 114–121, Hearing of the accused Wilhelm Greiffenberger, 1 July 1960, here fol. 121: *'[. . .] der nur sein Weiterkommen im Auge hatte [. . .].'*
5. Mann, 'Were the Perpetrators of Genocide "Ordinary Men" or "Real Nazis"?', p. 332 (emphasis in the original). Mann's is the largest and most representative sample of Nazi mass murderers yet studied.
6. Dicks, *Licensed Mass Murder*, p. 222.
7. Stanley Milgram, *Obedience to Authority: An Experimental View* (New York: Harper & Row, 1974), p. 142 (emphasis in the original).
8. See Christopher R. Browning, 'Perpetrator Testimony: Another Look at Adolf Eichmann', in Christopher R. Browning, *Collected Memories: Holocaust History and Postwar Testimony* (Madison, WI: University of Wisconsin Press, 2003), pp. 3–36, here pp. 6–7 (quote: p. 7). Browning describes Eichmann's claim that he was not an anti-Semite as a 'monstrous falsehood' (see ibid., p. 9). On the Sassen interviews see Irmtrud Wojak,

210   Notes to pages 123–124

Eichmanns Memoiren: Ein kritischer Essay (Frankfurt am Main: Fischer Taschenbuch, 2004 [2001]), pp. 48–66. For the dates of the interviews see ibid., p. 24.

9. See the criticism in Paul, 'Von Psychopathen, Technokraten des Terrors und "ganz gewöhnlichen Deutschen"', pp. 62–64; Bernd Weisbrod, 'Generation und Generationalität in der Neueren Geschichte', *Aus Politik und Zeitgeschichte*, Vol. 8 (2005), pp. 3–9, here pp. 6–7. See also Götz Aly, 'Saubere Mörder. Andrej Angrick verfolgt die Spur der Einsatzgruppe D im Süden der deutsch besetzten Sowjetunion', *Die Zeit*, 26 February 2004.

10. Mark Roseman, 'The Lives of Others – Amid the Deaths of Others: Biographical Approaches to Nazi Perpetrators', *Journal of Genocide Research*, Vol. 15, No. 4 (2013), pp. 443–461, here p. 452.

11. See Mallmann, '"Mensch, ich feiere heut' den tausendsten Genickschuß"', p. 124. Jürgen Matthäus is right to question the validity of anti-Semitism as a *monocausal* explanation for the Holocaust. It remains unclear, however, whom he is directing his argument against, because it is not apparent who, if anyone, still puts forward such an interpretation. See Jürgen Matthäus, 'Holocaust als angewandter Antisemitismus? Potential und Grenzen eines Erklärungsfaktors', in Frank Bajohr and Andrea Löw, eds., *Der Holocaust. Ergebnisse und neue Fragen der Forschung* (Frankfurt am Main: Fischer Taschenbuch, 2015), pp. 102–123.

12. Mallmann, 'Die Türöffner der "Endlösung"', pp. 458–459. The outstanding dissections by Klaus-Michael Mallmann ('"Mensch, ich feiere heut' den tausendsten Genickschuß"' and 'Die Türöffner der "Endlösung"') and the excellent Lower, *Hitler's Furies*, esp. pp. 152–166, are foremost among those works that have helped to resurrect the importance of anti-Semitism and ideology in general as a decisive motivating factor for Holocaust perpetrators.

13. See Friedländer, *The Years of Extermination*, pp. 107–108, 159 and 211–212; Thomas Kühne, *Belonging and Genocide: Hitler's Community, 1918–1945* (New Haven, CT/London: Yale University Press, 2010), pp. 105–107, 131–132 and 156–157.

14. Kühne, *Belonging and Genocide*, p. 4.

15. As proposed by Donald Bloxham, 'Motivation und Umfeld. Vergleichende Anmerkungen zu den Ursachen genozidaler Täterschaft', in Cüppers et al., eds., *Naziverbrechen*, pp. 62–74, here p. 73.

16. See Mann, 'Were the Perpetrators of Genocide "Ordinary Men" or "Real Nazis"?', p. 333.

17. Baumeister and Campbell, 'The Intrinsic Appeal of Evil', p. 218.

18. See Brad J. Bushman and Roy F. Baumeister, 'Threatened Egotism, Narcissism, Self-esteem, and Direct and Displaced Aggression: Does Self-love or Self-hate Lead to Violence?', *Journal of Personality and Social Psychology*, Vol. 75, No. 1 (1998), pp. 219–229; Baumeister and Campbell, 'The Intrinsic Appeal of Evil'.

19. This summary of the studies' findings is quoted from Baumeister and Campbell, 'The Intrinsic Appeal of Evil', p. 219. For the original presentation of the studies' findings see Bushman and Baumeister, 'Threatened Egotism', esp. pp. 227–228. On narcissism, Baumeister and Campbell

write: 'Narcissism is defined by highly favorable, even grandiose views of self, as well as the desire to be admired by others. Hence, when others evaluate them negatively, narcissists are extremely upset and prone to respond in an aggressive or violent manner.' (p. 219) Bushman and Baumeister make the following distinction: 'High self-esteem means thinking well of oneself, whereas narcissism involves passionately wanting to think well of oneself. The present findings suggest that it is the latter (emotional and motivational) sense of egotism that is decisive for aggression.' (p. 227)

20. Bushman and Baumeister, 'Threatened Egotism', p. 221.
21. Dicks, *Licensed Mass Murder*, p. 223. See also Chapter 9.
22. See Snyder, *Bloodlands*, pp. 399–400.
23. Quoted in Gerlach, *Kalkulierte Morde*, pp. 588–589: '*Bei den ersten Wagen [die die Opfer brachten] hat mir etwas die Hand gezittert, als ich geschossen habe, aber man gewöhnt das. Beim zehnten Wagen zielte ich schon ruhig und schoss sicher auf die vielen Frauen, Kinder und Säuglinge. Eingedenk dessen, dass ich auch zwei Säuglinge daheim habe, mit denen es diese Horden genau so, wenn nicht zehnmal ärger machen würden. Der Tod, den wir ihnen gaben, war ein schöner, kurzer Tod, gemessen [an] den höllischen Qualen von tausenden [sic] und Abertausenden in den Kerkern der GPU. Säuglinge flogen in grossen Bogen durch die Luft und wir knallten sie schon im Fliegen ab, bevor sie in die Grube und ins Wasser flogen. Nur weg mit dieser Brut, die ganz Europe in den Krieg gestürzt hat und jetzt auch noch in Amerika schürt. [. . .] Ich freue mich eigentlich schon, und viele sagen hier das [sic] wir in die Heimat zurückkehren, dann kommen unsere heimischen Juden dran.*'

Sources and literature cited

Primary sources

Archival sources

Germany

Amtsgericht Bottrop
'Beschluß für Todeserklärung', 2 II 57/51, Amtsgericht Bottrop, 15 October 1951

Bundesarchiv Berlin-Lichterfelde (= BArch Berlin)
Reichsfinanzministerium
    R 2/12150
Reichssicherheitshauptamt
    R 58/214–219, /240, /272, /825, /826, /840
Polizeidienststellen in der Sowjetunion
    R 70 Sowjetunion/31, /32
Präsidialkanzlei
    R 601/1813
SS-Wirtschafts-Verwaltungshauptamt
    NS 3/401
Sonstige zentrale Dienststellen und Einrichtungen der SS
    NS 48/19
Ortsgruppenkartei NSDAP
    MF-OK-32/E0045
Sammlung BDC, SSO/SS-Führerpersonalakten
    VBS 286/6400010138 SSO-Akte Dr. Alfred Filbert
Sammlung BDC, Akten des RS/Rasse- und Siedlungshauptamts SS
    VBS 283/6010010064 RuSHA-Akte Dr. Alfred Filbert

Bundesarchiv-Militärarchiv, Freiburg im Breisgau (= BArch-MA)
Befehlshaber rückwärtige Heeresgebiete
    RH 22/12, /224
102. Infanteriedivision
    RH 26–102/9
403. Sicherungsdivision
    RH 26–403/2, /4a
OKW/WFSt/Qu
    RW 4/v. 578

36. Waffen-Grenadier-Division der SS
    RS 3–36/10, /12
Brigaden, Legionen, Standarten sowie Kampfgruppen und Einheiten der Waffen-SS
    RS 4/932
Ergänzungsfilme aus dem ehemaligen Militärarchiv der DDR
    WF-03/13302
Bundesarchiv Außenstelle Ludwigsburg (= BArch Ludwigsburg)
Zentrale Stelle der Landesjustizverwaltungen zur Aufklärung natio-
nalsozialistischer Verbrechen
    B 162/2400, /2401, /3633, /3921, /3922, /4113, /4114, /4133,
    /14138, /20580, /20862, /21177, /30134, /30135
Bundesarchiv Zwischenarchiv Dahlwitz-Hoppegarten (= BArch D-H)
Sammlung Dok/P des Dokumentationszentrums der Staatlichen
Archivverwaltung im Ministerium des Innern der DDR
    Dok/P 12569
Sammlung 'NS-Archiv des Ministeriums für Staatssicherheit
der DDR'
    ZR 537, A. 6
*Der Bundesbeauftragte für die Unterlagen des Staatssicherheitsdienstes der
ehemaligen Deutschen Demokratischen Republik, Archiv der
Zentralstelle, Berlin (= BStU)*
Ministerium für Staatssicherheit
    MfS, HA IX/11, ZUV 9, Bd. 31
    MfS, HA IX/11, RHE 4/85 SU, Bd. 7
    MfS, HA IX/11, RHE 75/68
    MfS, HA IX/11, AV 1/80, Bd. 5
    MfS, HA IX/11, AK 3101/83
Landesarchiv Berlin (= LArch Berlin)
Staatsanwaltschaft beim Landgericht Berlin
    B Rep. 058, Nr. 3016, 3059, 5199, 7166, 7167, 7168, 7171,
    7172, 7174, 7175, 7178, 7179, 7184, 7186, 7187, 7189,
    7191, 7196, 7208, 7218
Generalstaatsanwaltschaft bei dem Kammergericht – RSHA-
Verfahren
    B Rep. 057–01, Nr. 1017
Senatsverwaltung für Justiz
    B Rep. 005, Nr. 584/1
Hessisches Staatsarchiv Darmstadt (= HStAD)
Justizministerium – Personalangelegenheiten
    G 21 B Personalakte Nr. 2862, Filbert, Alfred
            Personalakte Nr. 3415, Jost, Heinz
Staatsanwaltschaft Darmstadt
    H 13 Darmstadt Nr. 1291/25 Hauptakte
    (Ermittlungsverfahren), Bd. 25
Zeitungen Staatsarchiv Darmstadt
    Ztg 136 Darmstädter Echo

Ztg 169 Darmstädter Tagblatt
Tonbänder
    Q 61, Nr. 188
Bildersammlung
    R 4, Nr. 31736 UF
    R 4, Nr. 29813 / 24 A
Staatsarchiv Hamburg (= StA Hamburg)
    Staatsanwaltschaft   Landgericht   –   Nationalsozialistische
    Gewaltverbrechen
    213–12, Nr. 33, Bd. 16
Staatsarchiv Ludwigsburg (= StAL)
    Landeskriminalamt   Baden-Württemberg: Ermittlungsverfahren
    gegen NS-Gewaltverbrecher (ca. 1940–1945)
    EL 48/2 I Bü 678
Staatsarchiv München (= StA München)
    Staatsanwaltschaften
    32970/5
Brandenburgisches Landesamt für Denkmalpflege und Archäologisches
Landesmuseum, Zossen
    Messbildarchiv
    44 L 37 / 7204.26
Stadtarchiv Mannheim – Institut für Stadtgeschichte
    Meldekarte Dr. Alfred Filbert
    Meldekarte Adolf Hille
Stadtarchiv Mainz
    Schlossgymnasium (Oberrealschule)
    202/59, /60, /61, /62, /87, /90
Einwohnermeldearchiv der Stadt Bad Gandersheim
    Familienkarte Dr. Alfred Selbert
    Meldekarte Käthe Filbert
    Meldeliste Heckenbeck – Hilprechtshausen 1945
Einwohnermeldearchiv der Stadt Hannover
    Meldekarte Dr. Alfred Filbert
Archiv des Standesamtes Darmstadt
    Geburtenregister Darmstadt
        Nr. 666, Geburtsurkunde Otto Filbert
        Nr. 1169, Geburtsurkunde Karl Wilhelm Alfred Filbert
    Heiratsregister Darmstadt
        Nr. 491, Heiratsurkunde Peter Filbert und Christiane Kühner
Archiv des Standesamtes Worms
    Sterberegister Worms
        Sterbeeintrag 427/1949, Sterbeurkunde Christiane Filbert,
        geb. Kühner, 22 July 1949
        Sterbeeintrag 845/1956, Sterbeurkunde Peter Filbert, 31
        December 1956
Archiv des Standesamtes Wilmersdorf von Berlin

Sterberegister Berlin
  Sterbeeintrag 1391/1990, Sterbeurkunde Alfred Filbert, 3
    August 1990
Universitätsarchiv Gießen (= UniA GI)
  Promotionen und Dissertationen an der Universität Gießen von
    1894 bis 1945
    Jur. Prom. Nr. 775 Promotionsakte Alfred Filbert
  Matrikelakten des Studierendensekretariats
    Stud. Mat. Nr. 5493 Matrikelakte Alfred Filbert
Universitätsarchiv Heidelberg (= UAH)
  Studentenakten
    StudA, Filbert, Alfred (1929)
    StudA, Schleyer, Hanns Martin (1937)
International Tracing Service Archives, Bad Arolsen (= ITS Archives)
  Konzentrationslager Buchenwald
    1.1.5.1 Listenmaterial
    1.1.5.3 Individuelle Unterlagen Männer
      Häftlingsakte FILBERT, Otto
Archiv der Gedenkstätte Buchenwald, Weimar (= BwA)
  Sammlungsbestand des Archivs der Gedenkstätte Buchenwald:
    Buchenwald-Archiv
Archiv des Instituts für Zeitgeschichte, Munich (= IfZ-Archiv)
  Zeugenschrifttum
    ZS-429/I
    ZS-429/II
*Archiv der Vereinigung der Verfolgten des Naziregimes – Bund der
  Antifaschistinnen und Antifaschisten (VVN-BdA) Bundesvereinigung,
  Berlin (= Archiv der VVN-BdA Bundesvereinigung)*
  Dossier Alfred Filbert

United States

*National Archives and Records Administration, College Park, MA (=
  NARA)*
  Records of the Army Staff
    RG 319, IRR, File D 158813
    RG 319, IRR, File XE 158813
  Records of German Field Commands: Rear Areas, Occupied
    Territories, and Others
    RG 242, T-501, Roll 1

United Kingdom

The National Archives, Kew (= TNA, Kew)
  Control Office for Germany and Austria and Foreign Office:
    Control Commission for Germany (British Element), Internal
    Affairs and Communications Divisions: Files
    FO 1050/312

War Office: Directorate of Military Operations and Intelligence, and Directorate of Military Intelligence; Ministry of Defence, Defence Intelligence Staff: Files
WO 208/4139

Poland

Instytut Pamięci Narodowej [Institute of National Remembrance], Warsaw, Poland (= IPN, Warsaw)
IPN GK 127/34 KL BUCHENWALD

Russia

Rossiiskii Gosudarstvennyi Voennyi Arkhiv [Russian State Military Archives], Moscow (= RGVA)
Reichssicherheitshauptamt
500/3/795
Arkhiv Rossiyskogo Nauchno–Prosvetitel'nogo Tsentra Kholokost [Archives of the Russian Research and Educational Holocaust Centre], Moscow
Letter from Sofiya Ratner, 6 and 8 September 1941

Lithuania

Lietuvos Centrinis Valstybės Archyvas [Lithuanian Central State Archives], Vilnius, Lithuania (= LCVA)
Photo number 12843
Valstybinis Vilniaus Gaono Žydų Muziejus, Holokausto ekspozicija, Žaliasis namas [Vilna Gaon State Jewish Museum, Holocaust Exhibition, Green House], Vilnius, Lithuania
Calendar for November 1941 from Kazimierz Sakowicz's diary

Israel

Yad Vashem Archives, Jerusalem
Photo Archive
Photo number 4613/916
Microfilm Collection
JM/19924

Printed primary sources

Memoirs, diaries and contemporary books, and official publications
Bundesgesetzblatt, 1949, No. 9, 31 December 1949.
Bundesgesetzblatt, 1969, No. 52, 30 June 1969.
Dicks, Henry V., *Licensed Mass Murder: A Socio-Psychological Study of Some S.S. Killers* (New York: Basic Books, 1972).
Filbert, Alfred, *Kann das Ablehnungsrecht des Konkursverwalters des Vorbehaltsverkäufers mit der Anwartschaft des Käufers auf den Eigentumserwerb ausgeräumt werden?* (Gießen: Buchdruckerei Meyer, 1935).
Gruchmann, Lothar, ed., *Autobiographie eines Attentäters: Johann Georg Elser. Aussage zum Sprengstoffanschlag im Bürgerbräukeller, München, am 8. November 1939* (Stuttgart: Deutsche Verlags-Anstalt, 1970).

Gründel, E. Günther, *Die Sendung der Jungen Generation. Versuch einer umfassendenrevolutionären Sinndeutung der Krise* (Munich: C. H. Beck, 1932).

Haffner, Sebastian, *Geschichte eines Deutschen. Die Erinnerungen 1914–1933* (Munich: dtv, 2002).

Internationales Forum des jungen Films / Freunde der deutschen Kinemathek, ed., *15. internationales Forum des jungen Films, Berlin 1985. 35. Internationale Filmfestspiele Berlin. Nr. 9: Wundkanal (Execution a Quatre Voix): Hinrichtung für Vier Stimmen* (Berlin: Internationales Forum des jungen Films, 1985).

'Interview mit Thomas Harlan. Von Noël Simsolo', in Internationales Forum des jungen Films / Freunde der deutschen Kinemathek, ed., *15. internationales Forum des jungen Films, Berlin 1985. 35. Internationale Filmfestspiele Berlin. Nr. 9: Wundkanal (Execution a Quatre Voix): Hinrichtung für Vier Stimmen* (Berlin: Internationales Forum des jungen Films, 1985), pp. 2–4.

Kogon, Eugen, *Der SS-Staat. Das System der deutschen Konzentrationslager*, 5th exp. ed. (n.pl.: Europäische Verlagsanstalt, 1959 [1946]).

Kruk, Herman, *The Last Days of the Jerusalem of Lithuania: Chronicles from the Vilna Ghetto and the Camps, 1939–1944*, edited and with an introduction by Benjamin Harshav, translated from Yiddish by Barbara Harshav (New Haven, CO/London: YIVO Institute for Jewish Research/Yale University Press, 2002).

Leibbrand, Robert, *Buchenwald. Ein Tatsachenbericht zur Geschichte der deutschen Widerstandsbewegung* (Stuttgart: Europa, n.d. [1945]).

Michaelis, Rolf, ed., *Erinnerungen an das SS-Sonderkommando 'Dirlewanger'* (Berlin: Michaelis, 2008).

Nationale Mahn- und Gedenkstätte Buchenwald, ed., *Buchenwald. Mahnung und Verpflichtung. Dokumente und Berichte*, 4th rev. ed. ([East] Berlin: VEB Deutscher Verlag der Wissenschaften, 1983 [1960]).

Personenbestand der Hessischen Ludwigs-Universität zu Giessen. Sommersemester 1927 (Giessen: Münchow'sche Universitäts-Druckerei Otto Kindt, 1927).

Personenbestand der Hessischen Ludwigs-Universität zu Giessen. Sommersemester 1928 (Giessen: Münchow'sche Universitäts-Druckerei Otto Kindt, 1928).

Personenbestand der Hessischen Ludwigs-Universität zu Giessen. Wintersemester 1927/28 (Giessen: Münchow'sche Universitäts-Druckerei Otto Kindt, 1928).

Personenbestand der Hessischen Ludwigs-Universität zu Giessen. Wintersemester 1928/29 (Giessen: Münchow'sche Universitäts-Druckerei Otto Kindt, 1928).

Personenbestand der Hessischen Ludwigs-Universität zu Giessen. Winter-Semester 1929/30 (Giessen: Münchowsche Universitäts-Druckerei Otto Kindt, 1929).

Reichsgesetzblatt, 1934, Part I, 20 December 1934.

Richter, Friedrich, 'Tuchfabrik Hinrichssegen in Workallen, Gemeinde Bolitten bei Liebstadt', *Mohrunger Heimatkreis-Nachrichten*, Vol. 33, No. 102 (Easter 2004), pp. 54–57.

Ronge, Paul, *Im Namen der Gerechtigkeit. Erinnerungen eines Strafverteidigers* (Munich: Kindler, 1963).

Sakowicz, Kazimierz, *Ponary Diary, 1941–1943: A Bystander's Account of a Mass Murder* (New Haven, CT/London: Yale University Press, 2005), ed. Yitzhak Arad, translated from Polish by Yad Vashem.

Schneider, Hans, and Georg Lehnert, *Die Gießener Burschenschaft 1814 bis 1936. Sonderdruck aus den Burschenschafterlisten, Band 2* (Görlitz: Verlag für Sippenforschung und Wappenkunde C. A. Starke, 1942).

Schur, Grigorij, *Die Juden von Wilna: Die Aufzeichungen des Grigorij Schur*, ed. Wladimir Porudominskij, translated from Russian by Jochen Hellbeck (Munich: dtv, 1999 [1997]).

Sereny, Gitta, *Am Abgrund: Gespräche mit dem Henker. Franz Stangl und die Morde von Treblinka*, translated from English by Helmut Röhrling, rev. ed. (Munich: Piper, 1995 [1974]).

Stephan, Jean-Pierre, *Thomas Harlan. Das Gesicht Deines Feindes: Ein deutsches Leben* (Frankfurt am Main: Eichborn, 2007).

von Wenz zu Niederlahnstein, Rolf, Heinrich Henß and Otto Abt, *Dreihundert Jahre Leibgarde Regiment: Blätter der Erinnerung an die ruhmvolle Vergangenheit des Leibgarde-Infanterie-Regiments (1. Großherzoglich Hessisches) Nr. 115* (Darmstadt: Kichler, 1929).

Contemporary articles in newspapers and periodicals

'Angeklagter: Damit werde ich mein Leben lang nicht fertig. Russische Lehrerinnen mußten sich entkleiden, bevor sie erschossen wurden – "Wir hatten üble Leute im Einsatzkommando"', *Augsburger Allgemeine*, 23 May 1962.

'Einsatzkommando-Prozeß in Berlin. Dr. Filbert: Heydrich entließ mich nicht – Murren im Zuhörerraum bei Selbstbemitleidung des Angeklagten', *Augsburger Allgemeine*, 15 May 1962.

'"Es war Sadismus". Erschütternde Aussagen im Einsatzkkommando-Prozeß', *Allgemeine Wochenzeitung der Juden in Deutschland*, 8 June 1962, p. 2.

'Ex-Nazis Sentenced', *AJR Information*, Vol. 17, No. 8 (August 1962), p. 5.

'Filbert: Ich selbst schoß vorbei. Zweiter Tag im Prozeß gegen das Einsatzkommando IX in Berlin', *Augsburger Allgemeine*, 17 May 1962.

'Filbert schwer belastet', *Augsburger Allgemeine*, 18 May 1962.

'Früherer SS-Führer entlassen', *Frankfurter Allgemeine Zeitung*, 7 June 1975.

Greiner, Ulrich, 'Über den Tod hinaus: Liebe und Haß. Die 41. Filmfestspiele von Venedig', *Die Zeit*, 14 September 1984, p. 52.

'Größter Judenmordprozeß in Berlin. Die Angeklagten nach dem Krieg in leitenden Stellungen tätig', *Augsburger Allgemeine*, 11 May 1962.

'Hauptaufgabe: Judenerschießungen. Erdrückende Aussagen im Berliner Einsatzkommandoprozeß', *Stuttgarter Nachrichten*, 18 May 1962.

'Hohe Zuchthausstrafen im Einsatzkommando-Prozeß. Lebenslänglich für den ehemaligen SS-Offizier Alfred Filbert – Aberkennung der bürgerlichen Ehrenrechte auf Lebenszeit', *Augsburger Allgemeine*, 23 June 1962.

'Immensee in Wilna', *Der Spiegel*, No. 38 (17 September 1984), pp. 210–211.

Joffroy, Pierre, 'Les faussaires de la mort', *Libération*, 30 November 1983.

'Schwurgericht Berlin: Befehlsnotstand lag nicht vor. Zuchthausstrafen im Prozeß gegen die Einsatzgruppe 9', *Stuttgarter Zeitung*, 23 June 1962.

'Staatsräson vor Recht. Moabiter Richter: Naziverbrecher werden geschont', *Berliner Zeitung*, 23 June 1962, p. 2.

Strothmann, Dietrich, 'Die gehorsamen Mörder. Das Heuser-Verfahren in Koblenz – Porträt eines Prozesses', *Die Zeit*, 7 June 1963, p. 4.
'Kriminelle Kriminalisten? Gestern SS-Sturmbannführer – heute Polizeidirektor', *Die Zeit*, 8 June 1962.
Suhrkamp, Peter, 'Söhne ohne Väter und Lehrer. Die Situation der bürgerlichen Jugend', *Die Neue Rundschau*, Vol. 43, No. 5 (May 1932), pp. 681–696.
WAZ Bottrop, 12 September 1984, p. 122/13 (obituary).
'Zeuge streckt Schwurhand zum Hitlergruß. Hauptangeklagter Filbert als "strenger und rigoroser Führer" geschildert', *Augsburger Allgemeine*, 25 May 1962.

Collections of documents

Angrick, Andrej, Klaus-Michael Mallmann, Jürgen Matthäus and Martin Cüppers, eds., *Deutsche Besatzungsherrschaft in der UdSSR 1941–1945. Dokumente der Einsatzgruppen in der Sowjetunion* (Darmstadt: Wissenschaftliche Buchgesellschaft, 2013).
Beluga, Z. I., et al., eds., *Prestupleniya nemetsko-fashistskikh okkupantov v Belorussii 1941 – 1944* (Minsk: Izdatel'stvo 'Belarus', 1965).
Die Verfolgung und Ermordung der europäischen Juden durch das nationalsozialistische Deutschland 1933–1945. Band 7, Sowjetunion mit annektierten Gebieten I: Besetzte sowjetische Gebiete unter deutscher Militärverwaltung, Baltikum und Transnistrien, compiled by Bert Hoppe and Hildrun Glass (Munich: Oldenbourg, 2011).
International Military Tribunal, ed., *Der Prozess gegen die Hauptkriegsverbrecher vor dem Internationalen Militärgerichtshof, Nürnberg, 14. November 1945 – 1. Oktober 1946*, Vol. 8 (Nuremberg: Sekretariat des Gerichtshofs, 1947), Vol. 29 (Nuremberg: Sekretariat des Gerichtshofs, 1948), Vols. 34 and 39 (Nuremberg: Sekretariat des Gerichtshofs, 1949).
Justiz und NS-Verbrechen. Sammlung deutscher Strafurteile wegen nationalsozialistischer Tötungsverbrechen 1945–1966, Vol. XVII, ed. Irene Sagel-Grande, H. H. Fuchs and C. F. Rüter (Amsterdam: University Press Amsterdam, 1977).
Justiz und NS-Verbrechen. Sammlung deutscher Strafurteile wegen nationalsozialistischer Tötungsverbrechen 1945–1966, Vols. XVIII and XIX, ed. Irene Sagel-Grande, H. H. Fuchs and C. F. Rüter (Amsterdam: University Press Amsterdam, 1978).
Justiz und NS-Verbrechen. Sammlung deutscher Strafurteile wegen nationalsozialistischer Tötungsverbrechen 1945–1999, Vol. XXIII, ed. C. F. Ruter and D. W. de Mildt (Maarssen: APA – Holland University Press, 1998).
Kárný, Miroslav, Jaroslava Milotová and Margita Kárná, eds., *Deutsche Politik im 'Protektorat Böhmen und Mähren' unter Reinhard Heydrich 1941–1942: Eine Dokumentation* (Berlin: Metropol, 1997).
Klein, Peter, ed., *Die Einsatzgruppen in der besetzten Sowjetunion 1941/42. Die Tätigkeits- und Lageberichte des Chefs der Sicherheitspolizei und des SD* (Berlin: Edition Hentrich, 1997).
Mallmann, Klaus-Michael, Andrej Angrick, Jürgen Matthäus and Martin Cüppers, eds., *Die 'Ereignismeldungen UdSSR' 1941. Dokumente der Einsatzgruppen in der Sowjetunion* (Darmstadt: Wissenschaftliche Buchgesellschaft, 2011).

Mallmann, Klaus-Michael, Jochen Böhler and Jürgen Matthäus, *Einsatzgruppen in Polen. Darstellung und Dokumentation* (Darmstadt: Wissenschaftliche Buchgesellschaft, 2008).
Matrikel des Corps Hassia Giessen zu Mainz 1815–1985 (Mainz: Selbstverlag des Verbandes der Alten Herren des Corps Hassia Gießen zu Mainz, 1985).
Trials of War Criminals before the Nuernberg Military Tribunals under Control Council Law No. 10, Nuernberg, October 1946 – April 1949: Volume IV (Washington, DC: US Government Printing Office, n.d. [1950]).
Witte, Peter, Michael Wildt, Martina Voigt, Dieter Pohl, Peter Klein, Christian Gerlach, Christoph Dieckmann and Andrej Angrick, eds., *Der Dienstkalender Heinrich Himmlers 1941/42* (Hamburg: Christians, 1999).

Interviews, written and telephonic notifications

Interview with Holocaust survivor and former Soviet partisan Fania Brancovskaya, Rudniki Forest, near Vilnius, 29 May 2012.
Interview with Robert Kramer's widow, Erika Kramer, Paris, 6 April 2013.
Interview with Ursula Langmann, Paris, 25 June 2013.
Interview with Alfred Filbert's nephew, Peter Filbert, Weinheim, 29 August 2013.
Telephonic notification from Ralph Filbert's wife, Erika Filbert, Media, PA, 12 June 2013.
Written notifications from Ursula Langmann, Paris, 12 March, 14 April, 15 May and 4 September 2013.
Written notifications from Dieter Filbert, Berlin, 17 and 31 March 2013 and 21 November 2014.
Written notification from Danièle Brey, Paris, 9 April 2013.
Written notification from Heike Geschonneck, Berlin, 11 April 2013.
Written notification from Manfred Hobsch, *Zitty*, Berlin, 8 June 2013.
Written notification from Ralph Filbert's wife, Erika Filbert, Media, PA, 29 July 2013.
Written notification from Ulrich Adomat, Berlin, 18 September 2013.

Online sources

Ancestry.com. *New York, Passenger Lists, 1820–1957* [database on-line]. Provo, UT, USA: Ancestry.com Operations, Inc., 2010 [last accessed on 25 February 2013].
Ancestry.com. *Philadelphia, Pennsylvania, Marriage Index, 1885–1951* [database on-line]. Provo, UT, USA: Ancestry.com Operations, Inc., 2011 [last accessed on 18 February 2013].

Films

Notre Nazi, dir. Robert Kramer (France/Germany: Reass Films/Quasar Film, 1984).
Thomas Harlan – Extrasplitter, dir. Christoph Hübner (Germany: Christoph Hübner Filmproduktion, 2007).

Wundkanal – Hinrichtung für vier Stimmen, dir. Thomas Harlan (Germany/France: Quasar Film/Reass Films, 1984).

Secondary literature

Printed literature

Altenhöner, Florian, 'Heinz Jost und das Amt III des SD-Hauptamtes: Ein MI5-Bericht aus dem Jahr 1945', *Journal for Intelligence, Propaganda and Security Studies*, Vol. 2, No. 2 (2008), pp. 55–76.

Al'tman, Il'ya, *Zhertvy nenavisti. Kholokost v SSSR 1941 – 1945 gg.* (Moscow: Fond Kovcheg, 2002).

Altshuler, Mordechai, ed., *Distribution of the Jewish Population of the USSR 1939* (Jerusalem: Centre for Research and Documentation of East European Jewry, 1993).

Aly, Götz, *'Endlösung'. Völkerverschiebung und der Mord an den europäischen Juden* (Frankfurt am Main: S. Fischer, 1995).

'Saubere Mörder. Andrej Angrick verfolgt die Spur der Einsatzgruppe D im Süden der deutsch besetzten Sowjetunion', *Die Zeit*, 26 February 2004.

Angrick, Andrej, 'Abendrot des Dritten Reichs – oder vom somnambulen Kannibalismus eines Regimes im Untergang', in Martin Cüppers, Jürgen Matthäus and Andrej Angrick, eds., *Naziverbrechen. Täter, Taten, Bewältigungsversuche* (Darmstadt: Wissenschaftliche Buchgesellschaft, 2013), pp. 117–131.

Besatzungspolitik und Massenmord: Die Einsatzgruppe D in der südlichen Sowjetunion 1941–1943 (Hamburg: Hamburger Edition, 2003).

Arad, Yitzhak, *Ghetto in Flames: The Struggle and Destruction of the Jews of Vilna in the Holocaust* (Jerusalem: Yad Vashem, 1980).

Auerbach, Hellmuth, 'Die Einheit Dirlewanger', *Vierteljahrshefte für Zeitgeschichte*, Vol. 10, No. 3 (July 1962), pp. 250–263.

'Konzentrationslagerhäftlinge im Fronteinsatz', in Wolfgang Benz, ed., *Miscellanea. Festschrift für Helmut Krausnick zum 75. Geburtstag* (Stuttgart: Deutsche Verlags-Anstalt, 1980), pp. 63–83.

Aust, Stefan, *Der Baader-Meinhof-Komplex*, exp. and rev. ed. (Hoffmann und Campe: Hamburg, 1997 [1985]).

Bajohr, Frank, *Parvenüs und Profiteure. Korruption in der NS-Zeit* (Frankfurt am Main: S. Fischer, 2001).

Banach, Jens, *Heydrichs Elite. Das Führerkorps der Sicherheitspolizei und des SD 1936–1945*, 3rd rev. ed. (Paderborn: Schöningh, 2002 [1998]).

Barth, Boris, *Genozid. Völkermord im 20. Jahrhundert: Geschichte, Theorien, Kontroversen* (Munich: C. H. Beck, 2006).

Baumeister, Roy F., and W. Keith Campbell, 'The Intrinsic Appeal of Evil: Sadism, Sensational Thrills, and Threatened Egotism', *Personality and Social Psychology Review*, Vol. 3, No. 3 (1999), pp. 210–221.

'Befehl ist Befehl'? Eine Ausstellung über die Polizei in der NS-Zeit mit Schwerpunkt auf dem Gebiet des heutigen Rheinland-Pfalz, Arbeitsgruppe 'Polizei im NS-

Staat' beim Ministerium des Innern und für Sport Rheinland-Pfalz, January 2004.

Benz, Wigbert, *Der Hungerplan im 'Unternehmen Barbarossa' 1941* (Berlin: Wissenschaftlicher Verlag Berlin, 2011)

Birn, Ruth Bettina, 'Zeitgeschichte und Zeitgeist', *Einsicht 06. Bulletin des Fritz Bauer Instituts*, Vol. 3 (autumn 2011), p. 70.

Blasier, Cole, 'The United States and the Revolution', in James M. Malloy and Richard Thorn, eds., *Beyond the Revolution: Bolivia since 1952* (Pittsburgh, PA: University of Pittsburgh Press, 1971), pp. 53–109.

Bloxham, Donald, 'Motivation und Umfeld. Vergleichende Anmerkungen zu den Ursachen genozidaler Täterschaft', in Martin Cüppers, Jürgen Matthäus and Andrej Angrick, eds., *Naziverbrechen. Täter, Taten, Bewältigungsversuche* (Darmstadt: Wissenschaftliche Buchgesellschaft, 2013), pp. 62–74.

Böhler, Jochen, *Auftakt zum Vernichtungskrieg. Die Wehrmacht in Polen 1939* (Frankfurt am Main: Fischer Taschenbuch, 2006).

Bölling, Klaus, 'Das Pflichtgefühl eines Mörders', *Süddeutsche Zeitung*, 5 April 2011, p. 2.

Borodziej, Włodzimierz, *Der Warschauer Aufstand 1944* (Frankfurt am Main: S. Fischer, 2001).

Bourdieu, Pierre, 'L'illusion biographique', in Pierre Bourdieu, *Raisons pratiques. Sur la théorie de l'action* (Paris: Éd. du Seuil, 1994), pp. 81–89.

Browder, George C., *Hitler's Enforcers: The Gestapo and the SS Security Service in the Nazi Revolution* (New York/Oxford: Oxford University Press, 1996).

Browning, Christopher R., *Fateful Months: Essays on the Emergence of the Final Solution* (New York/London: Holmes & Meier, 1985).

Ordinary Men: Reserve Police Battalion 101 and the Final Solution in Poland, exp. ed. (London: Penguin, 1998 [1992]).

'Perpetrator Testimony: Another Look at Adolf Eichmann', in Christopher R. Browning, *Collected Memories: Holocaust History and Postwar Testimony* (Madison, WI: University of Wisconsin Press, 2003), pp. 3–36 and 87–95.

Browning, Christopher R., with contributions by Jürgen Matthäus, *The Origins of the Final Solution: The Evolution of Nazi Jewish Policy, September 1939 – March 1942* (Lincoln, NE: University of Nebraska Press, 2004).

Bülte, Christian, 'Erich Bley', in Mathias Schmoeckel, ed., *Die Juristen der Universität Bonn im 'Dritten Reich'* (Cologne: Böhlau, 2004), pp. 48–79.

Bushman, Brad J., and Roy F. Baumeister, 'Threatened Egotism, Narcissism, Self-esteem, and Direct and Displaced Aggression: Does Self-love or Self-hate Lead to Violence?', *Journal of Personality and Social Psychology*, Vol. 75, No. 1 (1998), pp. 219–229.

Cesarani, David, *Eichmann: His Life and Crimes* (London: William Heinemann, 2004).

Corni, Gustavo, *I ghetti di Hitler: Voci da una società sotto assedio 1939–1944* (Bologna: il Mulino, 2001).

Cüppers, Martin, *Wegbereiter der Shoah. Die Waffen-SS, der Kommandostab Reichsführer-SS und die Judenvernichtung 1939 – 1945* (Darmstadt: Wissenschaftliche Buchgesellschaft, 2005).

Cüppers, Martin, Jürgen Matthäus and Andrej Angrick, eds., *Naziverbrechen. Täter, Taten, Bewältigungsversuche* (Darmstadt: Wissenschaftliche Buchgesellschaft, 2013).

Curilla, Wolfgang, *Die deutsche Ordnungspolizei und der Holocaust im Baltikum und in Weißrußland 1941–1944* (Paderborn: Schöningh, 2006).

Dams, Carsten, and Michael Stolle, *Die Gestapo. Herrschaft und Terror im Dritten Reich*, 3rd rev. ed. (Munich: C. H. Beck, 2012 [2008]).

Dehmel, Horst-Gerhard, *Die Geschichte der Wormser Polizei* (Guntersblum: Horst-Gerhard Dehmel, 1997).

Dehnicke, Diether, 'Karlheinz Meyer – Leben und Werk', in Klaus Geppert and Diether Dehnicke, eds., *Gedächtnisschrift für Karlheinz Meyer* (Berlin/New York: De Gruyter, 1990), pp. 1–3.

Deiseroth, Dieter, 'Die Legalitäts-Legende. Vom Reichstagsbrand zum NS-Regime', *Blätter für deutsche und internationale Politik*, Vol. 53, No. 2 (February 2008), pp. 91–102.

Dieckmann, Christoph, 'Bewaffnete jüdische Untergrund- und Widerstandsbewegungen. Litauen 1941–1944', *Einsicht 09. Bulletin des Fritz Bauer Instituts*, Vol. 5 (spring 2013), pp. 28–34.

'Der Krieg und die Ermordung der litauischen Juden', in Ulrich Herbert, ed., *Nationalsozialistische Vernichtungspolitik 1939–1945: Neue Forschungen und Kontroversen* (Frankfurt am Main: Fischer Taschenbuch, 1998), pp. 292–329.

Deutsche Besatzungspolitik in Litauen 1941–1944, Vol. 1 (Göttingen: Wallstein, 2011).

Drössler, Stefan, and Michael Farin, eds., *Thomas Harlan. Wundkanal* (Munich: Filmmuseum München/Goethe-Institut München, 2009) [twelve-page booklet accompanying the DVD].

Earl, Hilary, *The Nuremberg SS-Einsatzgruppen Trial, 1945–1958: Atrocity, Law, and History* (Cambridge: Cambridge University Press, 2009).

Eichmüller, Andreas, *Keine Generalamnestie. Die Strafverfolgung von NS-Verbrechen in der frühen Bundesrepublik* (Munich: Oldenbourg, 2012).

Engelmann, Jonas, 'Sauvater, du Land, du Un, du Tier', *Jungle World*, 18 February 2010.

Figaj, Thilo, 'Die blutige Karriere des Heinz Jost', *Darmstädter Echo*, 23 March 2012, pp. 16–17.

Fiks, Norbert, *1869–1994. 125 Jahre Ostfriesische Volksbank – ein geschichtlicher Abriß* (Leer: MaYa-Ebooks, 2002 [1994]).

Frei, Norbert, *Karrieren im Zwielicht: Hitlers Elite nach 1945* (Frankfurt/New York: Campus, 2001).

Vergangenheitspolitik. Die Anfänge der Bundesrepublik und die NS- Vergangenheit, rev. ed. (Munich: C. H. Beck, 2012 [1996]).

Friedländer, Saul, *The Years of Extermination: Nazi Germany and the Jews, 1939–1945* (New York: HarperCollins, 2007).

Ganzenmüller, Jörg, *Das belagerte Leningrad 1941–1944: Die Stadt in den Strategien von Angreifern und Verteidigern* (Paderborn: Schöningh, 2005).

Gerlach, Christian, 'Die Einsatzgruppe B 1941/42', in Peter Klein, ed., *Die Einsatzgruppen in der besetzten Sowjetunion 1941/42. Die Tätigkeits- und Lageberichte des Chefs der Sicherheitspolizei und des SD* (Berlin: Edition Hentrich, 1997), pp. 52–70.

Kalkulierte Morde. Die deutsche Wirtschafts- und Vernichtungspolitik in Weißrußland 1941 bis 1944 (Hamburg: Hamburger Edition, 1999).

Gerwarth, Robert, *Hitler's Hangman: The Life of Heydrich* (New Haven, CT/ London: Yale University Press, 2011).

Geschichte des Corps Hassia Giessen zu Mainz 1815–1965 (Mainz: Selbstverlag des Verbandes der Alten Herren des Corps Hassia Gießen zu Mainz, 1965).

Giovannini, Norbert, *Zwischen Republik und Faschismus. Heidelberger Studentinnen und Studenten 1918–1945* (Weinheim: Deutscher Studien Verlag, 1990).

Goda, Norman J. W., 'The Nazi Peddler: Wilhelm Höttl and Allied Intelligence', in Richard Breitman, Norman J. W. Goda, Timothy Naftali and Robert Wolfe, *U.S. Intelligence and the Nazis* (Cambridge/New York: Cambridge University Press, 2005), pp. 265–292.

Habel, F.-B., ed., *Lexikon Schauspieler in der DDR* (Berlin: Neues Leben, 2009).

Hachmeister, Lutz, *Der Gegnerforscher. Die Karriere des SS-Führers Franz Alfred Six* (Munich: C. H. Beck, 1998).

Schleyer. Eine deutsche Geschichte, rev. paperback ed. (Munich: C. H. Beck, 2007 [2004]).

Hammerschmidt, Peter, '"Daß V-43 118 SS-Hauptsturmführer war, schließt nicht aus, ihn als Quelle zu verwenden". Der Bundesnachrichtendienst und sein Agent Klaus Barbie', *Zeitschrift für Geschichtswissenschaft*, Vol. 59, No. 4 (2011), pp. 333–348.

Hancock, Eleanor, *Ernst Röhm: Hitler's SA Chief of Staff* (Basingstoke: Palgrave Macmillan, 2008).

Harris, Henriette, 'Die menschenfeindlichen Potenziale', *Die Tageszeitung*, 7 May 2014, p. 15.

Harshav, Benjamin, 'Introduction: Herman Kruk's Holocaust Writings', in Herman Kruk, *The Last Days of the Jerusalem of Lithuania: Chronicles from the Vilna Ghetto and the Camps, 1939–1944*, edited and with an introduction by Benjamin Harshav, translated from Yiddish by Barbara Harshav (New Haven, CT/London: YIVO Institute for Jewish Research/Yale University Press, 2002), pp. xxi–lii.

Hasenclever, Jörn, *Wehrmacht und Besatzungspolitik. Die Befehlshaber der rückwärtigen Heeresgebiete 1941–1943* (Paderborn: Schöningh, 2010).

Headland, Ronald, 'The *Einsatzgruppen*: The Question of their Initial Operations', *Holocaust and Genocide Studies*, Vol. 4, No. 4 (1989), pp. 401–412.

Messages of Murder: A Study of the Reports of the Einsatzgruppen of the Security Police and the Security Service, 1941–1943 (Rutherford: Fairleigh Dickinson University Press, 1992).

Heise, Thomas, 'Das Projekt "Wundkanal"', *Der Freitag*, 23 February 2010.

Herbert, Ulrich, *Best. Biographische Studien über Radikalismus, Weltanschauung und Vernunft, 1903–1989* (Bonn: Dietz, 1996).

'"Generation der Sachlichkeit". Die völkische Studentenbewegung der frühen zwanziger Jahre in Deutschland', in Frank Bajohr, Werner Johe and Uwe

Lohalm, eds., *Zivilisation und Barbarei: Die widersprüchlichen Potentiale der Moderne* (Hamburg: Christians, 1991), pp. 115–144.

Hoch, Anton, 'Das Attentat auf Hitler im Münchner Bürgerbräukeller 1939', *Vierteljahrshefte für Zeitgeschichte*, Vol. 17, No. 4 (October 1969), pp. 383–413.

Holler, Martin, *Der nationalsozialistische Völkermord an den Roma in der besetzten Sowjetunion (1941–1944)* (Heidelberg: Dokumentations- und Kulturzentrum Deutscher Sinti und Roma, 2009).

'Extending the Genocidal Program: Did Otto Ohlendorf Initiate the Systematic Extermination of Soviet "Gypsies"?', in Alex J. Kay, Jeff Rutherford and David Stahel, eds., *Nazi Policy on the Eastern Front, 1941: Total War, Genocide, and Radicalization* (Rochester, NY: University of Rochester Press, 2012), pp. 267–288.

Ingrao, Christian, *Croire et détruire: Les intellectuels dans la machine de guerre SS* (n.pl. [Paris]: Fayard, 2010).

Les chasseurs noirs: La brigade Dirlewanger (n.pl. [Paris]: Perrin, 2006).

Jäckel, Eberhard, 'Einfach ein schlechtes Buch', in Julius H. Schoeps, ed., *Ein Volk von Mördern? Die Dokumentation zur Goldhagen-Kontroverse um die Rolle der Deutschen im Holocaust* (Hamburg: Hoffmann & Campe, 1996), pp. 187–192.

Jäckel, Eberhard, Peter Longerich and Julius H. Schoeps, eds., *Enzyklopädie des Holocaust. Die Verfolgung und Ermordung der europäischen Juden, Band III: Q–Z* (Munich/Zürich: Piper, 1995).

Jäckel, Hartmut, *Menschen in Berlin. Das letzte Telefonbuch der alten Reichshauptstadt 1941* (Stuttgart/Munich: Deutsche Verlags-Anstalt, 2000).

Jäger, Herbert, *Verbrechen unter totalitärer Herrschaft. Studien zur nationalsozialistischen Gewaltkriminalität* (Olten/Freiburg im Breisgau: Walter-Verlag, 1967).

Jäger, Klaus, 'Die "Medaille zur Erinnerung an die Heimkehr des Memellandes"', *Orden und Ehrenzeichen*, Vol. 2, No. 6 (April 2000), pp. 2–5.

Judt, Tony, with Timothy Snyder, *Thinking the Twentieth Century* (London: Heinemann, 2012).

Katz, Dovid, 'Review Article. Detonation of the Holocaust in 1941: A Tale of Two Books', *East European Jewish Affairs*, Vol. 41, No. 3 (December 2011), pp. 207–221.

Kay, Alex J., 'Death Threat in the Reichstag, June 13, 1929: Nazi Parliamentary Practice and the Fate of Ernst Heilmann', *German Studies Review*, Vol. 35, No. 1 (February 2012), pp. 19–32.

Exploitation, Resettlement, Mass Murder: Political and Economic Planning for German Occupation Policy in the Soviet Union, 1940–1941 (New York/ Oxford: Berghahn Books, 2006).

'Nicht nur Erschießungsmeldungen', *Einsicht 07. Bulletin des Fritz Bauer Instituts*, Vol. 4 (spring 2012), p. 64.

Review of Ernst Piper, *Alfred Rosenberg. Hitlers Chefideologe* (Munich: Blessing, 2005), *University of Sussex Journal of Contemporary History*, No. 10 (spring 2006).

'"The Purpose of the Russian Campaign is the Decimation of the Slavic Population by Thirty Million": The Radicalization of German Food Policy in early 1941', in Alex J. Kay, Jeff Rutherford and David Stahel, eds., *Nazi Policy on the Eastern Front, 1941: Total War, Genocide, and Radicalization* (Rochester, NY: University of Rochester Press, 2012), pp. 101–129.

'Transition to Genocide, July 1941: Einsatzkommando 9 and the Annihilation of Soviet Jewry', *Holocaust and Genocide Studies*, Vol. 27, No. 3 (winter 2013), pp. 411–442.

'Ungleiche Brüder. Der SS-Massenmörder und der KZ-Häftling', *Einsicht 10. Bulletin des Fritz Bauer Instituts*, Vol. 5 (autumn 2013), pp. 49–55.

Kay, Alex J., Jeff Rutherford and David Stahel, eds., *Nazi Policy on the Eastern Front, 1941: Total War, Genocide, and Radicalization* (Rochester, NY: University of Rochester Press, 2012).

Kershaw, Ian, *Hitler 1889–1936: Hubris* (London: Allen Lane, 1998).

Hitler 1936–1945: Nemesis (London: Allen Lane, 2000).

Kierkegaard, Søren, *Papers and Journals: A Selection*, translated from Danish by Alastair Hannay (London: Penguin, 1996).

Klausch, Hans-Peter, *Antifaschisten in SS-Uniform. Schicksal und Widerstand der deutschen politschen KZ-Häftlinge, Zuchthaus- und Wehrmachtsgefangenen in der SS-Sonderformation Dirlewanger* (Bremen: Edition Temmen, 1993).

Klee, Ernst, *Das Personenlexikon zum Dritten Reich. Wer war was vor und nach 1945*, rev. ed. (Frankfurt am Main: Fischer Taschenbuch, 2005 [2003]).

Klein, Peter, 'Der Mordgehilfe: Schuld und Sühne des Dr. Otto Bradfisch', in Klaus-Michael Mallmann and Andrej Angrick, eds., *Die Gestapo nach 1945. Karrieren, Konflikte, Konstruktionen* (Darmstadt: Wissenschaftliche Buchgesellschaft, 2009), pp. 221–234.

'Die Wannsee-Konferenz als Echo auf die gefallene Entscheidung zur Ermordung der europäischen Juden', in Norbert Kampe and Peter Klein, eds., *Die Wannsee- Konferenz am 20. Januar 1942. Dokumente, Forschungsstand, Kontroversen* (Cologne/Weimar/Vienna: Böhlau, 2013), pp. 182–201.

'Einleitung', in Peter Klein, ed., *Die Einsatzgruppen in der besetzten Sowjetunion 1941/42. Die Tätigkeits- und Lageberichte des Chefs der Sicherheitspolizei und des SD* (Berlin: Edition Hentrich, 1997), pp. 9–28.

Knörrer [Knörer], Ekkehard, 'Der Täter im Spiegelkabinett', *Die Tageszeitung*, 10 December 2009.

Krausnick, Helmut, 'Die Einsatzgruppen vom Anschluß Österreichs bis zum Feldzug gegen die Sowjetunion. Entwicklung und Verhältnis zur Wehrmacht', in Helmut Krausnick and Hans-Heinrich Wilhelm, *Die Truppe des Weltanschauungskrieges: Die Einsatzgruppen der Sicherheitspolizei und des SD 1938 – 1942* (Stuttgart: Deutsche Verlags-Anstalt, 1981), pp. 11–278.

'Hitler und die Befehle an die Einsatzgruppen im Sommer 1941', in Eberhard Jäckel and Jürgen Rohwer, eds., *Der Mord an den Juden im Zweiten Weltkrieg: Entschlussbildung und Verwirklichung* (Stuttgart: Deutsche Verlags-Anstalt, 1985), pp. 88–106.

Krausnick, Helmut, and Hans-Heinrich Wilhelm, *Die Truppe des Weltanschauungskrieges: Die Einsatzgruppen der Sicherheitspolizei und des SD 1938 – 1942* (Stuttgart: Deutsche Verlags-Anstalt, 1981).

Kruglov, Alexandr, 'Sekretnoye delo imperii. Massovoye unichtozheniye mirnogo naseleniya zonderkomandami SD na vremenno okkupirovannoi territorii SSSR v 1941–1944 gg. (dokumenty i materialy)', unpublished manuscript, 2011.

Kruse, Falko, 'Zweierlei Maß für NS-Täter? Über die Tendenzen schichtenspezifischer Privilegierungen in Urteilen gegen nationalsozialistische Gewaltverbrecher', *Kritische Justiz: Vierteljahresschrift für Recht und Politik*, Vol. 11, No. 3 (1978), pp. 236–253.

Kühne, Thomas, *Belonging and Genocide: Hitler's Community, 1918–1945* (New Haven, CT/London: Yale University Press, 2010).

'Der nationalsozialistische Vernichtungskrieg und die "ganz normalen" Deutschen: Forschungsprobleme und Forschungstendenzen der Gesellschaftsgeschichte des Zweiten Weltkrieges. Erster Teil', *Archiv für Sozialgeschichte*, Vol. 39 (1999), pp. 580–662.

Kühnel, Karsten, 'Archivierung beim Internationalen Suchdienst in Bad Arolsen', *Archivnachrichten aus Hessen*, Vol. 9, No. 1 (2009), pp. 25–28.

Kunz, Norbert, 'Das Beispiel Charkow: Eine Stadtbevölkerung als Opfer der deutschen Hungerstrategie 1941/42,' in Christian Hartmann, Johannes Hürter and Ulrike Jureit, eds., *Verbrechen der Wehrmacht: Bilanz einer Debatte* (Munich: C. H. Beck, 2005), pp. 136–144.

Kwiet, Konrad, 'Rassenpolitik und Völkermord', in Wolfgang Benz, Hermann Graml and Hermann Weiß, eds., *Enzyklopädie des Nationalsozialismus* (Munich: dtv, 2001 [1997]), pp. 50–65.

Lehnstaedt, Stephan, 'The Minsk Experience: German Occupiers and Everyday Life in the Capital of Belarus', in Alex J. Kay, Jeff Rutherford and David Stahel, eds., *Nazi Policy on the Eastern Front, 1941: Total War, Genocide, and Radicalization* (Rochester, NY: University of Rochester Press, 2012), pp. 240–266.

Linck, Stephan, *Der Ordnung verpflichtet: Deutsche Polizei 1933–1949: Der Fall Flensburg* (Paderborn: Schöningh, 2000).

Longerich, Peter, *Goebbels. Biographie* (Munich: Siedler, 2010).

Heinrich Himmler. Biographie (Munich: Siedler, 2008).

Politik der Vernichtung. Eine Gesamtdarstellung der nationalsozialistischen Judenverfolgung (Munich: Piper, 1998).

Lower, Wendy, *Hitler's Furies: German Women in the Nazi Killing Fields* (Boston, MA: Houghton Mifflin Harcourt, 2013).

Mallmann, Klaus-Michael, 'Die Türöffner der "Endlösung". Zur Genesis des Genozids', in Gerhard Paul and Klaus-Michael Mallmann, eds., *Die Gestapo im Zweiten Weltkrieg. 'Heimatfront' und besetztes Europa* (Darmstadt: Wissenschaftliche Buchgesellschaft, 2000), pp. 437–463.

'Menschenjagd und Massenmord. Das neue Instrument der Einsatzgruppen und –kommandos 1938–1945', in Gerhard Paul and Klaus-Michael Mallmann, eds., *Die Gestapo im Zweiten Weltkrieg. 'Heimatfront' und besetztes Europa* (Darmstadt: Wissenschaftliche Buchgesellschaft, 2000), pp. 291–316.

'"Mensch, ich feiere heut' den tausendsten Genickschuß". Die Sicherheitspolizei und die Shoah in Westgalizien', in Gerhard Paul, ed.,

Täter der Shoah. Fanatische Nationalsozialisten oder ganz normale Deutsche? (Göttingen: Wallstein, 2002), pp. 109–136.

Mallmann, Klaus-Michael, and Gerhard Paul, eds., *Karrieren der Gewalt. Nationalsozialistische Täterbiographien* (Darmstadt: Wissenschaftliche Buchgesellschaft, 2004).

Mann, Michael, 'Were the Perpetrators of Genocide "Ordinary Men" or "Real Nazis"? Results from Fifteen Hundred Biographies', *Holocaust and Genocide Studies*, Vol. 14, No. 3 (winter 2000), pp. 331–366.

Margolis, Rachel, 'Foreword', in Kazimierz Sakowicz, *Ponary Diary, 1941–1943: A Bystander's Account of a Mass Murder* (New Haven, CT/London: Yale University Press, 2005), ed. Yitzhak Arad, translated from Polish by Yad Vashem, pp. vii–xii.

Matthäus, Jürgen, 'Holocaust als angewandter Antisemitismus? Potential und Grenzen eines Erklärungsfaktors', in Frank Bajohr and Andrea Löw, eds., *Der Holocaust. Ergebnisse und neue Fragen der Forschung* (Frankfurt am Main: Fischer Taschenbuch, 2015), pp. 102–123.

Mende, Berliot von, and Erling von Mende, 'Ein Bürokrat der mittleren Ebene', unpublished manuscript, 2013.

Michaelis, Rolf, *Die SS-Sturmbrigade 'Dirlewanger'. Vom Warschauer Aufstand bis zum Kessel von Halbe* (Dresden: Winkelried, 2006).

Michman, Dan, *The Emergence of Jewish Ghettos during the Holocaust,* translated from Hebrew by Lenn J. Schramm (Cambridge/New York: Cambridge University Press, 2011).

Milgram, Stanley, *Obedience to Authority: An Experimental View* (New York: Harper & Row, 1974).

Mitteilungen der Forschungs- und Arbeitsgruppe 'Geschichte des BND', ed. Bundesnachrichtendienst, special issue 'Kassationen von Personalakten im Bestand des BND-Archivs', 22 December 2011.

Mußgnug, Dorothee, 'Die Juristische Fakultät', in Wolfgang U. Eckart, Volker Sellin and Eike Wolgast, eds., *Die Universität Heidelberg im Nationalsozialismus* (Heidelberg: Springer, 2006), pp. 261–317.

Mühlhäuser, Regina, *Eroberungen. Sexuelle Gewalttaten und intime Beziehungen deutscher Soldaten in der Sowjetunion 1941 – 1945* (Hamburg: Hamburger Edition, 2010).

Naftali, Timothy, 'Reinhard Gehlen and the United States', in Richard Breitman, Norman J. W. Goda, Timothy Naftali and Robert Wolfe, *U.S. Intelligence and the Nazis* (Cambridge/New York: Cambridge University Press, 2005), pp. 375–418.

Ogorreck, Ralf, *Die Einsatzgruppen und die 'Genesis der Endlösung'* (Berlin: Metropol, 1996).

Orbach, Wila, 'The Destruction of the Jews in the Nazi-Occupied Territories of the USSR', *Soviet Jewish Affairs*, Vol. 6, No. 2 (1976), pp. 14–51.

Paehler, Katrin, 'Making Intelligence Nazi: The SD, Foreign Intelligence, and Ideology', revised doctoral thesis, 2014.

Paul, Gerhard, 'Von Psychopathen, Technokraten des Terrors und "ganz gewöhnlichen Deutschen". Die Täter der Shoah im Spiegel der Forschung', in Gerhard Paul, ed., *Täter der Shoah. Fanatische*

Nationalsozialisten oder ganz normale Deutsche? (Göttingen: Wallstein, 2002), pp. 13–90.

'Zwischen Selbstmord, Illegalität und neuer Karriere. Ehemalige Gestapo-Bedienstete im Nachkriegsdeutschland', in Gerhard Paul and Klaus-Michael Mallmann, eds., *Die Gestapo – Mythos und Realität* (Darmstadt: Wissenschaftliche Buchgesellschaft, 1995), pp. 529–547.

Pawley, Margaret, *The Watch on the Rhine: The Military Occupation of the Rhineland, 1918–1930* (London/New York: I. B. Tauris, 2007).

Peck, M. Scott, *The Road Less Travelled*, 25th Anniversary Edition (Rider: London, 2003 [1978]).

Piper, Ernst, *Alfred Rosenberg. Hitlers Chefideologe* (Munich: Blessing, 2005).

Pohl, Dieter, *Die Herrschaft der Wehrmacht: Deutsche Militärbesatzung in der Sowjetunion, 1941–1944* (Munich: Oldenbourg, 2008).

Holocaust. Die Ursachen, das Geschehen, die Folgen (Freiburg im Breisgau: Herder, 2000).

Potthast, Jan Björn, *Das Jüdische Zentralmuseum der SS in Prag. Gegnerforschung und Völkermord im Nationalsozialismus* (Frankfurt am Main/New York: Campus, 2002).

Querg, Thorsten J., 'Spionage und Terror – Das Amt VI des Reichssicherheitshauptamtes 1939-1945', unpublished doctoral thesis, Freie Universität Berlin, 1997.

'Ralph Filbert. Obituary', *The Daily Times*, 26 February 2014.

Rathert, Ronald, *Verbrechen und Verschwörung. Arthur Nebe, der Kripochef des Dritten Reiches* (Münster: LIT, 2001).

Rebhandl, Bert, 'Aus der Generation der Unbedingten', *Frankfurter Allgemeine Zeitung*, 26 October 2010.

Rhodes, Richard, *Masters of Death: The SS-Einsatzgruppen and the Invention of the Holocaust* (New York: Alfred A. Knopf, 2002).

Richter, Klaus, Review of Wolfram Wette, *Karl Jäger. Mörder der litauischen Juden* (Frankfurt am Main: Fischer Taschenbuch, 2011), *Zeitschrift für Ostmitteleuropa-Forschung*, Vol. 63, No. 3 (2014), pp. 482–483.

Rieger, Berndt, *Creator of Nazi Death Camps: The Life of Odilo Globocnik* (London/Portland, OR: Vallentine Mitchell, 2007).

Robel, Gert, 'Sowjetunion', in Wolfgang Benz, ed., *Dimension des Völkermords. Die Zahl der jüdischen Opfer des Nationalsozialismus* (Munich: Oldenbourg, 1991), pp. 499–560.

Romanovsky, Daniel, 'Ianovichi', in United States Holocaust Memorial Museum, *Encyclopedia of Camps and Ghettos, 1933–1945, Volume II: Ghettos in German-Occupied Eastern Europe, Part B*, ed. Martin Dean (Bloomington, IN/Indianapolis, IN: Indiana University Press, 2012), pp. 1679–1680.

'Vitebsk', in United States Holocaust Memorial Museum, *Encyclopedia of Camps and Ghettos, 1933–1945, Volume II: Ghettos in German-Occupied Eastern Europe, Part B*, ed. Martin Dean (Bloomington, IN/Indianapolis, IN: Indiana University Press, 2012), pp. 1745–1748.

Römer, Felix, *Der Kommissarbefehl: Wehrmacht und NS-Verbrechen an der Ostfront 1941/42* (Paderborn: Schöningh, 2008).

'The Wehrmacht in the War of Ideologies: The Army and Hitler's Criminal Orders on the Eastern Front', in Alex J. Kay, Jeff Rutherford and David Stahel, eds., *Nazi Policy on the Eastern Front, 1941: Total War, Genocide, and Radicalization* (Rochester, NY: University of Rochester Press, 2012), pp. 73–100.

Roseman, Mark, 'The Lives of Others – Amid the Deaths of Others: Biographical Approaches to Nazi Perpetrators', *Journal of Genocide Research*, Vol. 15, No. 4 (2013), pp. 443–461.

Rückerl, Adalbert, *NS-Verbrechen vor Gericht. Versuch einer Vergangenheitsbewältigung*, 2nd rev. ed. (Heidelberg: C. F. Müller, 1984 [1982]).

Ruprecht, Uwe, 'Ein offenes Geheimnis', *Jungle World*, No. 20, 7 May 2003.

'Für eine Schachtel Zigaretten', *Die Gazette. Das politische Kulturmagazin*, 15 March 2003.

'SS-Mann 52729. Ein ganz gewöhnlicher deutscher Verbrecher', unpublished manuscript, 2003.

Russell, John, 'Art View: In Search of the Real Thing', *New York Times*, 1 December 1985.

Scheffler, Wolfgang, 'Die Einsatzgruppe A 1941/42', in Peter Klein, ed., *Die Einsatzgruppen in der besetzten Sowjetunion 1941/42. Die Tätigkeits- und Lageberichte des Chefs der Sicherheitspolizei und des SD* (Berlin: Edition Hentrich, 1997), pp. 29–51.

Schmiedecker, Andreas, 'Fassungslose Geschichtsschreibung. Geschichtliche und biografische (De)Konstruktionen bei Thomas Harlan', in Thomas Marchart, Stefanie Schmitt and Stefan Suppanschitz, eds., *reflexiv. Geschichte denken, SYN. Magazin für Theater-, Film- und Medienwissenschaft*, Vol. 2 (Berlin/Münster/Vienna/Zürich/London: LIT, 2011), pp. 69–83.

Schneider, Christoph, 'Täterarbeit', *Einsicht 03. Bulletin des Fritz Bauer Instituts*, Vol. 2 (spring 2010), p. 82.

Schneppen, Heinz, *Walther Rauff. Organisator der Gaswagenmorde: Eine Biographie* (Berlin: Metropol, 2011).

Schröder, Henning, and Hans H. Lembke, *Nikolassee. Häuser und Bewohner der Villenkolonie* (Berlin: H. Schröder, 2008).

Seeger, Andreas, *Gestapo-Müller. Die Karriere eines Schreibtischtäters* (Berlin: Metropol, 1996).

Siekmeier, James F., *The Bolivian Revolution and the United States, 1952 to the Present* (University Park, PA: The Pennsylvania State University Press, 2011).

Simpson, Christopher, *Blowback: America's Recruitment of Nazis and its Effects on the Cold War* (London: Weidenfeld & Nicolson, 1988).

Smelser, Ronald, and Enrico Syring, eds., *Die SS: Elite unter dem Totenkopf. 30 Lebensläufe* (Paderborn: Schöningh, 2000).

Smilovitskii [Smilovitsky], Leonid, *Katastrofa evreev v Belorussii, 1941–1944 gg.* (Tel Aviv: Biblioteka Matveia Chernogo, 2000).

Snyder, Timothy, *Bloodlands: Europe between Hitler and Stalin* (New York: Basic Books, 2010).

Spierenburg, Pieter, *The Prison Experience: Disciplinary Institutions and Their Inmates in Early Modern Europe* (New Brunswick, NJ/London: Rutgers University Press, 1991).

ed., *The Emergence of Carceral Institutions: Prisons, Galleys and Lunatic Asylums 1550–1900* (Rotterdam: Erasmus Universiteit, 1984).

Stang, Knut, 'Dr. Oskar Dirlewanger – Protagonist der Terrorkriegsführung', in Klaus-Michael Mallmann and Gerhard Paul, eds., *Karrieren der Gewalt. Nationalsozialistische Täterbiographien* (Darmstadt: Wissenschaftliche Buchgesellschaft, 2004), pp. 66–75.

Stephan, Jean-Pierre, 'Fritz Bauers Briefe an Thomas Harlan. Eine deutsche Freundschaft', *Einsicht 09. Bulletin des Fritz Bauer Instituts*, Vol. 5 (spring 2013), pp. 36–44.

Steur, Claudia, *Theodor Dannecker: Ein Funktionär der 'Endlösung'* (Essen: Klartext, 1997).

Stollhof, Alexander, 'SS-Gruppenführer und Generalleutnant der Polizei Otto Ohlendorf – Eine biographische Skizze', unpublished doctoral thesis, Vienna, 1993.

Streim, Alfred, 'Zur Eröffnung des allgemeinen Judenvernichtungsbefehls gegenüber den Einsatzgruppen', in Eberhard Jäckel and Jürgen Rohwer, eds., *Der Mord an den Juden im Zweiten Weltkrieg: Entschlussbildung und Verwirklichung* (Stuttgart: Deutsche Verlags-Anstalt, 1985), pp. 107–119.

Streit, Christian, *Keine Kameraden: Die Wehrmacht und die sowjetischen Kriegsgefangenen 1941–1945*, 4th rev. ed. (Bonn: Dietz, 1997 [1978]).

'Ostkrieg, Antibolschewismus und "Endlösung"', *Geschichte und Gesellschaft*, Vol. 19 (1991), pp. 242–255.

Studienkreis Deutscher Widerstand 1933–1945, ed., *Heimatgeschichtlicher Wegweiser zu Stätten des Widerstandes und der Verfolgung 1933–1945, Band 8: Thüringen* (Frankfurt am Main: VAS, 2003).

Ullrich, Christina, *'Ich fühl' mich nicht als Mörder'. Die Integration von NS-Tätern in die Nachkriegsgesellschaft* (Darmstadt: Wissenschaftliche Buchgesellschaft, 2011).

Ungváry, Krisztián, *Battle for Budapest: 100 Days in World War II*, translated from Hungarian by Ladislaus Löb (London/New York: I. B. Tauris, 2011 [1998]).

Unverhau, Dagmar, *Das 'NS-Archiv' des Ministeriums für Staatssicherheit. Stationen einer Entwicklung*, 2nd rev. ed. (Münster: LIT, 2004 [1998]).

Vieregge, Bianca, *Die Gerichtsbarkeit einer 'Elite'. Nationalsozialistische Rechtsprechung am Beispiel der SS- und Polizei-Gerichtsbarkeit* (Baden-Baden: Nomos Verlagsgesellschaft, 2002).

Vinnitsa, G., 'Lepel', in I. A. Al'tman, ed., *Kholokost na territorii SSSR: Entsiklopediya* (Moscow: ROSSPEN, 2009), p. 521.

Wagner, Patrick, *Volksgemeinschaft ohne Verbrecher: Konzeptionen und Praxis der Kriminalpolizei in der Zeit der Weimarer Republik und des Nationalsozialismus* (Hamburg: Christians, 1996).

Walbrach, Carl, ed., *Geschichte der Giessener Burschenschaft Alemannia 1861–1961* (Giessen: Selbstverlag der G. B. Alemannia, 1961).

Weinke, Annette, 'Amnestie für Schreibtischtäter. Das verhinderte Verfahren gegen die Bediensteten des Reichssicherheitshauptamtes', in Klaus-Michael

Mallmann and Andrej Angrick, eds., *Die Gestapo nach 1945. Karrieren, Konflikte, Konstruktionen* (Darmstadt: Wissenschaftliche Buchgesellschaft, 2009), pp. 200–220.

'Der Eichmann-Prozess, Hannah Arendts "Eichmann in Jerusalem" und die Semantik des industrialisierten Massenmords', in Martin Cüppers, Jürgen Matthäus and Andrej Angrick, eds., *Naziverbrechen. Täter, Taten, Bewältigungsversuche* (Darmstadt: Wissenschaftliche Buchgesellschaft, 2013), pp. 289–302.

Eine Gesellschaft ermittelt gegen sich selbst. Die Geschichte der Zentralen Stelle Ludwigsburg 1958–2008 (Darmstadt: Wissenschaftliche Buchgesellschaft, 2008).

Weisbrod, Bernd, 'Generation und Generationalität in der Neueren Geschichte', *Aus Politik und Zeitgeschichte*, 8/2005, pp. 3–9.

Welzer, Harald, *Täter. Wie aus ganz normalen Menschen Massenmörder werden* (Frankfurt am Main: S. Fischer, 2005).

Westermann, Edward B., 'Stone Cold Killers or Drunk with Murder? Alcohol and Atrocity in the Holocaust', unpublished manuscript, 2014.

Wette, Wolfram, *Karl Jäger. Mörder der litauischen Juden* (Frankfurt am Main: Fischer Taschenbuch, 2011).

Wildt, Michael, *Generation des Unbedingten. Das Führungskorps des Reichssicherheitshauptamtes*, rev. ed. (Hamburg: Hamburger Edition, 2003 [2002]).

An Uncompromising Generation: The Nazi Leadership of the Reich Security Main Office, translated from German by Tom Lampert (Madison, WI: University of Wisconsin Press, 2009).

Wilhelm, Hans-Heinrich, 'Die Einsatzgruppe A der Sicherheitspolizei und des SD 1941/42 – Eine exemplarische Studie', in Helmut Krausnick and Hans-Heinrich Wilhelm, *Die Truppe des Weltanschauungskrieges: Die Einsatzgruppen der Sicherheitspolizei und des SD 1938 – 1942* (Stuttgart: Deutsche Verlags-Anstalt, 1981), pp. 279–643.

Winkler, Heinrich August, *Weimar 1918–1933. Die Geschichte der ersten deutschen Demokratie* (Munich: C. H. Beck, 1993).

Wippermann, Wolfgang, 'Nur eine Fußnote? Die Verfolgung der sowjetischen Roma: Historiographie, Motive, Verlauf', in Klaus Meyer and Wolfgang Wippermann, eds., *Gegen das Vergessen: Der Vernichtungskrieg gegen die Sowjetunion, 1941–1945* (Frankfurt am Main: Haag u. Herchen, 1992), pp. 75–90.

Wojak, Irmtrud, *Eichmanns Memoiren: Ein kritischer Essay* (Frankfurt am Main: Fischer Taschenbuch, 2004 [2001]).

Wolgast, Eike, 'Die Studierenden', in Wolfgang U. Eckart, Volker Sellin and Eike Wolgast, eds., *Die Universität Heidelberg im Nationalsozialismus* (Heidelberg: Springer, 2006), pp. 57–94.

Yelenskaya, I. E., and Ye. S. Rozenblat, 'Viléyka', in I. A. Al'tman, ed., *Kholokost na territorii SSSR: Entsiklopediya* (Moscow: ROSSPEN, 2009), pp. 155–156.

Zimmermann, Volker, *Die Sudetendeutschen im NS-Staat. Politik und Stimmung der Bevölkerung im Reichsgau Sudetenland (1938–1945)* (Essen: Klartext, 1999).

Interviews, written and telephonic notifications

Written notification from Jürgen Holler, Standesamt Darmstadt, 9 June 2010.

Written notification from G. Potthoff, Gauß-Gymnasium, 2 August 2010.

Written notification from Thomas Brünnler, Landeshauptarchiv Sachsen-Anhalt, Abteilung Dessau, 27 August 2010.

Written notification from Jenny Kempkes, Deutsche Bank, 1 September 2010.

Written notification from Group Human Resources, Commerzbank, 3 September 2010.

Written notification from Dr Frank Teske, Stadtarchiv Mainz, 8 September 2010.

Written notification from Group Human Resources, Commerzbank, 9 September 2010.

Written notification from Dr Detlef Krause, Historisches Archiv der Commerzbank, 10 September 2010.

Written notification from Dagmar Lerch, Standesamt Worms, 21 September 2010.

Written notification from Dr Carsten Lind, Archiv der Philipps-Universität Marburg, 8 March 2011.

Written notification from Bernhard Loh, Vorstandssekretariat/Recht, Berlin-Hannoversche Hypothekenbank AG, 19 October 2011.

Telephonic notification from Gregor Klusmann, Personalabteilung, Ostfriesische Volksbank, 5 December 2011.

Written notifications from Manfred Kielhorn, Pressesprecher/Öffentlichkeitsarbeit, Stadt Bad Gandersheim, 21 November 2011, 9 January 2012 and 28 February 2012.

Written notifications from Christa Bischof, Bürgeramt Mitte, Hanover, 30 December 2011 and 3 January 2012.

Written notification from the Deutsche Dienststelle für die Benachrichtigung der nächsten Angehörigen von Gefallenen der ehemaligen deutschen Wehrmacht (WASt), Berlin, 13 January 2012.

Written notification from Laura Kempers, Bundesamt für Verfassungsschutz, Cologne, 10 April 2012 and 9 January 2013.

Written notification from Ulrich Utis, Leiter der Arbeitsgruppe Archiv, Bundesnachrichtendienst, Berlin, 19 April 2012.

Written notifications from Michele Meeks, Information and Privacy Coordinator, Central Intelligence Agency, 16 May 2012 and 25 January 2013.

Written notification from Ronald Langer, Stadtarchiv und Stadtmuseum, Stadt Fürth, 23 August 2012.

Telephonic notification from the director of the JVA Stuttgart, Ltd. Regierungsdirektorin Regina Grimm, 5 September 2012.

Written notification from Lars Hoffmann, Beauftragter für Öffentlichkeitsarbeit der Justizvollzugsanstalt Tegel, 10 September 2012.

Written notification from Ulrike Leuchtweis, Staatsarchiv Ludwigsburg, 21 September 2012.

Written notification from Michele Meeks, Executive Secretary, Agency Release Panel, Central Intelligence Agency, 26 September 2012.

Written notification from Dr Andreas Elbach, Leiter der Arbeitsgruppe Archiv, Bundesnachrichtendiesnt, Pullach, 4 January 2013.
Interview with Henning Pferdmenges, grandson of Heinrich Pferdmenges, 7 March 2013.
Written notification from Henning Schröder, Berlin-Nikolassee, 10 March 2013.
Written notification from Erling von Mende, Berlin, 26 June 2013.

Online articles

Kay, Alex J., 'Brothers – The SS Mass Murderer and the Concentration Camp Inmate', *Tr@nsit online*, 8 August 2013: http://www.iwm.at/read-listen-wat ch/transit-online/brothers-the-ss-mass-murderer-and-the-concentration-ca mp-inmate/ [last accessed on 10 August 2013].
Nazi War Crimes and Japanese Imperial Government Records Interagency Working Group: Final Report to the United States Congress, April 2007: https://www.ar chives.gov/iwg/reports/final-report-2007.pdf [last accessed on 3 November 2015].
'The CIA and Nazi War Criminals: National Security Archive Posts Secret CIA History Released Under Nazi War Crimes Disclosure Act', in *National Security Archive Electronic Briefing Book*, No. 146, ed. Tamara Feinstein, 4 February 2005: http://www2.gwu.edu/~nsarchiv/NSAEBB/NSAEBB146/ [last accessed on 3 November 2015].
Wiley Online Library, International Transactions on Electrical Energy Systems; Article: 'A parameter-identification-based diagnosis for detecting static air-gap eccentricity', T. Bradatsch and D. Filbert; Author Information: http://onlineli brary.wiley.com/doi/10.1002/etep.4450050407/abstract [last accessed on 21 May 2014].

Films

Babi Jar – Das vergessene Massaker, dir. Christine Rütten and Lutz Rentner (Germany: Hessischer Rundfunk, 2012).

Index

Protectorate of Bohemia and Moravia 14,
    See also Czechoslovakia;
    Sudetenland
Prussia 24
Pullman Works 37

RAF *See* Red Army Faction (RAF)
Rahm, Karl 129
Rasspe, Jan-Carl 114
Rath, Karl 65, 100, 105
Ratner, Sofiya Isidorovna 67, 69
Rauff, Walther 1
Ravensbrück *See* concentration camps
Red Army 66, 68, 86
    commissars 42, 48, 62, 71, 75
Red Army Faction (RAF) 14, 108,
    111–112, 114–115, 206
Reich Criminal Police 2, 28, 43–45, 79,
    81–83, 88, 154
    Berlin Criminal Police 45
    Reich Criminal Police Office 28
Reich Ministry for the Occupied Eastern
    Territories 89
Reich Ministry of Economics 192
Reich Ministry of Finance 38
Reich Security Main Office (RSHA) 5,
    27–30, 38, 41, 43–45, 58, 71, 75,
    78–79, 81–82, 87, 103,
    105–107, 110
    Office I 38, 39, 41, 45
    Office II 2, 38, 143
    Office III 39, 87
    Office IV 39
    Office V 40, 81, 87, 206
    Office VI 14, 28–30, 38, 78, 81,
        87, 115
    Office VII 2
Reichstag 21, 99
Rembrandt 106
Reserve Police Battalion 9 *See* Order Police
Rheinische Kreditbank 12, 135
Rhenish Hesse 12–13, 22
Rhineland 12, 26, 143
Richter, Friedrich 192
Ronge, Paul 97, 103, 196
Rosenberg, Alfred 39, 89
Rostock 110
RSHA *See* Reich Security Main Office
    (RSHA)
Russia 39, 41, 60, 69, 99–105, *See also*
    Soviet Union

SA 21, 110
Sachsenhausen *See* concentration camps
St Petersburg 45, *See also* Leningrad

Sakowicz, Kazimierz 52, 165
San Francisco 116
Sassen, Willem 123
Sastarinya 66
Saxony 40
Scenes from the Class Struggle in Portugal
    (film) 116
Schäfer, Oswald 70–71, 105
Schauschütz, Franz 50, 52, 55
Schellenberg, Walter 39, 78, 81
Schenckendorff, Max von 69
Schleswig-Holstein 87
Schleyer, Hanns Martin 14, 137, 138
Schneider, Gerhard 45–46, 51, 55, 57–62,
    65, 69, 71, 76, 92, 99–101, 103,
    154, 167
Schneller, Ernst 99
Schulz, Erwin 100, 148
Schulz, Karl 81–82
Schulz-Isenbeck, Kurt 46, 65
SD *See* SS Security Service (SD)
Secret State Police Central Office *See*
    Gestapo Central Office
Secret State Police *See* Gestapo
Security Police 28, 40, 45, 48, 53, 56, 60,
    63, 80, 96, 160, 193
    Main Office of the Security Police 28
Seidel, Hans-Dieter 120
Seidel, Rudolf 202
Siauliai 159
Six, Franz Alfred 2, 38, 76
Slovakia 85–86
Smolensk 62, 159
South Africa 114
Southampton 11
Soviet Communist Party *See* Communist
    Party of the Soviet Union
Soviet partisans *See* partisans, Soviet
Soviet Union 39–43, 57, 96, 103, 122, *See*
    also Belarus; Estonia; Lithuania;
    Russia; Ukraine
Sparkasse Hannover 92
Sredzki, Siegmund 99
SS 1–3, 7, 14, 20–22, 25, 30–31, 37–38, 40,
    46, 49, 59, 63, 68–69, 75, 78–79, 81,
    83, 88, 91, 96, 101, 110, 114–115,
    122–123, 138, *See also* Waffen SS
    1st SS Infantry Brigade 164
    SS Cavalry Regiment 2 67
    SS-Sturm 2/I/32 138
    SS-Sturm 4/II/33 21–22
    SS-Sturm 8/33 21
SS Security Service (SD) 5, 22–28, 30, 40,
    43–46, 48, 51, 59, 75, 79–81, 88,
    110, 154, 193